W9-CKF-964

AMERICAN COMMONWEALTHS SERIES

W. Brooke Graves, *Editor*

The Government and Administration of Mississippi

The Government and Administration of

AMERICAN COMMONWEALTHS SERIES

W. Brooke Graves, *Editor*

MISSISSIPPI

ROBERT B. HIGHSAW

Professor of Public Administration and
Director of the Bureau of Public Administration
University of Mississippi

and

CHARLES N. FORTENBERRY

Professor of Political Science
University of Mississippi

THOMAS Y. CROWELL COMPANY

New York

Library of Congress Catalog Card Number: 54-11152

MANUFACTURED IN THE UNITED STATES OF AMERICA

American Commonwealths Series

THE STATES have always been, and they are today, the key units in American federalism. As Professor Charles E. Merriam has said, "The fact is that if we did not have states, it would be necessary to create them, with the same fundamental purpose that is now our goal, of maintaining the balance between liberty and authority, between central and local, and with an adequate division of functions and responsibilities. We need not apologize for our American states."

There have been books and articles in great numbers on most phases of the organization and administration of the Federal government. The number of organizations and the quantity of literature relating to municipal government and administration have reached staggering proportions. For some reason not readily apparent, the states—vital though they are to our federal system—have seldom been given the attention they deserve. Students in the state field have long felt the need for more adequate information on government and administration in the individual states, on which few books have been published, and still fewer good ones.

The publication of the American Commonwealths Series represents a long-range attempt to meet this end. Students of state government everywhere will hail this effort to provide parallel studies of the governments of each of the forty-eight states and the four major territories. These studies are being written by carefully selected scholars, each particularly qualified to write on the government of his own state. Many of the authors are political scientists with nation-wide reputations. Working together as members of a team, they are attempting, in many states for the first time in the history of the state, to present a complete description and analysis of state governmental institutions and procedures on a sound scholarly basis.

It is believed that these volumes will have a wide variety of uses. They will provide suitable text material for a growing number of college and university courses, many of them required by law, dealing with the governments of the individual states. They will provide reference material and supplementary reading for high school seniors, and for libraries of all types —public and private, general and specialized, school and college. They will also provide reliable information on state matters for a large number of citizens and citizen organizations whose members are in a position to provide civic leadership—editors, journalists, radio commentators, the clergy, members of the bar and of the teaching profession, and others, as well as service clubs, veterans' groups, taxpayers' organizations, chambers of commerce, and many, many more. These volumes should also be of use to such women's organizations as the League of Women Voters, the American Association of University Women, and a large number of women's literary, civic, and other clubs. Government officials in all three branches of government, and at all levels, will find in them a wealth of information on all sorts of questions, outside of their own fields of interest or specialization, on which they need to be informed. Most important of all, perhaps, is the fact that, as this Series grows, it will provide for scholars a vast storehouse of comparative information on the history, development, and present functioning of government in the American states.

W. BROOKE GRAVES

Editor's Introduction

I AM SURE that the citizens of Mississippi will forgive me if I repeat once more an unpleasant fact—for it is a fact—that various self-appointed critics have from time to time referred to Mississippi as a politically backward and benighted community. It would seem to me that the splendid description and analysis of Mississippi governmental institutions by Professors Highsaw and Fortenberry in this volume should make abundantly clear that any such charge against Mississippi—or, for that matter, against any other one of our forty-eight states—is in 1954 both erroneous and unjustified.

To be sure, not all of our states discharge all of their governmental responsibilities equally well, but each of them seems to excel in some particular areas. The states are not all alike, nor do they always do things in the same way, but then, there is no good reason why they should. One of the outstanding merits of our Federal system is that it provides a maximum amount of latitude to the states to deal with their own domestic problems in their own ways.

This survey shows that Mississippi has the full complement of laws and governmental services and agencies that one now expects to find in a modern American state. These services are well organized and well administered. In Mississippi, as elsewhere throughout the South, momentous changes in the social and economic life of the State are gradually being reflected in changes in governmental institutions.

In some areas Mississippi citizens and their government have demonstrated a sense of public responsibility that other states might do well to emulate. Since 1946 the State has developed and put in operation a program for medical education and an integrated health program to improve medical care and hospital services for the people. Under the leadership of one of the nation's most distinguished authorities in the field of public health and medicine, real progress has been made in all the fields of endeavor—increase in the supply of physicians in the State, new programs and facilities for medical and nursing education, thirty-eight new hospitals and five more under construction, and the establishment of the fastest-growing state-wide plan of voluntary hospitalization and surgical insurance in the country.

Recognizing the economic peril to its citizens created by a one-crop agricultural economy, the State has for some years been making intensive efforts not only to develop a diversified agriculture, but also to "balance agriculture with industry"—BAWI. Mississippi is a rural state, 70 per cent of its people living in rural areas and securing their income from farm production. It will probably continue to be predominately rural for some years, but trends toward both industrialization and urbanization are in evidence.

In education, Mississippi's people and their government get a rating of A-plus for effort, if not yet for the excellence of their school program. The Council of State Governments reports that "in general the states which are low in the average current expense per pupil are low in ability to support education and are making a greater than average effort as measured by the ratio of revenue receipts for public schools to total personal income." This applies to Mississippi. At the same time, nine of the twelve poorest states were among the twelve having the largest number of children to be educated. This also applies to Mississippi. Yet, despite a low income level and a more than average school population, Mississippi taxes itself more heavily, its citizens dig more deeply into their pockets—in proportion to their income—for the support of their schools than do the citizens of the large, wealthy industrial states.

The percentage of individual income devoted to public schools through state and local taxes is higher in Mississippi than it is, for example, in New York—2.318 per cent (rank 28) as against 2.158 per cent (rank 41). Such evidence of interest in education, such evidence of a willingness to tax until it hurts for the support of the things that matter most—these, I submit, are the attributes of courage and vigor, not of weakness.

W. Brooke Graves

The Library of Congress
July, 1954

Preface

ALTHOUGH INTEREST in the government and administration of Mississippi is now higher than perhaps it has ever been, there is still available little in the way of published materials that bring together in an integrated narrative the organization and functioning of the State's government. This book has been planned to fill the obvious gap. It should be useful to a wide variety of persons and groups: students in institutions of higher learning, interested State administrative and legislative officials, officers of local government, and citizens of Mississippi generally.

In the South the state governments commonly perform directly more functions and render more services than do the governments of states where traditionally a larger share of governmental activities has been allocated to local units, and Mississippi follows closely this regional pattern. As new services are added and old ones expanded, the growth of state government continues. In a sense, this growth is reflected in state expenditures, which rose from $58,000,000 in 1942 to more than $161,000,000 in 1952 and still higher in 1953. The structure and organization through which these funds are expended, as well as the management of the personnel engaged in public functions, warrant careful examination and evaluation.

As in the case of all books of this type, many persons have provided real assistance. Grateful acknowledgment is due to the officials of state and local government in Mississippi who gave freely of their time and knowledge and furnished documents, statistical data, and other materials included in the volume. Special acknowledgment must be made to several individuals. Professor Huey B. Howerton, Chairman of the Department of Political Science at the University of Mississippi, read portions of the manuscript and offered valuable suggestions. Our wives, Mary Wagner Highsaw and Mae Edwards Fortenberry, also reviewed the manuscript and suggested improvements that have been incorporated. Mrs. Marjorie D. Latham and Mrs. Maudie R. Nipper of the staff of the Bureau of Public

Administration, University of Mississippi, prepared the manuscript for publication through its several revisions. We are especially indebted to Dr. W. Brooke Graves, Legislative Reference Service, Library of Congress, who, as Editor of the Series in which this volume appears, was both patient and helpful.

Most studies of social science contain errors, both of fact and interpretation. Responsibility for the materials in the present book and for their interpretation rests with the authors.

ROBERT B. HIGHSAW
CHARLES N. FORTENBERRY

University, Mississippi
July, 1954

Contents

AMERICAN COMMONWEALTHS SERIES

W. Brooke Graves, *Editor*

The Government and Administration of Mississippi

CHAPTER 1

The State and Its People

HISTORICAL BACKGROUND

MISSISSIPPI BECAME the twentieth American state with its formal entry into the Union on December 10, 1817. Back of the admission lay more than two centuries of history, for less than fifty years after the discovery of America Spanish explorers moved up the Mississippi Valley. A century and a half later Sieur d'Iberville landed on the Gulf Coast, and the French began settlement near what is now Biloxi.

France lost control of the territory to Great Britain in 1763 after the French and Indian War, and English sovereignty over the lands continued until 1779. In this period colonists came in increasing numbers, from New England and the Middle Atlantic colonies down the Ohio and Mississippi rivers and from the Carolinas, Georgia, Maryland, and Virginia across the mountains. Meanwhile, Spain recognized the independence of the United States and took rule of the territory. The United States acquired title in 1795, and on April 7, 1798, Congress formally created the Mississippi Territory, which was enlarged in 1804 to embrace the present states of Alabama and Mississippi and again a few years later to include West Florida. By 1810 the territorial population residing within the present state boundaries had grown to 40,000 inhabitants, and agitation began for admission to the Union. In 1817 Congress divided the territory into two sections and authorized the western portion to organize a state government. A constitutional convention was held with representatives from fourteen counties, all of which were located in the southern third of

Mississippi. David Holmes was elected governor, and Congress approved the admission of the new state to the Union.

In the next decade or two population grew as settlement of the state continued. By 1832 both the Choctaw and Chickasaw Indians had ceded their lands, and one of Mississippi's early "cotton booms" was on. Prices were high, so that the new, fertile lands of the state gave rich rewards compared with soils to the east, already losing their fertility because of exhaustive farming practices. The great planters of the Natchez-Vicksburg area witnessed the rise of a threat to their political power as the number of small farmers increased rapidly with new settlers.

The development of the state was reflected in increased trade, which moved largely over waterways. Natchez grew on the banks of the Mississippi and Yazoo City on the Yazoo River. Communities developed in the northeast Mississippi hills around Grenada on the Yalobusha River and to the east in the prairie country near Columbus and the Tombigbee River. In the southern part of the state Columbia, situated on the Pearl River, linked the small municipality of Jackson with the plains of the Gulf Coast. Roads developed naturally to supplement waterways, and in the early part of the nineteenth century one of these, the Natchez Trace, running northeasterly from Natchez 500 miles to Nashville, at first provided a convenient return route for the workers who manned the one-way flatboats to New Orleans, and later a highway for traders and settlers.

The great land boom of the 1830's together with the development of roads and the advent of the railroad coincided with the spread of cotton farming into the hill country like Lafayette County and, by the time of the War between the States, into the swampy lowlands of the Mississippi Delta. The main movement of people into Mississippi—except for considerable Negro migration in the Reconstruction Period—was completed in the early years of the fitful 1850's. Slavery, upon which much of Mississippi's agricultural wealth seemed to be erected, was now a great national issue, and in the Mississippi elections of 1851 candidates under the astute direction of Henry Foote were victorious with a platform accepting the Compromise of 1850. Within ten years the irreconcilable conflict was a reality, and Mississippi cast her lot with the Confederacy. The Reconstruction years came and passed, and Mississippi generally was caught in the vortex of national economic development. Wars and floods, drought and depression all have afflicted Mississippi over the years; sometimes, it would seem, more than other states.

In 1890 a constitutional convention drafted the present state constitu-

MISSISSIPPI COUNTIES AND PRINCIPAL CITIES

tion. At this time a trend to urbanism became apparent as Jackson and Meridian grew, along with the continued expansion of numerous smaller municipal corporations. The great depression of the 1930's placed a severe economic strain on the state; cotton prices went down and remained low throughout the decade. The periods of the two world wars were years of industrial prosperity, though, and they had important effects upon the state. Industries in other states needed workers and had the wages to pay them; many young men and women, white and Negro, left Mississippi, and in these years population fell somewhat.

Since 1936 Mississippi and her leaders have made conscious efforts to balance agriculture with industry, to achieve an economic base that is less precarious than agriculture has proved in the past. What lies ahead cannot be foretold.[1] Mississippi is something more than history, however; it is people who live in a specific physical and social, economic and political environment. It is chiefly the framework of politically organized society erected by these people in their environmental location with which this volume deals.

MISSISSIPPI GEOGRAPHY—LAND USE PROBLEMS

A few basic geographic facts can be briefly stated. The state occupies a portion of the Gulf Coastal Plain Province of the United States. Its total land area is 47,716 square miles, and the inland water area comprises 296 square miles. The extreme length, north to south, of Mississippi is 330 miles and the point of greatest width 180 miles. In physical size Mississippi ranks thirty-first in the Union.

Topography and Climate

Contrary to popular impression, Mississippi is not a plain. Its surface features are divisible into ten major areas that describe roughly the geologic features of the state.* The state slopes gently from a maximum height of about 800 feet in the north to sea level along the coast. Into this slope numerous streams have cut over the years so that few level uplands remain. The country, therefore, is hilly with the exception of the Alluvial Plain and the prairies of northeast Mississippi.

Climatically Mississippi has sometimes been characterized as a state of

* These are: the Mississippi Alluvial Plain (the Delta), Loess Bluffs, Pine Hills, Jackson Prairie Belt, North Central Hills, Flatwoods, Pontotoc Hills, Black Prairie, Fall Line Hills, and Coastal Terrace.

"warm winters and even warmer summers." Although there are differences between areas, the temperature varies from an average minimum of 39 degrees in the northern counties and an average minimum of 54 degrees on the coast to respective annual mean temperatures of 61 and 65 degrees. Average precipitation is between 50 and 60 inches of rainfall annually, and the frost-free season approximates 200 days annually.

Land Use Problems

The physical features of the Mississippi environment are such that a number of important problems of land use have arisen in the past. Among these are agricultural land use, forest land, soil erosion, mineral resources, water resources, and water problems.

Agricultural Land Use. As late as 1945 much of the land of Mississippi then in crops should have been withdrawn from use. Of 30,348,000 acres, 10,150,000 acres comprised areas suitable for permanent vegetation that could be used for grazing or woodland, usually with moderate limitations, and another 3,357,000 acres could be employed only occasionally for crops.[2] Decades of misuse of the land, cut by numerous small streams and leached by heavy rainfall, have been a drain upon the economy of the state, so much so that in 1938 the Mississippi Planning Commission estimated that Mississippi's land held 200,000 people on farms too poor to return a minimum satisfactory living to them.

Forest Land. Mississippi once was covered almost completely with forests. Today more than 16,000,000 acres, or about 53 per cent of the land area, are in forests. Forest industries have supported a sizable portion of Mississippi's people, and the wise and effective utilization as well as conservation of this resource has been made largely a state program in which the Federal government also participates. Although many remedial steps have been taken since 1935 to initiate reforestation programs on the 12,000,000 acres requiring such aid, much still remains to be done.

Mineral Resources. Except for oil, the state's mineral deposits are not spectacular. Mineral research has demonstrated that Mississippi possesses wealth in clay minerals. Many of the counties have been investigated and some testing facilities have been established. Extensive geologic study remains to determine Mississippi's hidden resources, and this story is alluded to in a subsequent chapter.

Water Resources. The people of Mississippi have a supply of water that is pure enough and abundant enough for domestic uses. Some areas of the state can produce large supplies of artesian water, but continued expansion for industrial uses will require installation of conservation practices. Early in 1954 conservationists were calling for serious study of this problem.

Sometimes Mississippians believe they have too much water; until 1917 much of the state had little or no protection against floods and overflows. Since that time Federal-state cooperation in a program of upstream engineering, improvement of surface drainage, and partial control of recurring backwaters has opened much fertile alluvial land to farming.

MISSISSIPPI'S PEOPLE

Mississippi is more than land and the problems that come with its use. Mississippi is also its people. How many of them are there? Where do they live? What do they do? What are some of their essential characteristics?

Total Population

Mississippi now ranks twenty-sixth in terms of population among the states of the Union. Table 1 shows the growth in number of inhabitants in Mississippi since 1800. It shows also the varying percentages between whites and Negroes. In every decennial census except two, Mississippi's population has grown; it fell slightly in 1920 and again in 1950, when the total number of inhabitants stood at slightly more than 2,000,000 persons. From 1850 to 1900 Negroes constituted almost 56 per cent of the population; in 1940 they were a little less than half; and by 1950, the nonwhite population totaled only 44.4 per cent. Since 1900 the ratio of Negroes to white population has consistently declined and can be expected to fall further as out-migration continues.[3]

Mississippi's people also are moving from farms to urban areas of 2,500 or more. Since 1900 the urban population has steadily increased, growing from less than 8 per cent in 1900 to almost a fifth of the state's population by 1940 and to more than a fourth by 1950. Conversely rural population has diminished. Moreover, rural nonfarm population, that is, persons living in smaller municipal corporations and in unincorporated areas but not on farms, has increased at the expense of rural population, growing since 1940 to 474,545 persons, or almost 23 per cent of the state's total population. It appears particularly significant that the Mississippi urban population is growing at the expense of the farm population, so

TABLE 1

POPULATION OF MISSISSIPPI, 1800–1950

	TOTAL POPULATION		RACE		RESIDENCE	
Year	*Number*	*Per Cent Change By Decades*	*White* (Per Cent)	*Nonwhite* (Per Cent)	*Urban* (Per Cent)	*Rural* (Per Cent)
1800	8,850[a]	—	—	—	—	100.0
1810	40,352[a]	356.0	—	—	—	100.0
1820	75,448	87.0	—	—	—	100.0
1830	136,621	81.1	—	—	2.0	98.0
1840	375,651	175.0	—	—	1.0	99.0
1850	606,526	61.5	48.8	51.2	1.8	98.2
1860	791,305	30.5	44.7	55.3	2.6	97.4
1870	827,922	4.6	46.2	53.8	4.0	96.0
1880	1,131,597	36.7	42.4	57.6	3.1	96.9
1890	1,289,600	14.0	42.2	57.8	5.4	94.6
1900	1,551,270	20.3	41.3	58.7	7.7	92.3
1910	1,797,114	15.8	43.7	56.3	11.5	88.5
1920	1,790,618	−0.4	47.7	52.3	13.4	86.6
1930	2,009,821	12.2	49.7	50.3	16.9	83.1
1940	2,183,796	8.7	50.7	49.3	19.8	80.2
1950	2,178,194	−0.2	55.6	44.4	27.9	72.1

[a] This figure represents the portion of the territorial population residing within present State boundaries.

Sources: Figures for 1800–1940 taken from John C. Belcher and Morton B. King, *Mississippi's People* (Bureau of Public Administration, University of Mississippi, 1950), Table I, p. 12; for 1950 from United States Department of Commerce, Bureau of the Census, "Mississippi General Characteristics," *1950 United States Census of Population* (Washington, 1952), Tables 10, 11, 12.

rapidly that the latter has decreased from 71 per cent in 1920 to 50 per cent today.

General Characteristics

Of the total number of Mississippians, 716,851 are in the labor force available for work. This total includes 78.7 per cent of the men, white and Negro, and 24.8 per cent of the women fourteen years and over. The median family income in 1950 of Mississippians was $1,028, and more than 72 per cent of the families had incomes of less than $2,000. Table 2 indicates the principal occupations by which Mississippi's people earn their livelihood. Casual analysis of the table will show that more than 339,000 persons of both races work as farmers, farm managers, unpaid farm labor, or paid farm labor. Employing slightly less than half of the total labor force, agriculture even today remains the predominant occupation in Mississippi.

TABLE 2

MISSISSIPPI OCCUPATION CHARACTERISTICS, 1950

	White	*Per Cent*	*Negro*	*Per Cent*
Professional, technical workers	33,548	8.4	7,775	2.5
Farmers, farm managers	95,696	23.9	111,144	35.2
Nonfarm managers, officials, and proprietors	40,109	10.0	3,316	1.0
Clerical, kindred workers	36,752	9.1	1,723	.5
Sales	31,055	7.8	1,960	.6
Craftsmen, foremen	43,675	10.9	9,938	3.1
Operatives	53,521	13.3	31,531	10.0
Private-household workers	1,135	.3	32,093	10.1
Other service workers	15,929	4.0	20,135	6.4
Farm-unpaid family	18,424	4.6	34,045	10.8
Farm-paid laborers and foremen	9,124	2.3	27,246	8.6
Laborers (nonfarm)	15,828	4.0	31,329	9.9
Others	5,792	1.4	4,028	1.3
TOTALS	400,588	100.0	316,263	100.0

Source: "Mississippi General Characteristics," Table 28-a.

Population Trends

A recent study of Mississippi's people discloses three important trends.[4] First, the rate of population increase will be slow. This conclusion is based upon several factors, including a stationary or declining white birth rate and an increasing mortality rate as the ratio of older people rises; the Negro birth rate will probably remain stable, while the death rate will decline for some years and then begin to ascend. Economic factors that may impinge on the rate of population growth are also present. Thus a major depression in the near future would probably result in an increase in the Mississippi population; conversely a continued acceleration of industrial activity in the nation and of prosperous economic conditions would drain many persons from the state. Mechanization of agriculture, if at the same pace as in recent years, would free a large number of farm laborers for other occupations, possibly out of Mississippi unless marked industrial development within the state permitted their local employment.

Second, the proportion of white persons in the total population will rise because the loss of population from migration to other states will be greater among Negroes than whites. This outmigration would be hastened with rapid mechanization of agriculture. Finally, the current trend toward concentration of population in the urban areas will persist. The results of this move are significant. Its development will change the manners and attitudes inherited in a traditionally agricultural society; it forecasts also a declining birth rate and employment of more Mississippians on a wage or salary basis. This last fact, in turn, will make the people of the state more dependent upon fluctuations of urban employment and hence upon the operation of the business cycle. The governmental patterns of Mississippi, therefore, may come to approximate more closely those of the largely urban states of the Middle West and the Northeast. It is in this light, perhaps, that the state government must plan and must act, not merely for the current problems of a rural state but also for the problems of a new population in future years.

SOCIAL, POLITICAL, AND ECONOMIC HERITAGE

To say that a state is influenced by its social, political, and economic heritage is but to utter a commonplace. Yet this obvious fact has a special significance when applied to Mississippi. For, to a greater degree than most states, its social, political, and economic characteristics are a result of its heritage; in many respects Mississippi is a product of its past.

Social Factors

The social background of the state is firmly rooted in the institution of slavery. As early as 1800 the Mississippi Territory contained 3,489 slaves, and the number increased rapidly during the next five decades. Between 1830 and 1840 slaves became more numerous than white residents, establishing a numerical superiority of Negroes over whites that was maintained for a hundred years. In 1860 the slave population stood at 436,631 as compared to 353,901 white people. At this date, however, the total of all slaveholders amounted to only 8.8 per cent of the white population, almost all of whom should be classed as family heads. Of this limited group 46.9 per cent, or slightly less than half, owned from one to five slaves.[5] The combined planter families of the antebellum period, dear to novelist and genealogist alike, constituted less than half of the white people.

The significance of the planters, however, was vastly greater than their numbers would indicate. From them sprang not only the social and political leaders of the time but the mores and habits that marked all social relationships. By common consent, large landowners were aristocrats; ownership of slaves was a mark of distinction.* Economically a sort of feudal barony, the slaveholders assumed the obligations of their class: paternalism toward the slaves, protection of plantation autonomy, leadership in politics and war.

Although the majority of the white people were not included in this group, it appears that they were no less influenced by the planter class because of nonmembership. The nonslaveholding whites, though manifesting some enmity toward the planters and jealousy toward the slaves, tended to acquiesce in the system of planter leadership. It is one of the anomalies of history that the South's battles in the War between the States—a major purpose of which was the defense of slavery—were fought largely by nonslaveholding soldiers.

The war and the unfortunate aftermath of Reconstruction obliterated many of the economic distinctions among the people of Mississippi. Slaves were freed, plantations were abandoned, wealth disappeared. The ravages of invasion and battle and the turmoil and misgovernment that followed left only poverty and the memories of happier days. Different political leaders appeared; the "carpetbaggers," the "scalawags," and the recently freed Negroes—all new to the political scene—had their brief period of ascendancy. But when this transitory phase had passed, the political situation settled down to something not too different from prewar days. And the social cleavages remained, with but slightly different emphases. Mississippi was still a society of planters, poor whites, and Negroes. As slow and painful economic progress was made, the "planter" class broadened to include all people of wealth or of wealthy ancestry, and the poor whites came to include many nonfarmers. The Negroes, citizens by the Federal and state constitutions, remained somewhat the same group they had always been.

The seven decades since Reconstruction have brought many changes. Succeeding generations have witnessed the declining prestige of the landowners, the increasing prominence of the lower economic group, and the gradual progress of the Negroes to a better status. The growth of cities, along with industrial and commercial development, has distributed wealth

* An interesting sidelight on this aristocracy was the case of Greenwood Leflore, a half-breed Indian and former chief of the Choctaw tribe. He was among the state's largest slaveowners, his holdings numbering almost 400 slaves. Leflore County and its principal city, Greenwood, are named for him.—Charles S. Sydnor, *Slavery in Mississippi* (Appleton-Century, 1933), p. 131.

among more and more people. Revolutionary improvements in travel and communication have promoted interchange of population and ideas with other regions, thus dampening the fires of provincialism. But traditions do not die easily; patterns of thought and social attitudes are long-enduring. In many respects, Mississippi clings to the culture of the past.

What are the modern evidences of this social heritage of slavery, of the coexistence of widely different racial groups, of a landed gentry and a much larger group of landless citizens? They are not hard to find. The widely publicized attitude of the people toward segregation of whites and blacks is not mere intolerance and bigotry; it is the product of a way of life that has existed for a century and a half. The restrictions of the suffrage are not merely a device to bar the Negro from political participation; they reflect a widespread belief, born of the planter aristocracy, that better government results when a large segment of the people, both white and black, do not vote. Hatred of the Negro by a small number of white people, an emotion that formerly expressed itself in physical intimidation and lynching, is a carryover of the prewar jealousy of poor whites toward the slaves who were, in many respects, more fortunate.

The outpourings of novelists and writers of which Mississippi and its people are the theme have presented two contrasting pictures. One, perhaps best painted by Stark Young, is the land of magnolias and moonlight, of fair and gentle womanhood, of men steeped in honor and gallantry, of patient and loyal Negroes, of picturesque cotton fields and romantic rivers. The other is the land of William Faulkner, the place of shiftless sharecroppers and grinding poverty, of decadent gentlemen and wayward women, of racial violence and moral ruin.[6] Neither of these pictures is nor was intended to be a true characterization of the life and social atmosphere of the state. Mississippi has people of uprightness, honor, and tolerance; it also has demagogues, ne'er-do-wells, and bigots. It has wealth and poverty, education and illiteracy, progressivism and reaction. The tendency of many of its people to nurture traditions and to remember the past is but the natural inclination to look back to what was, and now seems to be, a brighter period. Their social heritage produces a fierce pride in their own history, customs, and institutions—the "Southern way of life." It also produces resentment against external criticism and resistance to outside reformers or their suggestions. Yet, these same reforms are constantly being effected by local decisions; institutions and habits change here as elsewhere. The social viewpoint is complex, but understandable. With such a background it could hardly be different.

Political Factors

Mississippi's political background parallels, in many ways, its social counterpart. This is but natural since the political, social, and economic factors in a people's behavior are interwoven and often indistinguishable. Political attitudes are frequently but a reflection of social or economic interests.

Political lines in Mississippi were defined well before the beginning of statehood. During the territorial period development and settlement were largely in the southern half of the state. Since this was a region of large-scale farming, the political power was lodged in the planter aristocracy of the Natchez-Vicksburg area. These men were conservative Democrats of the Jeffersonian school, and their influence was evident in the political events that attended the admission of the territory to statehood. The first constitution of the state, which contained provisions for a limited number of elective offices, restricted suffrage, and similar conservative features, showed clearly the influence of the planter group.* This leadership continued through the 1820's and into the period generally described as Jacksonian democracy. With the acquisition of the Choctaw and Chickasaw Indian lands, however, there was rapid development and settlement of the northern half of the state, and the period from 1830 to 1840 saw the population increased from 136,621 to 375,651 and the number of counties more than doubled. Since this tremendous increase in voting strength in the newly-settled sections represented adherents of the Jacksonian school of democracy, the control of the planters of the southwest was threatened. The new influence was revealed in the Constitution of 1832, which abolished property qualifications for voting, provided for popular election of judges, and in other ways reflected the democratic sentiments of the frontier.

The national party battles of this period had their counterpart in Mississippi. The conservative Democrats, opposing and detesting the more radical measures of the party, became Whigs, and this party experienced considerable success in the elections of the state during the decade 1835-1845, electing a governor and a United States Senator, and carrying the electoral vote for William Henry Harrison in 1840.[7] As the national fortunes of the Whig Party ebbed in the bitter controversies over slavery, a similar decline was evident in Mississippi. The conservative element,

* The most influential leader in the writing of the 1817 constitution was George Poindexter, the state's first representative in Congress and governor from 1820 to 1822.

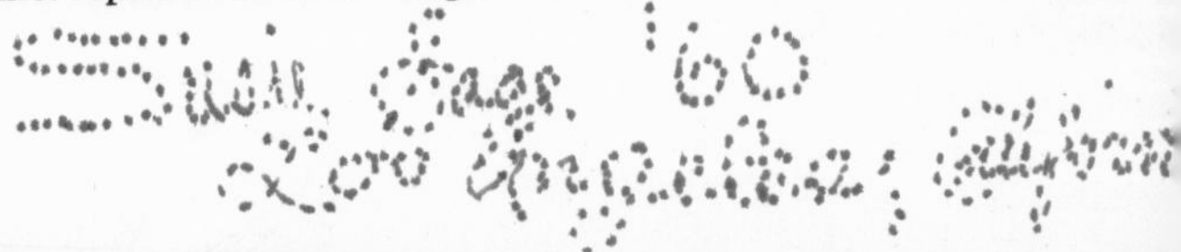

represented by the planter group of the Natchez region and inclined toward the Whig Party, was overpowered by the Democratic voters from the northern portion of the state.

The political leaders of the state during the decade prior to the War between the States were Democrats who adhered to the doctrines of John C. Calhoun. Men like Jefferson Davis and Jacob Thompson, though ardent defenders of slavery, did not draw their political support from the planter aristocracy, but rather from the frontier sections of the state. These areas, although not holding great numbers of slaves, felt that their future development depended on slave labor and thus could support the most outspoken advocates of slavery and secession.

The Republican Party in Mississippi was born of the war and nurtured by Reconstruction. It disappeared, for all practical purposes, with the end of the Reconstruction Period. Its leaders were chiefly "visitors" from northern states, but a number of Negroes filled important political offices. It drew no support from the conservative elements of the population, that group having been driven firmly into the Democratic Party by the excesses and mismanagement of the Republican administrations of these turbulent Reconstruction years. Recent efforts to reorganize and build up this party in Mississippi have found the Republican record during these years the most difficult obstacle to overcome.

The dominance of the political scene by the Democratic Party that began in 1876 was threatened slightly with the rise of the Populist movement in the 1890's. This party, which showed its greatest strength in the year 1895 when it polled 17,466 votes,[8] drew its support from the small farmers. Fear of the strength of this group was evident in the convention that wrote the Constitution of 1890 with its restrictive provisions on the suffrage.

Political conditions in Mississippi in the middle years of the twentieth century reflect much of this heritage. The seventy-five years of solid Democratic control would indicate to the casual observer that the allegiance to one party is unshakable. Within this party, however, the old cleavages remain. The element that formed the old Whig Party and endured membership in the Democratic Party for most of the years since remains adamantly conservative; the element that formed the Populist Party of the 1890's, joined now by most of the small group of Negro voters, inclines toward liberalism. One author sees the picture as "The Delta and the Hills"—the Delta representing conservatism and the hill sections the liberal element.

Although this characterization has little geographical basis, it reveals much of the political background of the state. The Delta, home of the large plantations, can trace its political lineage back to the planter aristocracy, although many groups and ideas have been injected along the way. The Hills represent a political belief that dates from the nonslaveholding whites of the antebellum period, also with numerous additions throughout the years. This view is over-simplified, but it indicates well the political heritage of the state.[9]

Economic Factors

The basic economic heritage of any people is the land. Land has an unusual significance for the people of Mississippi, since it has always been the direct source of their income through the production of agricultural crops and timber. Ownership of land also has been important as a social and political yardstick. Earlier reliance on a one-crop agriculture, however, has brought poverty to much of the agricultural population.

In recent decades more attention to its basic heritage has been evident in the state's economy. The discovery of oil and gas and subsequent production in various parts of the state has enlarged its values and added a new element to the natural wealth. Persistent activities of the friends of conservation and reclamation, also described earlier, have reforested and restored many thousands of wasted or cutover acres. Agricultural reform is evident in more scientific methods of farming that make for greater production with improvement of the soil at the same time. The introduction of cattle raising, dairying, poultry production, and vegetable culture as well as other forms of diversification has lessened the dependence of the farming population on cotton.

Perhaps the greatest potential boon to the economy lies in the newly-discovered possibilities of industrial development. A large labor supply, sufficient water, abundant power resources, and a mild climate are attractions that have already brought a number of industries to the state with indications that the pace of industrialization is being rapidly accelerated.

The economic background of Mississippi has its limiting factors. There is still present much of the inherited devotion to cotton as the primary type of agriculture. Much of the labor supply of the state is unskilled and better adapted to farming than to industry. The people are generally of low income. None of these limitations appear to be too severe. The relative increase in the average income of the people has in recent years surpassed the increase for the people in the nation as a whole.[10] The economic future appears bright.

GOVERNMENT AND ITS ENVIRONMENT

This chapter has sought to sketch the background of Mississippi's history, its geography, and its people as well as to relate their social, political, and economic heritage. The state government and administration, in fact, cannot be considered apart from the physical and cultural environment, for, although many comments on them can be made that are generally applicable to all state governments, other conditions grow out of the state's own peculiar background and development. Thus specific problems are often an outgrowth of physical, social, or economic features of the state, problems such as the resistance to political change, the devoted adherence to a rigid constitution, the fear of an integration of administrative authority, among others. These problems are issues of the mind of Mississippi as well as issues of the mechanics of government. Again and again in the chapters that follow will they arise. Sometimes solutions will seem improbable, and the political mores too powerful. In other instances this same heritage will be found to have had a marked positive effect. These results are as they should be, for, perhaps, the problem of state government is only a segment of the broader story of Mississippi's people.

FOOTNOTES

[1] A number of common sources have been employed heavily in these pages. Among them are the following: John C. Belcher and Morton B. King, *Mississippi's People* (Bureau of Public Administration, University of Mississippi, 1950); Federal Writers' Project, *Mississippi, A Guide to the Magnolia State* (Viking Press, 1938); John W. Monette, *History of the Discovery and Settlement of the Valley of the Mississippi* (Harper, 1846), vol. 1; and Mississippi State Board of Development, *Mississippi: America's State of Opportunity* (Jackson, 1944).

[2] Soil Conservation Service, *Soil and Water Conservation Estimates for the Southeastern Region* (rev. ed., Washington, June, 1945), p. 19.

[3] Belcher and King, *op. cit.,* pp. 11-12.

[4] *Ibid.,* pp. 75-76. This passage is largely restated from this source.

[5] Charles S. Sydnor, *Slavery in Mississippi* (Appleton-Century, 1933), pp. 192-93.

[6] See Stark Young, *Heaven Trees* (Scribner's, 1926), *So Red The Rose* (Scribner's, 1935); William Faulkner, *Sanctuary* (Random House, 1931), *Absalom, Absalom!* (Random House, 1936).

[7] Charles Lynch, Governor, 1836-1840; John Henderson, U. S. Senator, 1839-1845. A. L. Bingaman, president of the state senate from 1838 to 1840, also was a Whig. See Dunbar Rowland, *History of Mississippi* (Jackson: S. J. Clarke Pub. Co., 1925), I, 586 ff.

[8] See William D. McCain, *The Populist Party in Mississippi* (Unpublished Master's thesis, University of Mississippi, 1931); *House Journal, 1896,* p. 74.

[9] V. O. Key, *Southern Politics* (Knopf, 1949), pp. 229 ff.

[10] U. S. Department of Commerce, *Survey of Current Business* (August, 1952), p. 17. See also David McKinney, *Income Payments to Mississippians* (Bureau of Business Research, University of Mississippi, 1952).

CHAPTER 2

The State Constitution

WRITTEN CONSTITUTIONS are fundamental in all American government. They exemplify a basic principle of our political philosophy—that ours is a government of laws and not of men. A constitution may be defined as a body of fundamental law upon which a government is built and in accordance with which that government operates. It thus establishes the machinery of government and at the same time protects the people from improper exercise of governmental authority.

THE BACKGROUND OF STATE CONSTITUTIONS

State constitutions have been in existence longer than any modern charters of government in the United States, antedating both the present national Constitution and an earlier ill-fated charter of the national government, the Articles of Confederation. Lineal antecedents of the first state constitutions, however, may be found in the charters originally granted to American trading companies and colonies by the British Crown. These charters included provisions relating to government as well as to trade, and contained clauses binding the governing country as well as the colonial authorities.[1] Although many of these earlier charters were revoked during the colonial period, 1607-1776, the charters of Rhode Island and Connecticut were adequate, with certain modifications, for use as state constitutions after these colonies had become states of the present Federal government.[2] The development of state constitutions, in short, has been a continuous process for the past 300 years. Present state constitutions, like the national Constitution, are the result of centuries of political experience.

The first constitutions adopted by the states after the Declaration of Independence were, for the most part, merely the instruments of colonial government adapted to the use of independent states. Most of them were drawn up and put into effect by the legislatures of the states. In 1779, however, Massachusetts set the pattern for constitution-making by calling a convention of elected delegates, chosen for the special purpose of writing the fundamental law of that state.[3] The precedent of a convention has been followed by states since that time.* Naturally, most states have found it necessary to rewrite their original constitutions, the average life of such documents being about sixty years.

Early Constitutions of Mississippi

Mississippi has had four constitutions since its admission into the Union in 1817. The Constitution of 1817 was marked by brevity and simplicity. Following the pattern of early American state constitutions, it provided for few elective officers, concentrating the political power of the state in the legislature and, to a lesser extent, in the governor.[4] The Constitution of 1832, however, revealed the influence of the Jacksonian era in which it took effect. It provided for more direct popular government, with most state officers elected by the people and the political power widely distributed. Minor executive officers and judicial officers were made subject to popular election, and more elective local offices were created with short tenure. This constitution served until the state seceded from the Union in 1861 and joined the Confederacy. The necessary modifications to conform to the change of allegiance were made by the Secession Convention of 1861.[5]

At the end of the War between the States, the Convention of 1865 made important changes in the constitution, and the state sought to re-enter the Union under the plan announced by President Johnson.† This attempt was rejected by Congress, and the state remained out of the Union for four more years. In 1868 another constitutional convention was called. This body, composed of Negro and white delegates chosen under the protection of occupation forces of the United States Army, wrote a constitution

* The Massachusetts constitution, which went into effect in 1780, also was submitted to a vote of the people. This precedent has not been followed so consistently.

† The meeting in Mississippi was the first of the southern state conventions to assemble in pursuance of the President's plan.—James W. Garner, *Reconstruction in Mississippi* (Macmillan, 1901), pp. 82-96, contains a discussion of this convention.

that was submitted to a vote of the people, where it was defeated.[6] After certain sections of the proposed constitution were separately resubmitted along with the whole document, it was finally ratified in 1869.* This constitution served to gain readmission of the state into the Union. This "Reconstruction Constitution" varied from the 1832 document chiefly in that it contained various provisions designed to guarantee the civil and political rights of the freed Negroes and to meet the requirements of Congress for readmission into the Union.[7] Under this constitution the control of the state government fell into the hands of the so-called carpetbaggers and scalawags through unscrupulous and dishonest manipulation of the Negro vote. Naturally, this engendered bitter feelings on the part of the white people, and the state was rocked with political turmoil. The success of the white Democratic nominees in the election of 1875, followed by the resignation of the Republican governor, Adelbert Ames, inaugurated one-party government in the state and laid the groundwork for a new constitution.† Although it was fifteen years before a new constitution was written, the unhappy experiences of the Reconstruction Period were still fresh in the minds of delegates when they assembled to write the Constitution of 1890.

The Constitutional Convention of 1890

After 1876 the government was solidly in Democratic hands. Although the 1869 constitution provided equal political rights, and a small number of Republican office-holders were Negroes, the white people were in full political control.‡ Under the able leadership of Governor John M. Stone, who served from 1876 to 1882, and Governor Robert Lowry, who was in office from 1882 to 1890, much progress was made in recovering from the effects of the war and Reconstruction.

With the election of Benjamin Harrison as President in 1888, and the introduction of a "force bill" in the 1889 Congress, new fears were expressed about Federal measures that would restore Negro control in the state under the equal franchise provisions of the 1869 constitution. Although this was probably the most important reason for the demand for

* The sections in question were the proscription clauses (art. 7, secs. 3, 5) affecting Confederate veterans and supporters. They were defeated and did not become a part of the constitution.

† Governor Ames resigned on March 29, 1876, after impeachment charges had been voted by the house of representatives.—Dunbar Rowland, *History of Mississippi* (Jackson: S. J. Clarke Pub. Co., 1925), II, 203-4.

‡ Blanche K. Bruce, a Negro Republican, served ably in the United States Senate until the expiration of his term in March, 1881.—*Ibid.*, p. 218.

a new constitution, other reasons, such as the regulation of corporations and the restriction of private legislation, were also expressed. An act of the 1890 legislature provided for the calling of a constitutional convention.[8] The governor's proclamation calling the convention was issued on March 11, 1890, and the convention assembled on August 12, 1890.[9]

The convention consisted of 134 delegates, of whom all but two were Democrats.* S. S. Calhoon of Hinds County presided over the sessions, which continued for nearly three months. On November 1, 1890, the convention completed its labors, and the new constitution was adopted by a vote of 104 to 8, with 21 delegates absent and not voting.[10] Eventually 129 of the 134 members of the convention signed the constitution. One member died during the convention, one was absent, and three who were present refused to sign.[11]

No provision was made for the submission of the document to a popular vote, although this question did not escape the attention of the delegates. A proposal was made by one delegate to submit the constitution to a referendum, allowing the electorate to vote on each of the different sections. This proposal was referred to the judiciary committee of the convention, which reported on October 30, 1890, that such submission was "unnecessary and inexpedient."[12]

The 1890 convention also assumed legislative functions and passed a number of "ordinances" providing for such things as the extension of the terms of state officials then in office until 1896, and the adoption of a new ballot system.[13] Adjournment was taken on November 1, 1890, and the new constitution took effect on that date.

THE CONSTITUTION OF 1890

The Mississippi constitution today retains the same general features it had at the time of its adoption. In addition to a preamble it contains fifteen articles, each of which is subdivided into sections. There is also a schedule of twelve sections providing for carrying the document into effect. In all, there are 287 sections, and the whole document, including the amendments added since its adoption, fills about sixty printed pages.

The subject matter of the constitution may be summarized by a brief explanation of the fifteen articles. They are: (1) distribution of powers—

* H. F. Simrall of Warren County was a Republican and James L. Alcorn of Coahoma County was a former Whig who had served as United States Senator and as governor under a Republican administration.—Rowland, *op. cit.*, p. 246.

a classification of the executive, legislative, and judicial powers of government with the provision that they remain separate; (2) boundaries of the state—establishment of the geographical boundaries of the state with provisions as to change; (3) bill of rights—series of twenty-eight sections designed to protect the rights of citizens against the state government; (4) legislative department—a detailed regulation of the election, powers, and procedure of the state legislature; (5) executive—provisions relating to the qualifications, election, and functions of the governor and other state and local officials; (6) judiciary—provisions concerning the organization and jurisdiction of state courts and for the election of judicial and court officers; (7) corporations—provisions for the chartering of corporations and for their regulation and taxation by the legislature; (8) education—provisions for the establishment of districts, funds, and revenues for public education and for the election of officials to administer them; (9) militia—authorization of legislation to establish a state militia, with provision for officers and funds; (10) the penitentiary and prisons—regulations concerning the employment of persons convicted of crime; (11) levees—establishment of a system of levee districts with provision for officials and tax support; (12) franchise—establishment of requirements for registration and voting, and fixing of the date for election of state officers; (13) apportionment—fixing the representation for various counties in the lower house of the legislature and the establishment of representative and senatorial districts containing more than one county, with strict limitations as to reapportionment; (14) general provisions—miscellaneous limitations as to local government, prohibiting miscegenation, providing oath of public office, and directing the payment of Confederate pensions; (15) amendments to the constitution—establishing the method of amendment.

The titles of these articles covered the principal aspects of state government as they appeared in 1890. A constitution written today probably would combine some of these subjects, omit some, and add new ones.

Bills of Rights

Bills of rights usually are among the most highly regarded provisions of state constitutions. In them the individual finds a direct and specific statement of those rights that he can enjoy free from interference by his government. All such provisions in state constitutions are quite similar in content and all are based primarily on the English Bill of Rights of 1689.

The Bill of Rights of the Mississippi constitution is found in article 3. It consists of twenty-eight sections that cover the general subjects of:

(1) political power and states rights; (2) freedom of speech, press, religion, assembly, and petition; (3) protection of persons and property; (4) definition of treason; (5) rights of accused persons; (6) miscellaneous rights.

All political power of the state is declared to be "vested in, and derived from, the people," by section 5. This, of course, is but a restatement of the basis of constitutional democracy. The "inherent, sole, and exclusive" right of the people to regulate the government and to change its constitution and government without violating the national Constitution, as expressed in section 6, also is well understood. The military power is made strictly subordinate to the civil power by section 9, and section 20 provides that all persons holding office in the state have a specified term of office. The right of the state to secede is expressly forbidden by section 7.

The basic rights of freedom of speech, press, religion, assembly, and petition are protected by three sections of the Bill of Rights. Section 11 protects the right "peaceably to assemble and petition the government." Section 13 declares that freedom of speech and press "shall be held sacred"; persons charged with libel as a result of the exercise of this freedom must be acquitted if the matter charged as libelous is true and is published with good motives and justifiable ends.[14] Section 18 prohibits any religious test for holding office and any law giving preference to a religious sect or mode of worship.* It also provides religious freedom, but stipulates that this right does not justify the exclusion of the Bible from use in the public schools.

Six separate sections deal with the protection of persons and property. Section 12 guarantees the historic right to "keep and bear arms" in aid of the civil power, when legally summoned, and to defend one's person, home, or property. The legislature is expressly authorized to regulate or prohibit the carrying of concealed weapons. Section 14 repeats a provision of the Fourteenth Amendment to the national Constitution that no person may be deprived of "life, liberty, or property without due process of law."† Section 15 prohibits slavery or involuntary servitude and thus repeats the provision of the Thirteenth Amendment to the national Constitution. Similarly, section 16, prohibiting ex post facto laws or laws impairing the obligation of contracts, repeats the prohibition on states found in Article I, section 10, of the national Constitution. Section 17 regulates the manner in which private property may be taken for public use under the power

* In this connection see section 265, which denies public office to any person who denies the existence of a Supreme Being.

† As in the case of the Fourteenth Amendment, there has been extensive litigation under this section.

of eminent domain. Due compensation must be paid and the determination of whether the proposed use is public is made a judicial question. Section 19 rather archaistically protects persons by prohibiting dueling and providing that participants in duels in or out of the state be disfranchised and disqualified from holding public office.

Sections 21 to 31 of the Bill of Rights deal with persons accused of crime. These rights include protection of the privilege of the writ of habeas corpus,* prohibition of double jeopardy, protection from unreasonable searches and seizures, and the requirement of proper warrant. All persons are assured access to the courts for the remedy of injuries, and the right of a person to prosecute or defend any civil cause in which he is a party is guaranteed. Every person is assured further of the right to jury trial, to be confronted by witnesses against him, and to obtain witnesses in his behalf; nor can he be compelled to testify against himself. Grand jury indictment is required in prosecution of crimes where the penalty is death or imprisonment. Other protections of accused persons include the prohibition of cruel and unusual punishment, excessive fines, excessive bail, and imprisonment for debt.

Various other provisions of a miscellaneous nature may be found in the Mississippi Bill of Rights. Treason is defined in section 10 as levying war against the state or giving aid or comfort to its enemies. Conviction of treason must be on testimony of two witnesses to the overt act or on confession in open court. This article operates as a protection of individual rights, both by the definition of treason and by the requirement for conviction. Section 8 declares that all residents who are citizens of the United States are citizens of Mississippi, again repeating a provision of the Fourteenth Amendment of the national Constitution. Section 32 provides that the enumeration of certain rights in the constitution does not deny or impair others retained by and "inherent in the people."

In these provisions the basic rights of the people seem to be amply protected. The only significant omission from the list of traditional guarantees is an article relating to the quartering of soldiers. No abuses resulting from this omission appear to have occurred.

Students of the Mississippi constitution may question the necessity for the inclusion in the Bill of Rights of sections 8, 14, 15, and 16, which repeat provisions of the national Constitution. Although these sections are, for

* The writ may be suspended when, in case of rebellion or invasion, the public safety demands it, but only on authority of the legislature. The power of the courts in determining propriety of acts during suspension is important.—*State* v *McPhail,* 182 Miss. 360, 180 So. 387 (1938).

the most part, unnecessary, they seem to have been included in order to make the body of guarantees more complete. Each of these sections was carried over from the 1869 constitution.[15]

AMENDMENT AND REVISION

State constitutions require changes or additions from time to time to make them fit new conditions. For this reason an amending article is considered an essential part of such documents. The most common method of amendment is by proposal of the legislature and ratification by the voters.* This is the only method provided by the Mississippi constitution. Article 15 covers the subject as follows:

Section 273. Whenever two-thirds of each house of the legislature shall deem any change, alteration or amendment necessary to this Constitution, such proposed amendment, change or alteration shall be read and passed by two-thirds vote of each house, respectively on each day, for three several days; public notice shall then be given by the secretary of state at least three months preceding an election, at which the qualified electors shall vote directly for or against such change, alteration or amendment, and if more than one amendment shall be submitted at one time, they shall be submitted in such manner and form that the people may vote for or against each amendment separately; and if it shall appear that a majority of the qualified electors voting shall have voted for the proposed change, alteration or amendment, then it shall be inserted at the next succeeding session of the legislature as a part of the Constitution and not otherwise.

This article provides substantially the same method of amendment as that of the constitutions of 1832 and 1869.[16] It will be noted that the process of amending consists of three steps: (1) proposal by the legislature; (2) ratification by the voters; (3) insertion by the legislature.

Proposal by the Legislature. The requirement that two thirds of each house of the legislature vote for a proposed amendment is construed to mean two thirds of the members present.[17] Although there is no requirement that amendments be proposed in regular sessions, the limitations on extraordinary sessions would prevent the proposal of an amendment unless recommended by the governor.[18] The provision that each amendment must be submitted separately is mandatory.[19]

Ratification. The voters register their opinions on a proposed amend-

* This method of amendment, with variations as to detail, is found in forty-six states. Delaware does not require popular ratification, and New Hampshire authorizes amendment only by constitutional convention.—Clyde F. Snider, *American State and Local Government* (Appleton-Century-Crofts, 1950), pp. 16-18.

ment at the next general election following proposal by the legislature. The secretary of state must give publicity to the proposal for three months preceding this election. In order to be approved the amendment must secure a majority of all votes cast at the election, not merely a majority of those voting on the proposition.[20]

Insertion by the Legislature. The effective date of an amendment, which has been approved by vote of the people, must await the "insertion" of the amendment by the next session of the legislature. This is a mandatory duty required by the constitution and does not allow the legislature any discretion. Apparently, amendments may be inserted by extraordinary as well as by regular legislative sessions.*

Constitutional Revision. Since 1890 the people of Mississippi have adopted thirty-five amendments to their constitution in an effort to keep it abreast of changing conditions. Nine of the fifteen articles have been amended one or more times. Naturally, a great many other proposed amendments have failed to secure the necessary vote for popular ratification. The judiciary article has been amended more frequently than any other with ten separate amendments. Seven amendments have been added to the legislative and legislative apportionment articles, five to the education article, four to the article on levees, three each to the articles on franchise and general provisions, and one each to the articles on the executive, civil rights, and amendments. The time of amending has been spaced fairly well throughout the period, except for the year 1916 when nine amendments were inserted by the legislature.

In general, the amendments have not been of great importance, dealing more with matters of administration than with governmental structure. Perhaps the more important basic changes were those making the judges of the courts elective rather than appointive,[21] the changes in the apportionment of the legislature,[22] and the establishment of a nonpolitical system of administration for the state's higher educational institutions.[23] Perhaps the most important change attempted was the amendment providing for direct legislation by the initiative and referendum. Adopted by the people in the election of 1914 and inserted by the legislature in 1916, it was used on several occasions before being declared unconstitutional six years later.[24]

The Voters and Constitutional Amendments. Voter participation in the amending process is small, due in part to the provision that amendments must be voted on at elections rather than primary elections. In a one-

* Three amendments were inserted by the extraordinary legislative session of 1935. The courts have never ruled on the constitutionality of this insertion.

party state it is natural that general elections do not attract many voters, and the popular interest in proposed constitutional amendments is not sufficient to bring them to the polls. Apathy also results from the fact that the voters often do not understand the meaning of the amendment upon which they are to vote. Whatever the reason, it is a fact that only a small percentage of the people vote on proposed changes in the constitution.* Changes in the fundamental law are the essence of the democratic process. They should command the active interest of a large majority of the electorate.

REWRITING THE CONSTITUTION

As previously indicated, the constitution contains no provision for change except by legislative proposal of amendments. With the passing years, there has been increasing opinion that this method of change is inadequate, and that only a rewriting of the fundamental law will bring it into line with modern economic and governmental conditions.

Although important constitutional changes have been made by other methods,† it is generally believed that a convention of popularly-elected delegates is the best method for complete revision of a constitution. The present document does not provide for the calling of a convention; however, it is well established that the legislature may call one as a regular exercise of legislative power.[25] Although the legislature may refer this question to the voters for advice, such a referendum is not necessary.[26]

There have been a number of proposals for rewriting the constitution. Perhaps the most significant effort was that of the Committee of Forty-five, a group of influential private citizens who sought unsuccessfully to have the legislature call a convention in 1926.[27] Governor M. S. Conner recommended the calling of a constitutional convention to the 1932 and 1934 sessions of the legislature, and a bill providing for a convention passed the senate in 1934.[28]

Renewed interest in a new constitution was expressed in 1950 following the publication of a book on the subject by a professor at the School of Law of the University of Mississippi.[29] Newspapers gave the matter considerable attention, and the Mississippi State Junior Chamber of Commerce accepted the proposal as a major project for civic improvement in 1950.

* The largest vote cast on a constitutional amendment in the 1950 election was 80,439. This may be compared with the 407,774 votes for governor in the first primary of the Democratic Party in 1951.—*Mississippi Bluebook, 1952,* pp. 356-58.

† The revisory commission has been used to good effect in Virginia and Missouri.

Bills providing for a convention were introduced in the 1950 and 1952 legislative sessions but died in committee or on the calendar.

There appears to be little question that the present constitution is out of date and in need of major revision. Nor is there good reason to believe that the reforms needed can be accomplished by constitutional amendment. Such problems as legislative reapportionment, administrative reorganization, and judicial reform can be solved only by a complete revamping of the fundamental law. The decision on constitutional reform is one that must be made ultimately by the electorate. The voters cannot make their choice, however, until proponents of constitutional reform induce legislative submission of the issue to popular decision.

FOOTNOTES

[1] Henry S. Commager, *Documents of American History* (4th ed., Appleton-Century-Crofts, 1948), pp. 6-13.

[2] Allan Nevins, *The American States during and after the Revolution, 1775-1789* (Macmillan, 1927), p. 164.

[3] *Ibid.*, pp. 179-82.

[4] George H. Ethridge, *Mississippi Constitutions* (Jackson: Tucker Printing Company, 1928), pp. 488-506.

[5] *Journal of the State Convention of Mississippi, 1861* (Jackson: 1861), pp. 136-38.

[6] James W. Garner, *Reconstruction in Mississippi* (Macmillan, 1901), p. 216.

[7] Constitution of 1869, printed in Ethridge, *op. cit.*, pp. 531-57. Note particularly art. 1, secs. 1, 18, 19, 20, 21, 24. There were also changes in the government, such as the substitution of appointive for elective judges and the lengthening of the term of the governor to four years.

[8] *Mississippi Laws, 1890,* ch. 35.

[9] *Journal of the Constitutional Convention, 1890* (Jackson, 1890), pp. 3-5.

[10] *Journal, op. cit.*, pp. 637-38.

[11] *Ibid.*, pp. 697-700.

[12] *Ibid.*, pp. 549-51. The 1869 document was the only Mississippi constitution ever submitted to a popular vote.

[13] *Ibid.*, pp. 685-96.

[14] For interpretation of this provision see *Williams* v *State,* 130 Miss. 827, 94 So. 882 (1922), and *Sullens* v *State,* 191 Miss. 856, 4 So. (2nd) 356 (1941).

[15] Constitution of 1869, art. 1, secs. 1, 2, 9, 19.

[16] Constitution of 1832, art. 7, sub-art. 2; Constitution of 1869, art. 13. The 1817 constitution provided for the convention method of amendment: Constitution of 1817, art. 6, sub-art. 3.

[17] *Green* v *Weller,* 32 Miss. 650 (1856).

[18] Constitution of 1890, art. 5, sec. 121.

[19] *Power* v *Robertson,* 130 Miss. 188, 93 So. 769 (1922).

[20] *State ex rel. McClurg* v *Powell,* 77 Miss. 543, 27 So. 927 (1900).

[21] *Mississippi Laws, 1912,* ch. 414; *ibid., 1916,* ch. 156.

[22] *Ibid., 1904,* ch. 172; *ibid., 1916,* ch. 160.

[23] *Ibid., 1944,* ch. 344.

[24] *Power* v *Robertson,* 130 Miss. 188, 93 So. 769 (1922). This decision overruled *State* v *Brantley, Ex Parte Robinson,* 112 Miss. 812, 74 So. 662 (1916), an earlier decision upholding the validity of the amendment. Invalidation was based

on the grounds that it did not differentiate between legislative and executive power and that it dealt with more than one subject.

[25] Walter E. Dodd, *The Revision and Amendment of State Constitutions* (Johns Hopkins University Press, 1910), p. 44; *Sproule* v *Fredericks,* 69 Miss. 898, 11 So. 472 (1892).

[26] *Ibid.*

[27] Ethridge, *op. cit.,* pp. 470-73.

[28] *Senate Journal, 1934,* p. 142.

[29] William N. Ethridge, Jr., *Modernizing Mississippi's Constitution* (Bureau of Public Administration, University of Mississippi, 1950).

CHAPTER 3

Nominations and Elections

MISSISSIPPI FALLS within that group of states politically classified as the "Solid South." The Democratic Party has been in complete control of the state government since the end of the Reconstruction regime in 1876.* By tradition and by choice, Mississippi is among the staunchest of the one-party states.

Although the state has been dominated by a single party for seven decades, political campaigns usually have included candidates of one or more additional parties. In no election, however, have Republican or minor party candidates seriously threatened Democratic control.† Without exception the general elections have been mere formalities. Although it usually offers candidates only for the highest state offices and for presidential electors, the Republican Party maintains an organization in the state, largely to carry on the routine duties necessary to party existence.‡ No

* Adelbert Ames, Republican, last of the Reconstruction governors, resigned under impeachment charges on March 29, 1876.—Dunbar Rowland, *History of Mississippi* (Jackson: Clarke Pub. Co., 1925), II, 204.

† A relatively large vote was cast by the Populist Party in the presidential campaign of 1892 and by the Republican Party in 1928.

‡ Since 1928 the Republican organization has been split into two factions, each with a separate organization. By a law of 1950, however, each party was required to register with the secretary of state; thereafter only the group registered could nominate candidates or conduct other activities in the name of that party. The "lily white" faction of the Republican Party, being the first to register, is thus the legally recognized organization of the Republican Party in Mississippi. Delegates of the other faction, the "Black and Tan" group, however, were recognized and seated in the Republican national convention in 1952.—*Mississippi Laws, 1950,* ch. 458. The constitutionality of this law has been upheld by the Mississippi Supreme Court.—*Hoskins* v *Howard,* 59 So. (2nd) 263 (1952).

minor party has a permanent organization in Mississippi. The legal requirements that party candidates for elective office must be nominated by primary election and that parties polling less than one third the total vote in the preceding presidential election must pay the cost of such primaries tend to discourage minor party activity.

(Naturally, the real political issues in the state are intraparty. These questions pertain chiefly to taxation, regulation, education, prohibition, and proposed national legislation affecting states' rights. Consequently, political alignments are factional rather than partisan and political contests are marked by personal rather than party politics.)

PARTY COMMITTEE ORGANIZATION

The state party machinery consists of a hierarchy of committees, selected every four years.[1] The committees constitute a part of the national organization and at the same time direct party affairs within the state. By contrast with several other southern states, notably Alabama, Georgia, North Carolina, and Virginia—where the machinery operates almost entirely by party rules—Mississippi has fairly detailed laws regulating the organization and functions of party committees. Among these functions is the conduct of all primary elections in accordance with the election laws of the state.

The State Executive Committee

The state party system is headed by the state committee composed of eighteen members—three from each of the state's congressional districts—chosen by the state convention, which meets on presidential election years.* The chairman is chosen by the committee and becomes the nominal head of the party in the state. Naturally, he occupies the most important position in the whole organization.

The state executive committee has general control over all party affairs. Persons seeking nomination for state and state district offices file their names with this committee, and it must certify all candidates to the county executive committees before their names can be placed on the primary ballot. It canvasses returns for state and state district offices the third day after the first primary and announces the official results. In contests where there is no majority, the committee certifies the two highest candi-

* Committeemen are nominated by the convention delegates from the different congressional districts, each district delegation acting separately.

dates to the county committees for the second primary ballot. The results of the second, or "run-off," primary are canvassed in like manner the third day after the election is held, and the nominees are officially announced.* An official tabulation of the results is furnished by the state chairman to the secretary of state. The state committee also may prescribe regulations for voting in primary elections in addition to those fixed by law.† The date of the state convention is determined by this committee.

District Committees

Below the state committee are senatorial and flotorial district committees. They exist only in those legislative districts composed of more than one county, and derive their names from the type of district, whether for electing senators or for electing "floater" representatives. Although established by law, these committees are not of great importance, their duties relating chiefly to certification of certain legislative candidates for the primary ballots and the official canvass of results of these contests. The law provides that the members from each county are to be chosen as provided by the executive committee of that county after the general election of that year. In practice, the county chairmen of the district usually serve as members of the senatorial and/or flotorial committees.

The County Executive Committee

The county executive committee is composed of fifteen members, three from each supervisor's district within the county, chosen every four years by the county convention.‡ It occupies a key position in the party organization, having virtually the same control over county primaries that the state committee exerts over state-wide primaries. Candidates seeking nomination for county and county district offices file applications with this committee, and it certifies all candidates before their names are placed on the primary ballot. It appoints officers for the primary elections and makes all arrangements for conducting primaries in accordance with the law. The first or second day after the election this committee reviews the results and declares the nominees and those candidates to be submitted

* Appeals from decisions of party committees concerning nominations may be taken to the courts.—*Mississippi Code, 1942,* secs. 3182, 3183.

† The voter must also be in accord with a "statement of principles" adopted by the state convention.—*Ibid.,* 1952 Supp., sec. 3129.

‡ As an alternate method the existing committee may submit the choice of its successors to a primary election. A county committee, in its discretion, may add three additional members from the county at large.

to a second primary. The vote on state and district candidates is tabulated and forwarded to the district and state executive committees.[2] Contests over nominations are decided by this committee, subject to an appeal to the courts.

The county committee designates the date for the county convention and apportions the delegates equally among the districts within the county, or in proportion to the votes cast for the party candidates in the last presidential election. The state committee fixes the date for the precinct elections at which these delegates are chosen.

Municipal Committee

The municipal committee is outside the regular hierarchy of committees and has no duties beyond the conduct of primaries for the nomination of municipal officers. It contains the same number of members as the legislative body of the city, chosen at the municipal primary election, with the term of office (four years) corresponding to that of city councilmen.[3]

THE CONVENTION SYSTEM

Another branch of the party machinery is the system of delegate conventions. It is also a hierarchy, consisting of three conventions—state, county, and county precinct meetings—that are held quadrennially on presidential election years.[4]

Precinct conventions are mass meetings of all electors of the party in the precinct, held at the "usual voting place" at ten o'clock on a date fixed by the state committee.* This meeting has the sole function of selecting by secret ballot delegates to a county convention in such number as fixed by the county committee. The county convention, meeting a few days later on call of the county committee, has the dual function of choosing the county committee and of selecting the county's delegates to the state convention in "a number equal to double its representation in the house of representatives."

The state convention meets at the state capitol on the call of the state committee shortly after the county conventions are held.† It has three primary functions to perform: (1) to select delegates to the national convention; (2) to nominate presidential electors; (3) to select the state committee that will serve for the next four years. Under a recent law it

* The law requires that ten days' notice be given for holding precinct conventions.
† The dates of all conventions are arranged to suit the date announced for the party's national convention.

may also nominate candidates for President and Vice-President of the United States, adopt a platform, promulgate principles and "take such further action deemed proper by the convention."*

The selection of delegates from the different congressional districts to the national convention, though theoretically done by the state convention in plenary session, is in fact merely the approval of persons nominated by preconvention caucuses of the delegates in the various congressional districts. Delegates from the state at large are chosen by the full convention.

Members of the state executive committee make up the governing organ of the party in the state for the four years following adjournment of the convention. Presidential electors perform only perfunctory duties in casting the electoral vote of the state in accordance with the popular vote.†

It is natural that the precinct, county, and state conventions are usually composed of the politically active men and women in the respective counties. Almost anyone who desires to attend a convention as a delegate may do so because of the lack of general interest and because few persons wish to incur the expense of the trip. The result is that a large number of political leaders, officeholders, and office-seekers may be found in the state convention, and to a lesser degree in the county conventions. Representation of the rank and file of the party voters in these meetings is, at most, a polite theory.

SUFFRAGE AND REGISTRATION

Qualifications for voting in Mississippi vary slightly for general and primary elections. All the qualifications for the election are required in the primaries, plus additional requirements fixed by law and party regulations. Since only the Democratic Party holds primary elections, the effect of these extra requirements is to make voting in the Democratic primaries more difficult.

All voters are required to register with the circuit clerk in their respective

* *Mississippi Laws, 1952,* ch. 391. This act also authorized the convention to recess and hold a later meeting. It was enacted because of the rift between the state and national organizations of the Democratic Party. The law would have legalized withdrawal from the party by the state organization, following the national nominating convention.

† By act of a special legislative session of 1944, the legislature specifically reserves the right to nominate presidential electors at any time before the election. This action was taken to assure that electors vote for the party nominees.—*Mississippi Code,* 1952 Supp., sec. 3298. However, under a 1948 law parties were authorized to nominate unpledged electors.—*Ibid.,* sec. 3107-5.

counties of residence. Registration may be made at any time, though if the voter registers during the four months preceding a general election he is disqualified for that election. Registration is permanent, but a reregistration may be ordered by the county board of supervisors because of the loss, destruction, or confusion of the registration books. The registration and poll books are revised each year by the county election commission. Each person registering is required to take an oath that he is qualified to vote, will answer any questions concerning these qualifications, and will support the state and national constitutions. Persons unable to read or interpret when read to them any section of the state constitution cannot be registered. Members of the armed services and allied branches may be registered by mail.*

In addition to making proper registration the eligible voter must be a citizen of the United States, at least twenty-one years of age, and a resident of the state two years and of the election district one year.† Payment of a poll tax of two dollars per year is required of all persons between the ages of twenty-one and sixty (except the deaf, blind, and maimed), and the tax must be paid for the two years preceding the election.‡

In order to vote in the primaries in Mississippi, one must possess all the preceding qualifications and meet any additional requirements of the party's state executive committee. The primary voter must be in accord with the principles of the party as stated by the party state convention, must have been in accord with the party for the past two years, and must intend to support the nominees in the ensuing election.**

Idiots, insane persons, those convicted of certain crimes,†† and Indians not taxed are denied suffrage under the Mississippi constitution.

* The principal regulations on registration are found in the Constitution of 1890, art. 12, secs. 242-45. Voters in municipal elections must also register with the clerk of the municipality.

† Ministers and their wives may vote with only six months' residence in the district.

‡ This tax may be increased to three dollars by the board of supervisors of any county. It must be paid by February 1. Persons who reach twenty-one after February 1 and before the election may vote without paying the tax if otherwise qualified. Members or recently discharged veterans of the armed forces who have not had an opportunity to pay the tax may vote. These persons and those exempt must present certificates of exemption or qualification. Voters in municipal elections must have paid all taxes due the municipality for the past two years and not have been convicted of violating the prohibition law within the city.

** Nominees for President and Vice-President of the United States were specifically omitted from this requirement by act of the 1948 legislature.—*Mississippi Code,* 1952 Supp., sec. 3129.

†† The crimes are: bribery, burglary, theft, arson, obtaining money or goods under false pretenses, perjury, forgery, embezzlement, and bigamy. This disqualification may be removed by the legislature by vote of two thirds of all elected members or by executive pardon before the sentence is served.

Absentee Voting

A qualified voter who is absent from his county on any election day by reason of occupation or one who is physically incapacitated may vote by absentee ballot. Application for an absentee ballot must be made to the registrar of voters within ten days of the election with sworn affidavit that the applicant must be absent for reasons of occupation or physical incapacity. The absentee ballot is delivered or mailed to the applicant by the circuit clerk, along with a certificate and affidavit. In this the voter again swears to the reason for his absence or incapacity and designates a person to deliver the ballot to the election managers of the precinct where he regularly votes. The affidavit, sworn before a proper officer, states that the ballot was shown to the officer unmarked and that the voter filled it out in his presence, without disclosing for whom he voted, and that no influence was exerted as to the way in which the person voted. The person designated to deliver the absentee ballot is required to be a qualified voter of the same precinct as the absentee voter and cannot be a candidate for any office.[5] A member of the armed services or allied branches also may vote by absentee ballot. Such person or a member of his family may make application, without affidavit, within sixty days of the election and ballots for all elections to be held (primaries and general election) are mailed on the same application. Such ballots are voted in the same manner as by other absent persons.[6]

Nonvoting

Mississippi has a very high percentage of nonvoting citizens. Even in the primaries, where competition is keenest, less than one third of the adult population actually votes. In the general elections the number is far less. Of a total population of two and one-sixth millions, more than half of whom are of voting age, slightly more than 400,000 vote in the leading primary contests.

Obviously the principal nonvoting segment of the population is the Negro group, which is almost half the total population. Until 1944 Negroes were barred from the primaries. Although now eligible to vote,* few Negroes exhibit any interest or take any part in voting. Naturally, the number voting may be expected to increase as the Negro increases in knowledge of, and familiarity with, state and local politics.

* *Smith* v *Allwright,* 321 U. S. 649 (1944) upheld the right of Negroes to participate in party primaries on an equal basis with white people.

The poll tax as a cause of nonvoting has been a subject of much interest in recent years. Doubtless the tax is a considerable deterrent to voting of both whites and Negroes, although proof of the actual numbers is, of course, unavailable. One study of political behavior in the state concludes that "the poll tax is less effective as a deterrent to voting than the habit patterns of urban living."[7] Considerable sentiment for repeal of the tax was evident a few years ago, and a lively discussion of the matter was noted in the 1939 gubernatorial campaign. More recently the subject has become a national-state controversy, with the result that the poll tax is no longer discussed on its merits but rather as a symbol of states' rights. There is no organized movement in Mississippi for its repeal.

Other reasons for nonvoting may be found in the exacting requirements of residence. The fact that Mississippi is a one-party state is an important cause, particularly in general elections, which are mere formalities and attract little attention. Indifference and inertia explain much nonvoting. Too, the voter finds the long ballot confusing and burdensome and often gives up in disgust.

Nonvoting, especially when it reaches the proportions found in Mississippi, is a serious threat to true democratic government. Although laws and constitutional changes cannot overcome the apathy and indifference of the electorate, they might be employed to remove some of the obstacles to voter eligibility and to simplify the task of the voter. Measures that would serve to increase the participation of intelligent citizens in elections can only improve popular government.

PRIMARIES AND ELECTIONS

The most important elections in Mississippi are the primaries. All party nominations for elective office in the state must be made by primary election. Since there is only one party of importance, nomination in the Democratic primaries is tantamount to election.*

The mandatory primary system was inaugurated by law in 1902,† and the first elections under the law were held in 1903. Two primaries are held; if no candidate receives a majority in the first election, a second, or

* The laws relating to primary elections are found in the *Mississippi Code,* 1952 Supp., secs. 3105-3203. When only one candidate has filed for the primary within the time limit, the party executive committee may declare the nominee without a primary. Republican candidates usually are nominated in this way.

† This was the second state-wide, mandatory primary law in the United States. The first was the Minnesota law of 1901.—*Minnesota Laws, 1901,* ch. 216.

"run-off," primary between the two highest candidates is held three weeks later.* Not all officials are elected in the same year, and the dates of primaries vary with the different elections. All state, state district, county, and county district officers, except judges of the state courts, are chosen in odd-numbered years. These elections come every four years, dating from the original election under the present constitution in 1891. The first nominating primary for these elections is held on Tuesday after the first Monday in August, and the second is held three weeks later. United States Senators and Representatives and judges of the state supreme court and district courts are chosen on even-numbered years. The first primary for these elections is held on the fourth Tuesday in August, and the second three weeks later. Under a 1950 law municipal elections are held on Tuesday after the first Monday in June every four years, dating from 1953. The first primary for this election is held on the second Tuesday in May preceding the election, and the second primary a week later.[8] Thus, every year primaries and elections of some kind are held in the state.

Conduct of Primaries

The conduct of primary elections is largely a local affair. State laws designed to safeguard and control elections are numerous and detailed. The control is legislative rather than administrative, however, since no state officials supervise or direct the process.

A candidate for nomination in a primary secures a place on the official ballot by filing his name with the proper executive committee sixty days before the date of the first primary.† The candidate is required to pay a filing fee fixed by the party committee, ranging from a maximum of $100 for state-wide office to $2.50 for county district office.‡ The state executive committee certifies the candidates for state and state district offices to the different county committees, and senatorial and flotorial committees certify their candidates in the same manner. The county committees then have the names of these candidates, along with those who have filed for county and county district offices, printed on the official primary ballot. Candidates for the same office must appear on the ballot in alphabetical

* In case of a tie between the two leading candidates these two and the next highest candidate are placed on the second primary ballot. The leading candidate wins. Withdrawal of a candidate eligible for the second primary makes the next highest candidate eligible.

† Candidates for municipal primaries can file thirty days before the first primary.

‡ This money is used for expenses of the executive committee. The cost of the primary, for any political party that polled one third of the total vote in the preceding national presidential election, is paid from the county treasury.

order. A sample ballot is furnished to the county committees by the state and district executive committees with the state and state district candidates properly arranged, in order that all ballots in the state can be of the same general form.*

The county committee makes the preliminary arrangements for voting. It appoints managers for each precinct poll, who in turn appoint the election clerks. Polls are required to be open from 8 A.M. until 6 P.M., except in cities of more than 1,000 registered voters, where the hours are from 7 A.M. to 6 P.M. If his name appears on the poll book, the voter must first put his signature in a "receipt booklet" and present poll tax receipts for the two previous years. He then receives a ballot with the initials of one of the managers on the back. The ballot is voted by making a "v" or "x" mark opposite the names of the candidates for whom he wishes to vote. Voting is done in a secret place, and the ballot must be folded so that the manager's initials show on the outside. These initials are checked by the initialing manager for genuineness, and the ballot is deposited in the box. Illiterate or physically incapacitated voters may have the assistance of one of the managers in signing the receipt booklet and in marking the ballot.

The ballots are counted at the precincts when the polls are closed, and the ballot boxes are locked and returned to the circuit clerk. The county executive committee canvasses the ballots the next day and declares the official results. The results on state and state district contests are certified to the state executive committee; those of local contests are certified to the circuit clerk.

The run-off primary is conducted in the same manner as the first for the purpose of securing an absolute majority in such contests as were not settled in the first primary.

General Elections

General elections are conducted under the same general regulations as primaries.[9] They are under the general supervision of the State Election Commission, a board consisting of the governor, the attorney general, and the secretary of state. This board appoints a commission of three persons for each county. The county commission has charge of all arrangements in connection with registration, revision of the registration books, appointment of election managers, printing of ballots, and the declaration of the election results.

* A recent law authorizes the governing authorities of any county or municipality to purchase or rent voting machines.—*Mississippi Laws, 1954,* House Bill 299.

The election ballot includes party candidates properly certified to the commission and independent candidates who file a petition containing the signatures of fifty qualified voters.* The form of the ballot is decided by the State Election Commission, but a blank space must be provided for write-in votes. The names of all candidates must be in the hands of the county election commission fifteen days before the date of the election. The requirements for polls, hours, and voting are the same as for primaries. Results of the election are reviewed by the county commission, and persons elected to county office are delivered certificates of election. The results are also certified officially to the secretary of state.

Special elections to fill vacancies in congressional, state, and local offices are conducted as general elections without the necessity of a primary. The leading candidate wins in all general elections for local office, but in all special elections a runoff must be held. Tie votes are settled by lot.

Prohibition of Corrupt Practices

Mississippi has elaborate and detailed laws to insure fairness in primary elections. These laws regulate strictly the details of handling and custody of ballots, the conduct of voting, and the counting and reporting of results. Candidates in the primaries are limited as to maximum expenditures† and can neither promise jobs during the campaign nor coerce employees as to voting. Candidates also are prohibited from making charges reflecting on the honesty and moral character of opponents unless these charges can be proved; such charges, whether true or untrue, cannot be made within five days of the election. Newspapers printing charges made by a candidate against his opponent must allow the same amount of space in a later issue for the opponent to reply. Violations of these and other corrupt practices laws, upon conviction, are punishable by fine or imprisonment or both.[10] In order to get his name on the ballot in primaries a candidate must file, with the circuit clerk if for a county office and with the secretary of state if for a state office, affidavits that he is not a subversive person and that he has read the corrupt practices laws.

* Only fifteen names are required on a petition for independent candidates for town, village, or county district offices.

† Maximum expenditures range from basic limitations of $25,000 for governor and United States Senator to $500 for county district offices. Post-election expenses and the salary of a central campaign manager are excepted. Candidates for state or supreme court or congressional district office also may spend an additional $1,000 for each county of 40,000 population and $500 in other counties, if the money is collected and spent in the particular county. This makes it possible for a candidate for governor to spend legally in excess of $70,000 in a campaign.—*Mississippi Laws, 1952,* ch. 395. These laws do not apply to general elections.

Contests over primary elections are filed with the county or state executive committee, depending on the contest or candidates concerned. Any delay or failure to grant proper relief by a party executive committee, however, authorizes the contestant to take the case directly to the circuit court of the county where the alleged irregularity occurred.* Appeals from the judgment of this court may be taken to the state supreme court. Cases involving contests over general elections are taken directly to the circuit court of the county.

ELECTORAL PROBLEMS IN MISSISSIPPI

Any analysis of the electoral problems in Mississippi would include attention to the social and economic factors involved. With an economy that is predominantly agricultural and a population that is almost evenly divided along racial lines, the interplay of social, economic, and political forces makes accurate analysis difficult, if not impossible.[11] Only the more general problems can be considered here.

The failure of the party system in Mississippi is clear to the most casual observer. Among the more important functions of political parties in a state are the formulation of programs based on state issues and the enactment of these programs into laws when the party candidates are elected to office. Carrying out of these functions requires party cohesion and stability and the presence of at least two parties in order that the voters may exercise a real choice. None of these exists in Mississippi. There is no party platform so far as state issues are concerned. With only one party the candidates in the primaries devise their own platforms. The campaign thus becomes one of personalities rather than of issues. Since nomination in the Democratic primary is equivalent to election, there is no necessary agreement on a party program among persons elected to executive and legislative offices. Consequently there is no party responsibility to the voters. Any personal responsibility is lost in the maze of divided authority and of constitutional or legal restrictions.[12]

A possible alternative for the two-party system might be the formalization of factions within the Democratic Party. Such factions certainly exist, but the tendency to associate factions with individuals and the reshuffling of these groups from election to election raises doubts as to whether they are stable enough to serve as responsible agencies for the expression of public opinion.[13]

* A judge of a district outside the county is appointed to hear the case.

The direct primary can be blamed for much of the lack of party solidarity. It can also be charged with encouraging mediocre candidates who confuse the voters with popular illusions, promises, and plain demagogism. A return to the system of nomination by delegate convention, which also would draft a party platform, might do much to locate party responsibility. In the absence of a competing party, however, there would be no way of enforcing this responsibility, and the platform would be meaningless. Moreover, the convention method of nomination would destroy effectively the direct participation of the voters, since nominations for all practical purposes are the elections. There appears to be no considerable sentiment among the people of Mississippi for abolishing the direct primary. The task is one of perfecting the primary so that it can best express the will of the voters.

The most important political development in Mississippi in recent years has been the result of national rather than of state issues. Largely because of the stand of the Democratic Party for national legislation on civil rights, and the adoption of a strong plank favoring such legislation in the national platform, the Mississippi delegation withdrew from the national convention in Philadelphia in 1948. Subsequently, delegates from certain southern states, including Mississippi, attended a "States' Rights Conference" held in Birmingham, where they adopted a statement of principles and nominated candidates for President and Vice-President of the United States. At the same time this convention affirmed its allegiance to the principles of the Democratic Party, though taking sharp issue with the Philadelphia convention as to what those principles were. Electors supporting the candidates of the States' Rights Conference were elected in November, and the electoral vote of the state was cast for them. Practically all the members of the state Democratic organization, as well as most state officials and members of Congress, announced their support of the States' Rights program and candidates. This rift between the state and national organizations and leadership of the party continued through the next four years and into the national convention of 1952.

Following the 1952 convention, however, most of the state leaders of the party, although in strong disagreement with certain parts of the national Democratic platform, announced their support of the nominees for President and Vice-President. The state convention, reconvening after the national meeting, endorsed the nominees and nominated a slate of electors pledged to them. A minority of the party leaders and other citizens promoted an active campaign for the Republican candidates. It is significant, though, that this was done by nominating a slate of independent electors pledged to the Republican nominees; most supporters of this group consistently proclaimed themselves "independent Democrats." Although the results of the election showed approximately 60 per cent of the votes for the Democratic electors, the unusually large vote for the independent group emphasized the widespread opposition to the national leadership and program. This problem, however, is of an intraparty nature. It has not altered the one-party situation.

The small but growing trend toward industrialization in the state may have some effect on politics in future years. This effect probably will be exercised through the activities of organized labor groups, which tend to be liberal. Of this there is no immediate prospect. In the last analysis, only the efforts of an aroused and intelligent public opinion can solve the problems of the state's political life. The enlargement of the electorate and the political education and training of those who vote are tasks to which patriotic citizens may well turn their attention.

FOOTNOTES

[1] The powers of party committees are found in sections 3105-3108 of *Mississippi Code Annotated,* 1942 with 1952 Supplement, hereinafter cited as *Mississippi Code,* with appropriate section number.

[2] *Mississippi Code, 1942,* secs. 3115-3118, 3142.

[3] *Ibid.,* 1952 Supp., sec. 3152.

[4] *Ibid.,* 1952 Supp., sec. 3107.

[5] *Mississippi Code,* 1952 Supp., secs. 3203-01–3203-10.

[6] *Mississippi Laws, 1952,* ch. 396.

[7] William Buchanan, *The Mississippi Electorate* (State College, Miss.: Social Science Research Center, 1953), p. 25.

[8] *Mississippi Code,* 1952 Supp., secs. 3374-62–3374-63.

[9] The constitutional and legal provisions regarding elections are found in the Constitution of 1890, art. 12, secs. 240-253 and *Mississippi Code,* 1952 Supp., secs. 3204-3316.

[10] Most of the corrupt practices laws may be found in *Mississippi Code, 1942,* and 1952 Supp., secs. 3158-3195. These laws do not apply to general elections.

[11] In this connection see V. O. Key, Jr., *Southern Politics* (Knopf, 1949), particularly pp. 229-53.

[12] For a discussion of this see the report of the Committee on Political Parties of the American Political Science Association, "Toward a More Responsible Two-Party System," *American Political Science Review,* XLIV (September, 1950), 15-36.

[13] Such a proposal has been made for the same situation in the state of Louisiana. See Alden L. Powell and Emmett Asseff, *Party Organization and Nominations in Louisiana* (Baton Rouge: University Bureau of Government Research, 1952), pp. 17-18.

CHAPTER 4

The Legislature:

COMPOSITION and ORGANIZATION

THE LEGISLATURE is the matrix of the state's activities. Its members, chosen by the voters, represent the different varieties and intensities of public opinion. From this body come the translated versions of this opinion—the laws and administrative agencies that provide the numerous services to the people of the state. The legislature not only determines what the state will do; it also decides how these things will be done.

The Mississippi legislature is fairly typical of such bodies in other states. It consists of two houses: a senate with 49 members and a house of representatives with 140 members. Its composition reflects a cross-section of the state's economy and politics. As might be expected in a state whose economy is primarily agricultural, farmers are the largest occupational group among its members. Lawyers are the next most important occupational group, though various other professions, businesses, trades, and callings are represented. A possible trend away from lawyers as legislators may be noted in the comparison of occupations in a recent legislature with those of a legislature two decades earlier, which showed lawyers leading the list with farmers second. Practically every degree of age and education is found among its members. Few women are elected, though it appears that not many women are candidates for legislative positions.*

The occupational distribution of the legislature is indicated in the fol-

* The 1948-1952 legislature contained five women, and five were elected in 1951 and served in the 1952 session. Special elections in 1953 added two more women, one of whom resigned. The 1954 session thus had six feminine members—the largest number ever to sit in the body. A total of twenty-six women have served in the legislature since the first was elected in 1923.

lowing table on the persons elected to membership for the 1948-1952 term. It should be noted that many members have more than one occupation, for instance, farming and banking, and the tabulation below includes only the primary or most important occupation.

TABLE 3

OCCUPATIONS OF MEMBERS OF THE LEGISLATURE OF MISSISSIPPI
(Regular Session, 1948)

Occupation	*House*	*Senate*
Farmers and planters	44	19
Lawyers	28	15
Teachers	14	3
Students	19	—
Automobile dealers	—	2
Minister	—	1
Merchants	7	2
Stockmen	1	1
Physicians	1	1
Insurance business	3	1
Newspaper business	2	1
Sawmill business	1	1
Writer	—	1
Electrician	1	—
Piano tuner	1	—
Repairman and mechanic	1	—
Advertising business	1	—
Salesmen	2	—
Theater business	1	—
Ice and storage business	1	—
Retired	1	1
Pharmacy and drug business	2	—
Contractors	2	—
Chamber of Commerce employment	2	—
Public health work	1	—
Miscellaneous	4	—

Source: This table was compiled from biographical data on members of the legislature found in the *Mississippi Blue Book, 1945-1949,* pp. 42-63, the periodic report of the secretary of state. Occupational listings were made by the members of the legislature.

A rapid turnover in membership is indicated by figures on legislative experience of the 1948-1952 legislature. Of the members of the house in the 1948 session, 56.4 per cent had no previous legislative experience, 23.6 per cent had been members of the legislature for one term, 11.4 per cent had served for two previous terms, and 8.6 per cent had served three or more terms. In the senate the turnover appears to be less though still significant. Of the senators elected for the same term, 38.7 per cent had no previous legislative experience, 32.6 per cent had served one previous term, 14.3 per cent had served two previous terms, and a like percentage had served three or more terms.* From these statistics of a typical legislature it may be seen that more than half the members are new to the task of lawmaking.

APPORTIONMENT OF REPRESENTATION

Apportionment in both houses of the legislature is purportedly based on the number of qualified electors.† Because of rigid provisions in the Constitution of 1890, however, such apportionment is impossible, and the actual system is the arbitrary allotment of members to the various counties and districts. Although the constitution authorizes reapportionment after each decennial census, there has been no real reapportionment for more than sixty years. Moreover, under the existing constitutional limitations reapportionment would only continue the present disproportionate ratio of representation. The result is that Mississippi has one of the most inequitable systems of representation to be found among American legislatures.

The Constitution of 1890 divided seventy-five counties of the state into three districts and assigned the number of representatives and senators to each. The districts were so drawn that two of them, the Northeastern and Southwestern, had a predominantly white population; the third, the Western, was largely Negro. The constitution further required equal representation from these districts, and limited any reapportionment by requiring uniform reduction or increase of members among the three districts. The constitution also provided that each county should have at least one representative, and an amendment in 1904 fixed this minimum for new counties that may be created. Seven new counties have been added since 1890, each with a single representative. The constitution was amended in 1916 to rearrange the senatorial districts in twelve counties and add four more districts. Thus the number of representatives, fixed at 133 by the constitution, has been raised to 140 by the constitutional power of

* *Mississippi Blue Book, 1945-1949* (Jackson: Secretary of State, 1949), pp. 42-63. Figures on the 1952-1956 legislature show the same general pattern, with 53.6 per cent of the house members and 42.9 per cent of the senate members without previous legislative experience.—*Ibid., 1952,* p. 100.

† Three other states—Tennessee, Rhode Island, and Massachusetts—use this method of apportionment. Texas bases representation in the senate on this plan.

the legislature to establish new counties. The number of senators has been raised from 45 to 49 by constitutional amendment. Except for these relatively minor additions, there has been no change in the apportionment determined by the constitution. No general reapportionment is possible except by constitutional amendment. Since a large number of counties would have their representation reduced by a general reapportionment, it is not surprising that the legislature does not propose such an amendment.* Although the legislature has the power to reapportion its membership within each district, provided the equilibrium between districts remains unchanged, this power is not mandatory and has not been exercised.†

Naturally, large shifts in population have been made during the last six decades, increasing the disparity in representation among the different sections of the state. A comparison of various counties reveals gross inequalities. Issaquena County, with a total population of 4,966 persons, sends one representative to the legislature. Jones County, with a total population of 57,235, also sends one representative. Noxubee County, with a population of 20,022, sends three representatives and elects one senator. Jones County shares its senator with another county. Similar disparities may be found where comparisons are made on the basis of qualified electors. The average representation is one for each 15,564 people in the house and one for each 44,468 in the senate. The general disproportion is revealed in the following table showing the counties, their representation, and the percentage of average representation in each house.

The original scheme of districts and apportionment and the constitutional limitation placed on reapportionment were designed to maintain a majority of legislators from the white counties. Since scarcely any Negroes have participated in state politics in more than fifty years, the system appears to have served a different purpose than its authors intended. Its chief effect has been to penalize white voters who are underrepresented by its provisions. It seems clear that constitutional changes providing for reapportionment are necessary, if a substantial portion of Mississippi's people are to have adequate representation.‡

The urban-rural conflict in the Mississippi legislature does not approach

* The only method of proposing constitutional amendments in Mississippi is by two-thirds vote of both houses of the legislature.—Constitution of 1890, art. 15, sec. 273.

† Reapportionment bills as well as resolutions to amend the constitution were introduced at the 1954 session. All died in committee or on the calendar.

‡ A recent study of this problem concludes that the only practical method of reapportionment is by a new constitution. William N. Ethridge, Jr., *Modernizing Mississippi's Constitution* (Bureau of Public Administration, University of Mississippi, 1950), p. 37.

TABLE 4

APPORTIONMENT OF MISSISSIPPI LEGISLATURE

County	*Population*	*Number of Representatives*	*Percentage of Average Representation*	*Number of Senators*	*Percentage of Average Representation*
Adams	32,256	2	96	1	138
Alcorn	27,158	2	115	⅓	55
Amite	19,261	2	162	½	115
Attala	26,652	2	117	1	167
Benton	8,793	1½	266	⅗	303
Bolivar	63,004	2	49	1	71
Calhoun	18,369	2	169	⅔	161
Carroll	15,499	2	201	½	143
Chickasaw	18,951	2	164	⅔	156
Choctaw	11,009	1	141	½	202
Claiborne	11,944	1½	195	½	186
Clarke	19,362	1½	121	½	115
Clay	17,757	2	175	½	125
Coahoma	49,361	2	63	⅓	30
Copiah	30,493	3	153	1	146
Covington	16,036	1	97	½	139
DeSoto	24,599	2	126	1	181
Forrest	45,055	1	34	½	49
Franklin	10,929	1½	214	½	203
George	10,012	1	155	⅓	148
Greene	8,215	1	189	⅓	180
Grenada	18,830	1½	124	½	118
Hancock	11,891	1	131	⅓	125
Harrison	84,073	1½	28	½	26
Hinds	142,164	3½	38	1½	47
Holmes	33,301	3	140	1	134
Humphreys	23,115	1	67	⅔	128
Issaquena	4,966	1	313	½	448
Itawamba	17,216	1½	136	⅔	172
Jackson	31,401	1½	74	⅓	47
Jasper	18,912	1½	123	½	118
Jefferson	11,306	1½	206	½	197
Jefferson Davis	15,500	1	100	⅓	96
Jones	57,235	1	27	½	39
Kemper	15,893	2	196	½	140
Lafayette	22,798	2	136	1	195
Lamar	13,225	1	118	⅓	112
Lauderdale	64,171	3	73	1	69
Lawrence	12,639	1	123	½	176
Leake	21,610	1½	108	½	103
Lee	38,237	2½	102	⅔	78

TABLE 4—*continued*

County	*Population*	*Number of Representatives*	*Percentage of Average Representation*	*Number of Senators*	*Percentage of Average Representation*
Leflore	51,813	1	30	½	43
Lincoln	27,899	1½	84	½	80
Lowndes	37,852	3	123	1	117
Madison	33,860	2	92	1	131
Marion	23,967	1	65	⅓	62
Marshall	25,106	3	186	⅗	106
Monroe	36,543	3	128	⅔	81
Montgomery	14,470	1½	161	½	154
Neshoba	25,730	1	60	½	86
Newton	22,681	2	137	½	98
Noxubee	22,022	3	233	1	222
Oktibbeha	24,569	2	127	½	90
Panola	31,271	3	149	1	142
Pearl River	20,641	1	75	⅓	72
Perry	9,108	1	171	½	244
Pike	35,137	2	89	½	63
Pontotoc	19,994	2	156	⅔	148
Prentiss	19,810	2	157	⅓	75
Quitman	25,885	1	60	⅓	57
Rankin	28,881	2	108	½	77
Scott	21,681	1	72	½	102
Sharkey	12,903	1	121	½	172
Simpson	21,819	1	71	½	102
Smith	16,740	1	93	½	133
Stone	6,264	1	248	½	355
Sunflower	56,031	1	28	⅔	53
Tallahatchie	30,486	1	51	½	73
Tate	18,011	2	173	⅗	148
Tippah	17,522	1½	133	⅗	152
Tishomingo	15,544	1	100	⅓	95
Tunica	21,664	1	72	⅓	68
Union	20,262	2	154	⅗	132
Walthall	15,563	1	100	⅓	95
Warren	39,616	3	118	1½	168
Washington	70,504	3	66	⅔	42
Wayne	17,010	1	91	½	131
Webster	11,607	1	134	½	192
Wilkinson	14,116	2	220	½	158
Winston	22,231	1½	105	½	100
Yalobusha	15,191	2	205	½	146
Yazoo	35,712	3½	152	1	124
TOTALS	2,178,914	140		49	

Source: Compiled from information contained in the *Mississippi Blue Book, 1952,* and the Bureau of the Census.

the intensity and importance of that found in many other states, because there has been no large urban group in the population. The essential elements of the controversy, however, may be found in the gerrymandered districts and in the failure of the legislature to reapportion within its constitutional power to do so. Many of the more rapidly growing cities of the state, such as Laurel, Gulfport, and Jackson, are located in counties that are underrepresented by comparison with other counties. The further growth of these and other cities similarly located will accentuate this disproportion and intensify the latent conflict.

COMPOSITION OF THE LEGISLATURE

The general features of the legislature of Mississippi follow the conventional American pattern. There are two houses, a senate and a house of representatives. The 140 members of the house are chosen from the state's eighty-two counties and nine flotorial districts. Each county elects from one to three members; nine districts, each consisting of two counties, elect one floater representative each. The forty-nine members of the senate are chosen from forty-two districts, each composed of from one to five counties. Three of these elect two senators each, and two elect three senators each.* Members of both houses are chosen for terms of four years, and the terms in both houses coincide. Each house is judge of the election of its own members.

Qualifications of Members

The minimum qualifications for members of the legislature pertain to age, residence, and citizenship.[1] A representative must be at least twenty-one years of age, a qualified elector, and a resident citizen of the state four years and of the county two years preceding his election. A member of the senate must be at least twenty-five years of age, a qualified elector of the state four years, and a resident of his district for two years preceding his election. United States citizenship is not a specific qualification but is implied in the oath required of members. Persons convicted of an infamous crime or bribery in securing election, or who are liable for public

* In nominating legislators from multimember districts the elector votes for the number of persons to be chosen from the district. Voting for one person only renders the ballot void for that office. The majority required for nomination is determined by dividing the total number of voters by the number of persons to be chosen. More than one half of this number constitutes a majority.—*Mississippi Code,* 1952 Supp., sec. 3110.

funds unaccounted for, are ineligible for membership.[2] Each house is judge of the qualifications of its own members.

Compensation, Privileges, and Immunities of Members

Each member of the legislature receives $2,000 for each regular session. For extraordinary sessions members are compensated at the rate of $15 per day. The travel allowance is quite liberal. For travel to and from the capitol for regular and extraordinary sessions ten cents per mile is paid. In addition, members are allowed six cents per mile for travel to and from home each week during sessions, if the travel is actually performed.* Members of the legislature are exempt from arrest during the legislative session and for fifteen days before and after each session, except in cases of treason, felony, or breach of the peace.[3]

Sessions

The legislature meets in regular session every even-numbered year at the state capitol on Tuesday after the first Monday in January. Special sessions convene on the call of the governor.[4] There is no constitutional or statutory limit on the length of either regular or special sessions. The governor is empowered to adjourn the legislature in case of disagreement between the two houses as to the date of adjournment.

ORGANIZATION OF THE LEGISLATURE

Both houses of the legislature organize at the beginning of the regular session in January following the election of members. This organization continues, except for minor changes due to vacancies, for the four years of the legislative term. Officers are chosen at the first meeting in both houses, though the committees are not completed until several days later. The lieutenant governor, elected by the people, presides over the opening session of the senate, and the secretary of state is in charge of the first session of the house. These officials accept the election certificates of members and administer to them the oath of office. The service of the secretary of state ends when officers of the house are chosen.

* The lieutenant governor (president of the senate) and the speaker of the house each are paid $3,000 per regular session. These officers are paid the same as other members for extraordinary sessions and draw the same travel allowances.—*Mississippi Code,* 1952 Supp., secs. 3345–3346-5; *Mississippi Laws, 1952,* ch. 326.

Legislative Officers

Each house of the legislature is authorized by the constitution to choose its own officers, except for the regular presiding officer of the senate, who is the lieutenant governor.[5] The senate elects a president pro tempore, a sergeant-at-arms, and doorkeepers by majority vote of its members. Pages, porters, and other necessary employees are appointed by the presiding officer. The house elects, by majority vote of the members, a speaker, clerk, sergeant-at-arms, and doorkeepers. Pages, porters, and other necessary employees are appointed by the speaker.*

Duties of Presiding Officers

The presiding officers of the two houses are the most influential members of the legislature. Their duties are important and numerous. Each in his respective house presides over sessions, enforces the rules, and maintains decorum among the members. Each signs all measures passed and all writs, orders, and subpoenas that his house orders to be issued. He has charge of all employees and certifies all pay rolls, with minor exceptions. The committees of each house are appointed by the presiding officer and in each house he is a member of the committee on rules. Each presiding officer may vote in case of a tie or if his vote is necessary to a decision by the body, and each can participate in debate when his house sits as a committee of the whole. The speaker of the house, as a member of that body, must vote when the house is voting by ballot.

Duties of Other Officers

The president pro tempore of the senate has the duty of presiding with full powers in the absence of the lieutenant governor. The chief clerical officers, the secretary of the senate and the clerk of the house, have similar duties. Each has charge of keeping and preserving all papers and records of his house. Clerical duties include reading bills, preparing and posting the calendar, and the keeping, reading, and publication of the journal. These officers must attest all bills, resolutions, writs, and other papers and documents signed by the presiding officers of the houses. The sergeant-at-arms in each house preserves order under the direction of the presiding

* In the 1952 regular session there were 32 house employees, 26 senate employees, and 3 persons employed by both houses. The number and compensation of employees is fixed by vote of the members, with payment from the contingent funds of the two houses.

officer and serves all writs and subpoenas issued. He is also in charge of the doorkeepers and servants and has general responsibility for the halls and meeting places. The duties of other employees are indicated by the titles assigned to them.

Legislative Committees

The committee system of the legislature is the most important part of the organization. Most lawmaking is done by committees; the action of a committee usually is the key to the passage or defeat of a measure on the floor. Since most committees of the Mississippi legislature are appointed by the presiding officers of the two houses, it is obvious that the power and influence of these officials in regard to legislation is enormous.*

Each house has a large number of standing committees. These committees are set up for four years and have the task of studying proposed legislation and recommending action to the full membership of the body to which they belong. There are 41 such committees in the senate and 45 in the house. Each house also has a number of select, or special, committees that exist until the task for which they were established has been accomplished. There are also joint committees, composed of members of both houses. Some of these are standing committees, and some are select. Of particular importance are the joint conference committees for the study of bills on which the houses disagree and joint ad interim committees, which are created usually for purposes of investigation of larger problems requiring legislative attention. The work of these committees is done during the interim period between regular sessions.† Each house also employs the committee of the whole, in which the whole membership sits as a committee for consideration of proposed legislation.

Table 5 reveals the serious need for revision of the committee structure. The number of committees is far too large for efficient operation or in fact for any useful purpose. The large number of committees

* The only committees not appointed are the judicial committee of each house and the rules committee of the senate. All lawyers and law students in each house are members of the judiciary committee of that house; the senate rules committee consists of the lieutenant governor, president pro tempore, and one senator from each congressional district, elected by the senators of that district.

The first person named on a committee serves as chairman and the second as vice-chairman. Joint committees have a chairman and vice-chairman from each house.

† Four joint ad interim committees were created by the 1948 session, two by the 1950 session, and one by the 1952 session. The general legislative investigating committee was created in 1946 with no statutory limit on its existence. It has thus become a joint standing committee until the legislature decides to abolish it.

TABLE 5

STANDING COMMITTEES IN THE MISSISSIPPI LEGISLATURE, 1952

Senate	*Number of Members*	*House*	*Number of Members*
Agriculture, Commerce, and Manufacturing	14	Aeronautics and Aviation	9
Aviation and Aerial Transportation	11	Agriculture	29
Banks and Banking	9	Appropriations	29
Claims	7	Banks and Banking	11
Constitution	9	Census and Apportionment	15
Contingent Expenses	3	Claims	7
Corporations	9	Conservation of Minerals and Natural Resources	29
County Affairs	12	Constitution	11
Conservation of Natural Resources	22	Contingent Expenses	7
Drainage	7	Corporations	11
Education	9	County Affairs	17
Engrossed Bills	5	Drainage	11
Federal Relations	5	Education	29
Fees and Salaries	9	Eleemosynary Institutions	15
Finance	26	Engrossed Bills	5
Forestry	11	Federal Relations	11
Highways and Highway Financing	22	Fees and Salaries of Public Officers	13
Humane and Benevolent Institutions	9	Fisheries, Commerce, and Shipping	11
Insurance	12	Forestry	17
Interstate Cooperation	5	Game, Fish, and Wild Life	11
Judiciary	[a]	Highways and Highway Financing	29
Juvenile Delinquency and Child Welfare	11	Insurance	11
Labor	9	Interstate Cooperation	5
Levees	9	Judiciary	[a]
		Juvenile Delinquency and Child Welfare	11

on which most members serve makes it impossible for them to give the best service to any. If the standing committee assignments in the senate were equally divided, each senator would have membership on eight separate committees. It is not uncommon for more prominent senators to serve on as many as twelve committees. The same situation, to a lesser degree, prevails in the house. Naturally, some committees are not of great importance and require less of the members than others. Some are practically moribund, having no important functions and meeting at rare intervals if at all. A sharp reduction in the number of committees, such

TABLE 5—*continued*

Senate	*Number of Members*	*House*	*Number of Members*
Local and Private Legislation	5	Labor	15
Military Affairs	10	Livestock and Poultry	21
Municipalities	7	Local and Private Legislation	7
Oyster Industry	5	Manufacturers	5
Penitentiaries and Prisons	12	Mileage	5
Pensions	11	Military Affairs	11
Printing	5	Mississippi Levees	12
Public Health and Quarantine	9	Municipalities	11
Public Lands	7	Penitentiary	17
Public Works	5	Pensions and Social Welfare	23
Railroads and Franchises	9	Public Buildings and Grounds	7
Registration and Elections	9	Public Health and Quarantine	9
Roads, Ferries, and Bridges	15	Public Lands	9
Rules	9	Public Printing	7
Temperance	9	Railroads and Public Service Corporations	11
Transportation	15	Registration and Elections	10
Unfinished Business	3	Roads, Ferries, and Bridges	25
		Rules	9
		Temperance	11
		Ways and Means	29

Joint Committees	*Number of Members*
Enrolled Bills	10
Executive Contingent Fund	8
Investigation of State Offices	16
State Library	8
University and Colleges	24

[a] All members of the legislature who are lawyers or law students are by legislative rules members of the judiciary committee of the house to which they have been elected.

Source: *Handbook Mississippi Legislature, 1952-1956* (Jackson, 1952).

as has been accomplished in the national Congress and in various states, would greatly improve efficiency of the legislature.*

FOOTNOTES

[1] Constitution of 1890, art. 4, secs. 40, 41, 42.

[2] *Ibid.*, secs. 43, 44.

[3] *Ibid.*, sec. 48.

[4] *Ibid.*, sec. 121. See Chapter 6, pp. 78-79.

[5] Constitution of 1890, art. 4, sec. 39.

* Alabama, Rhode Island, and South Carolina are among the states that have reduced the number of committees. See Council of State Governments, *The Book of the States, 1952-53* (Chicago, 1952), p. 100.

CHAPTER 5

The Legislature:

POWERS and PROCEDURE

THE MISSISSIPPI LEGISLATURE, as all such bodies, operates within the limitations of the national Constitution. These restrictions are the Tenth Amendment, which prevents the state from legislating on subjects delegated to the national government, and Article I, section 10, which prohibits states from enacting certain specified laws. Other provisions of the national Constitution, notably the Fourteenth Amendment, limit the state even when it enacts laws within its own field. In addition, the state constitution contains many provisions, positive and negative, that restrict the powers and procedure of the legislative body.

POWERS AND LIMITATIONS

By the terms of the Mississippi constitution the "legislative power" of the state is vested in the legislature.[1] Other provisions of the constitution, however, contain such detailed requirements on laws to be enacted and not to be enacted that little is left to legislative discretion. The more important legislative duties prescribed in the constitution relate to taxation, municipalities, corporations, property, suffrage, elections, and public officers. On many of these subjects the constitutional provisions are comprehensive and explicit.* On subjects of lesser importance the legislature also operates in many instances under detailed constitutional mandate.

* Illustrating this explicitness is the provision that the legislature must regulate the election of officers of corporations in the state, stipulating the manner of voting and the voting strength of stockholders.—Constitution of 1890, art. 7, sec. 194.

The most important constitutional provisions relating to the legislature, however, are the numerous prohibitions placed on its powers. The legislature can make no distinction in its laws between the rights of men and the rights of women to acquire, own, and dispose of property. Neither can it donate lands to private corporations,* permit lotteries, pay the salary of a deceased person, grant extra compensation to an officer or contractor after service rendered, retire an officer on pay, or elect any officer other than legislative officers, the state librarian, and presidential electors.† Many more could be listed.

Local and Special Legislation

The number of limitations indicates a lack of confidence in the legislature by the authors of the 1890 constitution. This loss of esteem resulted from a series of legislative misdoings that extended back to the period before the War between the States and involved the undermining of the public credit, land scandals, and improper relations with corporations and individuals.[2] Many of these mistakes arose because the legislature undertook to legislate on particular matters and individuals instead of passing general laws. There were also instances of legislative meddling in purely local affairs.[3] Consequently, the constitution contains specific limitations on the power of the legislature to pass local and special legislation.‡

Five sections of the constitution deal with this problem. Section 87 prohibits local or special laws when general laws will suffice and prohibits the suspension of general laws for the benefit of individuals or private corporations. Section 88 directs the legislature to pass general laws by which local and private interests can be provided for, municipalities chartered, and corporations created and regulated. Section 89 requires the appointment of a standing committee on local and private legislation in each house of the legislature. These committees must consider each local and private bill and recommend passage, stating that the objectives of the bill cannot be accomplished by general law or court proceeding, before the bill can be passed. The courts are prohibited from nullifying bills so passed because of their local or special nature. Section 90 enumerates twenty-one cases in which local or special laws cannot be passed. Section

* An exception is made in the case of railroads. They may be granted a right-of-way, not exceeding 100 feet in width.—*Ibid.*, art. 4, sec. 95.

† The Bill of Rights of the constitution, of course, limits the legislature as well as other branches of the government.—*Ibid.*, art. 3, secs. 5-32.

‡ In the three earlier constitutions the only limitation of this nature was the prohibition of special laws granting divorces.—Constitution of 1817, art. 6, sec. 17; Constitution of 1832, art. 7, sec. 15; Constitution of 1869, art. 4, sec. 22.

91 prohibits special legislation applying to one or more counties, but not all counties, regarding fees of local officers.*

These provisions indicate the emphatic desire of the constitution's framers to prohibit local and special legislation. In effect, they have done little to prevent such laws. By conforming to the procedural requirements of section 89, the legislature can pass practically any local or special law it desires, except for the enumerated cases in section 90. Where municipalities are concerned, the familiar device of classification has been used to cover up much special legislation.†

Generally the courts have upheld these laws. A study in 1948 found that ninety-nine cases had been in the supreme court litigating the constitutionality of local and special laws. In only fourteen of these cases were the statutes declared unconstitutional.[4] The large volume of local and special laws enacted at each session of the legislature attests to the ineffectiveness of such limitations on its powers.‡

Miscellaneous Powers

In addition to its primary function of making laws, the Mississippi legislature has other assorted powers. It serves as an electoral college for the election of the governor and other state officers.[5] The house of representatives also elects a governor from the two highest candidates when no person receives a popular and electoral majority in the election.[6] The legislature has the exclusive power to propose amendments to the constitution.[7] It has the power to impeach and try civil officers of the state for "treason, bribery, or any high crime or misdemeanor in office." Impeachment is by two thirds of all members present in the house of representatives, and trial is by the senate, where a like vote is required for conviction.[8] A further judicial function of the legislature is the power to address the governor, by two-thirds vote of each house, for removal of judges of the state courts when the charges are insufficient for impeachment. In such cases the person charged must be given notice and hearing.[9] The senate exercises a limited amount of executive power through its authority to confirm the appointment of certain military and civil officers made by the

* Sections 80 and 85 direct the legislature to pass general laws relating to fiscal affairs in municipalities and the working of public roads in counties.

† Typical of such legislation is the 1948 law authorizing any city with a population exceeding 30,000 and not exceeding 40,000, now operating under a commission form of government, to adopt a council-manager plan of government.—*Mississippi Laws, 1948,* ch. 385. This law could apply only to Meridian.

‡ The 1950 regular session enacted 882 laws. Of these, 562 were general and 320 were local and private.

governor.[10] Finally, the legislature has important powers of investigation of state officers, which may be exercised independently of other departments of government.[11]

Legislative Aids

The modern state legislature finds its work increasingly difficult. Present-day legislation is often technical and may apply to a variety of situations and individuals. It must withstand the scrutiny of the courts and lend itself to convenient application by administrative officials. The task of writing such laws, consequently, requires the aid of persons with specialized knowledge and training that the legislator frequently lacks and has no time to acquire.

The first provision for such aid was the creation of the Legislative Reference Bureau in 1938.[12] Its purpose is to provide members of the legislature with information on particular problems before them. Through this organization legislators may obtain laws of other states, model bills, data on specific bills, and other necessary or helpful information. The bureau is a part of the state library, thus all the materials of the library are readily available to the members of the legislature.

In 1944 the positions of revisor of the statutes and legislative draftsmen were created by the legislature. These persons are appointed by the attorney general of the state. The revisor of the statutes studies, compares, and analyzes the laws of the state and makes reports at each regular session on errors, duplications, and conflicts in such laws with recommendations for correction. He also advises members during sessions and at other times on the constitutionality and effect of statutes and furnishes advice on the preparation of any bill or resolution.[13] Two legislative draftsmen are employed during regular sessions to assist members in drafting bills and in obtaining data in connection with their legislative duties.[14]

In addition to these aids services are provided for the legislature by various semiofficial agencies. The Bureau of Public Administration of the state university conducts studies for legislative committees upon request and publishes biennially a handbook on legislative procedure for use of members. In 1952 representatives of the state's higher educational institutions conducted a training course in procedure for new legislators.[15]

In recent years considerable use has been made of interim committees as an aid to legislators. These committees, which have varied from five in 1947 to two in 1952, have included groups investigating some of the most important legislative subjects such as reorganization of the state government and the equalization of educational facilities. Interim committees have generally been hard-working groups, and valuable information has been contained in their recommendations and reports. The necessary cost of such investigations, however, has made them an expensive method of gathering facts, and the need for a legislative council, or similar body, to provide a permanent research agency for the study of legislative problems has been voiced by members of the legislature. Bills creating one were introduced in both the 1952 and 1954 legislative sessions, but failed of passage.

THE PASSAGE OF BILLS

Procedure in the Mississippi legislature is basically similar to that in other state legislatures and in the Congress of the United States. It is regulated severely by the provisions of the constitution, which contains a total of twenty-four articles limiting legislative procedure. These limitations relate to the style of legislation, to the process of legislating, and to appropriation and revenue measures.[16] Naturally they hamper the work of the body by denying, to a large extent, the power to make its own rules. The legislature has not always adhered strictly to these provisions, and the courts have upheld a liberal interpretation of them.[17] Nevertheless, there is much to indicate that the legislature might function more efficiently with a larger degree of control over its internal operation.

Introduction of Bills

Bills may originate in either house of the legislature and may be introduced by a member at any time except during the last three days of a session. For purposes of this explanation, the measure will begin in the house of representatives.* To introduce a bill, the author places it at any time in a box at the front of the clerk's desk. When in the order of business the time arrives for the introduction of new bills, the clerk of the house reads the titles of all bills deposited since the previous day's reading.† The constitution requires that all bills must be read on three separate days, but this provision may be dispensed with by two-thirds vote of the house considering the measure.[18] Consequently, it is customary at this point to

* Contrary to the national Congress and many state legislatures, there is no requirement that money bills originate in the house of representatives.

† The constitution requires that all laws begin with the words, "Be it enacted by the Legislature of Mississippi." The title must also clearly indicate the subject matter.—Constitution of 1890, art. 4, sec. 71.

dispense with the first and second readings. Following a lapse of one legislative day, the speaker then refers the bill to the appropriate committee.*

Committee Consideration

The committee is charged with making a thorough examination of the form, contents, and title of each bill referred to it. The house may empower the committee to summon persons and papers, administer oaths, and generally make its investigations effective. Usually hearings are conducted on all important measures, and parties interested in the proposed legislation are given an opportunity to speak.

After study and investigation the committee is ready to report on the bill. It may recommend by majority vote passage or defeat of the measure. It also may recommend passage with amendments added by the committee.† Or, it may make no report, as a result of which the bill may be killed.‡

In its report on a bill the committee must include an expression as to the sufficiency of the title. Favorably reported bills are printed upon recommendation of the committee chairman so that copies may be available to members of the house.

The Calendar

When a bill is reported by a committee it is placed on the calendar. The calendar is a record of bills favorably reported and of the order in which they were reported, maintained by the clerk of the house. From this calendar bills are taken up for consideration in order unless, on recommendation of the rules committee, a bill is advanced to the head of the list for immediate consideration. In addition to the general calendar, separate calendars are maintained for certain committees, and bills are taken from these calendars according to the order of business of the house.**

* Most bills are considered by standing committees. Some bills, because of their content, may require consideration by two standing committees. A few bills are considered in committee of the whole (the whole house sitting as a committee), although a two-thirds vote is required for forming such a committee.

† The amendments cannot be so extensive as to change the original purpose of the bill.—Constitution of 1890, art. 4, sec. 60.

‡ When a bill has not been reported for twenty legislative days, it may be withdrawn from the committee by majority vote of all members elected to the house.—*House Rules,* no. 98.

** Separate calendars are kept in the house of representatives for the ways and means, appropriations, and local and private legislation committees. The senate maintains separate calendars for the finance, rules, and local and private legislation committees.

Third Reading, Amendments, Debate, and Voting

When a bill is taken from the calendar on regular or special order, it is read in its entirety by the clerk, and amendments and debate are in order. If an amendment is proposed and adopted, it becomes a part of the bill, though no amendment can change the original purpose of the bill. Debate usually is opened by the affirmative side. Speakers are limited to ten minutes when speaking on the main question and five minutes when debating "subsidiary questions," though this time may be extended by vote of the members. When the final vote on the bill has been called for, each side is allowed only five minutes, and the affirmative side always closes the debate. The rules of debate require courtesy and proper decorum on the part of the members, and the presiding officer is in charge of enforcing such regulations.

When the bill is put to a final vote, the members register their votes in alphabetical order by an electrical voting device. Each member pushes a button at his desk that records his vote as "aye" or "no," and the vote appears on the scoreboard at the front of the chamber. Each member present is required to vote unless excused by the house.* A majority vote of the members present is required to pass most bills. However, an appropriation measure requires the vote of a majority of all elected members; a bill granting a gratuity or donation for any person or object requires a two-thirds vote of all elected members; and a revenue bill or a bill assessing property for taxation, or exempting property from taxation, must have a vote of three fifths of the members present.[19] A quorum must be present before any bill can be passed.

After a bill has received a favorable vote, it remains subject to reconsideration for one legislative day. The member moving a reconsideration must have voted with the majority. Since votes on a bill may be changed at any time before the final vote is announced, a member who sees that the vote is going against him may change his vote in order to be on the side of the majority and thus be eligible to move for reconsideration. The vote on reconsideration is cast in the same manner as the first vote. When a bill finally has passed, it is signed by the clerk and is transmitted to the senate.

* No person absent from the chamber when the question was put, or who has a pecuniary interest in the measure, may vote.—*House Rules,* no. 24.

Procedure in the Senate

When a bill reaches the senate it is given to the presiding officer. From that point on, it follows the same procedure as a bill originating in that body: first and second readings, reference to committee, consideration and report by the committee, third reading, amendments, debate, and the final vote, which is subject to reconsideration just as on any other bill. The vote requirements are the same in both houses, though the senate members vote by roll call, since that body has no electrical voting equipment.

Two minor differences in procedure between the two houses may be pointed out. A committee of the senate must report on all bills submitted to it and thus cannot kill a bill by mere failure to report. Also, the time limit on debate in the senate is twenty minutes for each speech on the main question instead of the ten minutes allowed in the house.

If the bill passes the senate in the same form as passed in the house, it is ready to be enrolled and signed. After being certified by the secretary, it is referred to the Joint Committee on Enrolled Bills. When this committee reports that it is properly enrolled, the bill is signed by the speaker of the house and the president of the senate in open sessions of their respective houses. It is then ready for transmittal to the governor.

Disagreement Between the Houses

All bills must pass both houses in identical form and language. Any change or amendment, however slight, in the second house requires that the bill be returned to the house where it originated. If the originating house concurs in the change by majority vote, the bill is then ready to be enrolled. Frequently, particularly if the bill is important, the originating house refuses to concur in the amendment. This means that the bill, at the request of either house, will be referred to a joint conference committee. The conference committee, consisting of an equal number of persons appointed from each house, meets and tries to reconcile the differences. When agreement has been reached, a written report is submitted to both houses. If accepted by both houses by majority vote, the bill is ready to be enrolled and signed as described above. If either house adheres to its disagreement, either in the conference committee or in the vote upon its report, the bill fails of passage.*

* Conference reports usually are accepted without debate. When a bill is finally defeated, it cannot be introduced again in the same session, except by two-thirds consent of the members of either house after three days' notice.—*Joint Rules,* no. 11; *House Rules,* nos. 73, 85.

Order of Business

Each house of the legislature prescribes in its rules an order of business that governs the daily proceedings. This order is followed, and matters cannot be taken up out of the regular order except by two-thirds vote of the members. However, by majority vote each house may adopt a special order for particular measures. The regular order in each house follows:

ORDER OF BUSINESS

Senate	*House of Representatives*
1. Reading of the journal	1. Reading of the journal
2. Presentation of petitions	2. Reports of select committees
3. Reports of standing committees	3. Reports of standing committees
4. Reports of select committees	4. Introduction of bills and constitutional amendments
5. Presentation of resolutions	5. Resolutions, petitions, and memorials
6. Introduction of bills	6. Disposition of pending business
7. Reference of bills	7. Consideration and passage of bills[20]
8. Unfinished business	
9. Considerations of bills and resolutions	

Action by the Governor

Upon final passage by both houses the bill is sent to the governor for his consideration and action.[21] No bills may be approved while the legislature is not in session.* Resolutions and measures affecting the prerogatives and duties of the legislature and its members, such as adjournment, constitutional amendments, and investigations of public officers, do not require action by the governor.[22]

PRESSURE GROUPS AND LOBBYING

The modern legislature does its work amid the importunities of numerous interest groups within and without the state. These groups may be business, commercial, industrial, agricultural, religious, educational, or pro-

* Constitution of 1890, art. 4, sec. 72. Because of this provision, the legislature completes its work five days before the adjournment date in order to allow the governor time to consider the large number of bills passed near the end of the session. Since the members go home at that time, legal adjournment is accomplished by a clerk in the presence of a few capitol employees or newspapermen.—*Memphis Commercial Appeal,* April 21, 1950.

fessional organizations; they may be associations of state or local employees. Although such "pressure groups" have varied and frequently clashing objectives, the aim of each is to influence legislation affecting that particular group.

The representatives of interest groups who frequent the state capitol during legislative sessions are referred to as "lobbyists" or, collectively, as "the lobby." Their task is to secure favorable or unfavorable action on bills relating to their employers. To accomplish this they employ various methods, ranging from supplying the legislator with accurate information to the use of money, political threats, and other illegal pressures. Much of the work of the lobbyist consists of cultivating the members most influential on the legislation in which he is interested by entertainment, favors, and the like. Of particular interest to the lobbyist are the members of the committee who will recommend action on the measure that concerns him. Sometimes the lobbyist inspires letters, telegrams, or visits to the legislator from his county or district, revealing, or purporting to reveal, the sentiment of the people on a particular measure.*

Much can be said in defense of the activities of pressure groups and their representatives. They provide much valuable information, one-sided but accurate, to legislative committees and individual members. They provide a kind of representation of economic or occupational interests not possible under the American system of choosing lawmakers. Basically, lobbying is but an exercise of the constitutional right of petition.[23] On the other hand, it may be used to defeat the interest of the general public and to make group or private interests the paramount concern of the elected representatives. Lobbyists operate in violation of the well-established principle that the legislator represents all of his constituents, rich or poor, strong or weak, without special pleading.

The lack of agreement as to the value or dangers of lobbying has not prevented states from regulating such activities.† Mississippi has both constitutional and legal provisions intended to prevent corruption in lobbying. The constitution prohibits members of the legislature from accepting any fee or reward for work done in behalf of any measure before the body. Members are forbidden to accept free passes or tickets at a discounted price from any transportation company. Conviction of bribery disqualifies a

* Much lobbying is done by individuals who visit their legislators in behalf of measures concerning their particular businesses or jobs. Such disorganized lobbying is rarely effective.

† Twenty-nine states have laws requiring registration of lobbyists, and nineteen states also require the filing of expense statements. *Book of the States, 1952-53* (Chicago: Council of State Governments, 1952), p. 111.

member from his legislative office, and either house may expel a member if convinced that he is guilty of corruption or has accepted a bribe.[24]

The law regulating lobbying was enacted in 1916. By its provisions any person, firm, corporation, or association that employs a person or firm as lobbyist must furnish to the secretary of state full information on the person employed, on the employer, and on the proposed legislation in which the lobbyist is interested. Such information must be filed five days after the lobbyist is employed. The secretary of state prepares a register of all such persons and organizations, including the information concerning them, that must be open to public inspection. A registration fee of one dollar is charged the employer of any lobbyist, upon payment of which the lobbyist receives a certificate. No person paid as a lobbyist can appear before any legislative committee or solicit any individual member without this certificate. The law prohibits the employment of any lobbyist on a contingent fee.

Within thirty days after adjournment of the legislative session, a full report on all expenses incurred in connection with lobbying must be filed by the employer of the lobbyist with the secretary of state along with the itemized statement of the lobbyist as to what he received and expended and to whom expended. These statements must be verified by oath, permanently recorded, and open to public inspection. Persons convicted of violating this law are subject to penalties up to a fine of $1,000 and three years' imprisonment, and firms or corporations so convicted may incur a maximum fine of $5,000.[25]

Although this law appears to provide comprehensive regulation, it contains important exemptions from its provisions. It does not require registration of persons not specifically retained, appointed, or paid for lobbying. All representatives of state institutions, local government officials or their representatives, and all persons who are invited to appear before committees are unaffected by its provisions.

It appears that in practice the measures regulating lobbying have little effect on these activities. The loopholes in the law, along with lax enforcement, leave the lobby largely free and generally unregulated. Few persons register under the law,* yet the activities of pressure groups and their representatives are widely recognized as an important influence on the legislature.

* A check of the register in the office of the secretary of state six weeks after the beginning of the 1950 legislative session revealed that only 12 persons were registered. Of these, 5 represented labor, 4 represented transportation companies, 2 represented jewelers, and 1 represented a food products company.

IMPROVEMENTS IN LEGISLATIVE PROCEDURE

The Mississippi legislature, like many others throughout the country, operates under procedure that is largely antiquated. Much of this results from the procedural limitations of the constitution, written more than sixty years ago. Naturally these limitations are not designed for the modern legislature, and many of them serve no useful purpose but only handicap the work of today's lawmakers. The constitutional basis of much of this procedure complicates the problem of improvement, since amendment or revision of the constitution is more difficult than revision of the statutes and rules.

Improvement of Committee Work

Most students and observers recognize that laws are written largely in the committees that report the bills. Yet far less attention is given to the needs of committees than to the needs of the whole body. Committees in the Mississippi legislature have few facilities for performing their work and almost no expert assistance in their important tasks. Many have no place to hold meetings and are forced to conduct hearings and investigations in downtown hotels and such places as are available. They are generally without staffs and printed materials to aid them in the study and investigation of bills. The provision of better assistance for standing committees would make for more efficient committee work and, of course, better laws.

A revamping of committee structure is a long-needed improvement. As indicated in the previous chapter, the number of standing committees could be reduced by two thirds, increasing the importance of each committee and lightening the committee work of individual members. Further simplification of the system might be effected by the general use of joint committees for the study of bills, thus avoiding the duplication in hearings and study that exists under the present system of separate committees and shortening the time needed to enact a measure into law.* Such improvements could result in great economy of legislative time and produce far better committee reports.

* The legislatures of Connecticut, Maine, and Massachusetts make considerable use of joint standing committees.—W. Brooke Graves, *American State Government* (Heath, 1953), p. 225. See also discussion in *American State Legislatures,* Report of the Committee on American Legislatures of the American Political Science Association (Crowell, 1954).

Replacement of Ad Interim Committees by Legislative Council

The use of joint committees for the study of legislative problems between sessions is a poor and expensive method of legislative planning. Although there is probably good reason to continue the General Legislative Investigating Committee, the study of specific problems now conducted in this manner could be handled far better and more economically by the creation of a legislative council with a permanent staff. Such a body would provide a valuable means of supplying legislative information and assistance and furnish the presession planning necessary for the best legislation.

Other Improvements

The constitutional requirement of three readings of every bill serves no useful purpose and wastes considerable time. Although the first two readings are largely a formality, because of the power to suspend the rule requiring full reading by two-thirds vote, there appears little reason for any reading except by title. Printing and distribution of bills several days before the final vote would serve the purpose better.

Other improvements in procedure or in organization that would affect procedure might include better bill-drafting and legislative reference services, annual sessions, better legislative records, and general streamlining of the rules under which the houses operate. Members of the legislature have a great amount of important work to do and a limited time in which to do it. The improvement and simplification of procedural rules, the employment of aids and devices that will improve the quality of their work, and the elimination of unnecessary practices that take up valuable time would enhance the prospects of good legislation.

FOOTNOTES

[1] Constitution of 1890, art. 4, sec. 23.

[2] Dunbar Rowland, *History of Mississippi* (Jackson: Clarke Pub. Co., 1925), I, 599 ff., II, 159 ff.

[3] George H. Ethridge, *Mississippi Constitutions* (Jackson: Tucker Printing House, 1928), p. 205.

[4] William N. Ethridge, Jr., *Modernizing Mississippi's Constitution* (Bureau of Public Administration, University of Mississippi, 1950), p. 26.

[5] Constitution of 1890, art. 5, sec. 140. Details of this election are explained in Chapter 6, p. 70.

[6] *Ibid.*, sec. 141.

[7] *Ibid.*, art. 15, sec. 273. The method of amendment is described in Chapter 2.

[8] *Ibid.*, art. 4, secs. 49-52. See also Chapter 6, p. 71.

[9] *Ibid.*, sec. 53.

[10] For example, *ibid.,* art. 4, secs. 213 A, 218.

[11] *Ibid.,* art. 4, secs. 60, 121.

[12] *Mississippi Laws, 1938,* ch. 163.

[13] *Mississippi Laws, 1944,* ch. 264, secs. 1, 2.

[14] *Ibid.,* sec. 3.

[15] See Charles Nolan Fortenberry, *A Handbook for Mississippi Legislators* (Bureau of Public Administration, University of Mississippi, 1952); "Classes for Mississippi Legislators," *State Government,* 25 (April, 1952), 85 ff.

[16] Constitution of 1890, art. 4, secs. 54-77.

[17] *Hunt* v *Wright,* 70 Miss. 298, 307, 11 So. 608, 610 (1892).

[18] Constitution of 1890, art. 4, sec. 59.

[19] Constitution of 1890, art. 4, secs. 64, 66, 70.

[20] *Senate Rules,* no. 53; *House Rules,* no. 48.

[21] For discussion of the governor's power, see Chapter 6.

[22] Constitution of 1890, art. 4, sec. 60.

[23] Constitution of the United States, First Amendment; Constitution of 1890, art. 3, sec. 11.

[24] Constitution of 1890, art. 4, secs. 44, 47, 55; art. 7, sec. 188.

[25] *Mississippi Laws, 1916,* ch. 105.

CHAPTER 6

The Governor

LIKE ALL STATES of the American Union, Mississippi has a governor. This officer has been provided in all four of the state constitutions, and under each his actual power has been limited. The development of the office of governor has represented a slow, gradual growth, pushed along by new statutes, court decisions, and relatively infrequent constitutional revisions.

The evolution of the office of governor covers four periods. First, the power and authority held by it in the territorial days was small. The bill creating the government of the Mississippi Territory made applicable the terms of the Northwest Ordinance* and provided appointment of a governor, a secretary, a common law court, and civil officers.[1] By this measure the governor and the three judges of the court, or a majority of them, were empowered to adapt the laws of the original states of the Union to the needs of the new territory, subject to the disapproval of Congress or the territorial assembly. The wide discretionary powers of the territorial governor were restricted by act of Congress in 1800 after some personal animosity had been aroused by the incumbent. A distrust of a strong executive had been created that still remains.

From 1817, when Mississippi became a state, until the middle of the century the governor was hardly more than a symbolic figurehead. Neither the 1817 nor the 1832 constitution gave more than bare recognition to the governor as chief executive. Not until the adoption of the latter instrument, for example, did he have either statutory or constitutional au-

* Excepting, however, the prohibition on slavery.

thority to make appointments,[2] and throughout the period any control he had over administration was insignificant.

In the third phase of development, which ended with the adoption of the Constitution of 1890, the powers of the governor gradually developed. The Constitution of 1869 vested in him limited appointing power and authorized a statute empowering him to fill all vacancies in the public offices of municipalities, counties, districts of the state, and all other public offices that were not included expressly in the appointing provision of the basic law.[3] A power of removal had been granted thirteen years earlier. The rapid accretion of independent and multitudinous boards and commissions, however, emphasized the administrative weaknesses of the office.

The office of governor has been characterized since 1890 by a lack of actual administrative authority, and the result of the continued addition of public services to the activities of the administrative branch has been to weaken its power still further by diffusion. At the same time, there have been fewer counter evidences. The power of appointment has increased slightly, perhaps, and the opportunity for assuming the leadership in forming fiscal policy has been ensured, at least in part, by the adoption of a statutory budget system. Even so, the Mississippi governor remains more of a "chief observer" than a chief executive.[4]

GENERAL CHARACTERISTICS OF THE OFFICE

A brief consideration of the main characteristics of the office must precede a review of its organization and powers. These characteristics include qualifications, nomination and election, term of office, vacancies, and removals.

Qualifications

The constitution establishes three qualifications for the governor: He must be at least thirty years of age, have been a citizen of the United States twenty years, and have resided in the state five years preceding the day of his election.[5] The Constitution of 1817 included these same requirements and contained in addition the proviso that the governor should possess "a freehold estate of 600 acres of land, or of real estate of a value of $2,000 at the time of his election" and for a year prior to it.[6] This property qualification was omitted from the Constitution of 1832, and the residence requirement was dropped to two years in the 1869 instrument. Qualifications for the office have remained the same, with these exceptions, throughout Mississippi's history.

Nomination and Election

Candidates for governor are nominated by direct primary, as are all other party candidates. A majority is necessary to nominate, a requirement that not uncommonly necessitates a second, or run-off, primary.

Mississippi's constitution provides that governors shall be elected in odd-numbered years on the first Tuesday after the first Monday in November every fourth year.* The effect of this timing of the general election is to prevent coincidence of state elections with the presidential elections and to make the gubernatorial contest an important and hard-fought race. The method of election, however, creates one important problem.

The division of the state into three districts is employed as a device in the election of the governor and other executive officers. The successful candidate must receive a majority of the popular vote and also of the electoral votes. The requirement provides that the candidate receiving in each county or district the highest number of votes shall receive as many electoral votes as the county or district is entitled to members in the house of representatives. If no candidate receives both a state-wide popular and electoral majority, the house selects one of the two highest candidates for the office.[7] By this requirement the basic law clearly is intended to safeguard white control of the office. Since the popular and electoral majorities have always coincided, the provision for electoral votes has never been of practical significance in the election process.

Terms and Compensation

The governor's term of office is four years. Early constitutions specified a two-year term, and not until 1869 was the tenure lengthened.[8] The Constitution of 1890 included provision that the governor shall be ineligible to succeed himself immediately in office, a departure from the state's previous experience.

Compensation for the office is fixed by the legislature with the usual limitation that it may not be increased or diminished for any specific incumbent of the governorship. The governor currently receives a salary of $15,000 and the use of the executive mansion without rentals.

* Constitution of 1890, art. 5, sec. 140. Only two other states, Kentucky and Virginia, have made similar provisions.

Vacancies and Removals

The governorship may be vacated temporarily or permanently in Mississippi by five methods: death, resignation, illness or other disability, temporary absence from the state, or impeachment.* The lieutenant governor succeeds to the office on the death of the governor. When the chief executive is absent from the state, the lieutenant governor also assumes the office and discharges its duties.† He is free to make important policy decisions and to exercise the powers of office just as the governor would.

If the lieutenant governor is incapable at the death or resignation of the chief executive, the president pro tempore of the senate succeeds to office, and following him the speaker of the house of representatives. When any doubt exists as to a vacancy in the governorship, the secretary of state is authorized to submit the question to the judges of the supreme court, whose opinion shall be in writing and is conclusive.[9]

The legislature possesses the customary impeachment power to remove the governor upon conviction of treason, bribery, or any high crime or misdemeanor. The house of representatives must bring the charges by a two-thirds vote, and the governor is tried by the senate with the chief justice of the supreme court presiding. A two-thirds concurrence is necessary for conviction. No governor has been removed by impeachment under the Constitution of 1890.[10]

CONSTITUTIONAL POSITION

Article 5 of the Constitution of 1890 prescribes the powers of the governor as in the summary that follows:

Section 116. The chief executive power shall be vested in a governor.

Section 119. The governor shall be commander-in-chief of the military and naval forces of the State except when they are in the service of the United States.

Section 120. The governor may require written reports from officers of the executive departments.

Section 121. He may convene the legislature in extraordinary session.

Section 122. He shall report from time to time to the legislature on the state of the government and make recommendations for its improvement.

* There being no recall provided, this method of removal is not operative.

† Constitution of 1890, art. 5, sec. 131. Even though the governor be absent no more than a day, this provision applies.—*Montgomery* v *Cleveland,* 134 Miss. 132, 98 So. 111 (1923).

Section 123. He shall see that the laws are faithfully executed.

Section 124. The governor shall have the power to grant reprieves and pardons in all criminal and penal cases, treason and impeachment excepted.

Section 137. He shall verify funds in the state treasury.

ORGANIZATION OF THE OFFICE

The governor is the legal head of a large public jurisdiction. Yet his office establishment is small and is devoted almost entirely to the handling of routine matters that develop in any executive office. The establishment consists of one executive assistant, an executive secretary, and the necessary clerical and stenographic employees.

Few staff aids are provided the executive. Students are generally agreed that all of the institutional activities of government that bear upon its day-to-day operation should be made the direct and immediate responsibility of the chief executive. One of his main tasks, indeed, is to assure the effective functioning of the executive departments. These institutional services are at least six in number: personnel, budgeting, accounting, purchasing, record keeping, and research and planning.

Not one of them is now so organized in Mississippi. Personnel matters are left to the individual offices in the absence of any central personnel office. The governor is the ex officio director of the State Budget Commission, established in 1932, without assuming the responsibility for the biennial budget it prepares; budgetary controls are applied, but chiefly to appropriated funds.[11] The accounting functions are the province of an independently elected officer, the auditor of public accounts, who conducts the postaudit, exercises a preaudit, and keeps the general state accounts.[12] Official records are maintained by the popularly elected secretary of state, and no executive establishment now exists for either state purchasing or planning and research. As a succeeding chapter will reveal, the absence of staff aids and auxiliary controls weakens considerably the administrative position of the Mississippi chief executive.

EXECUTIVE POWERS

Ministerial and Discretionary Powers

A distinction must be made between ministerial duties whose performance permits no exercise of judgment and discretionary powers where gubernatorial judgment may be employed. The former are subject to judicial order; an example is the commissioning of all state officers when their election has been properly certified. Where the power leaves discretion for action in the governor, his exercise of it cannot be compelled by the courts. Examples of discretionary powers include those to convene the legislature in extraordinary session and to grant pardons and reprieves. The Mississippi Supreme Court, however, decided in the leading case of the *Vicksburg and Mississippi River Railroad* v *Lowry* that the courts have no power to compel the governor to perform any of the acts of his office.[13]

Powers of Administration

The constitution vests "the chief executive power of this state" in the governor, and from it he is to possess, on the basis of this provision, the general administrative power of direction and supervision of his subordinates. The grant is made along with the constitutional delegation of powers to other specific executive officers, namely the lieutenant governor, secretary of state, state treasurer, and the auditor of public accounts.[14] The courts early imposed a limitation upon this executive power by ruling that the grant does not authorize the governor to bring suit in the name of the state and for its benefit.[15] As a result this officer has been empowered by statute to institute suit in his own name for the state should the proper officers fail or neglect to do so upon his request.

The constitution also enjoins the governor to "see that the laws are faithfully executed." The fact is, however, that this official may exercise only such means in discharging his power as are explicit in the constitution or are spelled out by legislative action. In one judicial instance the effect of the supreme court's decision was to broaden executive power by stating that it is the governor's duty as chief executive to enforce the law where the local enforcement machinery has broken down.[16]

Mississippi is one of thirty-four states that empower the chief executive "to require information in writing from officers in the executive departments of the state on any subject relating to the duties of their respective offices."[17] However, no independent power of investigation is vested in the governor. In effect this power is a declaration; no means are provided in the constitution for implementing it or for ensuring that the reports are informative and not merely perfunctory. The legislature has supplemented the constitutional grant by permitting the executive to require special reports of any officers and to supervise the official conduct of all executive and ministerial officers.[18]

Power of Appointment

The governor has no wide power of appointment vested in him by the constitution. Of the offices created by that document, only one, that of the adjutant general, is filled by gubernatorial appointment; one officer is appointed by the legislature, and the remainder are elected. Most of the governor's appointments, therefore, are founded on statutes. Today this statutory power extends independently to two dozen offices, boards, and commissions and a dozen offices or agencies, with senatorial approval.[19] No more than a third of the administrative establishments are affected by the appointing power. The governor is charged with seeing that the laws are executed faithfully and with exercising the chief executive power without the grant of authority necessary to enforce the laws or to supervise effectively official acts of administration.

Power of Removal

As a corollary to the restricted appointing power, the governor lacks constitutional authority to remove executive and administrative officers, whether appointed by him or elected by the people.* The usual constitutional method prevails; public officers shall be removed from office after indictment and conviction.

Some limited suspending power is allowed the governor in the case of defaulting state and county treasurers and tax collectors. In such instances he may make temporary appointments pending the investigation of their accounts. Even so, this power does not extend to the state insurance commissioner, although the latter collects taxes for the state.[20] Nor has the legislature taken advantage of its permissive power to authorize the governor to remove and appoint officers in any county or municipal corporation of the state.

The sum of this indicates that the governor possesses only such removal powers as the legislature cares to delegate to him with respect to statutory officers. The legislature has acted in few instances, although occasionally removal of specific officers for specific causes is permitted.† Coupled with

* The opinion in an early case, *Bursan* v *Cocke,* 44 Miss. 352 (1870), indicated an acceptance of the idea that the power to appoint carries with it the power to remove. No later opinion conveys acceptance of this concept.

† For example, trustees for the state deaf and blind institutes may be removed by the governor for failure to attend three consecutive meetings. Again, he can remove members of the Board of Trustees of Mental Institutions for willful neglect of duty or for misdemeanors in office that are liable to indictment.

the limited appointing power, the absence of an effective removal power deprives the Mississippi governor of a real tool for discharging the obligations placed upon him by his office.

Military Powers

The executive's position as commander in chief of the state's militia is assured. Since these forces may be employed constitutionally to execute the laws, repel invasions, and suppress riots or insurrection, they are an important body. The governor is responsible, subject to senate confirmation, for appointment of all commissioned officers in the militia, but he cannot remove them, the executive power here extending merely to recommendations to the senate.[21] As governor and as commander in chief, he must be responsible also for its organization, training, and general well-being.

LEGISLATIVE POWERS

The legislative authority of the governor falls into two categories, constitutional and extraconstitutional. The constitutional powers are four in number: the veto power, the power to send messages to the legislature, authority to call extraordinary sessions, and the power to adjourn the legislature when its two houses cannot agree upon adjournment. The extraconstitutional powers embrace all those means by which the chief executive endeavors to secure popular and legislative support for his program.

Veto Power

All four Mississippi constitutions have vested a veto power in the governor; their provisions have changed but little over the years. In accord with the checks and balances theory of the Mississippi constitution, the veto serves as a potential curb on legislative action and enhances the rather weak administrative power of the executive.

The governor has three alternative courses when a measure has passed both houses of the legislature and has come to his desk for action. He may sign it and thus make it law. He may disapprove the bill by returning it to the house whence it originated; in this event the proper house enters his objections on its journal and proceeds to reconsider the measure, a two-thirds affirmative vote of both houses being necessary to override the veto.

Finally, the governor may permit the bill to become law by holding it for five days (Sundays excepted). If the legislature adjourns before the expiration of this period, the measure becomes law unless the governor returns it within three days after the beginning of the next session. He can approve no bill when the legislature is not in session.[22]

The implications of these veto provisions are significant. First, the Mississippi constitution confers the commonly authorized suspensive veto. It is possible for the legislature to pass any measure over the governor's head at the session during which the veto power was used. The suspensive character of the power is emphasized further by the elimination of the pocket veto; the bill shall become a law unless it is returned to the legislature within the time limit at the beginning of the next session. Second, the governor is given only five days in which to study, consider, decide upon, and return a bill to the legislature after it has been presented to him. Third, the executive is compelled either to act unfavorably upon a specific bill or to approve it by act of commission or omission; he cannot veto it by holding it until adjournment.

Several aspects of the veto power in Mississippi require brief comment. Clearly five days are a very short time to hold a bill, particularly toward the end of a session when the legislative mills grind faster. It is true that twenty-one states have established this same period of consideration and that nine allow only three; but six days are allowed in four states, and ten in twelve states.[23] Ten days would not seem an unreasonable maximum for the consideration of much important legislation.

The rather sharp time limit carries over in the prohibition of executive approval of a bill after the adjournment of the legislature. In contrast, twenty-seven states require the governor to dispose of all bills submitted to him in three to thirty days after adjournment; otherwise they become law. Another five give the governor thirty days after adjournment to approve measures that become law if unsigned.[24] No Mississippi constitution before the current instrument forbade approval after adjournment. The constitutional prohibition appears to rest on the theory that, since the governor's veto is a legislative power, it is beyond his jurisdiction to approve or disapprove a measure when the legislature is not in session.[25] Three years before the present constitution was adopted the Mississippi Supreme Court ruled that the governor could approve legislation any time, including after the legislative adjournment, but this decision was explicitly reversed by the constitutional convention of 1890.[26]

If the veto restrictions prevent the death of a bill by executive failure to act, they also may delay approval of legislation by this same prohibition. The governor on his part may postpone action by holding a bill until the next biennial session, but if he desires to approve it when the legislature is not in session, he is powerless to act. The constitutional restrictions compel ultimate executive action without encouraging the making of deliberative decisions.

The governor, in addition, is given an item veto: he may approve parts of any appropriation bill while rejecting other parts.[27] The purpose of the item veto is to allow the executive to delete excessive, unconstitutional, or otherwise improper appropriations without endangering the passage of essential appropriations measures. The power is an important one because the Mississippi constitution expressly provides that all appropriations shall be made by separate bills embracing a single subject with the exception of those for the executive, legislative, and judicial departments, for interest on state bonds, and for school support. The latter may be general or lump sum appropriations. The Mississippi Supreme Court has interpreted this proviso for the item veto, ruling that it applied to both general and special appropriations acts and that the governor may not eliminate the section of a special appropriation act establishing the conditions on which the money may be drawn.

The frequency with which the governor exercises the veto and the reasons for its use vary with the individual occupying the office. In the decade 1937-1947 inclusive, some 9,227 bills were introduced in the Mississippi legislature and 3,410 passed. Of these measures only 66, or 2.4 per cent of all bills enacted, were vetoed.[28] Only in Georgia, South Carolina, Tennessee, and West Virginia, among the states of the South, was the veto employed less. Common reasons for the exercise of this power include faulty draftsmanship, gubernatorial objection to the policy to be established, duplication of existing statutes, unconstitutionality of the measures, and fiscal reasons, such as the failure to provide revenue to meet a proposed expenditure.

Messages

Just as the President presents an annual message to the national Congress, so the Mississippi governor is directed "to give the legislature information of the state of the government and recommend for consideration such measures as may be deemed necessary and expedient."[29] However, no specific time is stipulated for the presentation of these messages, as contrasted with the Federal Constitution.

The grant of authority to give information and to make recommendations is not merely an authorization. It is a definite duty with which the strong governor frequently complies. The governor's message, customarily presented to the legislature at the beginning of a session, reviews the condition of the state and outlines the program of the executive.[30] The constitution provides that the governor's messages shall be made from time to time, thereby affording an opportunity for repeated reports and recommendations throughout the session.

The effectiveness of the message power as a device for molding legislative action depends upon a number of facts: the strength of the governor, the political and factional composition of the legislature, the economic condition of the state, and a congeries of personal relationships. In the turbulent depression days of Governor Bilbo's second term, the legislature acted favorably on but 10 of the 75 measures he proposed. His immediate successor made 35 recommendations, of which 19 became law. Despite variations of this sort, messages are a potentially effective means for a statement of executive policy.

Special Sessions and Adjournment

Like the governors of all the states, the Mississippi governor may call special or extraordinary sessions of the legislature. He has had this authority under all the state constitutions.

Several aspects of the power should be observed.[31] The Mississippi constitution makes the power an exclusive one, providing that the call shall be by public proclamation "wherever, in his judgment, the public interest requires it." The governor also must state the subjects and matters to be considered by the legislature in extraordinary session. The legislature then is limited to the matters designated in the governor's proclamation with the exception of impeachments, examination into the accounts of state officers, and other matters that the executive may submit in writing to them while they are in session.*

Mississippi is one of fourteen states where the governor may convene the legislature at a place other than the seat of government if that place is in danger "from an enemy or from disease." Although a special session is expensive to the state and inconvenient to the legislators, Mississippi governors frequently have exercised the power. Thirteen extraordinary sessions have been called under the 1890 constitution, five of which were

* An 1890 statute curiously granted the governor authority to convene the senate in special session to concur in appointments.

summoned to deal with the economic problems in the depression of the mid-thirties.

Although section 1 of the Mississippi constitution states the familiar doctrine of separation of powers, and section 2 forbids any officer or officers of one branch of government to exercise the powers of either of the others, the governor may adjourn special sessions of the legislature when the house and senate are unable to agree on a time of adjournment. He may not adjourn them, however, beyond the day of the next stated meeting of the legislature.

Extraconstitutional Powers

A good deal of the governor's legislative influence flows from the extra-constitutional and nonlegal powers that adhere to the office he holds. First of all, by bargain and compromise and by the threat of a special session he can seek to fulfill his program. Second, by virtue of his position as a party or factional leader he can with some force focus attention upon legislative action or inaction. By news releases and press conferences he can state his views on pending legislation favorably or unfavorably.[32] In recent years daily newspapers within the state, such as the *Jackson Daily News* and the *Meridian Star,* and outside the state, such as the widely read *Memphis Commercial Appeal* and the *New Orleans Times Picayune,* have provided a means for reaching the reading public. Governor Fielding L. Wright (1946-1952) employed a personal appearance before the members of the 1948 legislature to emphasize his financial policy. Public addresses have been utilized by some governors to build up public support on controversial issues, and the radio has supplied a medium of reaching still more people. It is, of course, quite possible for a governor to go too far in his efforts to marshal legislative support, as in the case of Governor Bilbo, who in 1931 attempted to extract signed pledges from the legislators that they would support his program as the price for calling an extraordinary session to deal with emergency relief.[33]

The techniques employed in legislative relationships not unnaturally differ with the individual governor. The frequent lack of harmony between the chief executive and the legislature illustrates well the conflict between actual practice and the theoretical concept that the legislature makes the laws and that the governor simply executes them. Not a few important measures originate in the executive branch of government. Yet the constitution and the statutes of the state give the governor no formal affirmative leadership in the legislative process.* It is apparent thus that much of the effectiveness of the governor as a legislative leader rests upon no more solid foundation than the variable qualities of his personality.

JUDICIAL POWERS

Executive Clemency.

The governor occasionally may perform duties of a judicial nature. His most important power of this kind is that of executive clemency. In all criminal and penal cases, "excepting those of treason and impeachment," the governor has "the power to grant reprieves and pardons, to remit fines, and in cases of forfeiture to stay the collection until the end of the next session of the legislature, and by and with the consent of the senate to remit forfeitures."[34] In the case of treason the chief executive may grant reprieves with the consent of the senate. After conviction of a felony he may grant no pardon until the applicant has published his petition for pardon for thirty days in the county where the crime was committed, this petition setting forth the reasons why the pardon should be granted. Thus, in addition to the obsolete power to remit fines and forfeitures, the Constitution of 1890 allocates to the governor an exclusive power to pardon, or to remit a penalty; a power of reprieve, or stay of execution, which is shared with the legislature in treason cases but not in other crimes and felonies; and by implication the power of commutation, that is, the reduction or lessening of the penalty. No constitutional provision is made for the parole or conditional release under supervision of persons convicted and already under sentence.

The courts have made several well-established interpretations of the power of executive clemency. A pardon restores the right to vote by eliminating the fact of any crime and hence the existence of any guilt.[35] It includes the power to pardon for contempt, but does not extend to punishments meted out under municipal ordinances unless expressly specified by the legislature.[36] The legislature is powerless on its part to delegate the pardoning power to any officer other than the governor.[37]

* For example, an attempt has been made to bridge the gap in Virginia, where the item veto has been extended to include general bills. The governor may return the bill with a veto of objectionable sections and also with suggested changes. If the assembly agrees to them by a majority of the members present in each house, the bill is returned to the governor as though for the first time. See William N. Ethridge, Jr., *Modernizing Mississippi's Constitution* (Bureau of Public Administration, University of Mississippi, 1950), p. 53.

Although the courts have not expressly so ruled, the governor probably has the authority to grant conditional as well as unconditional pardons.[38]

Treatment of paroles is a statutory matter. Before 1944 the governor was without the assistance this power requires. Under a parole, violation of the conditions of release forfeits the parole, and the prisoner returns to serve out the unexpired portion of his sentence. Effective exercise of the parole device assumes the operation of a staff of parole officers and an administrative arrangement to supervise their work. In its 1942 session the legislature created the State Board of Pardons, a part-time body charged with reviewing petitions for pardon and reprieve and with reporting its findings and recommendations to the governor.[39] Without power and without employees, this agency was unable to implement a parole system. Two years later it was abolished and succeeded by the State Parole Board, whose membership consists of a full-time chairman and two part-time board members. This board serves two purposes. First, it must examine at the request of the governor the merit of any petition for pardon and recommend action thereon. Second, the board is empowered to recommend for parole eligible prisoners of the state; the terms and conditions are decided upon by the board, the prisoner remaining in the legal custody of the superintendent of the state penitentiary.[40] There is ample evidence that the exercise of executive clemency is a heavy burden on the governor. The current parole statute mitigates it by providing an advisory group on pardons and reprieves, by encouraging the governor to make releases on good behavior by parole rather than by conditional pardon, and by constructing the machinery for a parole system without encroachment upon the chief executive's basic authority.

Other Judicial Powers

Two powers of a judicial nature include the rarely, if ever, exercised suspension of the writ of habeas corpus and the consideration and decision on requests made by governors of other states for the extradition of persons charged with crimes. All Mississippi constitutions have safeguarded the writ of habeas corpus, and the present instrument prohibits its suspension, "unless when in case of rebellion or invasion, the public safety may require it, nor ever without the authority of the legislature."[41] Article IV of the Federal Constitution requires that the governor shall deliver to the state having jurisdiction any person charged with crime on the demand of the executive of the state from which the alleged criminal has fled. This command is clear, but the United States courts have ruled that the article places a discretionary rather than a mandatory duty upon the governor of the asylum state.[42] The latter may refuse to extradite a fugitive, and his decision is final. Before any decision is made, the governor not infrequently conducts hearings and passes upon both the law and the fact of the case. This power, which necessarily rests upon the governor as the chief executive authority, is a drain upon his time and energies.

FOOTNOTES

[1] George H. Ethridge, *Mississippi, A History* (Jackson: Historical Record Association, 1940), I, 58.

[2] Constitution of 1832, art. 5, sec. 13.

[3] Constitution of 1869, art. 12, sec. 7; *Mississippi Laws, 1870,* ch. 60.

[4] Oklahoma Legislative Council, *Constitutional Study No. 3* (Oklahoma City, 1948), p. 17.

[5] Constitution of 1890, art. 5, sec. 117.

[6] Constitution of 1817, art. 4, sec. 3.

[7] Constitution of 1890, art. 5, sec. 140. Section 143 extends this provision to other state officers.

[8] Constitution of 1869, art. 5, sec. 1.

[9] Constitution of 1890, art. 5, sec. 131. See also judicial interpretations found in *In re Opinion of the Justices,* 148 Miss. 427, 114 So. 887 (1927).

[10] See Chapter 3, p. 28.

[11] *Mississippi Laws, 1932,* ch. 120.

[12] *Mississippi Code, 1942,* Title 5, *passim.*

[13] 61 Miss. 102 (1883).

[14] Constitution of 1890, art. 5, secs. 116 ff.

[15] *Henry* v *State,* 87 Miss. 1, 39 So. 856 (1905).

[16] Compare *ibid.* with *State* v *McPhail,* 182 Miss. 360, 180 So. 387 (1938).

[17] Constitution of 1890, art. 5, sec. 120.

[18] *Mississippi Code, 1942,* sec. 3975.

[19] See Chapter 7, p. 87.

[20] Compare Constitution of 1890, art. 5, sec. 125, with *Henry* v *State,* 130 Miss. 855, 95 So. 67 (1922).

[21] Constitution of 1890, art. 9, sec. 216.

[22] *Ibid.,* art. 4, sec. 72.

[23] W. Brooke Graves, *American State Government* (Heath, 1953), p. 338.

[24] *Ibid.,* p. 341.

[25] Compare with *Hardee* v *Gibbs,* 50 Miss. 802 (1874).

[26] *State* v *Coahoma County,* 64 Miss. 358 (1887).

[27] Constitution of 1890, art. 4, sec. 73.

[28] Frank W. Prescott, "The Executive Veto in Southern States," *Journal of Politics,* X (1948), p. 667.

[29] Constitution of 1890, art. 5, sec. 122.

[30] For example, see Governor Conner's initial message to the 1932 legislature.—Stella A. O'Neal, *The Legislative Leadership of Governors Bilbo and Conner* (Unpublished Master's thesis, University of Mississippi, 1944), p. 31.

[31] Constitution of 1890, art. 5, sec. 121.

[32] For example, "Wright States Stand on Highway Program," *The Memphis Commercial Appeal,* December 4, 1949, sec. II, p. 12.

[33] "Sign on the Dotted Line," *State Government,* March, 1931, pp. 18-20.

[34] Constitution of 1890, art. 5, sec. 124.

[35] *Jones* v *Registrars of Alcorn County,* 56 Miss. 766 (1879).
[36] *Allen* v *McGuire,* 100 Miss. 781, 57 So. 217 (1912).
[37] *State* v *Kirby,* 96 Miss. 629, 51 So. 811 (1910).
[38] *Ex Parte Fleming,* 60 Miss. 910 (1883).
[39] *Mississippi Laws, 1942,* ch. 283.
[40] *Ibid., 1944,* ch. 334.
[41] Constitution of 1890, art. 3, sec. 21; *State* v *McPhail,* 182 Miss. 360, 180 So. 387 (1938).
[42] *Kentucky* v *Denison,* 24 Howard 66 (1861).

CHAPTER 7

Administrative Organization

THE ADMINISTRATIVE ORGANIZATION of Mississippi is characterized by its extreme complexity and wide diffusion of responsibility for execution of the laws. It consists of the governor and more than 100 additional offices and agencies.[1] It is the present purpose to sketch in broad outline the development of this administrative structure, the significant practices that are found, and the principal efforts that have been made to reorganize Mississippi's administration.

GROWTH AND DEVELOPMENT

In 1823 the state had only eight offices and agencies. These offices performed mainly the functions of general government, providing for the maintenance of order, disposition of public lands, and the necessary financial administration involved in the collection and disbursal of public moneys. In the period that ended with the *Code* of 1839, the number of administrative agencies had increased by only five, but two new services, state printing and the popular "internal improvements" program, had been added. The administrative structure remained fairly constant until the Reconstruction year of 1871. Since then it has experienced rapid and steady expansion, the peak period falling between 1917 and 1930, when no less than twenty-five new executive agencies were created. During its history the state has never decreased the total number of agencies; on the contrary, there has been a continuing accretion of administrative machinery.[2]

The distribution of administrative bodies among the functional fields of activity is significant. The most rapid—certainly the most recent—growth in the number of administrative units has been in the field of development and conservation of natural resources, where twenty-three agencies were functioning in 1950. In only two phases, education and hospitals and institutions for the handicapped, has there been any substantial reduction of administrative machinery. In both cases changes were effected, apparently as a result of Mississippi's sole attempt at reorganization, when a number of agencies were consolidated under the boards of trustees for Institutions of Higher Learning and for State Eleemosynary Institutions in 1932 and 1936 respectively. The growth of the administrative structure, in fact, has affected every principal functional field and has contributed to the broadening scope of state activity.

In 1823 seven offices found their legal basis in the Constitution of 1817 and only one rested upon a statutory basis. Twenty-five years later nine statutory agencies and offices existed compared to seven constitutional administrative positions. The margin has steadily widened between the two types of agencies until today there are ninety-odd offices and administrative bodies functioning with statutory authorization and only twelve based upon the constitution. Among the latter are the traditional offices of governor, lieutenant governor, attorney general, secretary of state, auditor of public accounts, and state treasurer as well as several more recently created positions including those of state librarian, the superintendent of education, and the board of education.[3] (See the table in the Appendix, pages 398-400.)

The number of constitutional offices and administrative bodies in Mississippi is small compared to all agencies for government. The difficulty encountered in amending the state constitution, the establishment of many administrative agencies to serve immediate needs, and the ease with which statutory bodies may be altered or abandoned are factors that doubtless have influenced the slow growth of constitutional offices in Mississippi. In general it may be stated that the mass of the state's administrative machinery rests upon a statutory basis and that the functions of state administration will continue to rest more on statutory than upon constitutional officers of administration.[4]

ADMINISTRATIVE OFFICIALS

One of the distinguishing features of Mississippi's administrative organization is its almost infinite variety. This variety is reflected in the types of administrative heads, the method of their selection, terms of office, compensation, and removal.

Types of Administrators

Twenty, or about one fifth, of the state's agencies are headed by single administrators; the remainder are directed by plural executives variously termed boards or commissions. Of the 83 bodies under the supervision of plural executives, 14 have full-time membership, 60 part-time membership, and 9 part-time membership combined with employment of an executive officer.

The single administrators include several traditional offices in addition to that of the governor. The office of lieutenant governor has no significant administrative duties and its value as a legislative liaison office is small because the incumbent is not necessarily of the same political faction as the governor. The attorney general is simply the legal adviser for the various state officers and agencies. The state treasurer receives and disburses state funds, and the auditor of public accounts is charged with both accounting and auditing functions of a wide scope. The secretary of state, a constitutional officer since 1817, discharges a group of miscellaneous functions that, apart from his regulatory powers under the blue-sky laws, are now largely clerical.[5]

In contrast, most of the newer offices are headed by plural executives. These offices include revenue, highways, labor, public welfare, public health, institutions, insurance, and the different aspects of the conservation of resources. Thirty-one plural executives have been established as recently as 1931. Their duties for the most part are primary and line services and reflect a broadened concept of the fields of responsible governmental activity. Neither the full-time commission nor the part-time board with a full-time executive, however, has been employed as extensively in these offices as the part-time boards and commissions.

Selection of Administrative Officers

The manner by which Mississippi's administrative offices are filled also offers variety. The governor, of course, is elected along with ten other state-wide administrative officers.* Most of these are constitutional offices,

* Attorney general, secretary of state, auditor of public accounts, treasurer, commissioner of agriculture, immigration, and statistics, commissioner of insurance, land commissioner, superintendent of education, lieutenant governor, and tax collector. Not included are two offices filled by election from special districts—public service commissioner and highway commissioner.

but several, notably the offices administering public lands, highways, and insurance, are statutory. Two officers, the state treasurer and the auditor of public accounts, are ineligible to succeed themselves or each other in office.*

Appointment by the governor, with or without senatorial approval, covered forty-one offices or agencies in 1930; by 1948 the scope of this power had fallen to twenty-four offices or agencies directly filled by gubernatorial appointment and twelve filled by appointment with senate confirmation. Among the free appointments are ten members of the Agricultural and Industrial Board, six members of the State Forestry Commission, and the membership of the Commission on Hospital Care. Senatorial approval is required for such appointments as the commissioner of public safety, the members of the State Tax Commission, and the long term appointments to the Board of Trustees of Institutions of Higher Learning.

Many offices, however, are filled on the ex officio principle. Beginning with one agency in 1839, the number has risen until forty executive bodies are composed wholly or partly of ex officio board members or commissioners. In the field of natural resources conservation in 1950 twenty-eight individual positions were filled by this method. Finally, several agencies are administered in effect by special interest groups. In this type of agency, which has received special attention in the last thirty years, the interest group serves as the administrative body itself, appoints the head, board, or administrator, or recommends to the governor a list of persons from which that official chooses the administrator or executive body.

Automatic selection by the ex officio method is by far the most popular means of selection. Appointment by the governor is second, although there are many elective offices. Only one method of selection has been employed for a period and then discarded—appointment by the legislature.†

Terms of Office

The two-year term of office was common in the early days of the state. By 1839 the four-year term accounted for most of the administrative terms and since then has been markedly preferred. All of the constitutional and all of the elective offices carry four-year terms.[6] Where statutory elective

* Constitution of 1890, art. 5, sec. 134. The governor is also ineligible to succeed himself immediately.

† This type was used between 1823 and 1880, and in 1839 was applicable to six agencies.

offices have been created, the same term prevails, and it has been extended widely to the membership of boards and commissions.

The legislators of Mississippi have not been inclined to fix the term for administrative officers for more than four-year periods. Most of these longer terms were restricted to trustees for the various educational institutions. By 1942 a definite trend was indicated toward the longer term of six years.* Only three agencies in 1950 had membership terms of longer than seven years.†

Methods of Compensation

Salaries for all single administrators are established by statute, ranging downward from the $15,000 annually paid the governor, although $10,000, as in the case of the attorney general, and $8,250 in the cases of the state treasurer, auditor of public accounts, and secretary of state, are not uncommon. Compensation by fees is employed in at least one case—the state tax collector. Although ex officio administrative officers normally serve without additional compensation, it is the standard practice to allow per diem payment to part-time commissioners. The legislature has not usually granted discretion to either the governor or the administrative boards to fix compensation for the working heads of the executive agencies. On the contrary, statutes spell out in detail both the method and amount in specific cases.

Methods of Removal

Removal by impeachment is prescribed for all constitutional officers[7] and, indeed, the constitution goes so far as to extend the impeachment process to "all civil officers." By statute, however, the governor is authorized to remove thirteen administrative officers and the members of three boards or commissions. In most instances, however, the laws of the state specify no method.‡

Summary of Administrative Organization

An over-all summary of Mississippi's administrative organization is now in order. The administrative structure of the state is today founded pri-

* For example, the Mississippi Commission on Hospital Care (1946), Board of Trustees of Mental Institutions (1946), Aeronautics Commission (1946).

† For example, Board of Trustees of Institutions of Higher Learning (1932).

‡ This condition applies to membership on forty-nine agencies, boards, or offices and, to a high degree, to two dozen ex officio bodies.

marily on statutes rather than the constitution, but a number of important offices derive their authority from the latter. The structure demonstrates a decided legislative preference for plural executives over agencies and offices headed by single administrators. Among the plural agencies, ex officio bodies have been regarded as capable organs for discharging administrative programs. Also evident have been the tendency to lengthen terms of office to four or more years and the trend toward a continued, but less emphasized, use of per diem payments as a method of compensation. The number of administrative bodies and the variety that they display among themselves have produced, finally, an administrative structure that has grown more complex with the assumption of each new activity.

THE ADMINISTRATIVE PATTERN

The 100 or more state administrative bodies now discharging public services demonstrate the interest Mississippi has taken in broadening the scope of governmental activity. Much of this action is recent, some twenty-seven agencies having been established since 1930. Since these agencies have been created one by one to administer a single field, for instance public welfare, or a single aspect of a public function, for instance forestry in conservation, the result is that Mississippi has failed to develop an effective administrative structure except as the discrete and independent agencies have cooperated with each other. The necessary legislative steps to provide an integration of structures and a coordination of activities have never been taken. The implications of the administrative pattern are of far-reaching importance for Mississippi. They are considered here from two points of view: the over-all administrative structure and the internal structure of state agencies.

Integration of Programs

Although integration of programs has been surprisingly complete in several fields,* the very existence of 106 agencies on the state level has precluded the development of either an administrative program for the state or integrated programs for most of the functional fields. Most administrative bodies, within limits, discharge their isolated programs with reasonable efficiency, but agencies that could cooperate often work at cross purposes, either through ignorance of related programs or occasionally for whatever special gains are to be had.

* Welfare and public health are notable examples.

Organization of Mississippi State Government, 1953

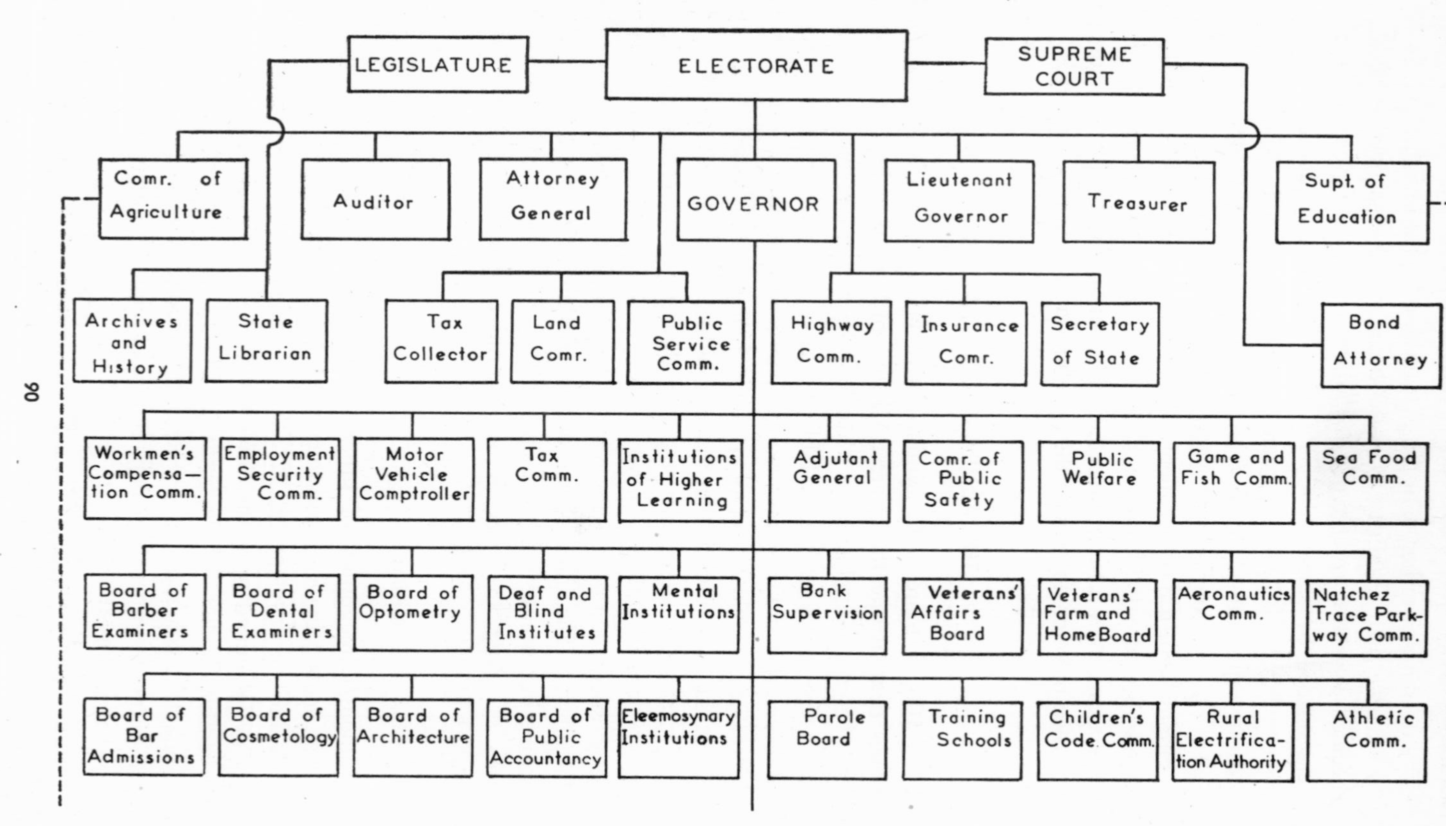

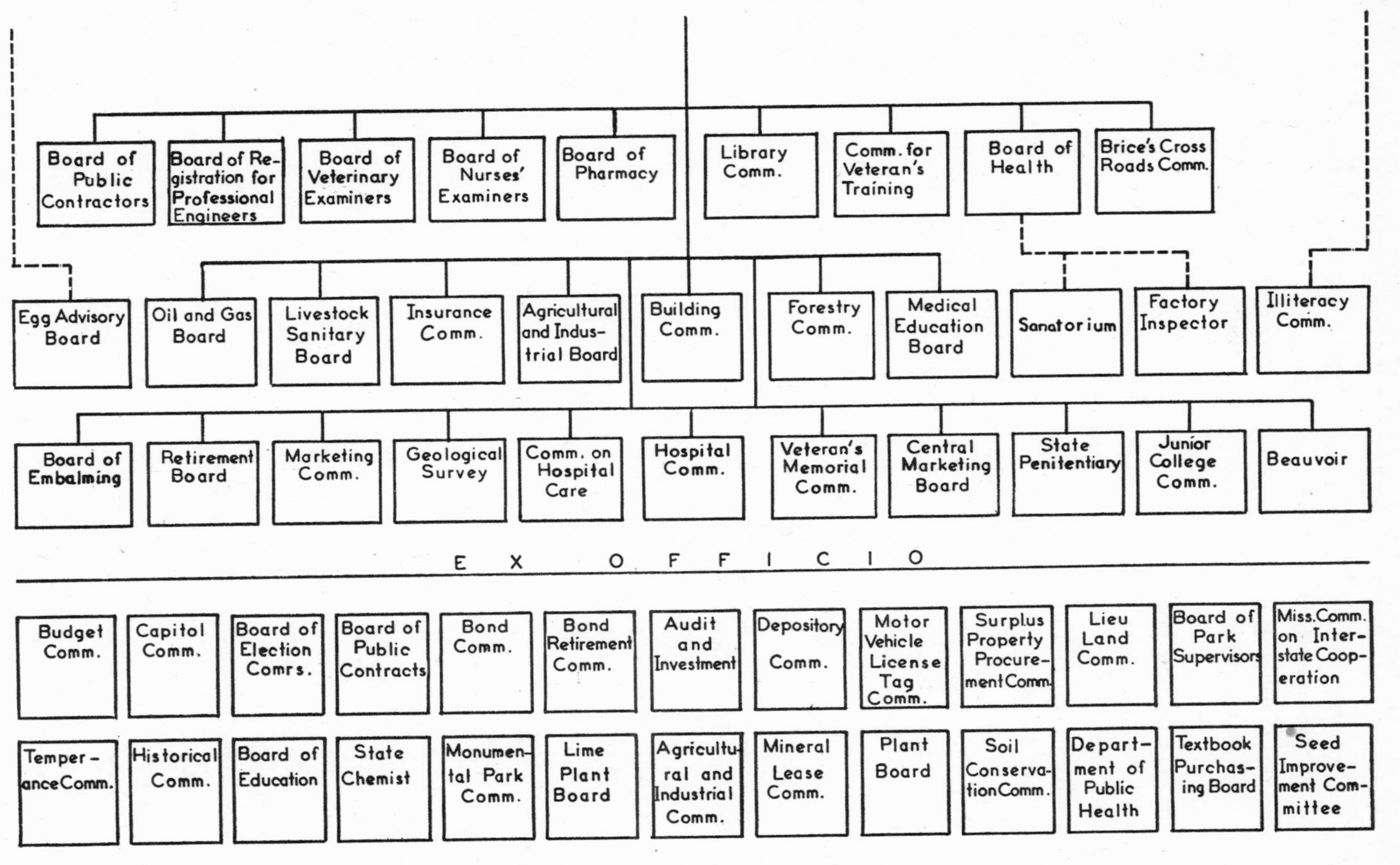

Board of Public Contractors
Board of Registration for Professional Engineers
Board of Veterinary Examiners
Board of Nurses' Examiners
Board of Pharmacy
Library Comm.
Comm. for Veteran's Training
Board of Health
Brice's Cross Roads Comm.
Egg Advisory Board
Oil and Gas Board
Livestock Sanitary Board
Insurance Comm.
Agricultural and Industrial Board
Building Comm.
Forestry Comm.
Medical Education Board
Sanatorium
Factory Inspector
Illiteracy Comm.
Board of Embalming
Retirement Board
Marketing Comm.
Geological Survey
Comm. on Hospital Care
Hospital Comm.
Veteran's Memorial Comm.
Central Marketing Board
State Penitentiary
Junior College Comm.
Beauvoir
E X O F F I C I O
Budget Comm.
Capitol Comm.
Board of Election Comrs.
Board of Public Contracts
Bond Comm.
Bond Retirement Comm.
Audit and Investment
Depository Comm.
Motor Vehicle License Tag Comm.
Surplus Property Procurement Comm.
Lieu Land Comm.
Board of Park Supervisors
Miss. Comm. on Interstate Cooperation
Temperance Comm.
Historical Comm.
Board of Education
State Chemist
Monumental Park Comm.
Lime Plant Board
Agricultural and Industrial Comm.
Mineral Lease Comm.
Plant Board
Soil Conservation Comm.
Department of Public Health
Textbook Purchasing Board
Seed Improvement Committee

A number of current consequences of administrative importance flow from Mississippi's disintegrated administrative structure. First is the obvious division of powers and duties among many separate agencies that results in a diffusion of objectives, direction, and responsibility for public action. Second, the sprawling administrative structure makes it difficult for the executive branch of government to present a well-rounded program for legislative consideration. On the one hand, the multiplicity of agencies may well prevent the legislative body from grasping clearly the administrative picture; on the other hand, responsibility for unified programs often falls to a dozen different agencies. Third, the intermittent creation of new departments, boards, and commissions develops administrative machinery that is rigid, complex, and difficult to adjust to new requirements. Fourth, the system lends itself to poor integration; that is, functions that are related are divided among two or more administrative bodies, while nonrelated activities are grouped together.* In short, Mississippi has a multitude of agencies that administer the commonly accepted functions of state government more or less independently of each other.

Position of the Governor

The lack of coordination among the operating activities is mirrored in the absence of the direction, supervision, and control required to provide a coordinating element. Reference has been made to the fact that the governor is the nominal chief executive of the state.[8] This nominalism flows from both legal and factual conditions.

The governor does not have broad and general powers to direct and control administration. He can appoint and remove heads of major departments in only a few instances. He is admonished to see "that the laws are faithfully executed," but is not charged to execute them. He may cajole, report to the legislature or to the courts; rarely may he remove the offending officer. He may require information in writing from the executive officers "on any subject relating to their duties,"[9] but any real power must come from his position as a party or factional leader. In Mississippi the administrative position of the governor is only that of one of several state executives.

Even if the governor did possess sufficient powers of direction, it is doubtful that he could perform the task of coordination that would fall to

* For example, mineral activities are divided between the Geological Survey and the State Oil and Gas Board. The secretary of state's office is apparently a catch-all for miscellaneous duties.

him. The effective span of control of any executive is limited; no governor can give close attention to five score agencies. The structure of administration imposes an excessive task upon him. The governor is technically responsible for the functioning of the administrative machine without being able to exercise much control over, or to offer much direction to, more than a few offices.

Managerial Controls

As the structure for administration fails to take account of the problem of direction, so also has it been deficient in providing a number of managerial controls. The first of these controls relates to fiscal management.

Although it will be observed that progress has been made in comprehensive fiscal management, the executive budget does not yet represent a complete fiscal plan.[10] Carefully drafted and prepared, the budget has suffered in the legislature because no one administrator claims responsibility for it. Transmitted to the legislature by the governor as the work of the secretary of the Budget Commission, the budget is credited by the secretary to statisticians of the commission. Budgetary controls that the executive may exercise over appropriations after they have been made are adequate to protect the state against incurrence of deficits on the part of agencies with appropriated funds. In several respects, however, there is no control: no officer reviews contracts; no purchasing system has been established; no prior review of expenditures is made. Nor do the budgeting controls apply to administrative bodies financed by special funds.*

Excepting departments and agencies whose course of action has been affected by the receipt of Federal funds, there is no organized system of personnel administration and, hence, no uniform personnel controls that can be employed. Since no regulations are in effect, personnel matters must be dealt with entirely at the level of the given office.

Where there are planning and research in either an administrative or functional sense, they too rest with the individual unit of administration. Aside from such fiscal planning as the Budget Commission discharges, there is no staff agency in Mississippi concerned with administrative planning and research. And functional planning has been replaced by industrial development as the chief function of the agencies that succeeded the Mississippi Planning Commission of the late depression years.[11] When planning and research are required to alter internal organization of an

* These funds, not subject to legislative appropriations, account for the major source of income for a number of agencies, for example, State Highway Commission.

agency, and hence its line performance, they fall to the administrator and his board. Where changes require no legislative authorization, they may be incorporated by administrative discretion; where legislative changes are needed, the individual agency presses for adjustment. Program planning and research similarly lack the unity of an integrated pattern.

Internal Structure

Internal structure of the agencies is also an important part of the administrative pattern. A large number of Mississippi's agencies for administration are headed by ex officio bodies; some forty are wholly or partly ex officio. These agencies suffer from the weaknesses inherent in this type of organization, and the number is too great for effective administration.

Most students of public administration are agreed that the ex officio board has failed as an administrative device. Some of the reasons assigned are plain to see. If an ex officio member takes his duties seriously, he is apt to find that they clash with those of his primary office; perfunctory interest means a diffusion of responsibility; the impartiality rule is hard to maintain; and political expediency sometimes receives undue consideration.[12]

The extensive use of boards and commissions, however, raises problems other than of their adaptability to specific functions. Where standards, objectives, and policies have been classified and well developed, the board or commission is almost wholly unsuited to the task of day-to-day administration. Responsibility cannot be fixed. Although some of the state's agencies have been constructed with an executive officer, this official cannot bear the responsibility, since his acts are subject to the approval or reversal of the board. A primary result of the commission-board system in Mississippi is to emphasize a loose organization for administration and to strengthen subject matter specialists and interest groups in their fight against departmentalization on the basis of major public functions and purposes.

Sound administrative performance is not lacking in Mississippi. However, the process of administration can be improved considerably from the points of view of cost, efficiency, and responsiveness. Effective functioning of the administrative organization indicates that its component parts require a higher degree of articulation than the current structure permits. The most impressive development in Mississippi government and law under the

Constitution of 1890 has been the tremendous growth in the number of state administrative agencies. Good organization would reverse this trend.

ADMINISTRATIVE REORGANIZATION

The administrative services of government in Mississippi have been established, as this chapter notes, when apparent need for them seemed to exist. Little or no consideration has been given at the time of their creation to any logical scheme of governmental organization. The result has been that the state is frequently, and often deservedly, criticized on the score of its administrative performance.

None of the four state constitutions dealt extensively with the question of administrative arrangement, and, since the writing of the Constitution of 1890, only twice have there been made definite and systematic efforts to reorganize the administrative structure, once in 1931 and again in 1950. There have been individual efforts by a few governors, but they were either completely ignored or regarded as political manipulations. For the most part these efforts lacked organized leadership, and the sincerity with which they were made was sometimes questionable.

The Brookings Survey

The movement that culminated in the Brookings survey of state and county government in Mississippi was initiated by the Mississippi State Board of Development, a nonprofit agency supported by private contributions.[13] Against a background of state indebtedness amounting to more than $30,000,000, with a record of treasury deficits during twenty-three of the twenty-nine fiscal years preceding 1930, this group began activities for reform. The legislature, at its instance, created the Research Commission of the State of Mississippi to be composed of the president of the Board of Development and ten to twenty-five citizens of the state.* The law directed the commission to study "the agricultural, commercial, industrial, economic, social and governmental" conditions and circumstances of the state and required it to make a full report to the governor and legislature during the 1932 session.[14]

The commission, because of a shortage of funds and because of time limitation, decided to restrict its scope to the administrative structure of

* *Mississippi Laws, 1930,* ch. 69. An appropriation of $150,000 was made to the Research Commission to defray partially costs of its work. Only so much could be expended, however, as was matched from private contributions or local governments.

state and county government. In conformity with the general desire to employ "an outstanding, non-commercial, non-partisan research agency," it selected the Institute of Government Research of the Brookings Institution to make the study. The survey work then was conducted in the fall and summer of 1931. Governor Martin S. Conner sent the study with a message to the 1932 legislature.

The Brookings Institution found that in general the chief defects in the organization of state government were the wide extent to which the elective system was used, the division of power among these elective officers and other agencies leading to a diffusion of responsibility and a lack of common direction of the state administrative system, the poor grouping of non-related functions in a single office and the scattering of related functions among many offices, overlapping of functions and lack of coordination among state agencies, and the general complex and inflexible character of the administrative machine.[15] In their report the representatives of the Brookings Institution claimed that these flaws were the basic reasons for the lack of economy and efficiency in the state government of Mississippi.

This was the general situation as the experts found it in 1931. The institution, therefore, recommended that the administrative system be reorganized on the basis of three generally accepted principles: (1) grouping of all services under a few departments to locate responsibility and authority and to facilitate financing and reporting; (2) placing the governor as head of the administration through widening of his appointive and removal powers and the short ballot; and (3) substitution of the bureau for the board type of organization.[16]

The *Brookings Report* recommended twelve major departments, namely, executive, taxation, treasury, justice, education, health, welfare, highways, conservation, banking and insurance, public service, and local government. Their heads were to be singular and appointed by the governor by and with the consent of the senate with the exception that the departments of health, education, welfare, and public service were to be administered by boards. A few boards were retained, but in almost every case these were to be attached to major departments. Institutions of higher learning were to be administered by a separate board. Centralized purchasing and personnel supervision were recommended, and there was to be an independent office of audit headed by an auditor of public accounts selected by the legislature. All agricultural activities were to be transferred to and administered by the Agricultural and Mechanical College (now Mississippi

State College). The office of secretary of state was to be abolished.[17]

The system thus recommended by the Brookings Institution would have placed the governor at the top with lines of authority running down through the departments and thence to the bureaus. All functions formerly carried out by the almost eighty separate boards and commissions were to be placed under appropriate bureaus, which were in turn to be broken down into divisions. The survey made specific recommendations for the abolition of many plural agencies and the assignment of their duties to the appropriate departments and bureaus.[18]

Reorganization Committee of 1950

House Bill 22 of the 1950 legislative session created the Legislative Fact-Finding Committee on Reorganization of State Government, composed of six members of the senate and six members of the house appointed by the lieutenant governor and the speaker, respectively. The legislation authorized a complete survey of state administrative agencies with a view to their reduction in number and anticipated economies in state government. The sum of $40,000 was appropriated for the committee's work.

The reorganization committee's proposals followed in general those made by the *Brookings Report* a decade and a half earlier. They proposed by eliminations, consolidations, and transferal of functions to reduce the number of administrative agencies to twenty-six, including sixteen major departments. An innovation was the proposal for an advisory board, without management powers, for each of the new departments. More significant, perhaps, was the recommendation for an Executive Office of the Governor in which would have been included a Bureau of General Administration to provide staff and auxiliary aids to the chief executive and to exercise in his behalf control of expenditures and over-all personnel policies.[19] Annual savings in excess of five million dollars were anticipated from adoption of the committee's recommendations.

Changes Resulting from Reorganization Proposals

An examination of the administrative system of state government in Mississippi today in the light of the *Brookings Report* and the report of the Legislative Fact-Finding Committee on Reorganization of State Government is revealing. True, some minor changes have been made in the two decades since the *Brookings Report* and in the few years since the reorganization committee submitted its report to the governor. It is by no means certain that they were a direct result of either report; they may just as well have resulted from conditions that made change imperative as from the stimulus of the reports.

The first principle recommended by both reorganization surveys was the grouping of services. Several attempts to carry out this principle have been made, but all have been on a minute scale. The establishment of the Board of Public Welfare (1936), of the Board of Trustees of Eleemosynary Institutions (1936), and of the Board of Trustees of Institutions of Higher Learning (1932) were steps in accord with the concept of grouping related services.[20] In 1944 the boards of trustees for the blind and deaf were combined.[21] In spite of this achievement, Mississippi now has more than eight dozen distinct boards, commissions, and other agencies. New bodies appear to have been created to meet immediate needs with no reference to existing agencies. Few steps, thus, have been taken in the direction of real departmentalization.

The second principle, that of placing the governor at the head of the administrative system in more than a nominal sense, seems to have received less consideration. Today the governor appoints only thirty-odd of the agency heads; in 1930 he was authorized to appoint the officers of forty-one of the seventy-seven administrative bodies. At present there are also eleven elective administrative officials responsible, not to the chief executive, but to the electorate. Since the surveys proposed that virtually all heads of departments be appointed by the governor, it can be said that this principle has been ignored.

The third principle, substitution of the bureau for the board type of organization, has not been followed. Analysis of present state agencies shows that almost all of the 1932 boards are still operative and that many more have been added since that date.

Perhaps the most significant change came with the enactment of the state budget law in 1932. This statute established the State Budget Commission, designated the governor director, and named the chairman of the State Tax Commission as his assistant.[22] The executive secretary of the budget agency has now assumed by statutory direction many of the budget duties of this latter official, who was charged to maintain a balanced budget and a system of budgetary controls.

It is clear that the recommendations embodied in Mississippi's two reorganization reports conform to the principles of reorganization that have found general currency among publicists, legislators, and governors throughout the United States. The practical effects of these principles in many states have been improved efficiency and performance. The sacrifice of democratic controls has not been involved. No one would argue that the governments of Tennessee or of Virginia, for example, where integration in the structure of state government has been accomplished, are any less democratic than that of Mississippi.

Doubtless the reasons behind the failure of the legislature to enact any considerable part of either the Brookings recommendations or the reorganization committee's proposals were many and varied. Among them, however, several deserve passing notice. First is the apparent preference Mississippians have for the long ballot over the short ballot implicit in reorganization. State officials, the general public, and the press reacted unfavorably, especially to the proposed reduction of the number of elective officials in both reports.[23] Fear of integrating administrative authority under the chief executive has overbalanced the desire to decrease the growing number of boards, commissions, and other bodies.

Second, Mississippi's legislators have been hesitant to abandon the patronage inherent in a sprawling administrative organization whose personnel management is weak. Both surveys were repugnant to some legislators and perhaps other state officials simply because sound administration rarely if ever can be reconciled with political patronage. Possibly more important has been the prevailing attitude that administrative conditions are not so bad as the two reports depicted them. The *Brookings Report* was initiated at a time when the state was almost bankrupt; when the final report was printed, the immediate emergency had lessened somewhat, and Mississippi was on the road to financial solvency. In contrast, the work of the 1950 reorganization committee was begun in a period of unparalleled prosperity for Mississippi, when each biennium the state treasury showed a surplus. Under these conditions, reorganization could wait.

A fourth reason for the substantive failure of the two reports to gain adoption lies in the fact that both the Brookings survey group and the reorganization study of 1950 lacked sufficient funds and staff for the preparation of legislation to embody the recommendations for a new administrative structure. Although the reorganization committee did succeed in the preparation of a few proposed measures, the task was too great for individual legislators and for the assistance available from the attorney general. Finally, the source of technical assistance employed in the 1932 study may have been a contributing factor to the reception of the report. The Brookings study was made largely by consultants from other states; the report that developed, although endorsed by the research commission, was a document prepared by technicians with no appreciable following in Mississippi. Governor Conner transmitted the survey to the legislature in 1932 with praise, but he also made the point clear that he had not read the report. The reorganization committee of 1950 employed as its technical staff, in contrast, members of the University of Mississippi faculty to avoid such criticism as that directed against the earlier report.

Doubtless there were other factors present in both instances, such as the absence of any well-organized citizens' movement to urge adoption of the recommendations. Whatever the causes may have been, the fact remains that two extensive reorganization plans, obtained and paid for by the people of Mississippi, have been put to no important use.

FOOTNOTES

[1] The number of agencies was determined by a careful examination of the Constitution of 1890 and the *Mississippi Code*. A convenient compilation is found in Robert B. Highsaw and Carl D. Mullican, Jr., *The Growth of State Administration in Mississippi* (Bureau of Public Administration, University of Mississippi, 1950), pp. 99-103.

[2] *Ibid.*, pp. 30-33.

[3] William N. Ethridge, Jr., *Modernizing Mississippi's Constitution* (Bureau of Public Administration, University of Mississippi, 1950), p. 41.

[4] Highsaw and Mullican, *op. cit.*, pp. 32-34.

[5] Ethridge, *op. cit.*, p. 59.

[6] Constitution of 1890, art. 5, secs. 116, 143; art. 8, sec. 202.

[7] Constitution of 1890, art. 4, sec. 50.

[8] Constitution of 1890, art. 5, sec. 116.

[9] *Ibid.*, sec. 120.

[10] See Chapter 9, pp. 122-27.

[11] Abolished 1940; replaced by the Board of Development. *Mississippi Laws, 1940,* ch. 147.

[12] Constitutional Survey Committee, Oklahoma Legislative Council, *Administrative Organization in Oklahoma* (Oklahoma City, December, 1947), p. 10.

[13] The full title of the report is *Report on a Survey of the Organization and Administration of State and County Government in Mississippi* (Jackson, 1932). Hereafter cited as *Brookings Report.*

[14] *Mississippi Laws, 1930,* ch. 69.

[15] *Brookings Report,* p. 445.

[16] *Ibid.*, pp. 447-48.

[17] *Ibid.*, p. 459.

[18] *Ibid.*, pp. 453-618.

[19] Legislative Fact-Finding Committee on Reorganization of State Government, *Mississippi: A Report on State Reorganization* (Jackson, December 15, 1950), pp. 21-23.

[20] *Mississippi Laws, 1936,* chs. 175, 180; *1932,* ch. 127, superseded by constitutional amendment, 1944; and Constitution of 1890, art. 8, sec. 213-A.

[21] *Mississippi Laws, 1944,* ch. 163.

[22] *Mississippi Laws, 1932,* ch. 120; amended by *Mississippi Laws, 1936,* ch. 215.

[23] For examples of this reaction to the 1950 proposals see *Tupelo Journal,* September 18, 1950; *Jackson Clarion-Ledger,* September 21, 1950; and *Laurel Leader-Times,* October 26, 1950.

CHAPTER 8

The Revenue System

THERE ARE THREE major problems involved in financing Mississippi's government: the determination of the sources of state income to be derived from taxes and sources other than taxes; the procedures established for the receipt, custody, supervision, and disbursement of public funds; and the budgeting system under which financial planning is conducted and a mutual adjustment of revenues and expenditures effected. The present chapter deals primarily with the first of these broad topics and concludes with a brief description of the administrative organization for revenue administration.

A GENERAL VIEW

The subject of revenues is of prime importance to state governments because the governmental machinery established to provide services and exercise controls would come to an abrupt halt if there were no funds to meet expenditures. Much of Mississippi's income comes from tax revenues of various kinds, and the system that has resulted from the adoption of taxes is subject to a number of common tests of soundness. Clearly the yields from the various tax and nontax revenues must provide sufficient funds to meet the expenditure program of the state, and additionally these returns must be made economically with low cost of collection. The Mississippi revenue system must also seek to distribute the cost of government equitably throughout the jurisdiction so that no one category of property or class of citizens bears an unjust load. Moreover, the revenue system must be flexible rather than rigid, adjusting easily to a need for increased or decreased funds, and simple in both structure and administration so that the ordinary citizen may readily understand it. Finally, it should possess a marked degree of stability, thereby assuring adequate yields regardless of prevailing business and economic conditions. With these general criteria in mind, our attention turns to a general survey of the Mississippi revenue system.

Growth of the Revenue System

The revenue system of this state, at least until the great depression, was largely the result of unplanned evolution. Historically, one of the first acts of the Mississippi Territory was passage of a statute directing the manner in which public funds should be raised. This early law set forth the principal characteristics of the property tax as the chief source of territorial income. Like other American states, Mississippi then developed its tax structure and revenue system by supplementing the basic property tax with other taxes. An inheritance tax was enacted, and various special privilege and business taxes also were developed. By 1930 the state had adopted an income tax as well as a number of miscellaneous revenue measures, among them motor vehicle taxes and estate and inheritance taxes. Ten years later the state was imposing many levies in addition to the property tax. These included personal taxes in the form of poll, commutation, and individual income taxes and business taxes, the latter embracing the corporation franchise tax, privilege taxes, corporation net income tax, and a gross sales tax. The tobacco tax and the general sales tax constituted additional and miscellaneous levies.[1]

The revenue system that had evolved in this fashion was the result of opportunism, and almost every legislative session altered it in some fashion. Nevertheless, expenditures consistently exceeded available revenue. With the coming of the great depression revenue yields declined, and consequently newer taxes assumed more importance in the reorganization of the revenue structure that came as the state sought to realize the potentialities of a broad array of excise levies.* A retail sales tax enacted in 1932 served as a model in the rapid expansion of this form of tax among the states during the depression years, and the revenue act of 1934 added a general sales tax. In the same year the state amusement tax was adopted, and since that

* For example, the yield of the property tax fell 52 per cent between 1930 and 1935 and that of the state privilege tax, 69 per cent.

time, as various rates have been modified or new taxes imposed, the current revenue system has taken its shape. This system now depends largely upon income from taxes on the purchase and sale of commodities and services rather than upon the traditional tax levies.

At the same time increased income has been realized from several sources besides taxes. Aid from other governments, chiefly the Federal, has assumed larger proportions since 1930, when only comparatively small subventions were received. Charges and miscellaneous sources, including department earnings, special donations, charges and fees for special services, and refunds, have yielded consistently large amounts.

Amount of Revenue Yields

Net state receipts from both tax and nontax sources have grown consistently since 1900. In terms of general growth, receipts from taxes and sources other than taxes have increased over fifty times, and revenue yields have almost quadrupled since 1930 alone. The distribution between tax receipts and nontax receipts shows, furthermore, that the ratio of taxes to nontaxes declined steadily from 1900 onward, with the exception of the year 1910. It rose slightly in 1947 and then fell again in 1950.

Material found in Table 6 indicates that the revenue base has shifted in recent years. Although the general property tax and the license and privileges tax were long counted on to furnish the necessary revenue to finance state operations, it is clear that they have been supplanted in importance by newer excise taxes, such as the general sales, use, and gross receipts levy and the income tax. Together excise taxes account for over 72 per cent of all tax receipts and nearly half of the total state revenue. These sources are extremely sensitive to the economic conditions of the state and nation, so that any noticeable change materially affects their yields. Since the excise taxes show almost at once any increase in the volume of business or the price structure, they will reflect conversely, and just as readily, any decline in business conditions.

While excise taxes thus have a paramount place in Mississippi's tax system, a trend has been discernible in revenue derived from conditional grants-in-aid and subventions from other governments. The many miscellaneous sources and charges, such as departmental earnings, account for a substantial proportion of state revenue, though, as Table 6 demonstrates.

Mississippi's revenue system is diversified even though it is largely dependent upon regressive and consumer levies. The state now utilizes most of the taxes that have been developed in other states of the American

Union. The ultimate stability of the revenue system creates some doubts, but clearly new levies can be justified only as supplemental revenue sources.

TAX SOURCES

A tax may be defined, for the purposes of our study, as a compulsory contribution exacted from the individual by government in order to finance the administration, controls, and services of politically organized society. It is impractical to impose taxes on the basis of benefits received by the individual, and students of government generally have agreed that the most equitable solution is for each citizen to pay in proportion to his ability without reference to special benefits. The diversity of its tax structure affords evidence that Mississippi has moved over the years toward some degree of equity in the distribution of the state tax burden. The main types of taxes are now considered in summary fashion.

General Property Tax

The general property tax in Mississippi consists of several different levies: the state, county, municipal, and separate school district, and special purpose levies. Discussion here concerns only the ad valorem tax levied for state purposes and deposited into the state treasury.[2] No maximum tax rate is prescribed by the Mississippi constitution, but a 1942 statute provides a four-mill rate unless it shall appear that the obligations of the state can be met by a lower millage. The statute fixes the minimum rate, however, at two mills.

The administration of the property tax is left mostly to the counties. Assessments are made locally, but the State Tax Commission is given the duty of examining the assessment rolls and equalizing assessments between both counties and classes of property. One important class of property is exempted from assessment by local officials: the present statute provides that assessments of public service corporations shall be made by the State Tax Commission. The law requires that the assessed value of property shall be its true value. Assessments are dated January 1st of each year.

There are numerous exemptions to the property tax. Among these are religious, educational, or charitable institutions, government bonds, hospitals, new factories and new enterprises for a five-year period, agricultural products grown in Mississippi, and homestead exemptions up to $5,000. A number of exemptions apply only to the state levy, whereas others, like homestead exemption, extend also to the taxes imposed by the localities.[3]

TABLE 6

STATE REVENUE BY PRINCIPAL SOURCES, 1900–1952
(In thousands of dollars)

	1900	*1910*	*1920*	*1930*	*1940*	*1950*	*1952*
Taxes	1,988	2,873[a]	5,651[a]	20,700[a]	27,786[a]	91,359[a]	109,826[a]
General Property	1,550	2,223	3,932	5,865	2,494	1,148	1,339
Sales, Gross Receipts, and Selected Commodities	—	200	478	11,020	19,954	61,301	63,314
License and Privilege	438	449	1,071	2,107	2,532	6,337	8,664
Individual Income	—	—	69	1,635	2,638	4,487	5,226
Corporation	—	—	74	34	52	7,637	10,042
Unemployment Compensation	—	—	—	—	—	4,118	6,115
Nontax Revenues	443	429	1,608	12,563	27,864	39,297	54,114
Aid from Other Governments	25	21	101	1,688	9,369	30,258	41,994
Charges and Miscellaneous	418	408	1,507	10,875	18,495	9,039	12,120
TOTAL	2,431	3,302	7,259	33,263	55,650	130,656	163,940

[a] Includes amounts for tax categories not shown separately, namely, death and gift, severance, and miscellaneous sources.
Source: Data from the Bureau of the Census.

Provision has been made, though, for reimbursement of local units and school districts for tax losses from the homestead exemption.

Sections 112 and 181 of the constitution apply restrictions on the legislature's use of the property tax. The former states that taxation shall be equal and uniform throughout the state and is the uniformity clause common to many American state constitutions. Section 181 applies the uniformity clause to the property of corporations.

The most evident trend in Mississippi's tax history has been the decline of the relative importance of the property tax. In 1930 the property tax yielded 17.6 per cent of net state receipts, and in 1952 considerably less than 1 per cent. With the development of other tax sources, the property tax in Mississippi has lost much of its significance for state government and has become instead the chief financial prop of local governments. No substantial trend is now apparent to abolish the ad valorem property tax for state purposes, however, and to allocate it exclusively, as many other states have done, to local units of government.

Corporation and Business Taxes

A number of levies apply directly to business enterprises, corporate or noncorporate. In Mississippi these levies include corporate organization and qualification fees, the corporate franchise tax, the chain store tax, insurance levies, severance taxes, and the state licenses and privileges code. Income taxes are considered in a separate section of this chapter.

Corporate organization and qualification fees are based on the authorized capital stock of the new corporation. Rates vary from $20 for $5,000 capital stock to $20 plus $2 for each $1,000 exceeding $5,000. The maximum fee, however, cannot exceed $500. The corporation franchise tax is measured by the amount of capital employed within the state; the current rate for this tax is $1.50 per $1,000 of capital. The franchise tax, of course, is simply an annual charge paid by a corporation for the privilege of doing business within this state.[4] The 1934 statute, under which the franchise tax is imposed, does not distinguish between foreign and domestic corporations.

A minor business levy, the chain store tax, is placed on businesses that operate three or more stores, at least one of which must be in Mississippi. The levy is based on the number of units in the chain and is graduated from $10 a store in chains having not more than five outlets to $300 per store in chains over 250.[5]

Somewhat more significant than the chain store tax are insurance and severance taxes. Insurance companies were subjected to taxation by 1910 and have contributed continuously to the support of state government in increasingly large amounts. Administered in Mississippi by the commissioner of insurance, the basic tax is levied on gross premiums collected within the state. Foreign and domestic establishments are taxed at the same rate, from 2.25 per cent to 3 per cent, depending upon the classification; domestic companies, however, are exempted from the application of certain other taxes. A classified flat fee also is charged all companies.

Although not corporation levies, severance taxes are business taxes and in Mississippi are of a selective type. The state entered this field in 1940 by levying a severance tax, measured by value at the point of severance, on timber and timber products produced for sale. The rate varies according to the type of timber. Four years later the legislature enacted an oil severance tax, which imposed a rate of six cents per barrel, or 6 per cent of the value of the oil at the point of production, whichever is greater.[6] Although severance taxes presently account for only a small part of state receipts, yields doubtless will expand throughout the periods of heavy production.

Mississippi also has an extensive system of privilege taxes upon specific businesses and occupations. The statute under which these taxes are now levied,[7] together with a 1944 amendment, embraces more than 200 types of activities. Few are omitted, and the list runs from "abstracting" through "weapons, deadly" and "wood years." There are almost as many charges as there are businesses enumerated, and these are based on flat rates, rates by classification, and rates graduated by some measure of the size of the enterprise. Privilege taxes had appeared in Mississippi by 1840, when an entry in the state auditor's report, "hawkers and peddlers," was the first evidence of the sale by the state of licenses and privileges.

Some indication of the significance of the yields of these specific taxes is found in the revenue derived from them for the fiscal year 1951-1952. The corporation franchise tax returned $1,285,000 in that year, the chain store tax $82,000, the severance taxes (state's share) $4,073,000 from oil and gas and $145,000 from timber, and the insurance taxes more than $2,000,000. Corporate organization and qualification fees yielded small returns. The total collections from these sources, then, account for hardly more than 6 per cent of Mississippi's revenues.

Sales and Use Taxes

Sales and use tax collections in contrast have contributed in recent years as much as a fifth of the state's revenues, the 1952 figures standing at more than $24,000,000 for the sales tax and a million more for the compensatory or use tax.

The Mississippi sales tax law, adopted in 1934,[8] may be defined as imposing an annual privilege tax, measured by the amount or volume of business; the amount of the tax is determined by applying its rates against values, gross income, or the gross proceeds of sales. Businesses are classified, and rates established. The rate for retailers is 2 per cent; for wholesalers or jobbers, .125 per cent; for automobile dealers, 2 per cent and milk dealers, 1 per cent; for certain public utilities and miscellaneous businesses, 2 per cent; and for sales prohibited by law, 10 per cent.

Exemptions from the general sales tax are numerous. They now include certain types of taxpayers, state and national banks, building and loan associations, nonprofit associations of various types, gross proceeds from the sale of cotton, the sale of farm products by the producer, and insurance companies, as well as many others.[9] Persons engaged in sales activities to which the tax applies are required to make monthly reports to the collecting agency, the State Tax Commission, but if the tax does not exceed $10 for any month, a quarterly report may be substituted. Annual statements must also be filed. Records of gross receipts must be preserved by the taxpayer for a two-year period. The State Tax Commission is given broad powers of enforcement of the law, and penalties are provided for those who do not fulfill its provisions. It should be observed here that the returns of this important tax are deposited in the general fund of the state.

Since 1938 a use tax has complemented the sales tax.[10] It applies a 2 per cent tax on tangible personal property, either purchased by retail or produced, rented, or leased for commercial use and brought into Mississippi for storage or consumption within the state. The tax applies also to persons receiving the benefits from the services of dyeing, cleaning, or laundering. A lower rate applies, though, to motor vehicles. Use tax payments must be made to the State Tax Commission by the fifteenth day of each month. Exemptions, record requirements, enforcement powers, and penalties do not differ greatly from those of the sales tax.

The sales and use taxes are essentially a single revenue source, for they seek to provide over-all coverage on both intrastate and interstate sales. Yields from the sales tax and the use tax have risen consistently since their adoption. By 1940 these two levies accounted for 13.3 per cent of all state revenue, and their ratio to total revenue now is above 18 per cent.

Sales taxes are more sensitive to general economic conditions than other levies, and in consequence their returns adjust more rapidly and more accurately to the trend of the times than any other single tax. A reduction in business sales and profits means a decline in sales tax receipts. This characteristic became evident in Mississippi with a slight decline in receipts in the latter part of 1949. It was reflected also in the budget document for 1950-1952, which predicted a 12 per cent decline by July 1, 1952, although increased yields failed to substantiate this prediction.

Selected Commodities and Services

In addition to the general sales levy, four important special sales and excise taxes merit specific attention. These are the special levies on motor vehicle fuels, alcoholic beverages, tobacco products, and admissions and amusements. Receipts from this tax group in 1952 amounted to 28 per cent of all revenue.

The motor vehicle fuels tax is a levy based on the number of gallons imported, manufactured, sold, or distributed within the state. Present rates are set at 7 cents per gallon for gasoline, at 7 cents per gallon on fuels other than gasoline, and at ½ cent per gallon on oil not employed in the operation of motor vehicles. The tax is collected by the comptroller of motor vehicles and, as in many states, the funds are segregated exclusively for highway purposes. By 1952 the fuels taxes amounted to 18 per cent of all state receipts.

The state derives revenue from alcoholic beverages in two ways. First, licenses founded on the classification of the business are sold. Licenses for wholesalers or distributors are fixed by a graduated schedule of charges, varying from $30 to $75, dependent upon the assessed valuation of the county; licenses for brewers of beer, wine producers, and retailers are set respectively at $500, $100, and $10-$25 for each place of business.[11] Second, an excise tax is levied upon light wines and beers with an alcoholic content of less than 4 per cent, the measure of the tax resting upon the number of weight gallons sold. Both levies are collected by the State Tax Commission and are deposited in the general fund of the state. Perhaps 2 per cent of Mississippi's revenue comes from this source.

The excise taxes on tobacco date in substantially their present form from the tobacco tax law of 1934.[12] Distributors, wholesalers, and dealers are required to have a permit and to pay a license fee. These licenses vary in cost from $5 to $100. Collections are deposited also in the general fund of the state.[13]

Although some taxes were placed on admissions and amusements before 1920, the present excise levy, like the tobacco tax, dates from 1934. The tax is based on the price of admissions; as amended by the legislature in 1952, the rate is one cent for each ten cents or a fractional part thereof received as admission to any amusement. For motion picture shows, though, the rate is fixed at 2 per cent on each dollar of gross revenues from the sale of admissions plus an additional tax of 3 per cent if the theatre belongs to a chain of more than ten.[14] This latter provision reflects a considerable discrimination favoring the small moving picture theatre owner and the lesser chains.

Income and Estate Taxes

Mississippi has imposed a tax on incomes since 1912. Locally administered and involving a levy equivalent to only five mills, the first income tax statute was thoroughly overhauled and revised by the income tax law of 1924.[15] The Mississippi courts shortly thereafter ruled that the income tax is an excise levy rather than a tax on property and so is beyond the scope of the constitutional prohibition on classification. The 1924 legislation also brought corporations within the scope of the income tax law for the first time, and the yields rose from $88,000 in 1921 to $1,635,000 in 1930.

The statute now in force is a general income tax applicable to the net income of "every resident, individual, corporation, association, trust or estate."[16] The statute taxes all net earnings within the state and, in the case of resident individuals and domestic corporations, income wherever earned. The current rate above all exemptions is 2 per cent on the first $5,000 of taxable income; 4 per cent on the next $5,000; 5 per cent on the next $10,000; and 6 per cent on all taxable income above $25,000. The personal income exemption stands at $4,000 for single persons and $6,000 for a married couple. These exemptions are in addition to allowable deductions for taxes, donations, and other authorized deductible expenses. The income tax statute, until amended in 1952, had contained specific exemptions of $1,000 for single persons and $2,500 for married persons, plus $400 for each dependent and medical exemptions of $200 for single and $300 for married persons. The income tax statute is administered by the State Tax Commission, and return and payment are due on March 15 if the return is made by the calendar year, or, if the taxpayer chooses, the fifteenth day of the third month following the close of his fiscal year. In 1952 this tax had the third most productive yield, trailing the sales tax and motor vehicle fuels levies. When that fiscal year closed, total collections from the income tax were slightly above $15,200,000.

A tax on the transfer of property at death first was adopted in Mississippi in 1918. This tax, a combination inheritance and estate levy, exacted a charge of .5 per cent on net estates of real and tangible personal property located within the state; it applied to both resident and nonresident decedents.[17] The inheritance levy, superimposed on the estate tax, was repealed in 1928. The estate tax statute of 1924 broadened the earlier levy, however, and with amendments it prevails to this day. Current rates on the net value of estates range from .8 per cent on estates up to $50,000 to 16 per cent on estates in excess of $10,000,000.[18] The rate schedule is adjusted so that each rate is 80 per cent of the given rate imposed by Federal law. The state obviously has availed itself of the Federal allowance. The tax, which is collected by the State Tax Commission, is due and payable one year after death. In 1952 upwards of $285,000 was covered into the general fund from the estate tax.

The income tax, which is not dependent upon a constitutional grant, is characterized by low rates and high exemptions. Although a general increase in income in Mississippi during the years of World War II and thereafter kept the yields from it high, the 1952 amendments to the statute may decrease future returns slightly. The estate tax no doubt is on the statute books chiefly to take advantage of the Federal credit. Rates differentiated by degree of relationship would utilize this tax more effectively.

NONTAX SOURCES

Analysis of state receipts demonstrates that an average of 40 per cent or more of Mississippi's public income is derived from sources other than taxes. The two categories considered here are aid from other governments and charges and miscellaneous collections.[19] Aid from other governments has been restricted chiefly to grants from the Federal government. Federal aid was first evidenced in a significant fashion through conditional grants to agricultural schools. Before 1930, though, comparatively small sums were received by Mississippi. The social and economic programs inaugurated largely by the New Deal augmented earlier programs, and in 1952 no less than $41,000,000 was received for programs in education, forest work, health, hospital construction, highways, social welfare, employment security, and agricultural research and marketing. In the decade of the forties fully 17 per cent of state revenues was received from Federal aid programs.

Since the charges and miscellaneous category is a catch-all group, no definite trend or description is feasible. This result is a consequence of the inclusion of administrative revenues, for instance fees and fines, received by the state. Also embraced within the classification are various entries such as refunds, special donations, and departmental earnings. Significant among the latter have been penitentiary farm sales. In 1860, through the sale of prison farm products and commodities, some $27,000 was realized; by 1949-1950, $962,295 was received from prison operations. In general, however, the variety of items included in the charges and miscellaneous classification has made for considerable fluctuation in receipts.

REVENUE ADMINISTRATION

Description of the tax sources in this chapter has included an occasional reference to a collection agency. The variety there indicated demonstrates that the function of tax administration is diffused among several offices. Concrete illustration is made at this point by a summary of the principal administrative agencies collecting significant revenues:

REVENUE COLLECTION IN MISSISSIPPI

Collection Agency	*Tax Collected*
State Tax Commission	Corporation franchise, income, property, business licenses, alcoholic beverages, severance, chain store tax, admissions, tobacco, sales, use, estate
Secretary of state	Corporate organization and qualification fees, other fees
Motor vehicle comptroller	Fuel use tax, motor vehicle fees
State insurance commissioner	Insurance privileges and premium taxes
State tax collector	Past due or unpaid taxes of the state or local taxing units

Not included in this summary are such special collections as game and fish licenses by the State Game and Fish Commission, fees collected by the commissioner of agriculture and commerce, and numerous other similar collections.

The most important of the agencies for revenue administration is the State Tax Commission. This body, established by statute in 1916, is composed of three members appointed by the governor, one from the state at large and one each from two state taxing districts.[20] The term of office is six years, and membership rotates so that a new commissioner is appointed every two years. Each commissioner must be a qualified elector with a "special knowledge of the subject of taxation" as it pertains to Mississippi.

Too many important statutory duties have been placed on the State Tax Commission to enumerate here. For example, the commission must investigate all tax matters and recommend changes in the tax laws to the legislature; at least one of its members must visit annually each of the eighty-two counties to obtain first-hand knowledge of its economic and tax problems; it must supervise administration of the property tax, assess the property of public service corporations, and equalize assessments among counties. Either collectively or through individual members, the State Tax Commission administers many of the parts of the state's extensive excise tax system. With a twenty-year history of freedom from political entanglements, the commission has exerted a continuous influence in the direction of improving the operation of the revenue laws entrusted to it.

Although the State Tax Commission today collects more than 90 per cent of the general fund revenues, its proportion of total revenue collections is considerably less. The administration of the revenue system is in fact divided among many agencies, each of which performs its assigned task with reasonable efficiency but independently of the others.* Just as the tax system was unplanned before 1930, so also has been the organization for tax administration.

It is axiomatic in administration that responsibility should be fixed definitely and that adequate authority should accompany the placing of responsibility. Although the State Tax Commission has made great strides in this direction since 1932, the present organization for revenue administration scatters in varying degrees among several independent offices responsibility for the business of assessing and collecting annually $130,000,000 of public funds. Mississippi has attained hardly more unity in revenue administration than in its general state organization.

FOOTNOTES

[1] *Brookings Report* (Jackson, 1932), p. 37.

[2] See Constitution of 1890, art. 4, sec. 112; art. 7, sec. 181; *Mississippi Code, 1942,* Title 39, div. 1-14.

[3] *Mississippi Code, 1942,* sec. 9714.

[4] *Ibid.,* secs. 9312-40.

[5] *Ibid.,* secs. 9300-9311.

[6] *Mississippi Laws, 1944,* ch. 134.

[7] *Ibid., 1940,* ch. 120; *1944,* ch. 138.

[8] *Mississippi Laws, 1934,* ch. 119.

[9] *Mississippi Code, 1942,* sec. 10116; Recompiled volume 7A (1952), sec. 10116.

[10] *Mississippi Laws, 1938,* ch. 114, as amended by *ibid., 1940,* ch. 120, and *ibid., 1948,* ch. 457.

[11] *Mississippi Laws, 1934,* ch. 127.

[12] *Ibid.,* ch. 125.

[13] *Mississippi Code, 1942,* secs. 10168-206.

[14] *Ibid.,* 1952 Supp., sec. 9057.

[15] *Mississippi Laws, 1924,* ch. 132.

[16] *Mississippi Laws, 1952,* ch. 402.

[17] *Mississippi Laws, 1918,* pp. 94 ff.

[18] *Mississippi Code, 1942,* sec. 9264.

[19] See Robert B. Highsaw and Carl D. Mullican, Jr., *The Growth of State Administration in Mississippi* (Bureau of Public Administration, University of Mississippi, 1950), pp. 68 ff.

[20] *Mississippi Code, 1942,* secs. 9197 ff.; see also, 1946, 1948, 1950, 1952 Supps.

* The Legislative Fact-Finding Committee on Reorganization of State Government recommended establishment of a single department of revenue through which all revenue collections would be made or channeled. The legislature has not acted on this recommendation. See *Mississippi: A Report on State Reorganization* (Jackson, December 15, 1950), pp. 28-31.

CHAPTER 9

Public Expenditures

THE PRECEDING CHAPTER examined the revenue, or income, side of Mississippi's state financial problems. Equally as important are the expenditures that the state makes in order to perform its functions effectively. Every act of government costs money, for services must be compensated and material supplied or equipment purchased. Expenditures are oil for the machinery of government, and to achieve effective financial administration governmental units everywhere have developed structures and procedures for financial administration. The growth in the number and scope of state activities has been great in Mississippi. Therefore, attention turns first to a brief resume of the state expenditures that support these activities.

INCREASE IN STATE EXPENDITURES

Review of governmental costs in Mississippi indicates a tremendous increase since 1900, from hardly more than $1,600,000 to $161,207,000 in 1952. This increase cannot be explained merely in terms of waste and unjustifiable extravagance. Population has grown by some 700,000 persons, or 45 per cent; a large population would mean more expensive government even if public services had continued to operate at the 1900 level. Two other factors, though, help to make clear the increase in the cost of state government. Since 1900 the number of services rendered by the state has doubled, the functions currently numbering 78 as compared to 39 a half century ago. This development, moreover, has come during a period of rising prices in which the public dollar was diminishing steadily in purchasing power.

Amount of Increase

Table 7 presents data for the purpose of illustrating this growth. From 1900 the increase in expenditures has been continuous without prolonged downward swings. Although the cost of government had risen greatly

TABLE 7

POPULATION AND STATE EXPENDITURES, SELECTED YEARS, 1900–1952

Year	*Population*	*Total Expenditures*	*Per Cent Increase*
1900	1,551,270	$ 1,624,133	—
1910	1,797,114	3,098,851	91
1920	1,790,618	7,956,933	157
1930	2,009,821	34,053,862	328
1940	2,183,796	53,252,263	56
1950	2,178,914	140,673,000	164
1952	2,164,000	161,207,000	15

Source: Data from the Bureau of the Census, and Biennial Reports of Auditor of Public Accounts.

before this century, the 1900 figure was only $562,000 greater than that for 1870. In contrast, greater percentage increases have been evident almost every decennial year for the past fifty years. These increases were accompanied, for the most part, by a larger income and greater assessed values. During the depression years of 1930-1935, however, state expenditures decreased a net of 22 per cent from the then peak year of 1930 and fell to a low of $25,000,000 in 1932. Viewed from a slightly different angle, the cost of state government to every inhabitant of Mississippi has risen from $1 in 1900 to $73.50 in 1952.

Change in Major Purposes

Since the turn of the century, the purposes for which the state expends public funds also have changed in their emphasis. Data illustrative of these changes are found in Table 8. From this table certain important facts emerge. Nothing was spent by the state on highways in 1900; they now consume a fourth of the state dollar. Although more money is expended currently on education, the percentage devoted to this figure has sharply declined. The newer charity and welfare functions have grown rapidly,

TABLE 8

STATE GOVERNMENTAL PAYMENTS BY MAJOR FUNCTIONS, 1900–1952

Major Function	*Per Cent 1900*	*Per Cent 1952*
Highways	—	25.1
Education	60.2	30.7
Welfare	—	12.4
Hospitals and institutions for handicapped	12.6	4.3
General government	15.00	2.3
Protection to persons and property	1.0	1.6
Conservation	—	4.4
Health and sanitation	.6	4.6
Recreation	—	—[a]
Debt service	3.3	1.5
Miscellaneous	7.3	13.1[b]
	100.0	100.0

[a] Percentage distribution less than 1 per cent.

[b] Includes Veterans' and Building Commission Revolving Fund, Transfers and Refunds, Permanent Improvements, and Repairs and Replacements.

Source: Biennial Reports of Auditor of Public Accounts.

and other services, such as health and conservation, have recorded significant increases. At the same time, the percentage allocated to general government (the overhead management, legislative, and judicial services) has fallen considerably.

The expanding functions of highways and welfare have been expensive developments once Mississippi has entered into them, accounting for 37.5 per cent of total expenditures in 1952. If education is added to these groups of services, the three together represent 68.2 per cent of all expenditures and explain the large increases in governmental costs.

FINANCIAL ADMINISTRATION

This review of financial administration concerns the procedures by which funds are made available to Mississippi's agencies for the discharge of their functions and by which their proper and lawful expenditure is ensured. Aside from revenue collection, which we discussed in the chapter immediately preceding, fiscal administration embraces four major operations: custody of funds, financial planning and supervision, procurement and disbursement, and audit and control. These operations are listed below in the order in which they occur along the mainline course of the state dollar through the fiscal offices:

FINANCIAL ADMINISTRATION IN MISSISSIPPI

Fiscal Operation	*State Agency*
1. Custody of funds	State treasurer State Depository Commission
2. Financial planning and supervision	Budget Commission, individual agencies, offices, boards, and commissions
3. Disbursement and purchasing	Board of Public Contracts, individual agencies, offices, boards, and commissions, state treasurer
4. Accounting and the audit	Auditor of public accounts, Department of the Audit

Custody of Funds

It is a basic function of the state treasurer to receive and keep the moneys of the state as they are turned over to the treasury by the revenue or special collection agency. The treasurer is a constitutional officer, elected in the same manner as the governor and ineligible to succeed either himself immediately or the auditor of public accounts in office. Most of his duties are outlined by statute, but essentially it is his responsibility to "receive and keep the moneys of the state . . . , to disburse the same agreeable to law, and to take receipts or vouchers for money which he shall disburse."[1] He is chiefly a ministerial officer, and his actions are controlled largely by those of the auditor of public accounts.

The treasurer performs essential functions in connection with the custody of funds. The Mississippi constitution requires him to make a report showing the transactions of his office for the preceding fiscal year and to publish twice yearly a statement under oath showing the condition of the treasury, together with a certificate of verification by the governor.[2] He thus must keep accounts of the receipt and expenditures of public funds, maintain separate accounts of revenues, retain documents showing the deposit of receipts, and make payments of interest and bonds.

The Mississippi treasurer does not possess the sole discretion for the selection of banks to be used as state depositories. The State Depository Commission, an ex officio body composed of the governor, attorney general, and state treasurer, is required to approve the depositories that are qualified to receive and hold public moneys for the state.[3] This commission approves also the securities pledged by the depositories, fixes the margin of security to be maintained by them, and approves surety bonds filed by them. The state treasurer executes under the law the decisions of the commission.

Financial Supervision and Planning

The problem of expending public funds has two aspects, that of the executive function of fiscal supervision and that of the individual operating official. The former begins in the governor's office and in the State Budget Commission with the preparation of estimates and carries through the execution of the budget within the limits prescribed by legislative enactment, which covers a period of two fiscal years. The operating agencies take part in financial planning by supplying the first estimates from which the budget is prepared and later by planning with the State Budget Commission for the allocation of appropriated funds. Moreover, each agency financed from the general fund budget must exercise internal controls. Although these controls usually are not prescribed by statute, auditing and budgeting requirements compel retention of copies of vouchers and requisitions. Monthly financial statements are sometimes prepared; less often a daily statement appears.

Disbursements

As the custodian of state funds the treasurer makes all disbursements on the warrant of the auditor of public accounts, all warrants being canceled after registration of the date received and of the date presented. Current statutes provide that the auditor shall supply the treasurer monthly with an account of all warrants drawn upon the treasury and that the treasurer and the auditor shall verify and reconcile receipts for the same period.[4] State agencies operating on appropriated funds must requisition the auditor of public accounts for pay warrants and keep on file a copy of every warrant. The requisition contains the name of the payee, the purpose of the warrant, and year of appropriation authorizing the expenditure. An agency requisitions either by a monthly check list, which includes itemized salaries, accounts, bills, and contracts, or individually for each payment.

Disbursement procedure for special or segregated funds is established by the statute that creates the funds. Moneys in these funds are deposited with the treasurer and issued upon auditor's warrant. The legislature has prescribed, often in detail, the manner by which administrative agencies may tap special funds. For example, the oil and gas supervisor of the State Oil and Gas Board pays all fees to the state treasurer, who deposits them in the "Oil and Gas Conservation Fund" and holds the fund in trust for the board. This fund then may be drawn upon by an auditor's warrant only by requisition approved by the board and for the purpose shown in itemized statements.[5]

Purchasing

Under a system of centralized purchasing all spending agencies requisition their needs from a single office, which buys for all or most of the agencies of government the materials and the equipment that they require to discharge their functions. Persons who favor central purchasing claim for it a number of advantages. Among them are a reduction of both overhead and unit costs, unified supervision of deliveries, storage, and distribution of purchased materials, maintenance of better accounting controls over expenditures, and the elimination of graft and favoritism. More than forty states have made some provision for an organized purchasing system. In addition to Mississippi, the only states that have not acted are Delaware, Florida, Nevada, New Mexico, and South Carolina. Few of the states stipulate that all expenditures must be made through a central agency, but they do provide for the purchase of a substantial portion of governmental supplies by this arrangement.

Before 1946 no system of centralized purchasing had been discussed seriously for Mississippi. A bill to create a purchasing commission passed one house of the 1946 legislature but failed of adoption. Additional legislative consideration of a purchasing system has occurred since that time. Mississippi is not without some provisions governing particular aspects of purchasing, for section 107 of the Mississippi constitution provides that:

> All stationery, printing, paper, and fuel, used by the legislature, and other departments of government, shall be furnished, and the printing and binding of the laws, journals, department reports, and other printing and binding . . . shall be performed under contract, to be given to the lowest responsible bidder, below such maximum and under such regulations as may be prescribed by law.

In order to carry out this order the 1912 legislature created the Board of Public Contracts, an ex officio body composed of the attorney general, secretary of state, auditor of public accounts, state superintendent of education, and the commissioner of agriculture and commerce.[6] The intent of the legislature did not extend beyond placing the responsibility on the board for contracting for all stationery and printing for public departments and agencies, educational institutions excepted,* and for fuel, heat, and light at the capitol buildings.

Actually most of the board's work has been concerned with printing and binding. An additional control has been imposed on the printing of departmental and agency reports. All of these reports are filed first with the State Budget Commission, and the Board of Public Contracts may not permit or pay for the publication of any report not approved by the State Budget Commission; furthermore, no agency possesses authority to finance printing of an unapproved report from either its appropriations or special funds.[7] These controls, though, leave the bulk of purchasing outside their scope, so that there are really as many purchasing agencies as there are boards, commissions, and offices.

A number of state offices and departments, particularly the larger units, have established departmental purchasing systems. A similar trend has been evidenced in the institutions of higher learning, where, for example, the University of Mississippi and Mississippi State College have established institutional purchasing offices. These offices have been able to economize on large scale purchases and have tied expenditures closely to budgetary controls and supervision. Nevertheless, Mississippi has lagged behind other states in establishing a purchasing system. Its administrative agencies expend more than $100,000,000 annually for all purposes, and legislative proponents of centralized purchasing have estimated that savings of $500,000 a year would result from establishment of a purchasing system.[8]

Accounting and the Audit

The keeping of the general state accounts is a function of the auditor of public accounts. Like the treasurer, this officer is elected for a four-year term and is ineligible to succeed immediately either himself or the state treasurer. With two exceptions related to the audit, all his important responsibilities have been established by statute. He is required chiefly to make a detailed report of receipts and expenditures of public funds to every regular session of the legislature and to furnish the governor periodically with complete information on the public finances of the state; he is forbidden to issue warrants without, or in excess of, appropriations except in the case of segregated funds and so exercises a preaudit. Detailed specifications are prescribed by statute for the issuance and contents of his

* Statutory requirements for public advertising and competitive bidding are imposed upon state institutions by *Mississippi Code, 1942,* sec. 9024.

warrants.[9] All of these devices have the common purposes of ensuring the accuracy of records kept and of determining that expenditures are made in accordance with the intent of the legislature and the law.

Other accounting controls are exercised by the Department of the Audit, established by the legislature in 1948. This department is a part of the state auditor's office, and its head is the auditor. Administration of the department rests with a director and auditors appointed by him.[10] The department is authorized to formulate and install in all public offices, municipalities included, a uniform and adequate accounting system; to perform both preaudits and postaudits of the fiscal records of any office or agency of the state government; to examine similarly the records of any agency or office empowered by the legislature to levy taxes and assess fees for special purposes; and to investigate unlawful practices in the handling of public funds. Several of these powers also are extended to the local governments.[11] These broad control powers are augmented by the authority given the auditor of public accounts to demand financial reports from all agencies for such periods and in such form as he may desire.

The power to formulate and install a uniform accounting system is an important control. Such a system should show the receipt, use, and disposition of all public funds and property, all sources of income and the amounts received from each, the supporting papers that establish the validity of transactions, internal and public reports of fiscal administration, and all funds received. Such a system is a significant one for establishing unity of fiscal administration.

There are two types of the audit for checking expenditures in Mississippi. The first is the administrative or preaudit, and the second is the independent or postaudit. The preaudit is an examination and approval of claims *before* they are sent from the spending unit to the treasurer for payment. Its objective is to ensure care and regularity in expenditures and to enable the chief executive to exert influence upon administrative policy and work programs reflected in expenditures. The independent or postaudit is an examination of payments and claims *after* they have been disbursed. Its objectives include determination of the regularity and legality of expenditures, a check of the accuracy of accounts and inventories, prevention of embezzlement or misappropriation, and the preparation of recommendations for the administrative agency, the legislature, and occasionally prosecuting officers. It is made on behalf of the legislature rather than the executive.

The preaudit is performed in Mississippi by the auditor of public accounts, the same officer who is charged to make the postaudit. This official is required specifically "to examine, state, settle, and audit" all claims against the state. As head of the Department of Audit, the auditor also has the powers of conducting the preaudit and the postaudit[12] and possesses in addition full power to inquire into the fiscal affairs of any state institution, office, or agency. Since 1932 postaudits have been made annually of all disbursements from both appropriated and segregated funds.

The need for both types of the audit is obvious. The preaudit, however, is strictly a function of management and should be performed by an agency directly responsible to the chief executive of the state. Most reorganized state governments thus have provided a comptroller, appointed by the governor and charged with the function of examining all payments claimed for or against the state. The postaudit, on the other hand, must be made as a legislative report or review of transactions that have taken place. This function should be performed by an officer completely independent of the executive. Election of the auditor of public accounts effectively removes him from control by the governor, but the over-all system of accounting and auditing created by the Mississippi laws fails to distinguish the preaudit and the postaudit. To make effective subsequent examination of payments and to determine their fidelity and legality, the auditor of public accounts should be divorced from the administrative function of the preaudit and freed from what is essentially a task of political management.

THE BUDGET SYSTEM

The three main phases of the operation of a budget system are (1) preparation of the budget; (2) action upon the budget by the legislature, which alone has the power to raise and appropriate public moneys; and (3) execution of the legislative budget. The system embraces then an organized and adjusted fiscal plan, presented by the governor to the legislature and acted upon by that body. The legislature requires the executive to carry out the details of the approved plan.

A movement of budget reform swept through the American states, beginning in 1911. This movement reached Mississippi in 1916, when the need for a budget system was recognized by the Legislative Committee on Taxation and Revenue of 1916-1918, which "urgently recommended" in its report adoption of a budget system to handle state finances.[13] The committee's recommendations covered chiefly budget formulation and enactment. In the ensuing budget law of 1918 the governor was required to submit to the legislature a balanced budget showing in detail the schedule of revenues. The budget document was to be based upon detailed departmental requests, executive recommendations, and comparative information from appropriations of the preceding biennium. The statute specified that the document as presented to the legislature should contain, properly summarized, these materials together "with the reason for the allowance or disallowance of any item . . . with any other recommendation or statement which the Governor may have to make as to any item or matter in [the] report."[14]

The 1918 statute did not work well in practice. Although it provided for conferences with the officers submitting budget requests, no evidence exists that such conferences were held or that if held, they were productive. The law did not authorize public hearings on the budget requests. Again, no governor complied with the duty to revise estimates submitted by operating officers, and actually the estimates were transmitted by the governor to the legislature substantially as he received them, no chief executive apparently having the time, inclination, or capacity to revise them.[15] Finally, budget formulation was weak because no governor until 1930 obeyed the statutory command that the budget document contain an estimate of prospective revenues.

Budget enactment was not affected measurably by this statute. Public funds continued as before to be appropriated by several independent legislative acts whose consideration and passage stretched out over a three and sometimes four month period without the guidance of an effective budget plan.[16] By 1930 it was evident that the budget law was good so far as it went, but that neither successive governors nor legislators had taken it seriously.

Current Budget Procedures

Enactment of a new budget statute, revising and extending the 1918 system, came in the depression year of 1932, perhaps partly as a result of the Brookings survey recommendation that the budget law should be revised to embrace not only budget formulation, but enactment and execution as well. This law established the framework for the present system.[17] It created a State Budget Commission with the governor ex officio director of the budget and the chairman of the State Tax Commission assistant director. The director (governor) appoints an executive secretary, who has charge of the State Budget Commission office and is responsible, as directed, for executing the budget laws.

It is made the specific duty of the assistant director to prepare the budget document for consideration by the governor. The former is charged, therefore, to familiarize himself with the needs and requirements of all establishments financed by general fund appropriations and is authorized to demand any information or records that may be required in the preparation of the budget.[18] This power is exercised by agents who biennially survey the various state institutions and departments through personal visits.[19] Although the budget act authorizes the assistant director to investigate the affairs of each agency before preparing the budget, the incumbent of the office has construed his powers narrowly. Neither this section nor any other gives

> . . . the Assistant Director supervisory authority over, nor charges him with supervisory responsibility for, the proper conduct of the State's institutions and governmental departments. . . . The authority granted is properly construed to apply only to the securing of such information as will enable the Assistant Director to appraise intelligently the needs of these institutions and departments, and make correspondingly intelligent recommendations for meeting such needs.[20]

During the preparation of the biennial budget, the assistant director holds hearings, at which time he goes over item by item the requests and needs of each expending agency with the heads of the agencies. By law he must note reasons for reduction or increase of any proposed item so that the governor can have all relevant information concerning the budget.

Recommendations of the assistant director to the governor are advisory only. The budget statute specifically provides for the appearance of any official aggrieved by his decisions before the proper legislative committee to urge revision or inclusion of some proposed appropriation. In refusing to allow requests, the assistant director doubtless has been influenced by several factors, among them, the general fiscal policy of the administration, the belief that a given request is excessive or improper, and the opinion that certain expenditures are both unwise and unnecessary.

The prepared budget must show a balance of proposed expenditures with revenues. The present statute provides that it shall be placed in the governor's hands by October 15 preceding each regular session of the legislature; in practice, it often reaches him in November or December. Although the budget normally is sent by the governor to the legislature accompanied by a letter of transmittal, the governor not infrequently sends a budget message with it. In past years the executive indicated that the budget was the work of the assistant director. The extent to which the executive secretary of the State Budget Commission has succeeded to those duties is not made clear by the 1952 legislation.

Budget Enactment

The Mississippi constitution limits general appropriation bills to the executive, legislative, and judicial departments; to payment of the interest on state bonds; and to support of the public schools. All other appropriations bills must be separate and contain but a single subject.[21] Prohibition of a single budget bill before the legislature thereby is made clear.

The power of the legislature over the executive budget is almost unlimited; it may and usually does modify that document by frequent revisions, mostly upward in recent sessions but sometimes downward.* The appropriations committees of the house and senate meet jointly in open session to consider the budget. At this time departments and agencies dissatisfied with the State Budget Commission's recommendations may appear to seek revisions. Neither house of the legislature in the meantime can consider special appropriations, except in emergencies, until the budget bills have been acted upon.[22] Recent legislative sessions have indicated that as long as 65 to 70 days are required to complete the enactment process.

Budget Execution

The third aspect of a sound budget system is the controls exercised over the budget after its enactment. Budgetary controls usually are applied to assure that moneys are not expended with undue haste or in excess of the amounts authorized by the legislature. Under the Mississippi statutes budgetary controls embrace all agencies and departments operating from appropriations from the general fund with five major exemptions; the legislature, governor's office, judiciary, institutions of higher learning, and any agency for which funds have been appropriated with the intent that they shall be expended immediately.[23] The controls, as generally employed, take the form of prior approval of quarterly allotments, which must be submitted to the State Budget Commission by the spending office in

* The budget document for the 1950-1952 biennium recommended a total of slightly more than $106,621,000 for all appropriations; as finally enacted, the total for ordinary support exceeded $116,805,000.

advance and approved before any part of the appropriation becomes available.

Upon approval of the quarterly estimates necessary for the work program, funds in the amount of the estimate are released for expenditure and constitute the maximum amount that the given agency may expend in the three-month period. However, this maximum is not rigidly imposed; amended estimates for expenditures in excess of the original allotment can be filed at any time before the end of the quarter. They must meet the approval of the State Budget Commission and fulfill two conditions: (1) additional obligations incurred above the quarterly estimates must not exceed the revenue actually received and on hand from other sources; and (2) supplemental estimates must be filed with the State Budget Commission prior to the end of the quarter when emergencies require this action.[24] If the director of the budget (the governor) refuses to approve the amended estimate, then the agency must operate within the balance of the original estimate. Incurrence of deficits thus is avoided by disbursing the appropriations through quarterly allotments; this consideration indicates that control of policy is implicit in approval by the State Budget Commission of the quarterly estimates.

Other expenditure controls also are imposed by the budget law. No office or agency expending general fund appropriations can spend more money than provided in its appropriation except "in emergencies or under unusual circumstances," and then only on the written approval of the director of the budget.[25] The latter shall limit the amount of emergency expenditures, prescribe the condition to which they apply, and explain his reasons for finding an emergency. Again, purchasing officers for state institutions must maintain a daily record of all orders and purchases. In addition, each agency financed from the general fund must file a quarterly report with the State Budget Commission within two weeks after the end of the quarter. This report must show separately the expenditures made during the quarter for which the report is filed, the expenditures made for obligations incurred during any period prior to the quarter for which the report is made, and obligations or indebtedness assumed during the quarter for which disbursements will not be made until a subsequent period.[26] Finally, the head of each office or agency is responsible for all obligations made in its name and personally liable for excess expenditures.

Mississippi's provisions for budget supervision and execution make it evident that an appropriation is not an order to spend the funds made available to each agency. Although there are lacking substantial contract, purchasing, and personnel controls, the system properly places, within restricted limits, the chief executive in a position to exercise considerable influence over policies and their financial implications. To this extent, it potentially augments his administrative powers.

SPECIAL AND SEGREGATED FUNDS

The Mississippi budget system does not extend fiscal controls to special or earmarked funds.* These include all public moneys collected for expenditures for public purposes that are segregated in special funds rather than deposited in the general fund of the state. They are moneys expended directly by the agencies benefited by them and are not subject to legislative appropriations. Hence, the State Budget Commission has no control over them at any stage in the expenditure process.

The use of special funds is characteristic of Mississippi, where in 1949-1950 thirty-five special funds produced 50 per cent of the state's total receipts. At least thirty state agencies are supported in whole or in part by special funds, among them the Office of the Motor Vehicle Comptroller, the Department of Public Safety, Department of Banking, the Highway Commission, the Sea Food Commission, the Forestry Commission, and the Board of Trustees of State Institutions of Higher Learning.[27] Most of the professional licensing bodies also are financed by earmarked funds.

Little can be said in favor of the extensive employment of segregated funds. Although it is true that employment of special operating funds means that an agency of administration is not wholly dependent upon the legislature to finance its programs and that these programs are in turn entirely or partly self-supporting, serious results follow from large scale use of earmarked moneys. First, they are expended outside of the general fund budget and make more difficult the task of over-all fiscal management. Second, special funds indicate that there is special money for special purposes. The program of the administrative body dependent upon them is set apart from those of other agencies and cannot be integrated with the latter, although all offices and agencies bear alike a public responsibility. Third, the use of special funds may identify a given office as the represent-

* The exception is the Game and Fish Protection Fund. Under *Mississippi Laws, 1952,* chapter 192 requires the Game and Fish Commission to submit a budget for proposed operations to the legislature. This measure and chapter 193 of the same legislative year subject the commission to the same general budget procedures and budgetary controls as agencies operating from general fund appropriations. The acts do not require legislative appropriation from the special fund, but do compel approval of budget requests and work programs.

ative of a special interest or industry rather than as an agency for the public welfare.

In addition, the place and use restrictions that frequently accompany segregated funds hinder considerably development of some state-wide programs. An illustration has been the Forestry Commission. Between 1938 and 1946 this commission derived 34 per cent of its total income from a county acreage tax, collected from scattered counties and restricted to use in them; an additional 38 per cent of the funds available to the agency came from Federal grants, chiefly for fire protection purposes. Thus almost three fourths of the funds available to the commission in this period carried with them the strings of employment in specific places and for specific purposes. Finally, the restraints in this case were emphasized because much of the funds used to match Federal grants came from the county levies rather than the commission's appropriation.[28] Difficulties of this sort are intensified by frequent fluctuations in the amounts of special fund collections from year to year. The administrator has little assurance as to the extent of obligations that can be incurred and, in consequence, cannot plan for needed policy changes or expansion of program activities.

Summarily stated, the significance of segregated funds for Mississippi's administrative system lies in the obstructions that they raise to effective financial planning, first to over-all executive control of fiscal policy and then to sound internal support of the individual agencies.

FOOTNOTES

[1] *Mississippi Code, 1942,* sec. 4289.
[2] Constitution of 1890, art. 5, sec. 137.
[3] *Mississippi Code, 1942,* sec. 9142.
[4] *Ibid.,* secs. 3868, 4299.
[5] *Mississippi Laws, 1932,* ch. 129; for other examples, see chs. 123, 194; *1936,* ch. 221; *1938,* ch. 178; *1944,* ch. 238.
[6] *Mississippi Laws, 1912,* ch. 205.
[7] *Mississippi Laws, 1932,* ch. 126.
[8] *Memphis Commercial Appeal,* February 17, 21, 1946. See, however, *Mississippi: A Report on State Reorganization* (Jackson, December 15, 1950), p. 100.
[9] *Mississippi Code, 1942,* secs. 3856 ff.
[10] *Mississippi Laws, 1948,* ch. 202, secs. 1, 2; *1952,* ch. 176, sec. 5.
[11] *Ibid.*
[12] *Mississippi Code,* 1952 Supp., secs. 3877-01 ff.
[13] *House Journal, 1918,* pp. 210-58.
[14] *Mississippi Laws, 1918,* ch. 225.
[15] See the frank statement of Governor Henry L. Whitfield in *House Journal, 1926,* p. 83.
[16] *Brookings Report* (Jackson, 1932), pp. 359 ff.
[17] *Mississippi Laws, 1932,* ch. 120; see also, *1952,* ch. 320.
[18] *Ibid.,* sec. 2.

[19] *Ibid.*, sec. 9.

[20] *General Fund Budget Proposed for the Fiscal Biennium 1938-1940 for the State of Mississippi* (Jackson: State Budget Commission, December 1, 1937), p. 7.

[21] Constitution of 1890, art. 4, sec. 68.

[22] *Mississippi Code, 1942,* sec. 9112.

[23] *Mississippi Laws, 1932,* ch. 120; *1936, 1st Ex. Sess.,* ch. 6; *1948,* ch. 364.

[24] *Ibid.; Mississippi Code,* 1952 Supp., sec. 9108.

[25] *Mississippi Code,* 1952 Supp., sec. 9108; compare with *Opinions of the Attorney General 1931-1933* (Jackson: Office of the Attorney General, 1934), p. 208.

[26] *Mississippi Code, 1942,* sec. 9109; *Mississippi Laws, 1932,* ch. 120; *1936,* 1st Ex., ch. 6.

[27] *Mississippi Code, 1942, passim.;* 1952 Supp., *passim.*

[28] Robert Baker Highsaw, *Mississippi's Wealth: A Study of the Public Administration of Natural Resources* (Bureau of Public Administration, University of Mississippi, 1947), pp. 116-17. In other cases, it is apparent that funds collected locally are to be expended, at least partly, in the area of collection. Compare *Mississippi Laws, 1932,* ch. 123, with *Opinions of the Attorney General 1931-1933* (Jackson: Office of the Attorney General, 1934), p. 82.

CHAPTER 10

Personnel Administration

ANY STUDY of government and administration in Mississippi must take account of its system of personnel administration. Employees no less than money are necessary to keep the machinery of government in operation. A large part of the daily effectiveness of government depends upon its employees,* the clerks, stenographers, engineers, technicians, inspectors, and field workers, who are directly and actively discharging its work. This chapter considers accordingly the organization of and the conditions in the state service, the departmental merit systems, and a summary of current problems.

GROWTH OF STATE PERSONNEL

Mississippi today employs more than 14,000 persons in its governmental agencies, of whom more than 10,000 are permanent full-time employees. The annual payroll alone approximates $25,000,000. Staffing the administrative establishment of the state government, then, is no small task; no business or industrial enterprise approaches the state government as an employer of Mississippians.

Full and complete information on the numerical growth in state personnel is not available for a number of reasons. There is no central state agency

* An officer of government is considered here as a person occupying position by election or appointment and responsible for the administration of some agency of government, for instance, department, office, commission, or board.—W. Brooke Graves, *American State Government* (4th ed., Heath, 1953), p. 476.

where information may be obtained concerning the number of public employees, employee turnover, salary scales, and other personnel matters. Resort must be had to two sources. The first is the boards, commissions, and departments themselves, but here there is a tendency to guess rather than to rely upon official records, which are not always maintained, or if kept, put in usable form. The second source, helpful for personnel estimates only since 1940, is the Federal Bureau of the Census.[1] This lack of reliable information restricts effective consideration of growth of personnel to 1940 and thereafter.

Certain observations, nevertheless, can be made with respect to selected categories of public employees before 1940. For example, until 1880 employees in general government, including such offices as those of the governor, secretary of state, attorney general, and general administrative officers, ranged from 46 to 148 persons and totaled 90 per cent of all state employees. From that date forward, though, employees engaged in activities related to protection of persons and property, conservation, and other new functions grew rapidly as the ratio of general administrative employees correspondingly fell.

Table 9 contains information for analysis of personnel growth from 1940 to 1950 by giving the number of state employees by years for ten major functional classifications of governmental activity. It indicates that state employment has doubled and more since 1940. Defense activities and war employment are reflected in the decreases shown for 1941 and 1942. The entry for the next year, however, exceeded the figure for 1940, and state employment continued to rise through 1950. Employment figures for the functional fields of highways, health, public welfare, and correction also show an absolute increase in the number of persons employed by the state, but a decrease relative to all the remaining functions, employment compensation and employment service activities excepted.

BASIC PROBLEMS OF PERSONNEL ADMINISTRATION

Employment statistics demonstrate that staffing is a major if auxiliary problem of Mississippi's state government. Its public service is conditioned by the fact that no central agency or central office for personnel administration has ever been established, and with the exception of a few boards or commissions participating in Federal social security programs, the merit principle of employment is almost unknown.

TABLE 9

NUMBER OF STATE EMPLOYEES, BY PRINCIPAL FUNCTIONS, 1940–1950

	1940	*1941*	*1942*	*1943*	*1944*	*1945*	*1946*	*1947*	*1948*	*1949*	*1950*
General Government	339	351	307	324	370	451	547	470	509	726	737
Public Safety	101	116	174	192	187	182	266	280	274	539	352
Highways	1,927	1,621	1,143	1,362	1,371	1,362	2,478	2,368	2,439	2,189	2,229
Natural Resources	228	253	284	319	414	540	452	1,727	1,703	2,467	2,553
Health	147	158	161	172	186	220	224	244	267	266	250
Hospitals and Institutions for Handicapped	574	687	719	1,183	1,016	973	1,087	1,203	1,440	1,475	1,622
Public Welfare	375	295	281	274	334	402	420	504	525	640	694
Correction	96	109	118	127	131	135	142	145	150	168	190
Education	1,091	1,216	1,342	1,689	2,038	2,249	2,617	2,875	3,180	3,638	4,235
Unemployment Compensation and Employment Services	77	84	69	80	80	79	170	425	507	476	734
Other	622	631	645	658	473	376	371	657	665	703	483
TOTALS	5,577	5,521	5,243	6,380	6,600	6,969	8,774	10,898	11,659	13,287	14,079

Source: Data from Bureau of the Census.

Personnel Conditions

Written two decades ago, the *Brookings Report* summarized conditions of the state service in these terms:

> Mississippi state government from the personnel viewpoint is largely being operated on the same basis that the national government was administered before 1883—namely, the spoils system. Some few state agencies, particularly the departments conducting scientific or professional work, have established high standards of employment but these are exceptions . . . it is necessary to improve the conception of public service on the part of all public officers.[2]

The survey went on to enumerate five specific conditions and factors that prevented sound personnel administration: (1) the spoils system and limited tenure of office; (2) lack of standards for recruiting personnel; (3) unscientific methods of determining compensation; (4) lack of any plan for advancements or promotions; and (5) neglect of minor personnel matters.[3] Of these, the limited tenure of office was deemed the most significant.

Recruitment and Selection

It is obvious at this point that no organized methods of attracting men and women in the state to the public service have been developed and that no positive effort has been made to find potentially capable public servants and to make them available. Thus no standard qualifications required for persons entering the service have been established. Each department head in effect serves as his own recruiting officer, and the absence of standardized qualifications means that appointments can be, and sometimes are, made on the basis of personal and political preferences. As a corollary to the absence of fixed qualifications, there is now no channel by which individuals may be informed of the opportunities in the state service.

From the spoils system also flows the result that scientific testing methods are not employed. Appointments usually are made by the administrative officer of the agency concerned, with the approval of the board or commission. Common recruitment and testing practices in such instances were summarized by one state employee who said his administrative chief "goes out and tries to find someone who knows something about the job, and if he likes him, he hires him."[4] With the exception of a few state agencies administering the Federal security programs, only a single agency, the State Game and Fish Commission, operates under a statute prescribing merit appointment of employees.

Twice the Mississippi legislature has declared that game wardens shall be appointed on the basis of merit.[5] The current statutes provide that no person shall be appointed a warden by the agency's director of conservation until the commission has issued to him a certificate stating that he has passed "the required examination." The law specifies additionally that the entrance examination shall embrace an investigation of the character, habits, and qualifications of the applicant for position of warden and that wardens shall be classified into three grades, removal of those rated in the first two grades requiring a statement of reasons and hearing.[6] No other employees of the commission are included, though. Even so, there are indications that the system has not functioned well, as, for example, when a member of the State Game and Fish Commission declared publicly a few years ago that "quite a few wardens . . . get political appointments, and they don't look to the director of the Game and Fish Commission for anything except their checks."[7]

The evils inherent in a personnel system where quaiification standards and examination are lacking are many and decisive. Among them are a frequent turnover of personnel, failure to select the most competent persons, and inability to induce even capable public servants to render the best services. All of these evils add up to a failure to develop an efficient service. Nevertheless, employees assigned to technical work generally appear to possess adequate training and technical qualifications. This has been the case especially with medical technicians, biologists, engineers, and personnel for other agencies engaging in large scale programs.

Executive officers or the administrative agents appointed by the various boards and commissions are tested presumably with no more thoroughness than are the stenographers and clerks. Not infrequently, though, the controlling statute will specify that the appointee must possess knowledge of and experience in his field, or both. In a few cases the executive officer must be a specialist with minimum professional training and experience.* No formal provisions for tests of competency or ability, however, have been established for these positions.

Classifications of Positions

Classification of positions means the distribution of positions, jobs, or employment into groups or classes upon the basis of their duties. It is a

* For example, the state oil and gas supervisor must be a petroleum engineer or a geologist with five years of experience in one of the two professions. *Mississippi Laws, 1948,* ch. 256.

systematic arrangement of positions by a determination of the duties of each and of the relationship of each position to various others. It rests, therefore, on the basis of a job analysis survey, although classification requires, in addition to finding out and recording the duties and distinctive characteristics of each position, preparation of a classification plan, development of job specifications for each class, and the allocation of individual positions to the respective classes.[8]

A classification system is essential for sound personnel administration even if the state has not established the merit principle of employment, because it makes possible the principle of equal pay for equal work. An adequate classification of positions on the basis of responsibilities and duties provides the means by which all persons doing stenographic work, for example, will receive salaries within the same general compensation level, by which all custodial work will be paid similarly, and by which compensation throughout the state service will be related to work performed. Mississippi has never adopted a classification plan,* and it is not unusual to find employees of two agencies performing similar work with widely varying salaries.

Compensation of Employees

Although closely related to the classification plan, a compensation plan is distinguished in that it is the foundation for evaluating positions by classes in relation to each other and for determining appropriate scales of compensation for each position. Good compensation practices now provide pay ranges for each position. Pay ranges normally fix a minimum and a maximum compensation, with a series of increments between.[9]

A few salaries in Mississippi still are specified by the legislature, but it is clear that neither house of the legislature can be familiar with the duties of any except the most important positions. Thus most salaries are now provided through lump sum appropriations to the departments, boards, and commissions. Individual compensation is then determined by the administrative head. In the absence of a central personnel agency, different salaries are set among the agencies for work involving the same duties and responsibilities. Equal pay for equal work is not and cannot be achieved under present personnel practices.

Other aspects of good personnel policy are also absent from the state scene. Aside from the highest administrative positions, where the pay is

* House Bill 600 of the 1930 legislative session provided for a classification and compensation system. It was killed in committee.

usually specified by statute,* salaries paid to state employees are generally low. Sometimes positions have had to be filled on a part-time basis, since competent persons were not available for the compensation offered.† Without a general compensation plan there can be no provisions for pay advancements or promotions. Finally, Mississippi's employees have had no systematic cost of living adjustments as part of the compensation system. During and after World War II state salaries generally increased because state offices had to compete with private enterprise for manpower. Even so, many state employees remain poorly paid.

Training

In any personnel policy, training occupies an important position and affects the quality and volume of work accomplished. It is useful to distinguish here the various kinds of training.[10] Three main types are preinduction, orientation, and in-service (including also on-the-job and off-the-job training). Preinduction training by definition takes place before the employee begins his duties, although he may or may not be already employed. Orientation training, occurring at the time of employment, explains to the new worker the organization and purposes of the agency. In-service training is designed to ensure better present performance and to prepare an individual for promotion. On-the-job training is given usually by the supervisor of the employee during working hours at the post of duty. Off-the-job training, which may or may not be given during working hours, is conducted mostly in groups by informational or conference methods.

Training does not necessarily require a central personnel agency, but it may be carried on by such a body in states where over-all personnel management has been established. The need for training has been recognized by a number of Mississippi agencies, although the programs that have developed are naturally different. The Mississippi State Board of Health trains field workers and technicians for its respective public health programs; the State Highway Patrol puts the new patrolman through a training school before he is assigned a regular post; the State Department of Wel-

* Examples of legislative determination of administrative salaries other than those for elective officers include the motor vehicle comptroller, his assistant comptroller, and division directors; members of the State Tax Commission; deputy state treasurer; director, Surplus Property Procurement Commission; comptroller, Department of Bank Supervision; director, State Game and Fish Commission; state forester; state librarian.

† As, for example, the position of librarian in the State Department of Archives and History during the 1948-1950 biennium.

fare holds training conferences for field personnel and uses various other training devices. Whether or not it is recognized, the new employee in any agency is trained day-to-day by instructions on how the particular task is to be done or the new procedure to be handled. Although there are many evidences of training in state agencies, its effectiveness and its development are hindered by impermanence of tenure and the absence of established lines of promotion.

Employee Relations

The subject of employee relations concerns the efforts of management to assist employees in the solution of personal problems and to provide the machinery for settling disputes that arise within the agency[11] Specific devices include counseling of employees, credit unions, recreational programs, agency bulletins, and the like. All of these are directed toward building and maintaining good morale among employees. Other personnel matters affect the conditions under which the individual employee works, such as vacations, sick leave, leave of absence, evaluation of work, and hours of work. Most of these problems in Mississippi are handled on an agency basis, since there are no uniform regulations governing them. Since regulations and practices should be standardized throughout the state's public service, no general high level of administration of personnel matters can be expected until there is created a central supervisory agency.

Promotion or Advancement

Every personnel system must take account of handling the problem of promotions. Promotion should be distinguished from advancement. In well-organized personnel systems promotion means a shift in duties, assumption of greater responsibilities, and the performance of more difficult work. It is accompanied usually by a change of title and an increase in compensation. Advancement means an increase of pay without corresponding changes in duties, responsibilities, or title.[12] Probably there is no more difficult or important aspect of good personnel management than the handling of promotions.

The reason for seeking sound promotions is primarily to serve the public interest by selecting the best employees for higher positions and secondarily to maintain high morale by providing reasonable opportunities for all qualified employees to advance in their work. Since the hope of promotion or advancement furnishes the employee with a powerful incentive for increased efficiency, the absence of a scientific and equitable system of rules and practices is a most serious indictment of Mississippi's personnel system.

Management of promotions is largely a technical problem that can be solved only through a predetermined system of personnel records and statistics, seniority, promotional tests, and other devices. Among these are performance ratings, which many jurisdictions have found useful in determining promotions because they tend to eliminate variable human factors and personal favoritism in making personnel changes. Promotion on the basis of influence, or salary increases that are dependent on biennial appropriations is a poor substitute for these. In the absence of a central personnel agency the average employee of the state, frequently limited in tenure, must wait for a death or resignation in his agency before promotion can be expected. The lack of just and expected recognition for services well done removes an incentive for effective job performance.

Separation and Retirement

Other significant changes in the status of employees are separations from the public service and retirement. Separations, that is, termination of employment, arise from removal, death, resignation, transfer to other agencies, or retirement of employees. Obviously all of these separations create problems. Although assurances must be present that inefficient or incompetent employees will be removed, adequate steps should be taken to protect efficient, competent employees of the state. Typically, Mississippi leaves determination of removal as well as all other disciplinary authority to the agency or department head. In most instances there are few if any legal restrictions on the exercise of this authority, and employees may be removed for any cause or no cause. So long as there are no bitter factional disputes within the Democratic Party of Mississippi, few wholesale dismissals occur. The possibility of serious damage is always present, though, in the unlimited responsibility placed in administrative heads. Formal transfers of employees to other agencies clearly are not provided in Mississippi's patronage system.

Opinion for many years held that the constitution prevented establishment of a state retirement system, section 93 of the fundamental law forbidding the legislature to retire any officer on pay, or part pay, or make any grant for a retiring officer. Certainly no over-all retirement program had been established, although a teachers' retirement system began operations in 1944 and participation in a Federal plan for employees of the Mississippi Agricultural Experiment Station and the State Extension Service was approved in 1944.[13] Legislation was enacted in 1952, however, bringing state employees under the Federal social security program.[14] A state retirement system also was created to supplement the Federal old-age and survivors insurance benefits, and Mississippi thereby instituted its first state-wide program for retirement of public employees.

Under the recent law state employees are required to come under social security, and the combined state and Federal programs are compulsory for new employees.* The state plan provides for full retirement at age sixty-five after ten years of employment; it permits retirement at age fifty-five after thirty years in the service. Other features of the plan allow retirement at age sixty after ten years employment with reduction in benefits of 3 per cent for each year below sixty-five; a "deferred" retirement at age sixty or later after twenty years of service, with benefits equaling the amount that normally would have been received for the number of years employed if the employee had remained in service; and disability benefits after ten years of employment equal in amount to 75 per cent of what the employee would have received as retirement payments for membership payments and prior service had he continued in active employment to age sixty.

The teachers' retirement act of 1942 was repealed with the adoption of this program, and teachers were brought under the new system. The result of Mississippi's entrance into the social security program for public employees and the adoption of a supplemental retirement system clearly will be to provide a greater measure of protection than would be afforded by either the Federal or state plans alone. The retirement system must be viewed as a major improvement in the state's personnel program. Its ultimate effect will be measured by the improved morale and efficiency that results from employee security, retention of the best employees in public service, and the relief of employees who cannot perform their work satisfactorily because of age or disability.

DEPARTMENTAL MERIT SYSTEMS

The preceding section has reviewed personnel organization and practices from the service-wide point of view. Merit systems are now in operation, however, that include state employees who are engaged in public health

* Both features of the system are optional for city and county employees, and persons employed by the state at the time of its adoption also may elect to remain outside the supplemental state program.

work and the Federal-state social security programs. These systems were brought into being by a 1939 amendment to the Social Security Act, which required an approved civil service system for employees in state departments receiving funds under the act.[15] In states where civil service agencies had already been established, standards of these programs usually were found adequate by the Federal government. In the remaining states, among them Mississippi, new agencies were formed to carry out the personnel policies required by the new legislation.

Quite commonly, "merit system councils" were established in the various states to assist all departments affected by the Federal requirement.* Mississippi, along with a few other states, limits the operation of the merit agency to a single department or board. Three agencies of this state are covered by departmental merit systems, as indicated in the following table.

TABLE 10

MISSISSIPPI DEPARTMENTAL MERIT SYSTEMS

Agency	*Name of Administering Body*	*Date Established*
Employment Security Commission[a]	Advisory Committee on Personnel	1938
State Board of Health	Merit System Council	1941
State Department of Public Welfare[a]	Merit System Council	1940

[a] Merit system also required by state statute.

In each case the supervisory body is charged with the function of recruiting and selecting employees for the department. Administration of the departmental merit system is the responsibility of the councils or the committees. These groups select merit system supervisors or directors who conduct the day-to-day operations of the merit systems. In addition to conducting examinations, the departmental merit agencies are concerned with assisting in such matters as certification, promotions, dismissals, demotions, transfers, and classification plans.† Personnel practices must, of course, receive Federal approval.

* Among such states are Arizona, Arkansas, Colorado, Delaware, Georgia, Iowa, Kansas, Missouri, Montana, Nebraska, New Hampshire, New Mexico, North Carolina, West Virginia, and Wyoming.

† For example, the Advisory Committee on Personnel of the Employment Security Commission examines and reports on these matters at least annually to the commission. It also may make recommendations to the commission for the development of merit system methods and maintenance of standards.—*Personnel Regulations of the Mississippi Employment Security Commission* (October 1, 1947), par. 1012.

It is obvious that the impact of the Federal security program has been to secure and to enforce generally sound practices in these three agencies. Salaries are somewhat above those of other state agencies, tenure is greater, and the effects of the patronage system are smaller. Still, there is much to be desired. Most significant, perhaps, is that personnel management plays little part, even here, in a system of general administrative control. In these agencies personnel is not one of the managerial powers of the executive. In 1950 the departmental merit systems, moreover, included a few more than 1,300 state employees, scarcely 10 per cent of the total number.

CURRENT PROBLEMS AND NEEDS

Most problems of personnel administration in Mississippi center about the overhauling and the improvement of present practices. The current failure of these practices can be viewed, for example, in the light of their inability to provide opportunities to Mississippians for a career in the state service. Although government employment does not yet receive the same favorable attention of young men and women that business does, the development of the many positive services offered by government today as well as the controls it maintains affords broad opportunities to well-trained persons. Many of the positions found in governments increasingly demand technical training in law, science, engineering, medicine, and other professions. Whether or not the public service attracts capable employees depends in no small measure upon the state's ability to combine the chance to render real service with opportunity to advance to higher posts without fear of abrupt dismissal or of undue political influences.

Conditions of public employment can be examined, conversely, from the standpoint of the administrator charged with executing some governmental function. The nature of the patronage system is such that too great a responsibility for recruitment, selection, and other personnel practices is placed upon the individual executive officer. An efficient staff for almost any state agency can be employed and kept only if the administrator, who himself usually serves only at the will of a board or commission, can win the confidence of his employees, if the work required stimulates professional pride, and if there is some reasonable continuity in service. The almost total absence of generally accepted personnel procedures militates against a satisfactory body of public employees, although a few agencies doubtlessly have attracted and maintained competent staffs in past years without formal merit selection, classification plans, compensation programs, or retirement systems. The correction of both these difficulties as well as others can result, however, only from control over personnel administration by a central agency.

A Central Personnel Agency

As previously observed,[16] the governor has little or no control over personnel, although he is nominally responsible for the efficiency with which the state government as an institution is operated. Whether responsibility for personnel matters is vested in the executive or in an independent agency, clearly there should be a single state office charged with administering personnel operations and with jurisdiction over all state agencies other than educational institutions.

The duties of this type of agency also admit of little argument. They should include recruitment and examination; certification and placement; continuous classification of positions on the basis of responsibilities and duties; establishment of service records; promulgation of a body of rules and regulations governing promotions, advancements, demotions, and transfers; development of suitable rules dealing with temporary and probational appointments; establishment of rules and regulations for the supervision of dismissals and lay-offs; and the construction of training courses to improve the performance of employees already in the service. As a necessary part of personnel operations in Mississippi, a central agency also must study on a current basis personnel problems and the personnel situation in state agencies, advise with administrative officers concerning their personnel problems, and maintain basic and necessary records.[17]

This recommendation is not new. It was made at the time of the survey of the Brookings Institution, and it still has the same advantages enumerated in that report: (1) assurance of wide publicity of vacant or newly created positions; (2) elimination of the incompetent by prescribing minimum qualifications before examination; (3) selection of the most desirable applicants on the basis of examination; (4) strengthening of morale in the service by lessening materially the influences of personal or political pressures; and (5) relief for the administrator of the work and pressure of selecting employees.*

Mississippi's state government is a large enough operation and employs

* *Brookings Report,* p. 465. The administrator would select the employee, of course, from a certified list of eligibles, usually three to five, at his discretion. This practice is customary in most merit systems.

sufficient personnel to justify a true personnel office. Organized personnel administration does not now exist, and constructive development of personnel practices is not imminent. There is little indication that many of the old practices will be abandoned or even modified. In any event, personnel administration represents a definite weakness in state government that should be speedily corrected.

FOOTNOTES

[1] United States Department of Commerce, Bureau of the Census series, *Government Employment*. Included in this series is an annual report of state employment.

[2] *Brookings Report* (Jackson, 1932), pp. 461-62.

[3] *Ibid.*, p. 462.

[4] Robert Baker Highsaw, *Mississippi's Wealth: A Study of the Public Administration of Natural Resources* (Bureau of Public Administration, University of Mississippi, 1947), p. 90.

[5] *Mississippi Laws, 1932,* ch. 123; *1946,* ch. 423.

[6] *Mississippi Code, 1942,* sec. 5852; *Mississippi Laws, 1952,* ch. 186.

[7] *Memphis Commercial Appeal,* May 12, 1946.

[8] William E. Mosher, J. Donald Kingsley, and O. Glenn Stahl, *Public Personnel Administration* (3rd ed., Harper, 1950), pp. 216 ff.

[9] Mosher, Kingsley and Stahl, pp. 266-69.

[10] For a discussion of public service training, see W. Brooke Graves, *Public Administration in a Democratic Society* (Heath, 1950), pp. 150-70.

[11] *Ibid.*, pp. 178-92.

[12] Leonard D. White, *Introduction to the Study of Public Administration* (3rd ed., Macmillan, 1949), p. 400.

[13] United States Department of Agriculture, *Federal Legislation, Rulings, and Regulations Affecting the State Agricultural Experiment Stations* (Mis. Pub. 515, March, 1943), p. 20. This system does not apply to any employees who are compensated entirely from state funds.

[14] *Mississippi Laws, 1952,* ch. 299.

[15] 53 U. S. Stat. 1360 (1939).

[16] Chapter 7, p. 92.

[17] See *Brookings Report,* p. 467.

CHAPTER 11

The Courts

THE COURT SYSTEM is an integral part of the state government. The generally accepted idea of the courts as a co-ordinate branch of the governmental machine, with the task of interpreting the constitution and laws, does not appreciate the wide range of their functions. A complete listing would include several other judicial as well as administrative duties.[1]

THE LAW OF THE STATE

To understand properly the work of the courts of Mississippi, it seems appropriate to look first at the laws that they must interpret. They are of four kinds: constitutional law, criminal laws, civil laws, and equity.

Constitutional Law

In Mississippi, constitutional law consists of the national Constitution and the constitution of Mississippi. When litigation involving provisions of these documents is before the courts, they perform the major function of judicial review—the determination of whether a national law, the state constitution, an act of the legislature, or a city ordinance is constitutional. Each of these acts must conform to the one preceding it, in the order named above, and all of them as well as any other acts of government, must conform to the Constitution of the United States. It is the supreme law.

Criminal Laws

Laws that are designed to maintain order, safety, and the peace of the state and that provide a punishment for their violation are called criminal laws. If the violation of such a law is punishable by death or imprisonment in the penitentiary the crime committed is defined as a felony.[2] When the punishment for violating the law is jail imprisonment or a fine, or both, the offense is referred to as a misdemeanor.

The major part of the criminal law consists of statutes passed by the legislature. It also includes the common law, which has been developed by custom and judicial decisions over a period of hundreds of years. The importance of the criminal law lies in the fact that it deals with the rights of society. Acts in violation of it, even though they involve only one or two individuals, are crimes against the whole social group, or the state. The state thus prosecutes all criminal cases and puts its prestige and force behind the enforcement of the criminal law. Consequently the protection of persons and property is much greater than if the enforcement is left to the individual directly affected.

Civil Laws

Laws designed to protect the rights of persons and groups without resorting to criminal procedure are called civil laws. The state is not directly concerned and merely provides the means, or courts, by which individuals or groups may protect their own rights. The person who is injured must prosecute. Naturally, the civil rights of persons include those against the government, such as are stated in the bills of rights of the state and national constitutions.[3] When these rights are infringed, by governments or by individuals, the aggrieved person may go into a court maintained by the state to enforce them.

Equity

Equity, strictly speaking, is not law but a system of justice that operates parallel to the law courts. Its origin goes back to fourteenth century England, where a royal officer was designated to award decisions on the basis of equity or justice to the parties in dispute when the law courts failed to provide a just and adequate remedy. This office developed into a system of equity courts that operated under its own rules and established its own precedents. These courts were transplanted to this country, along with the other features of the English judicial system. In the national judiciary, however, and in most state judicial systems, equity and law cases were handled by the same courts, though under different rules and procedure. In time, the distinction between law and equity became fainter, and an increasing number of state courts came to administer equity and law cases under the same tribunals. Today Mississippi is one of four states—Arkansas, Delaware, Mississippi, and Tennessee—that maintain separate equity courts.[4] The law jurisdiction of such courts is fully as important as their jurisdiction in equity.

COURT ORGANIZATION

The court system of Mississippi is relatively simple. Although distinguished by separate law and equity courts, the over-all organization reveals a smaller number of courts and levels of jurisdiction than is generally found in American states. It does not differ greatly from the system originally established in 1817. It is highly decentralized and is almost wholly lacking in administrative supervision.

Justice of the Peace Courts

The lowest courts of the state for rural areas are justices of the peace. One justice is chosen for each of the five districts in each county, but the number may be increased to two for each district at the discretion of the county board of supervisors.[5] The justice of the peace usually is a layman. His jurisdiction extends to civil cases where the amount in controversy does not exceed $200, and in criminal matters where the punishment does not exceed fine and imprisonment in the county jail. Justice courts are required to convene at regular times, such sessions to be at least once a month and not more than twice a month, and are courts of record.

Police Courts

Parallel to the justice of peace courts are the police courts of municipalities. In cities of 10,000 or more population, a police justice must be chosen, usually by the governing authorities; in smaller municipalities, the mayor may act as police justice. Police courts have jurisdiction over all violations of municipal ordinances as well as concurrent jurisdiction in misdemeanors with justices of the peace in all cases arising within the municipal limits. Sessions of the court are held each day except holidays, if the business requires it.

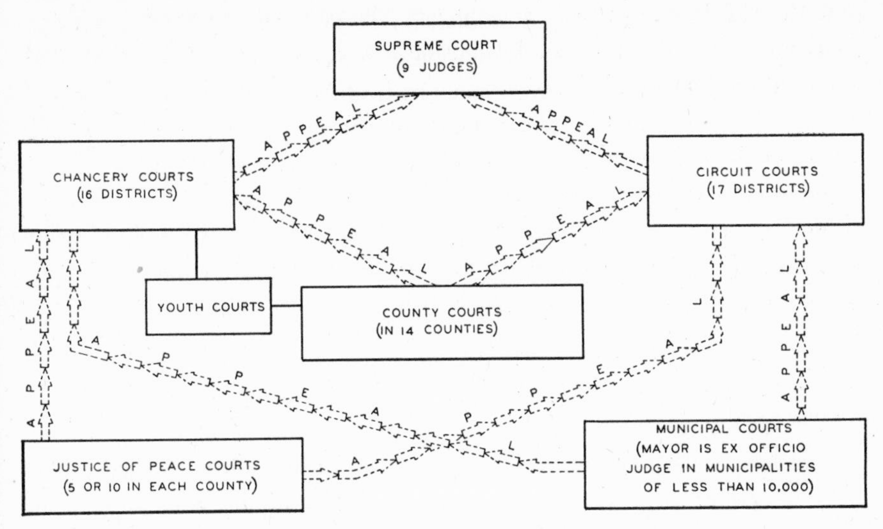

COURT ORGANIZATION OF MISSISSIPPI

County Courts

Fourteen counties of the state have county courts. The first of these was established in 1926, and a court is now required by statute for all counties that meet certain standards of population and property valuation. The matter is optional with other counties.* These courts exercise concurrent jurisdiction with circuit and chancery courts in cases at law and equity up to a maximum of $3,000, and concurrent jurisdiction with justices of the peace over misdemeanors. They have exclusive jurisdiction over cases of eminent domain, partition of personal property and actions of unlawful entry and detainer. Sessions of the court are held once a month, except in counties having two circuit court districts, where a session is held in each of the districts each month. Special sessions may be called by the county judge after ten days' public notice.[7]

Youth Courts

The legislature of 1946 created a special court for the handling of

* The requirements are a population of 35,000 or an assessed valuation of real and personal property exceeding $17,000,000, provided in either case the county has a municipality of 5,000 or more people. Counties having less than 35,000 population and property valued at between $7,500,000 and $17,000,000 and a municipality of between 10,000 and 11,000 inhabitants, which is not a county seat, also must have a county court.—*Mississippi Code, 1942,* 1952 Supp., sec. 1604. Counties not meeting these requirements may have a court if so decided by majority vote of the electors.—*Ibid.,* sec. 1618.

juvenile cases. This court is a division of the county court where one exists and in other counties is a division of the chancery court. It has jurisdiction over all cases involving persons from ten to eighteen years of age in matters of neglect or delinquency, except that persons of thirteen to eighteen charged with capital crimes must be tried in the circuit court. The circuit court, at its discretion, also may retain jurisdiction over persons of that age group charged with felonies. Special procedures for the youth court are provided that make for informality, exclusion of the public, and the elimination of a jury. Appeals from decisions of this court may be taken to the supreme court.[8]

Circuit Courts

The law courts of intermediate or general jurisdiction are called circuit courts. Although such courts are provided for in the constitution, the number and size of the districts is left to legislative discretion. At the present time there are seventeen circuit districts.[9] Jurisdiction of the circuit courts extends to all civil and criminal cases not otherwise provided for in the constitution; consequently, they are the principal trial courts for law cases. They also serve as appellate courts for cases appealed from justice of peace, police, and county courts. Sessions of the court are held at least twice each year in each county comprising the district; certain districts have sessions three or four times each year. Nine counties each have two judicial districts, with court sessions in each. The number of terms in each county, above two, as well as the maximum number of days for each term are fixed by law. However, the legal length of the term may be extended to complete a case in progress.[10] The law also may designate certain terms for civil business and others for criminal cases. Special terms of the court may be called by the judge when the business requires it, though two weeks public notice is required.

Chancery Courts

Of equal standing with the circuit courts are the district chancery courts, which are primarily courts of equity. Thus, theoretically, they administer a different system of law, though their jurisdiction over regular law cases has been affirmed both by constitutional and legal provisions.[11] The state is divided into sixteen chancery court districts, and each court holds regular sessions in each county comprising the district; the number of terms and their length are determined by law.[12] Jurisdiction of the courts includes all matters in equity, divorce and alimony, matters testamentary and of administration, minors' affairs, cases of idiocy and lunacy. Chancery courts also have concurrent jurisdiction with the circuit courts over suits on bonds of public officers, fiduciaries, and suits involving mutual accounts. The wide range of their jurisdiction, covering probate, administrative, and legal matters as well as equity, thus makes the chancery courts equally if not more important than the circuit courts in original trials. They also serve as appellate tribunals for minor courts in matters coming within their jurisdiction.

Supreme Court

The supreme court is the highest court of the state in all matters of law and equity. To it go all appeals from the chancery and circuit courts. The highest court also has limited original jurisdiction, such as the power to determine whether a vacancy exists in the governorship, when such an opinion is properly requested, and the power to issue the writs necessary to exercise its powers.[13] The court consists of nine judges, though they may sit in two divisions of five and four judges, respectively, for hearing and adjudging most cases. Terms of the court are required by law to begin on the first Monday of March and the second Monday of September, and the court must remain open at least nine months of the year if its business requires it. The judge with the longest continuous service on the bench is legally designated as the chief justice.

SELECTION AND TENURE OF JUDGES

Most judges in the courts of Mississippi are chosen by popular election. This method of selection is required by the constitution, although previous constitutions have not been consistent on this point. Under the original constitution of the state all judges were appointed and held their offices during good behavior.[14] The document of 1832 provided for popular election of judges and was among the first state constitutions to require an elective judiciary.[15] Under the 1869 constitution the state reverted to the appointive system of selection, except for justices of the peace, though limited terms were stipulated.[16] This arrangement was continued in the 1890 constitution as originally adopted. However, an amendment to the constitution in 1912 provided for popular election of circuit and chancery judges, and another amendment in 1916 extended the elective system to include the supreme court.[17] Judges of the county courts, established by statute, always have been elected. Thus the state has wavered between the elective and appointive systems. For approximately sixty years the appointive system has been used; for approximately seventy-four years the system of election has been preferred. Districts for electing supreme court judges are designated as northern, central, and southern, with three judges chosen from each district for terms of eight years. The terms are staggered so that only one judge from each district is elected in the same year. Circuit and chancery judges also are chosen from districts, designated by numbers, for terms of four years. The county is the district for electing county judges, and the supervisors' districts within the county are the districts used for electing justices of the peace. Both county judges and justices are elected for four-year terms.

Justices of the peace are chosen in odd-numbered years at the same time as state and local political officers. Police justices, required in cities of 10,000 or more population, are appointed by the governing authorities of the municipality. Other judges are chosen in even-numbered years at the same time as members of Congress. Special provisions in the corrupt practices law prevent candidates for circuit, chancery, or supreme court judgeships from being aligned with political factions and prohibit any contributions to their campaign expenses except by members of the bar who are not themselves candidates.[18]

Removal of Judges

All judges, as civil officers of the state, are subject to impeachment and, upon conviction, removal from office by the legislature. For reasonable cause, not sufficient for impeachment, the governor too may remove judges on address of each branch of the legislature, after the accused person has been allowed proper notice and hearing.[19] Judges, as public officers, are subject to the ordinary judicial processes for neglect of duty and commission of crimes or misdemeanors and, upon conviction, may be removed. Removal of persons officially adjudged to be of unsound mind also would apply to the judiciary. Vacancies in judicial positions in the county, circuit, chancery, and supreme courts are filled by appointment by the governor until the next regular state or congressional election occurring more than nine months after the vacancy exists. Vacancies in the minor courts are filled in the manner prescribed for other county and municipal officers.[20]

In order to be eligible for a supreme court judgeship a person must be a qualified elector, have five years' citizenship, have practiced law in the state for five years, and be at least thirty years of age. The same qualifications apply to circuit, chancery, and county judges, except that the age requirement is twenty-six years. Police justices must be attorneys and qualified electors. The only qualifications for justices of the peace are that they be qualified electors and have two years' residence in the district.

Except in the minor courts the compensation of judges is fixed by statute and cannot be changed during the terms to which they are elected. Present annual salaries of members of the supreme court are $11,000;* for judges of the circuit and chancery courts, $7,500; and for county judges from $4,200 to $7,200, depending in general on the population of the county.[21] Salaries of judges of police courts are determined by the municipalities. Justices of the peace are paid on a fee basis, though a statute provides for payment of a maximum of $100 per year to each justice for cases that the state loses.

Officers of the Courts

Each court has one or more officers to assist in the conduct of its business. For each justice of the peace there is a district constable, elected by the people, who arrests offenders, produces them in court, serves citations, collects fines, and in general waits upon the court. The sheriff and his deputies are officers of all the courts that sit in the county. They have the duty of serving citations and papers, arresting offenders, handling prisoners, and maintaining order in court.

Except for justices of the peace, all courts have clerks, who keep records, collect fees and costs, receive and process papers in regard to litigation, and attend to minor matters for the court. For police courts the city clerk serves in this capacity. Each county elects a chancery clerk and a circuit clerk who serve their respective courts, along with many other duties pertaining to the administration of the county's affairs. The circuit clerk is also clerk of the county court where such courts exist. The clerk of the supreme court is elected by the voters of the state. Circuit, chancery, and supreme court clerks are chosen for four-year terms, and their compensation is fixed by law.

In each county that has a county attorney this officer prosecutes cases for the state in the justice of peace and county courts. Each circuit court district has a district attorney who prosecutes civil and criminal cases for the state in the circuit court. The attorney general represents the state

* Effective at the end of the present terms, associate justices will be paid $12,500, and the chief justice $13,500.—*Mississippi Laws, 1954,* House Bill 95.

in cases before the supreme court. All these officers are elected for four-year terms. Miscellaneous officers such as court reporters, law clerks, marshals, and porters are appointed by the district courts and the supreme court.

PROCEDURE AND PROCEDURAL PROBLEMS

Judicial procedure is a vital part of the administration of justice. However well organized the courts may be, they cannot serve their purpose unless they actually operate in an effective manner. The rules of procedure determine, to a very large degree, the operation of the courts. They influence decisions that in turn affect the life, liberty, or property of persons and the welfare of the public. Procedure in the Mississippi courts, as in those of other states, reflects the result of long judicial experience, though the courts themselves have limited control over it. Procedural rules are made chiefly by acts of the state legislature.

Trial Procedure

Trial procedure in the Mississippi courts varies as to civil cases, criminal cases, and equity cases. There is also some variation among the different courts when trying the same type of case. The following brief description of each type of procedure may be helpful.

Civil cases in the county and district courts begin with the filing of a declaration with the court clerk. This declaration states the nature of the plaintiff's complaint or reasons for his grievances against the defendant and asks for the remedy to which he feels he is entitled. Upon receipt of this declaration the clerk of the court issues a summons addressed to the sheriff or constable of the county of the defendant upon whom a copy of the summons must be served. The summons contains the substance of the plaintiff's declaration and other matters, including the date of the next term of court. If the defendant wishes to contest or fight the suit, he files a written answer with the clerk stating his defense. The dates of these proceedings are legally regulated in relation to the time of the court term. The clerk, under the direction of the judge, fixes the date for trial. The place usually is in the county of the defendant, though the law allows certain exceptions to this rule.

The parties to a civil suit, with the assent of the judge, may waive the right to trial by jury. However, a jury may be demanded by either party.

If requested, a jury will be selected from a jury panel set up at the beginning of the court term.* Four prospective jurors may be peremptorily refused by each party to the suit, and others may be refused for cause. When a jury of twelve men has been agreed upon, the plaintiff presents his case to the court through the testimony of sworn witnesses and other evidence. The defendant then presents his case in the same manner. The judge instructs the jury as to its duties and provides it with written copies of instructions as to the law in the case. The jury then retires and renders a decision. Agreement of nine or more of the twelve jurors is necessary for a decision.

In criminal cases the procedure is much the same with some exceptions. The state is the plaintiff in such cases, and a case is brought to trial after the accused person has been indicted by a grand jury. This body, consisting of fifteen to twenty persons and empaneled in the same manner as a trial jury, hears evidence by the prosecuting attorney and witnesses that it may summon and decides whether the evidence is sufficient to warrant a trial. If it so decides, by concurrence of twelve members, it finds a bill of indictment. The indicted person is then arraigned and tried.† He makes no written pleading, as does the defendant in a civil case, but simply pleads guilty or not guilty. In capital cases the state and defendant are each allowed twelve peremptory challenges of jurors; in other criminal cases each side is allowed six such challenges. Since many persons on the jury list may be refused for cause, it is sometimes necessary to have a special venire in order to complete a jury. The verdict of the twelve members‡ as to the guilt or innocence of the person must be unanimous in criminal cases.[22]

Procedure in equity or chancery cases is similar to that in civil cases at law, except for certain particulars. In an equity proceeding the aggrieved person files with the chancery clerk a petition or bill of complaint setting forth the facts on which the complainant seeks relief and the insufficiency of a remedy at law. When this process has been served on the defendant he must make an answer or file a demurrer to the complaint. If the

* The judge draws the jury panel from a list compiled annually by the board of supervisors of the county.—*Mississippi Code, 1942,* secs. 1764-72. The exemptions from jury service are numerous and liberal. Legally, women are not competent jurors in Mississippi.

† Misdemeanor cases in a county court may be tried upon affidavit of the prosecuting attorney or "any reputable citizen."—*Mississippi Code, 1942,* 1952 Supp., sec. 1605.

‡ A judge, in his discretion, may direct that one or two alternate jurors be impaneled to prevent mistrial in the event of illness or death of a regular juror.—*Mississippi Laws, 1954,* Senate Bill 1202.

demurrer is overruled by the judge, the defendant then files an answer and the case goes to trial before the court, usually without a jury.* The decision of the court is rendered in the form of a decree.

Appeals

The procedure in appealing a case that has been decided in the trial court is important, since the power to appeal is broad and clearly defined. All cases tried in the justice of peace courts and municipal courts may be appealed to the county or circuit court, though not therefrom to the supreme court unless constitutional questions are involved.† Cases decided in the county court may be appealed to the circuit court or chancery court. All final judgments of the circuit court, except by plea of guilty, and all final decrees in the chancery court, except by consent, may be appealed to the supreme court.

Appeals to the supreme court are accompanied by a full transcript of the proceedings in the trial court, together with all pertinent papers including the bill of exceptions—the record of objections made by attorneys to decisions of the judge during the trial. It is on this record of the case, which is explained and argued by attorneys, that the supreme court decides the appeal. The high court may uphold or reverse a decision of the lower court or it may remand the case for a new trial.

Procedural Problems

Procedure in the courts of Mississippi offers many problems. Most of them stem from the fact that there has been little change in the practice, pleading, and procedure of trial courts during the past twenty-five years. Thus they lack the modern improvements that have been made in many other states.

The use of the jury in civil and misdemeanor cases appears to be a procedure that has outlived its usefulness. It is slow and expensive and contains no protection to the litigant not included in the broad right of appeal. However, the jury might well be retained in civil cases involving the public interest. The grand jury also is an antiquated procedure that other states have seen fit to abolish. The business of the criminal courts would be greatly expedited if persons were prosecuted on the affidavit of the prose-

* Certain cases before the chancery courts make use of a jury. In such cases the selection of a jury is similar to that in civil law cases.—*Mississippi Code, 1942,* secs. 1275, 1276.

† Appeals from justice of peace and municipal courts to the circuit court are trials *de novo.*—*Mississippi Code, 1942,* sec. 1201.

cuting attorney. Other problems involve the system of jury administration, which permits people who so desire to avoid jury service; the judge's lack of power to instruct the jury on the facts as well as the law; and the long delays, continuances, and postponements that occur in every court.

Many of the procedural problems are caused by the failure of the courts to make their own rules of procedure. Although such authority is not given the courts by the constitution, a limited power of this sort is found in statutory grants. However, the legislature has not allowed the courts to act on this grant but has instead regulated the details of procedure by law. There is no power in the supreme court, as is the case in some twenty other states, to prescribe rules for the lower courts. The trial courts exercise a very limited rule-making power. Naturally rules of procedure prescribed by the legislature lack the modernity and flexibility that would result from judicial rule-making.*

COURT ADMINISTRATION AND ADMINISTRATIVE PROBLEMS

Court Administration

Generally it may be said that there is no one system of administration of the courts of Mississippi. Instead the administration may be described as one of many systems, since each court, for the most part, is a separate unit. As indicated earlier, the legislature has regulated many aspects of the judicial system in detail. It has not prescribed any over-all plan of administration, and the limited power that the courts have to regulate their own affairs is exercised differently by the different courts.

The chancery and circuit courts of the state handle most of the trial work of the Mississippi courts. They are the district courts, with their areas of jurisdiction prescribed by act of the legislature. Since the legislature has the authority to change the system at any time by shifting counties from one to the other as well as the power to create new districts, it would appear that this method might keep the work load approximately equal in the different districts. Such is not the case. A recent survey revealed that during the year 1948 one circuit court district had more than ten times as many cases as another district. A similar disparity is revealed by a

* The Mississippi State Bar Association has repeatedly recommended statutes to the legislature providing expressly for the supreme court to make rules for pleading, practice and procedure in all courts. No action has been taken on these recommendations. "Report of Committee on Procedural Reform," *Mississippi Law Journal,* 19 (1948), 404-6; 20 (1949), 507-9.

comparison of the number of days the different courts actually sat in session.* Although certain courts pretermit several terms in the course of a year because of a lack of cases, others remain in almost continuous session and still are compelled to carry over cases because of a lack of time.†

Clerical Staff and Work

The clerks of all courts in Mississippi are popularly elected, with the result that the two clerks chosen in each county as well as the clerk of the supreme court function independently of each other. Although the duties of the clerk in regard to court records are regulated by law of the state, there is no provision for supervision of these duties except, in a limited way, by the judge. Naturally, there is much duplication as well as prolixity in the records of the various counties. Court clerks are required to make two reports to state officials each year. Both are financial reports and contain no information on other aspects of judicial statistics. Moreover, many clerks disregard the law by failing to make the reports.

The problems arising from this method of handling the clerical business of the courts are obvious. The judiciary has no effective control over its clerical force. There is no unified supervision or control of the clerical work by any authority. Nor is there any uniformity of records, or adequate system of reports. Furthermore, the system of election of the clerks makes the clerical work subject to all the evils of patronage common to political offices.

Advisory Council

Mississippi courts have no advisory body such as the judicial council found in some thirty-one other states. Such a body, usually composed of members of the bench and of the bar and lay citizens, is an important adjunct of a state judiciary. Its functions of research in procedure and organization, with periodic recommendations to the legislature or courts, are invaluable in the improvement of the judicial process. The judicial conference organized in Mississippi in 1945 appears to be a voluntary

* William N. Ethridge, Jr., *Modernizing Mississippi's Constitution* (Bureau of Public Administration, University of Mississippi, 1950), pp. 82-88. No complete judicial statistics are available for the Mississippi courts. This information was obtained by questionnaire sent to the chancery and circuit clerks and is sufficient to show the general maldistribution.

† A 1950 law permitting a judge to sit in another district with consent of the judge of that district limits the compensation for such extra service to $250 per year and does not greatly change the situation.—*Mississippi Laws, 1950,* ch. 338.

body that exists merely for the interchange of ideas. It does not discharge the usual duties of a judicial council.[23]

The administration of the court system does not differ materially from the administration of any other department of the state government. All the courts are engaged in the same task; all are performing the judicial function. The same need for unification, supervision, and efficiency exists in the judicial branch as in the executive branch insofar as administrative matters are concerned. The cost of the operation of the court system is considerable.* A properly reorganized administrative system probably would reduce the cost and at the same time provide the adequate and efficient service necessary to the proper functioning of the judiciary.

REFORM AND REORGANIZATION

The need for reorganization and reform in the state judicial system has long been recognized. Its archaic features are apparent to all students of the subject. Although piecemeal changes have been made from time to time, there has never been any general reform, and the system is much the same as it was when the state was established. The following suggestions on reform are advanced with the view of bringing the state judiciary in step with more modern practices.

Reduction of Small Claims Courts

The large number of courts handling petty litigation seems unnecessary, expensive and confusing. Justices of the peace, municipal courts and county courts (where they exist) exercise concurrent jurisdiction over petty causes. This duplication and overlapping of functions is wasteful. Justices of the peace should be abolished entirely and the jurisdiction of the municipal courts should be reduced to cases involving violations of municipal ordinances. A county court in each county could handle all small causes better and at far less expense and inconvenience to the litigants.

Combination of Law and Equity Courts

Separate courts for law and equity cases is an expensive way of maintaining traditional distinction in courts that for practical purposes does not

* For the biennium ending June 30, 1952, the appropriation was $1,053,744, exclusive of the cost of operating the offices of the circuit and chancery clerks in the 82 counties.—Mississippi State Tax Commission, *Service Bulletin,* No. 44 (1952), p. 7.

exist. Chancery courts have a large amount of law jurisdiction. One study of the jurisdiction of Mississippi chancery courts concluded that not more than 15 per cent of the cases were equity proceedings.[24] Moreover, the distinction is not recognized in the county courts, which administer both equity and law cases. Separate courts mean separate judges, separate clerks and staffs, and separate records. A combination of the two district trial courts would save money and facilitate justice.

Unification of All Courts under a Supreme Court of Judicature

The nature of the judicial function indicates the logic of combining all courts of the state under a general organization. Proper discharge of the function is the obligation of the state, regardless of the locale of the litigants. Judges are state officers, not local functionaries. To unite the courts under a general system would but recognize these facts and simplify the task. This system might be organized in three divisions, consisting of a supreme court, the requisite number of district courts, and a county court for each county. Other courts could be abolished. All judges would be members of one court, thus making it simple to interchange judges and equalize the judicial load. Such action would not preclude any classification of jurisdiction deemed desirable, nor would it prevent any specialized work such as juvenile cases.*

An Administrative Agency for Courts

The administration of the courts should be unified under an administrative director appointed by the chief justice of the supreme court. The administrative director and his staff would have the task of fixing the boundaries of court districts, assigning judges, apportioning judicial work, supervising the clerical staff, handling reports, collecting statistics, and generally attending to the housekeeping functions of the judiciary.

Better Selection and Tenure for Judges

Popular election of judges, particularly for short terms, is not conducive to obtaining the best caliber of judicial personnel. The qualifications of a good judge are not necessarily those of a good candidate. More important than the actual method of selection is the need for restricting the office to

* Unification of the court system along these lines has been advocated individually and collectively by members of the Mississippi bar. See "Report of Committee of Twelve on Unified State Court Plan," *Reports of Mississippi State Bar Association,* 13 (1918), pp. 101, 104; Ethridge, *op. cit.,* pp. 103 ff.

persons of high qualifications. This aim might be accomplished by filling vacancies from a panel of three persons recommended by a nonpolitical commission. A committee of the state bar association might serve as the recommending body, though lay members might also be included. From this panel a judge could be elected by popular vote or appointed by the governor for a limited term. At the end of the term the judge would be approved or rejected by the people on a noncompetitive ballot. If approved, the judge would continue in office for a longer term.*

Other proposals for improvement of the judicial system include the modernization of rules of procedure, establishment of a judicial council, and better compensation for judges. The courts can be good and efficient only so far as their organization, personnel, and procedure will permit.

FOOTNOTES

[1] One authority lists nine distinct functions of the courts. Westel W. Willoughby, *Principles of Judicial Administration* (The Brookings Institution, 1929), p. 211.

[2] *Mississippi Code, 1942,* sec. 677.

[3] See Chapter 2, pp. 20-21.

[4] Council of State Governments, *Book of the States, 1952-53* (Chicago, 1952), p. 462.

[5] Constitution of 1890, art. 6, sec. 171; *Mississippi Code, 1942,* sec. 1803.

[6] *Mississippi Code, 1942,* 1952 Supp., sec. 3374-35, 103.

[7] *Ibid.,* sec. 1613.

[8] *Mississippi Laws, 1946,* ch. 207.

[9] Constitution of 1890, art. 6, sec. 151; *Mississippi Code, 1942,* secs. 1394-1411.

[10] *Ibid.,* 1952 Supp., secs. 1395-1410.

[11] Constitution of 1890, art. 6, sec. 147; *Mississippi Code, 1942,* sec. 1262.

[12] *Mississippi Code, 1942,* secs. 1215-26, as amended by 1952 Supp., secs. 1215–26-9.

[13] *Ibid.,* secs. 1657, 4003.

[14] Constitution of 1817, art. 5, sec. 6.

[15] Constitution of 1832, art. 4, secs. 2, 11, 16, 23.

[16] Constitution of 1869, art. 6, secs. 2, 11, 17, 23.

[17] *Mississippi Laws, 1912,* ch. 415; *1916,* ch. 154.

[18] *Mississippi Code, 1942,* secs. 3191, 3192.

[19] Constitution of 1890, art. 4, secs. 49-53.

[20] *Ibid.,* art. 6, secs. 175, 177; *Mississippi Code, 1942,* secs. 3190, 4053; 1952 Supp., sec. 1608.

[21] *Mississippi Code, 1942,* 1950 Supp., sec. 4175; *Mississippi Laws, 1952,* chs. 238, 335.

[22] The jury in justice of peace courts consists of only six persons.

[23] Arthur T. Vanderbilt (ed.), *Minimum Standards of Judicial Administration* (Law Center of New York University, 1949), p. 69.

[24] Pressly S. Sikes, "Judicial Administration in Mississippi," *Mississippi Law Journal,* 6 (1934), pp. 233-37.

* The essentials of this plan are found in the reorganized judicial systems of Missouri and California.

CHAPTER 12

Law Enforcement

LAW ENFORCEMENT in the United States, although of concern to both state and national governments, is of special significance to the state. Most criminal law is state law, and its enforcement is one of the principal functions of state government. In most states, however, the task of law enforcement has devolved upon county or other local governments, with the state maintaining only nominal control. Mississippi is no exception to the general rule.

STATE AGENCIES FOR LAW ENFORCEMENT

An explanation of state law enforcement organization must begin with the governor, who has the constitutional duty of seeing that the laws are faithfully executed. The governor's power in this respect is by no means commensurate with his responsibility, since most officers concerned with law enforcement are popularly elected and generally not subject to control by the chief executive. The governor does command the military forces of the state, which, in certain circumstances, may be employed for law enforcement purposes.

The National Guard

The state militia consists of all able-bodied male citizens and prospective male citizens of Mississippi between the ages of eighteen and forty-five.* Most of these persons, however, are in the unorganized militia, which means they are subject to military duty if called. Those who have volunteered and have been accepted are in the organized militia, known and designated as the Mississippi National Guard.

The National Guard is organized, armed, and equipped in accordance with national law. Most of the cost is borne by the national treasury, and the guard conforms to the same regulations as the regular military forces, except that its officers are appointed in the state. Under the national Constitution the National Guard may be ordered into Federal service, whereupon it becomes part of the armed forces of the United States with the President as commander in chief.† During ordinary times, however, it serves as the organized militia under the command of the state governor. The adjutant general is chief of staff of the National Guard and is in direct charge of its activities. All officers are appointed by the governor with consent of the senate.

Although the National Guard is not organized or designed primarily for law enforcement, it may be employed for this purpose. It may be ordered out when the state is threatened with invasion, flood, or other catastrophe, or when there exists insurrection, mob activity, riot, or other situations that, in the opinion of the governor, the civil authorities are unable to control. Or, it may be ordered out if the sheriff or circuit judge in any county request it. Thus the situation may be one where civil law and authority have failed and the governor proclaims martial law, or may be simply a case of aiding a local law enforcement officer.‡

Although the state militia is thus available to the governor for the enforcement of the law under the stated circumstances, it is obvious that it is unsuited for the work of general law enforcement.** It is, however, the only force available for such work, since the State Highway Patrol is

* Persons from seventeen to eighteen and from forty-five to sixty-four years of age may be accepted as volunteers. State and local officers, ministers, and teachers are exempt.—*Mississippi Code, 1942,* secs. 8519-20.

† The Mississippi National Guard was in the active military service of the United States during World War II, from 1941 to 1946. It was reorganized in 1946, and most units were mobilized again from August 14, 1950, to May 1, 1952, for a period of twenty-one months.

‡ The leading case interpreting the governor's power to order out the National Guard is *State* v *McPhail,* 182 Miss. 360, 180 So. 387 (1938).

** When the National Guard, or any part of it, is in national service, the governor is empowered to organize, equip, train, and maintain a State Guard, for use as a temporary state militia.—*Mississippi Code, 1942,* 1952 Supp., sec. 8601.

limited for the most part to the enforcement of laws governing the highways.*

The Attorney General

The attorney general, as the chief attorney for the state, is naturally concerned with law enforcement. This officer is provided for in the constitution, which requires that he be elected every four years and have the same qualifications as judges of the circuit and chancery courts.[1] His compensation is fixed by statute. The law also provides for five assistant attorneys general† and as many as six persons for a clerical staff.

Although the attorney general has important duties as the state's chief legal officer, he is not empowered to direct the prosecution of violators of the general criminal law.‡ In fact, he is authorized to assist a district attorney in general prosecution only "when directed by the governor" or "when required by the public service."[2] Naturally, in view of this limited authority and because it is politically inexpedient, the attorney general seldom interests himself in prosecutions in the trial courts.

The importance of the attorney general to law enforcement thus is confined to specific aspects of enforcement, such as the prosecution of antitrust suits, suits for past due taxes, and suits against state officers. He also assists various state and local departments, agencies, and officers in their tasks of law enforcement through his duty to give opinions to them on any question of law.

LOCAL ORGANIZATION FOR LAW ENFORCEMENT

The general duties of local law enforcement officers are explained in chapters dealing with county and municipal government. These local officers include the county sheriff and the district constable in rural areas and the police or marshal for cities and towns. To these may be added the district attorney, who investigates crimes and prosecutes criminals in

* The Highway Patrol is authorized to enforce the traffic laws and regulations, including the power to pursue an offender to any other place. It may also, when so directed by the governor, enforce any of the laws of the state on the highways. It is specifically prohibited from exercising the powers of the state militia or the authority of the peace officers of the State. See *Smith* v *Rankin County,* 208 Miss. 792, 45 So. (2nd) 592 (1950).

† *Mississippi Code, 1942,* secs. 3827, 3828; 1952 Supp., sec. 3830. The revisor of the statutes, an assistant attorney general whose work is primarily with the legislature, is in addition to the five mentioned.

‡ The duties of this officer are listed in *Mississippi Code, 1942,* secs. 3832-51.

the circuit courts, and the county attorney, who performs similar duties in the county and justice of peace courts. The county board of supervisors, under the legal provision that makes its members conservators of the peace, has some small duties in regard to law enforcement. The duties of all these officers are discussed in some detail in later chapters.

It should be noted that all local law enforcement officers, except for some city policemen, are popularly elected in the areas that they serve. Also of importance is the fact that such officers are generally restricted in the exercise of their duties to the localities in which they were elected.* Although cooperation between these officers is possible, and doubtless is practiced frequently, this cooperation does not alter the general picture of state law enforcement as the particular locality, or the particular officer, desires that it be enforced. There is generally no state authority to compel the enforcement of a law by local officers, except the power of the governor to remove a sheriff for failure to protect prisoners from mob violence.* The result of this arrangement is what amounts to local option on the enforcement of state law. Although the greater part of the law is enforced generally and with some degree of uniformity, the more controversial statutes may vary from strict enforcement to almost complete disregard. Notable among such legislation is the famous prohibition or "dry" law, first enacted in 1908. In certain counties and towns the law is completely ignored, and retailers and dispensers operate as in a state where no such law exists. Certain cities have levied taxes on the sale and licensing of liquor dealers, which implies a recognition of its legality. Moreover, the state legislature has placed the sale of intoxicating liquors in a semi-legal status by levying a tax on illegal sales, commonly known as the "black market" tax and applying chiefly to the sale of intoxicants.[3] Naturally, under such conditions there is no state prohibition law worthy of the name. The experience with its enforcement indicates what might happen to any law.

The problems of law enforcement in Mississippi suggest the necessity for a state police force such as has been established in approximately three fourths of the states. As indicated above, the State Highway Patrol,

* The law enforcement duties of the sheriff are confined to his county except in the case of the pursuit of an escaping offender.—*Mississippi Code, 1942,* sec. 4255; *McLean* v *Miss.,* 96 F (2nd) 741 (1938). A constable cannot go beyond the confines of his district and serve process.—*Boutwell* v *Grayson,* 118 Miss. 80, 79 So. 61 (1918). Acts of a marshal outside the town limits are invalid.—*Riley* v *James,* 73 Miss. 1, 18 So. 930 (1895).

* *Mississippi Code, 1942,* sec. 4256. Although the governor may order out the National Guard for purposes of law enforcement, this is done at the request of a local officer.

although a police force, has no powers of general law enforcement. The beginnings of such an agency might have been a law of 1947 authorizing the governor to employ investigators who would have power to investigate, apprehend, and arrest persons committing crimes of violence, terrorism, or intimidation "anywhere in the State." This law, passed at a time when violence had been precipitated in connection with a strike of bus drivers, did not lead to the establishment of a "Mississippi Bureau of Investigation" as was predicted, but instead has remained a dormant statute. Apparently in deference to legislative sentiment, no investigators are now employed under it. A 1950 law, amended in 1952, authorizes the commissioner of public safety to employ a maximum of seven investigators to enforce laws preventing the theft of "livestock, poultry, and agricultural products and implements." Like highway patrolmen, these officers have no general police authority.[4]

Official action in connection with the laws described above reveals the strong popular sentiment for local autonomy in law enforcement. There appears little prospect for the creation of any general state law enforcement agency in Mississippi.

PENAL SYSTEM AND PAROLE

Related to the subject of law enforcement is the system for handling persons convicted of crimes. Students of law enforcement long have recognized that management of convicted persons frequently determines whether these persons return to society as law-abiding citizens or as habitual criminals. In keeping with this fact, many states have reorganized and modernized prison administration in recent years.[5] Mississippi is not among those states making important changes.

State Penitentiary

The state penal farm, located at Parchman, is governed by a board of commissioners of four members, serving for four-year terms. One member is appointed from each of the three supreme court districts and the governor serves as an ex officio member. The commission selects one of its members as chairman to preside over its meetings. Members are compensated at the rate of $15 per day and official expenses with a limit of ten days' pay per month, except for the chairman, who is limited to fifteen days' compensation. Bond also is required in the amount of $50,000 for the chairman and $10,000 for the other commissioners. Duties of the board include the establishment of rules and regulations for government of the penitentiary, the employment of the superintendent and certain other officials of the institution, the handling of all business matters, such as the purchase of supplies and the sale of crops and goods, the investigation of all matters of discipline and conduct of employees, and the examination and approval of claims, salaries, and other financial affairs of the institution. The board is required to make monthly and annual reports to the governor and a biennial report to the legislature on the financial condition of the penitentiary.[6]

The administration of the penitentiary is entrusted to a superintendent appointed by the board. The board shares in his responsibility by appointing some of the administrative officers while the superintendent, with approval of the board, appoints the others. The maximum number of employees and maximum salaries for them are fixed by statute. The total number of employees approximates 150. The superintendent exercises supervision over the institution, including the management of convicts, the transportation of prisoners to the penitentiary, and the maintenance of the proper records.

The penal program generally is designed to employ the hands and minds of convicts in the production of farm crops and certain commercial products, at the same time teaching the prisoners useful trades that they may follow upon release. The physical well-being of inmates is provided for by proper housing, food, and health facilities.* The employment of inmates as "trusties" is permitted, though the law limits the handling or management of convicts by other convicts. Prisoners cannot be used for work outside the penitentiary except when ordered by the governor in the event of floods or disasters. The only exception to this is the authorization of a limited number of persons to work on roads in Sunflower and Quitman counties, where the penitentiary farms are located.

The operation of the penitentiary has generally been a profit-making enterprise for the state. This profit is realized through the sale of farm crops, chief of which is cotton and cotton seed, and the sale of canned goods and such surplus industrial products as result from the vocational rehabilitation program. During the fiscal biennium ending June 30, 1951, the institution showed a net profit of $466,632.[7]

State Parole Board

The release of prisoners from the penitentiary prior to the end of their

* Corporal punishment of recalcitrant prisoners is forbidden by law, except on written permission of the superintendent.

terms, upon evidence of reform and rehabilitation, is an important phase of the penal program. Control of probation matters in Mississippi is vested in a board of three persons, one from each of the supreme court districts, appointed by the governor for staggered terms of six years. To assist the governor in selecting competent persons, a nominating committee has been established composed of the attorney general, the director of the Department of Public Welfare, the chief justice of the supreme court, the president of the State Bar Association, and a person with special knowledge of parole and probation appointed by the governor. This committee submits a list of from three to six eligible persons from which the governor makes appointments to fill vacancies on the Parole Board. This body is required to devote full time to its duties, and members receive salaries and reimbursement for official expenses.[8] The board has the duties of maintaining and studying the records of prisoners legally eligible for parole, including the power to interview such prisoners and make other investigation to determine whether and under what conditions they should be released. It also makes rules and regulations concerning the supervision and assistance of paroled persons. Upon request of the governor the board makes investigations on any case of pardon, commutation of sentence, reprieve, furlough, or remission of fine or forfeiture.* It has no control over release of persons from state training schools.

The law makes eligible for parole those prisoners with a record of good behavior who have completed one third of their terms, except that in sentences of more than thirty years, at least ten years of the sentence must have been completed. No person is eligible until one year has been served, and habitual criminals or those convicted three times of a felony are not eligible. Persons convicted of sex crimes can be paroled only after examination and approval by a competent psychiatrist chosen by the board. No parole can be ordered without written consent of the governor. The supervision of paroled persons is the duty of the welfare agent and sheriff of each county. Parolees must report to these officers once a month, and these reports are forwarded to the State Parole Board. These officers also are required to assist parolees in obtaining employment and in other matters and generally to exercise supervision over them. All paroled persons remain under the custody of the penitentiary and may have their paroles revoked by the board for any violation of the parole conditions.

* The power to grant pardons and reprieves and to remit fines and forfeitures is a constitutional power of the governor.—Constitution of 1890, art. 5, sec. 124. On the governor's power to grant paroles see *Mississippi Laws, 1952,* ch. 382.

JUVENILE DELINQUENCY AND CORRECTION

The problem of juvenile delinquency in Mississippi was long neglected. Perhaps because of an erroneous belief that delinquents are found only in large cities, as well as for other reasons, the state did little until recent years to indicate a recognition of the fact that juvenile offenders constitute a special problem in law enforcement and that their proper handling and rehabilitation are factors in crime prevention. The generally accepted fact that the rate of juvenile delinquency is higher among the lower income groups might indicate that Mississippi has a special problem in this respect.

The first correctional institution for young offenders to be provided by the state was created in 1916. Admission to the school was restricted to white children, however, and it was not until 1942 that a correctional school for Negro youth was established. In 1948 the legislature provided for youth courts (described in the previous chapter) where children may be tried under circumstances and procedures appropriate to their age. Thus considerable progress has been made in this field, but the inadequate facilities of the correctional institutions, particularly for Negroes, indicates that much remains to be done.

Reformation and training of the delinquent youth of the state is provided in two institutions officially designated as the Mississippi Training Schools. Both are governed by the same board of five trustees appointed by the governor for staggered six-year terms. All members of the board must be qualified electors, one must be an experienced educator, one an active licensed physician, one an active social welfare worker, and one a businessman or woman.[9] The board has general supervisory duties over the institutions, including the management of funds and property, the establishment of rules and procedures of operation of the schools, the appointment of superintendents, and the preparation of biennial reports on the schools to the governor. The superintendents, who hold office at the pleasure of the board, employ personnel, determine and supervise their duties, and effectuate the policies and regulations of the board.

The objectives of the institutions, as set forth by law, are the physical, moral, mental, and spiritual rehabilitation of the youths committed to them. Delinquents must be grouped as to age and disciplinary needs and must be trained in mechanical and industrial occupations as well as in literary subjects. One school, located at Columbia, is maintained for whites and the other, located at Oakley, is for Negroes.

Admission to the institutions is restricted to those youths who have violated laws involving moral turpitude or upon certificate of a circuit or chancery judge that the child is immoral, delinquent, or incorrigible. Only youths from ten to eighteen years of age are admitted. Provision is made for discharge of students, with approval of the court, and for their release on probation in the same manner. Except for sale of products produced on the farms operated at each school, the cost of the schools is borne entirely by the state. The current biennial appropriation (1952-1954) is $247,900 for the Columbia school and $185,000 for the Oakley school.[10]

SPECIAL KINDS OF LAW ENFORCEMENT

Although enforcement of the general laws is by locally chosen officers with little state supervision, certain special laws are in the hands of state agents. These laws are concerned chiefly with tax collection, conservation of wild life, and various inspection services. By its very nature such legislation requires state enforcement.

Tax Agents

The state tax collector, elected for four years, has important powers of law enforcement in regard to tax legislation. This officer, who is authorized to hire as many as ten deputies to assist in this work, is empowered to proceed by suit against all persons, corporations, companies, and associations for any due and unpaid taxes, whether owed to the state or to one of its subdivisions. By statute the state tax collector or his representatives may examine records, books, and accounts of any taxing body, such as a county board or municipal council, and determine whether public funds have been illegally appropriated or erroneously accounted for. Furthermore, this officer has authority to examine and investigate the records, papers, and accounts of any state or local official to determine whether embezzlement has occurred, and he may make additional assessments of property that has escaped assessments.[11] Cases of violation of law are reported by the state tax collector to the proper district attorney for prosecution. Delinquent taxes or illegally expended funds are recovered by suit maintained in the proper court by him on behalf of the state or local governmental unit.

The State Tax Commission, as the principle collection agency for state taxes, maintains accountants, appraisers, inspectors, attorneys, and other agents to assist in the enforcement of the tax laws. The commission has the duty of making and promulgating rules for the collection of taxes and distributing them to revenue officers and taxpayers; its agents have the power to audit books, examine records, or make other examination necessary to establish liability for taxes under the income, privilege, sales, and excise tax laws of the state. At the instigation of the commission, the attorney general or any district or county attorney may bring action in the name of the State to collect taxes due.[12]

The motor vehicle comptroller has, along with other duties, the task of enforcing the tax laws on gasoline and petroleum products. These include taxes on sales of such products as well as motor vehicle privilege license taxes. The comptroller is authorized to appoint field agents, inspectors, and auditors, who have the power to examine and inspect the books and papers of any person liable for the taxes collected by this office.[13]

Inspection Services

The enforcement of certain laws pertaining to standards of quality and quantity is entrusted to state agents. Weighing scales for the sale of livestock must conform to the requirements of the national Bureau of Standards, and the state commissioner of agriculture and his representatives are responsible for the enforcement of this law. The standards of other weights and measures are set forth by law, the list covering all agricultural products as well as coal, timber, and food products. These standards, however, are enforced by an inspector appointed in each county or city, under the direction of the governing board of the particular locality. In case no inspector is appointed, the circuit clerk of the county, or the clerk of the city, is designated as the enforcement officer.[14] Weights and measures statutes pertaining to the sale of petroleum products are enforced by the office of the motor vehicle comptroller as a part of its duties. Agents of this office have power to inspect all storage facilities, check samples, and inspect pumps or instruments to determine that they meet the requirements of the United States Bureau of Standards. This duty includes the inspection of liquefied compressed gas equipment and facilities. In addition, the motor vehicle comptroller has the duty of inspecting the size, weight, and physical qualifications of vehicles operating on the streets and highways of the state. For this purpose inspection stations are established at appropriate places along the highways of the state, a large number of which are open at all times.[15]

Other inspection services designed to aid and promote agriculture and allied industries are provided by the commissioner of agriculture, the Livestock Sanitary Board, and the State Plant Board.

The commissioner of agriculture and his agents have authority to inspect and analyze the quality of agricultural seeds offered for sale, including the inspection of handling and storage facilities, packaging, and branding. This power also extends to commercial feeds and fertilizers, where the law provides for a chemical analysis and proper tagging. Full power to establish such rules and regulations as may be necessary to enforce these standards is provided, though wherever standards have been established by the national Department of Agriculture the task is merely one of requiring compliance. This power has been extended further to include grades and standards for all farm products, such as fruits, vegetables, and eggs. In like manner agents of the commissioner of agriculture have power to inspect dairies, creameries, barns and cattle, and all facilities connected with the sale of dairy products. This includes the power to test such products to determine that standards of sanitation and content are complied with. Offenders in all these cases may be forbidden to sell such products, after proper process has been served, and may be punished for misdemeanor.[16]

The Livestock Sanitary Board, the executive secretary of which is a veterinarian, has powers of inspection designed to prevent diseases in livestock. The secretary is empowered to appoint, with consent of the board, inspectors and agents to make examinations and inspections to carry out the functions of the agency.[17]

The State Plant Board, through an entomologist and qualified inspectors, has power to inspect all plants, plant products, and bees, and the facilities for growing and shipping them, in order to detect pests, diseases, and poisons. This includes the power to require proper certificate of inspection before shipment into the state and the power to designate prohibited areas outside the state from which shipments are barred. Economic poisons on plants or plant wrappings are given special attention. Plants and products found to be infected or poisoned may be destroyed, shipments may be prohibited, and offenders may be prosecuted for misdemeanor.[18]

Mississippi has strict legislation regulating the development, production, and utilization of the oil and gas resources within its borders. This legislation concerns the drilling of wells, efficiency of production, the prevention of fire hazards, and the elimination of waste. The enforcement of such laws is entrusted to the State Oil and Gas Board, which has the power to employ a supervisor, inspectors, and other persons who have full authority to inspect all operations and facilities relating to the industry to determine whether the laws are observed. Such agents have access to whatever property and records are necessary to perform their duties, including the power to subpoena witnesses, books, and papers. The ordinary judicial processes are provided to enable these representatives to fulfill their duties.[19]

Another state agency having powers of inspection to enforce state laws is the Board of Health, which has important duties in regard to factories, food, and water facilities, and other matters relating to the public health. Other inspection functions of the Board of Health are carried out chiefly by local health officers and local inspectors of weights and measures, though authority to enforce its standards is lodged in the state agency. The state auditor of public accounts has important powers of inspection to determine whether the laws requiring uniform and proper accounting of public funds are enforced. The Public Service Commission has inspection powers in regard to its duties to see that laws pertaining to common carriers and their facilities are observed.

Game and Fish Wardens

In recent years Mississippi has given an increasing amount of attention to the conservation of wildlife. In 1932 the State and Game Commission was created for the purpose of propagating, protecting, and managing the wildlife of the state. This body was reorganized in 1952 and now consists of five members from five different areas, with an executive officer known as the state director of conservation. Although there is considerable prohibitory legislation to be enforced by the commission, it also has broad powers to formulate rules and regulations to carry out its functions.

The enforcement of the state laws on fish and game as well as the regulations of the commission is carried out by the law enforcement division headed by a chief law enforcement officer. In order to accomplish the work of this division the state is divided into thirteen districts, each with a supervisor. Under each supervisor a number of wardens are assigned to patrol the proper areas to prevent violations of the conservation laws, as well as to police any state lands in the vicinity.

Although all the wardens are under direction of state authority, they have the right to call upon local officers for aid in the performance of their duties. These duties include the execution of warrants and search warrants, the serving of subpoenas, the examination, inspection, or search of houses, buildings, or premises, the seizing of illegally taken game or fish, the arrest of offenders, and such other powers of peace officers as may be necessary in the performance of their work. Any violation or attempt to violate the laws pertaining to game and fish is legally declared a misdemeanor and appropriate fines are fixed.[20]

Enforcement of Sea Food Laws

Another portion of state law that is enforced by special officers of the state is that pertaining to the sea food industry. Sea food is one of Mississippi's most important natural resources, and special laws relating to the industry have been in effect since 1902.

Generally the laws are designed to regulate, conserve, and protect the industry. The administrative agency in control is the Sea Food Commission, consisting of five members who are appointed by the governor for staggered terms of five years. The task of inspection and law enforcement is the responsibility of the chief inspector and an assistant chief inspector, selected by the commission. In addition the chief inspector may appoint nine deputy inspectors to assist in the performance of his duties.

Duty of the inspectors consists of the enforcement of the laws for the protection, conservation, and propagation of sea foods of the state. To accomplish this they have authority to visit and inspect all factories, boats, trawls, and other facilities used in the industry. The inspectors are peace officers of the state with full power to carry arms, make arrests, confiscate illegally taken fish, and generally to do such acts as may be necessary to the enforcement of the laws. They are authorized to call upon all captains of licensed fishing vessels to assist them in carrying out their duties.[21]

IMPROVING LAW ENFORCEMENT

As indicated above, the general picture of law enforcement in Mississippi is one of state laws with local application. Except in the case of special categories of laws, such as those mentioned, the state does not undertake to enforce its laws and generally, as in the case of the Highway Patrol, forbids its agents to assume the duties of peace officers. Nor is there any effective state supervision of local enforcement of the general laws. Under these conditions, together with the highly decentralized court system, anything approaching uniform enforcement is obviously impossible.

These considerations raise the question of state enforcement of the general law by its own officers. Because a state police force is necessarily of considerable size, with appropriate funds it can maintain modern equipment for crime investigation and detection, training of officers in the latest police methods, and otherwise provide the state with an efficient and up-to-date system of law enforcement. The experience of states that have employed such a force for many years is that it results in far better legal protection for the people, with no objectionable intrusion on local autonomy.

Other suggestions for improving law enforcement might include training courses for local law enforcement officers to enable them to learn and apply modern techniques of criminal identification and detection. The Federal Bureau of Investigation has made its training facilities available to a limited number of local officers, though the number that can be trained in this manner is far too small for effective improvement. Certain states, notably California, have provided police training courses at the state university or other institutions, with the result that most of the state's officers at one time or another can receive better training in their duties.*

FOOTNOTES

[1] Constitution of 1890, art. 6, sec. 173.

[2] *Mississippi Code, 1942,* sec. 3845.

[3] *Mississippi Laws, 1944,* ch. 139, secs. 1-8.

[4] For these laws see *Mississippi Code,* 1952 Supp., sec. 3980-5; *Mississippi Laws, 1952,* ch. 173.

[5] See Austin H. MacCormick, "Progress in American State Prisons," *State Government,* XXII (April, 1949), 112-15.

[6] For legal provisions relating to the penitentiary see *Mississippi Code, 1942,* 1952 Supp., secs. 7921–8008-5.

[7] Mississippi State Penitentiary, *Biennial Report, 1949-1951* (Jackson, 1951), p. 4.

[8] See *Mississippi Code, 1942,* 1952 Supp., secs. 4004-01–4004-22, 4004-5.

[9] Legal provisions relating to these schools may be found in *Mississippi Code, 1942,* secs. 6744-63; 1950 Supp., secs. 6744-01–6744-21.

[10] *Mississippi Laws, 1952,* chs. 61, 63.

[11] *Mississippi Code, 1942,* secs. 9177-96. This officer has control of the administration of the "black market" tax referred to above.

[12] *Mississippi Code, 1942,* sec. 9197 ff.

[13] *Ibid., 1942,* secs. 9352-01 ff. Recompiled volume 7 (1952).

[14] *Mississippi Code, 1942,* secs. 5132-45; 1952 Supp., secs. 5132-5, 5145-5.

[15] *Ibid.,* secs. 1008-01 ff.

[16] *Ibid.,* secs. 4397-01–4397-31, 4415-74, 4424-69, 4536-44, 4545-01–4560-06.

[17] *Ibid.,* sec. 4835.

[18] *Mississippi Code, 1942,* secs. 4978-5011; 1952 Supp., secs. 5000-01–5000-33.

[19] *Ibid.,* secs. 6132-01–6132-51.

[20] The laws pertaining to this agency may be found in *Mississippi Code, 1942,* secs. 5841-5943, and Recompiled volume 5 (1952), 5841-5929-17; *Mississippi Laws, 1952,* chs. 186-93.

[21] *Mississippi Code, 1942,* secs. 6047-6131; 1952 Supp., secs. 6049-6121.

* The first effort of this kind in Mississippi was the Mississippi Law Enforcement Officers Institute, held at the University of Mississippi on February 15-27, 1953.

CHAPTER 13

Public Education

FOR WELL OVER A CENTURY Mississippi has been active in two primary educational functions, the establishment and operation of institutions of higher learning and the supervision of local educational systems. The legislature authorized the establishment of the University of Mississippi in 1844, and its first students were admitted in 1848. Two years earlier a system of common schools received legislative approval, although supervisory power was vested in the county governing bodies, then called police courts. Today the state's educational system consists of eight senior colleges, fifteen public junior colleges, more than 600 high schools, and 1,000 or more grade and grammar schools. Obviously, the administration of this sprawling system requires extensive administrative arrangements.

STATE EDUCATIONAL ORGANIZATION

State officials have extensive authority over the public school system in Mississippi in such matters as compulsory school attendance, textbook selection, certification of teachers, school transportation, and school finances. Accrediting agencies such as the Southern Association of Secondary Schools and Colleges also influence and sometimes compel public action. The emphasis in state activities, however, is placed upon ensuring equal educational opportunities throughout Mississippi, with primary responsibility for education resting at the local level of government.

State Board of Education

Mississippi is one of two remaining states, the other being Florida, whose board of education is composed entirely of ex officio officers. The Constitution of 1890 provides that the Board of Education shall consist of the secretary of state, attorney general, and superintendent of education and that its purpose shall be "the management and investment of school funds according to law and for the performance of such other duties as may be prescribed."[1] The members of the board serve the length of their primary terms—four years—with continuity in service depending upon re-election to the primary office.

The powers of the State Board of Education are substantial. It apportions the available equalizing funds to all public schools under conditions established by statute; it possesses some supervisory and appellate authority over county school officials, acting upon appeals from decisions of the county superintendents of education or the state superintendent; and it may remove county superintendents for neglect of duty, official misconduct, or drunkenness after a hearing, if one is desired. The State Board of Education also may adopt a course of study for the public schools, establish trade schools and classes, prescribe rules and regulations for a program of adult education, and regulate various matters that arise in the practical administration of the school system.

The State Board of Education is also the State Board of Vocational Education. As such it appoints and removes the directors of three divisions of the State Department of Education—Vocational Education, Vocational Rehabilitation, and Crippled Children's Services—as well as subordinate employees of these units. Most of its functions are fixed by statute and may be changed at legislative will.[2]

Superintendent of Public Education

Administration and management of the State Department of Education are vested in the superintendent of public education. This office was first established in 1869 as a constitutional position, and under the current constitution the state superintendent is elected in the same manner and for the same term of office (four years) as the governor.[3] Qualifications for the office are a minimum age of twenty-five years and residence in Mississippi for five years preceding election. Compensation is determined by statute.

The state superintendent, who is provided with an assistant superintendent, administers a department organized on the basis of major functions into the following divisions: instruction, administration and finance, school building and transportation, vocational education, vocational rehabilitation, and crippled children's services.* The assistant superintendent of public education, the directors of the divisions with the exception of those of the three divisions whose heads are appointed by the State Board of Education, and other employees are selected by the state superintendent and serve at his will.

The powers vested by statute in the superintendent of public education are many and extensive. He not only is charged with the supervision of the free public schools, agricultural high schools, and junior colleges; he also is given the means to enforce this mandate. Among the duties and responsibilities of the state superintendent are the following: to prescribe rules and regulations for the efficient conduct and organization of the public schools; preside over meetings of the State Board of Education; to collect materials for determining the proper distribution of common school funds;† to maintain records of his official acts and of those of the State Board of Education; meet with the county superintendents and advise them upon school matters; and require detailed reports from the county superintendents of education.[4] Other important educational functions, such as teacher certification, school plant inspection services, and curriculum matters are discharged by the various division directors.

Related Educational Agencies

A tendency—one common to the entire state administrative system—to create a new administrative body to administer a newly assumed educational function or a new variation of some old function has long been evident. Some five or six such agencies, both active and inactive, are upon the statute books, including the Mississippi Illiteracy Commission charged to study and assist in eliminating adult illiteracy, the State Temperance Commission intended to prepare instructional materials for the public schools in aid of

* These divisions and the consequent allocation of functions were established under the educational reorganization plan of 1946.—*Mississippi Laws, 1946,* ch. 297.

† Constitution of 1890, art. 8, sec. 206. This constitution provides a common school fund to be appropriated from the general fund of the state. Together with the county common school fund, which consists of poll taxes collected within the county, it is designed to finance a minimum, constitutional four-months school term. The state common school fund is distributed among the 82 counties and the separate school districts in proportion to the total number of educable children in each. See *State Board of Education* v *Pridgen,* 106 Miss. 219, 63 So. 416 (1913); *Miller* v *State,* 130 Miss. 564, 94 So. 706 (1923). The common school fund is distinct from the equalizing fund, and the courts have sustained the equalizing fund as valid additional support.—*Miller* v *State, op. cit.*

the temperance cause, and the State Committee for Certifying In-Institution Training for Veterans. Only the last body has been operative in recent years.

Probably the most important ancillary educational agency is the Mississippi State Textbook Purchasing Board, established in 1942.* The primary function of this body is to adopt, contract, and purchase textbooks for free use by public school students. Adoptions are made on the recommendation of rating committees, appointed by the state superintendent, for the purpose of making recommendations in the various courses of study. Although specific recommendations of these committees are not binding upon the textbook board, the latter must adopt some volume that has the approval of the particular rating group.

Recommended Improvements

Changes in the structure for administering the state's educational system have been proposed frequently. The report of the Brookings Institution recommended that the ex officio State Board of Education be transformed into a body of five to nine members appointed by the governor for staggered terms of ten years; it suggested also that the elective superintendent of public education be appointed by the reconstituted board of education.[5] The first of these two recommendations was repeated in 1950 by the final report of the Legislative Fact-Finding Committee on the Reorganization of State Government, which recommended that the governor appoint the state superintendent on recommendation of the board of education. Neither set of proposals has been favorably received by the legislature where constitutional amendments must be initiated.

The current internal structure of the State Department of Education resulted from the findings of the 1946 Joint Legislative Education Committee, which reported a "real need for a reorganization" of the department in the interests of avoiding duplication of work, maintaining adequate supervision, and reducing the cost of administration. Contrary to usual practice the Mississippi legislature accepted the committee's recommendations almost without change.[6] The state's educational system, however, has not developed in such a fashion that the separate officers and agencies are completely integrated into a working organization and support each other in providing an economical administration of the education function.

* The board consists of five members, namely, the governor as ex officio chairman, the superintendent of public education, and three members appointed by the governor for a four-year term, one member from each of the three supreme court districts.—*Mississippi Code, 1942,* sec. 6634 as amended by *Mississippi Laws, 1946,* ch. 444.

LOCAL SCHOOL ORGANIZATION

A review of early educational history in Mississippi shows a large number of private academies, largely operated by religious groups, to which parents of moderate means and occasionally of wealth sent their children. The legislature authorized the establishment of a public school system in 1846 and vested supervisory authority, as we have noted, in the county governing bodies. The Constitution of 1869 provided financial encouragement to the modest public school system, and the 1890 constitution made it mandatory for the legislature to organize a "uniform system of free public schools . . . for all children between the ages of six and twenty-one years."*

Local educational organization in Mississippi has taken the form of autonomous school districts governed by boards of school trustees. In these bodies is placed the principal authority, subject to state supervision in many respects, over local school administration.

Types of Districts

The several kinds of school districts currently used include the common school, special consolidated school, consolidated school, and separate school districts, the last of these units embracing both rural and municipal separate districts. Each of the different types is established by statute.† A common school district is simply an ordinary rural district organized by the county school board, while the consolidated and special consolidated districts must contain not less than ten square miles and not less than twenty-five square miles respectively, nor fewer than 250 pupils. A rural

* Compare Constitution of 1869, art. 8, sec. 6 with Constitution of 1890, art. 8, sec. 201. Section 207 of the latter document specifies that separate schools shall be kept "for the children of the white and colored races." In view of judicial developments, the legislature in 1952 created a legislative recess committee to study and prepare legislation concerning the public school system in view of possible attacks, judicial and otherwise, on the segregated school system, and also to facilitate the expansion and equalization of educational opportunities within the state.—*Mississippi Laws, 1952,* ch. 453.

†*Mississippi Laws, 1953 Ex. Sess.,* ch. 12, enacted in pursuance of the report of the Recess Committee on Education, abolished these school districts, but provided that all "such school districts shall continue to exist with all the powers, rights, privileges, and prerogatives thereof as now provided by law until . . . [such school districts] shall be reconstituted or the territory thereof consolidated with other territory. . . ." This act further authorizes the creation of county-wide districts and school districts lying in two or more counties, provides that the reorganized districts must meet approval of the newly established State Educational Finance Commission, and repeals *Mississippi Code, 1942,* sec. 6276, *ibid.,* 1952 Supp., secs. 6295-99, 6300, 6333-34, 6368, 6397, 6422, and *Mississippi Laws, 1950,* ch. 278.

separate school district must have an assessed valuation of $200,000 or more, or an area of sixteen square miles that has been organized by the county board of education and in which a school is operated at least seven months with no fewer than twenty-five students. Finally, the municipal separate school district consists of either the territorial boundaries of a municipal corporation or these boundaries and added territory.[7]

The 1953 special session of the Mississippi legislature, meeting to equalize educational opportunities in the state, reduced the types of districts to three: (1) municipal separate school districts, which are defined as in the preceding paragraph; (2) consolidated school districts, which are all districts in one or more counties other than municipal separate and county-wide school districts; and (3) county-wide school districts which, under the new equalization legislation, embrace all the territory of a county exclusive of the area "embraced within the limits of a municipal separate school district."* Reorganization from the pattern that prevailed until recently will no doubt consume the greater portion of the three-year period allowed for local conformity to the new statute. The legislature also created "line districts," that is, school units including territory embraced in two or more counties.

Administrative units totaling 1,417 in 1953 operate in Mississippi. This total consists of 695 county and consolidated districts, eighty municipal separate districts, twenty-three special consolidated districts, eleven rural separate districts, and 608 schools in the counties[8] for Negro children.

Special Schools

In addition to the various kinds of school districts, there are the special high school districts, which may include the territory of any school district or districts, the county high school districts, which embrace all areas outside of any separate or line school district, and the county unit school districts, which cover all territory not in a separate district and which are created by the county board of education. The special high school district is intended to enable consolidation of high schools at that level of education, while the county high school district seeks to provide secondary educational facilities for students who are not included in one of the separate school districts. Fifteen of these special schools are operating.†

* *Mississippi Laws, 1953 Ex. Sess.,* ch. 17, sec. 1. The report of the Recess Committee on Education, which prompted the session, and the legislation which resulted from it are discussed generally in the concluding pages of this chapter.

† For a discussion of the relationship of these schools to the public junior colleges, see pp. 189-90.

Board of Trustees

General control and management of the local school in each district are vested in a board of trustees. The 1953 equalization legislation continued in office the boards of trustees of all school districts in existence at the time of enactment of the new statutes, and until such time as the county boards of education reconstitute or reorganize the school districts in the newly established pattern. Thereafter the boards of trustees of municipal separate school districts will consist of five members chosen for staggered terms of five years each. Should the district contain territory outside the municipality in which reside 15 per cent of the students enrolled in the district, one member must be a resident of the outside territory, and, if 30 per cent or more of the pupils reside in the added territory, it may be represented by not more than two trustees.* Municipal separate school trustees will be elected by a majority of the governing authorities of the municipality.

The governing body of reconstituted districts that lie wholly in one county, but are not municipal separate or county-wide school districts, will be composed of five-man boards of trustees. The first board will be appointed by the county board of education, but thereafter the trustees will be elected by the qualified electors of the district for staggered five-year terms. The county board of education, however, will be the board of trustees, although each attendance center will be "in the custody" of a board of five trustees appointed by the county board for five-year terms, one expiring each year, from the residents of the attendance center.

In the event that some of the newly constituted districts, municipal units excluded, embrace territory in two or more counties, the board of trustees will be composed of five persons, the territory of each county being represented on the board in the ratio that the number of educable children is to the total number of educable children in the district; the territory of each county included in a multi-county district, though, must have at least one trustee. After the first trustees, who are to be appointed by the county boards of education, the board will be popularly elected. Term of office is five years.

* *Mississippi Laws, 1953 Ex. Sess.,* ch. 12. Where the district embraces territory of another county and 15 per cent of the pupils reside in this county, one trustee must reside in the county other than that in which the municipality is located. He is popularly elected.

County School Board

Chapter 10 of the Mississippi statutes enacted in 1953 established a county board of education to consist of five members, one to be elected by the resident and qualified electors of each supervisor's district of the county. After the first board, elected in May, 1954, has served, the term of office will be six years with part of the membership of the board expiring at two year intervals. Compensation of $5 per diem is specified for a maximum of 60 days in any one year. The new board replaces a similar agency composed of the county superintendent of education and five elected members, selected by the trustees of the county public schools from each supervisor's district.

The county boards of education, only recently selected under the new legislation, have substantial powers. Provisions thus are made for it to act as a central purchasing agency; to have full control of the distribution, allotment, and disbursement of Minimum Education Program funds provided for support of the county school system; to abolish or alter school districts other than municipal districts; to fix dates for opening of the school terms; and in general to exercise a wide range of authority vested in it by the state legislature.

County Superintendent of Education

The office of county superintendent of education, which is filled by popular election, has constitutional basis.[9] The Mississippi constitution reads that the county superintendent "shall be appointed by the board of education by and with the advice and consent of the senate . . ." for a term of four years; it also permits, however, the legislature to make the office elective.

Mississippi's reorganized system of local school officers continues the county superintendent as a traditionally elective officer. In order to be eligible for the office candidates must be qualified electors and citizens of the state for four years and of the county for two years preceding election. Nevertheless, the office may be made appointive in any county following petition of 20 per cent of the qualified electors of the county and a special election at which a majority of the qualified electors voting must favor the appointment of the superintendent by the county board of education.[10] However selected, the county superintendent must meet specified qualifications of education and experience.

The functions and responsibilities imposed upon the county superintendent are numerous. Stated generally, they are largely administrative in nature, and many of them deal with questions of educational finance and fiscal administration. The functions and responsibilities are sufficiently important, however, to make the county superintendent an important figure in the county-local system of administration that prevails in this state.

STATE SCHOOL ADMINISTRATION

Problems of Administration and Supervision

Although school systems in Mississippi, as in other states, are essentially local, the functions and services provided by the State Department of Education are significant in a number of areas, including the following: attendance, audio-visual education, curriculum development, school bus transportation, school health, the school lunch program, and vocational education.

School attendance is compulsory for all children between the ages of seven and sixteen years, with exemptions for those who have completed the common school course of study or its equivalent, mentally defective or physically incapacitated children, and those who live more than two and a half miles from the nearest school, and for whom no transportation is provided, as in the case of the consolidated schools. The county superintendent of education requires reports of absences from all school principals, public or private, on forms prescribed by the State Department of Education, and he makes monthly and annual reports to the state superintendent. A small fine and ten days imprisonment may be imposed upon conviction of parents or guardians who do not comply with these attendance regulations. Average daily attendance in 1953 of more than 464,000 indicates that only slightly more than half the number of educable children are attending classes, although school enrollment exceeds 540,000 pupils.

Among the many improved educational techniques is audio-visual education. A sub-unit of the state department's Division of Instruction is entrusted with this program on the state level. Its supervisor seeks to promote teacher training in audio-visual education through both in-service and pre-service courses, and makes routine visits to schools to inaugurate new programs, counsel with teachers, assist in setting up physical facilities, and promote established programs. He is available for school faculty, community organization, and special educational meetings, prepares photographic materials of instruction and directs the film library maintained by the State Department of Education, and assists in other work such as curriculum planning. In a recent biennium for example, the supervisor visited more than 130 schools, appeared before fifty-eight community and professional groups, and prepared numerous film strips. The department estimates that there are from 1,200 to 1,500 16 millimeter motion picture projectors in the public schools, and that more than 400 schools have joined forces to institute film libraries. The number of cooperative libraries of this sort, though, is insufficient to satisfy current needs, and the supervisor has recommended that legislative action be taken to supply audio-visual materials of all kinds without cost.

An acute need for adequate school buildings was reported by the Recess Education Committee of the Mississippi legislature in 1953. The committee found that 4,301 school buildings were in operation in the state, with only 1,291, or less than a third, "in good condition and needing only normal maintenance." Some 1,585 buildings, many of which are Negro schools, were found in need of "immediate replacement," and another 1,180 structures require major repairs.[11] These deplorable conditions were found despite appropriations of more than $7,000,000, of which $2,000,000 was earmarked for Negro school construction, in the 1946-1950 period. Supervision of common school construction in Mississippi is provided by the School Building Service, acting chiefly in an advisory capacity, which fosters the construction of educationally efficient school plants, eliminates waste in school plant planning and construction, and stimulates sound use and care of the buildings. Standard plans and specifications thus are furnished the schools, whose applications for state assistance in plant construction must have approval of the proposed construction by the State Department of Education.

Curriculum development is a power given to the State Board of Education, and services as well as supervision in this area are the responsibility also of the Division of Instruction. Thus this division promotes and participates in curriculum planning and development at the primary and secondary levels, including the agricultural high schools, the cooperative preparation of materials for the common school secondary level, the stimulation of programs of child study to be used as the basis for curriculum development for the Negro schools, and assistance in such fields as library service, music education, narcotics education, and audio-visual education. Although the legislature has not specified the course of study in unnecessary detail and has left considerable freedom to the state department and the school districts, state administrative supervision has tended to mold the course of study with some degree of uniformity among the schools of the state.

Mississippi is still primarily a rural state, and school bus transportation is necessary to transport a large portion of the educable children to and from the state's schools. Supervision of this function is the responsibility of the Division of School Transportation. Virtually all of Mississippi's counties own some of their school buses, of which there are more than 2,000, a number equalled or exceeded by privately-owned school buses. Annually these buses travel an approximate 25,000,000 miles and carry over 196,000 school children. The average annual cost of transportation per pupil now is slightly under $28. A number of problems have arisen concerning school transportation. Some areas have too many buses and too many routes; a fair number of the buses have unsafe wooden bodies, and hardly more than half of the counties by 1951 had established reorganized routes, bus maintenance shops, and driver training programs. Even so, considerable progress has been made since 1944 when the legislature authorized counties to purchase and own transportation equipment; formerly only one sixth of the state's school children were provided this service, today 38 per cent are transported.

The school health program in Mississippi is jointly administered by the State Board of Health and the State Department of Education through the Mississippi School Health Service. The program, hardly more than a decade in duration, seeks to utilize the available state and local resources in solving school health problems and to establish and maintain a balanced school health program in the schools of the state. The services provided are several in number. Health services include the detection and correction of physical, mental, and emotional defects in school children through medical examinations and services to secure educational adjustment. Although every county in the state has benefited, the program has been limited by a shortage of available funds.

A school lunch program is administered by the State Department of Education under the National School Lunch Agreement by which Federal assistance is distributed to schools participating in this program. In recent years Federal funds approximating $2,200,000 annually and commodities valued at more than $1,500,000 have been supplied the school lunch program, which includes 1,100 or more schools. Responsibilities of the state agency are clear in this work. Among them are preparation of the state plan of operation, supervision of the plan in force and maintenance and standards established by it, administration of the program in accordance with the National School Lunch Agreement, distribution of Federal commodities donated to the program, provision of consultative services in school lunch management and nutrition education, assistance in planning and conducting training programs and the purchasing of new equipment, and distribution of Federal funds allotted Mississippi for school lunch work.

Programs of special education in Mississippi are limited. Some 10,000 or more children now receive assistance through the Crippled Children's Service, initially organized as a part of the vocational rehabilitation program in 1936 and assisted with funds made available under the Federal Social Security Act. A separate unit of the State Department of Education since 1946, the service provides medical assistance to crippled children through regular weekly clinics in several cities and additional field clinics; since 1947 it has also provided, with Federal assistance, a program for cerebral palsy victims. Although this service has made considerable progress, future advances will require better educational facilities for crippled children throughout Mississippi's common school system as well as expansion of particular phases of its work, such as treatment of rheumatic heart cases and epilepsy cases, and correction of speech and hearing defects. Also needed are personnel training programs in several specialized areas and improvement in follow-up care of the children served.

The Federal Smith-Hughes Act marked the entry of the national government into a cooperative program of vocational education with the states. In Mississippi the State Board of Education functions also as the State Board of Vocational Education and cooperates with the local school boards in educational programs that meet conditions for Federal grant-in-aid funds in a single or several vocational fields. These fields, in which 95,000 persons study annually, embrace vocational agriculture, homemaking education, trade and industrial education, and distributive education. Vocational education work, which is supported financially by local units and the state as well as by the national government, reflects a demand for widened educational opportunities in an increasing number of schools. At the same time, this work is less controlled by the state superintendent of education than most programs because, along with the directors of the Division of Vocational Rehabilitation and the Crippled Children's Service, its director is directly responsible to the State Board of Education acting as the Board of Vocational Education.

Problems of Teachers

Mississippi has not solved a problem besetting most states—the acute shortage of public school teachers. The reasons for this shortage, perhaps, are both economic and psychological, the latter reflecting the relatively low esteem in which the teacher is held by the general public.

Teachers' salaries in Mississippi have not been large enough to attract people to the teaching profession on a permanent basis, a difficulty enhanced by the essential insecurity of work on a single year's contract that may or may not be renewed. The Recess Education Committee thus reported in 1953 that the average Mississippi teacher's salary for the 1951-1952 school year was $1,534 compared to $3,167 for the forty-eight states. Within the South, the salaries of Mississippi's teachers were also at the bottom, far below even the $2,130 average annual salary paid South Carolina's teachers who ranked immediately above those of this state. It was this finding that prompted the committee to recommend a minimum average salary scale, which would improve, though not equalize with other states, the compensation of Mississippi's public school teachers.

Since 1944 public school teachers have had retirement benefits. At first teachers were covered under a statute of specific applicability, there being no general state retirement system. In 1952 the teachers retirement act was repealed, and legislation enacted that covers state employees, including teachers, under the Federal social security system. A supplemental state retirement system creates additional benefits.* The net effect of Mississippi's new retirement system will be to provide more adequate retirement income to the teachers of the common schools than was possible under the older statute.

Two other aspects of school administration pertaining to Mississippi's teachers require special mention, the first of which is teacher certification. Licensing requirements, effective May 1, 1954, establish seven different types of certificates for elementary and secondary teachers. The teachers are classified by training and experience.† Administration of the program is vested in the Division of Instruction of the State Department of Education. Mississippi's program of teacher certification follows the accepted pattern by stressing training and experience; although it may perhaps operate to lift the professional competence of the teaching profession in the state, the program is not retroactive and will not invalidate any life-time certificate isued prior to May 1, 1954.

The second aspect involves the so-called loyalty oaths that have become common in American education since World War II. Mississippi's teachers, however, are not singled out as a specified category of persons whose

* Provisions of this legislation are summarized in Chapter 10, p. 139.
† Certification requirements are discussed in Chapter 20, pp. 307-8.

loyalty to the state and Federal constitutions may be questioned. The Subversive Activities Act of 1950 has wider application, forbidding the appointment or employment of any "subversive person" by the state, any county, municipality, or other political subdivision.[12] The act further requires each public employee to sign a statement, as a condition of employment, that he is not a subversive person, that is, one "who commits, attempts to commit, or aid in the commission of any act intended to overthrow, destroy, or alter or to assist in the commission of any act intended to overthrow, destroy, or alter the constitutional form of the government of the United States, or of the State of Mississippi. . . ." The employee must also assert that he is not a member of a "subversive organization or a foreign subversive organization," as defined by the law. Each agency of state government establishes rules and regulations providing for notice and hearing on accusations and the discharge of disloyal persons. Penal sentences ranging from five to ten years are established for persons committing subversive acts. Employees who file false statements are subject to the penalties of perjury. To date no public employee has been accused of signing a false statement or of subversive activities, yet the statute is severe and perhaps not as solicitous of the rights of the accused as it might be. Many public employees as well as many teachers in Mississippi inquire why they are more likely to be disloyal to their state and nation than the banker, the butcher, the baker, or candlestick maker.

PUBLIC SCHOOL FINANCE

Sources of School Support

Funds for Mississippi's public schools are derived from local taxes, sale or rent of sixteenth-section lands, tuition, Federal grants, gifts, athletic receipts, and several miscellaneous sources. The largest portion comes from local taxes collected by the counties and municipalities and from state funds that are allocated by legislative appropriation. Purely local sources include an ad valorem tax levied on real estate, personal property, and public utilities, and the poll tax. Separate school districts receive support from all property within the district, while schools in the county system secure funds from the tax on property within the district as well as from the general county property tax levied uniformly on all property within the county.[13] Since 1929, when local funds accounted for 65 per cent of all school support, the ratio of local to state financial support has consistently declined until in 1952 it approximated only 40 per cent.

The ratio of local to state financial support doubtless will change under the Minimum Education Program adopted in 1953 and 1954. Under current statutes the state assures each child this program, which is financed by both the state and local governments, the latter's share being determined upon the ability to pay. Fiscal capacity of a district will be determined by an economic index, incorporated in the statute, which ascertains local economic ability by such measurements as retail sales tax paid, assessed valuation of public utilities, the value of farm products and others. Thus, if a county has 3 per cent of the state's economic capacity as determined by the index, the law requires that it pay 3 per cent of the local cost of the minimum program. Separate districts will bear their proportionate fraction of the county's share, the amount to be determined on the basis of assessed valuation within the district. Under present statutes, the local districts probably will pay somewhat over $11,000,000 from local revenues in each of the school years of the 1954-1956 biennium; they are also expected to expend $10,000,000 for enrichment of the program beyond the minimum level.[14]

State Support

The Mississippi legislature biennially appropriates a large sum for allocation among the public schools. Included in this appropriation are the State Per Capita Fund and the State Equalizing Fund. The former, required by section 206 of the Mississippi constitution, consists of half the appropriation and is distributed to school systems on the basis of the number of educable children living within the jurisdiction of the system. The other half of the appropriation, the State Equalization Fund,* is administered by the State Department of Education and is intended to assist the weaker school districts and counties to meet minimum educational standards. Some sixty odd counties and more than twenty separate districts receive equalizing funds in addition to the per capita distribution that goes to all systems. The legislature makes an occasional, additional appropriation for school use, as in the 1947 special session when it appropriated $5,000,000 more to be expended on schools in 1947 and 1948.

The significance of this state support is readily grasped when one views a few of the recent biennial appropriations for school purposes. For 1942-1944, $15,575,000 was appropriated for the common school fund

* *Mississippi Laws, 1953 Ex. Sess.*, ch. 14, sec. 5, repealed this fund and replaced it with the Minimum Education Program Fund. The law provides that the new fund, together with the State Per Capita Fund, shall equal the state's part of the cost of the Minimum Education Program.

and an additional $2,000,000 for all grade and secondary activities; by the 1946-1948 biennium the total had risen to $29,247,000 of which $28,000,-000 was earmarked for common school support; and in 1952-1954, $52,284,000 was appropriated for the public schools of which $50,000,000 was earmarked for common school support.

Other Funds

Federal-aid funds are granted school units offering special work in agriculture and in such areas as home economics and diversified occupations. The school lunch program in 1950-1952, for example, received support totaling $7,124,520 from sources other than state appropriations, which totaled only $125,000 for this purpose. Additional support comes from funds derived from the sixteenth-section lands, that is, lands set aside by the national government for school purposes. Some districts charge tuition, based on average expenditure per student, for students who live outside the district. Most of the miscellaneous sources, however, furnish negligible income.

Financial Handicaps

A number of major difficulties hamper the adequate financing of the state's public schools. A recent study divided these handicaps into two major classifications, rural and urban. Among the handicaps of the rural schools have been a sparsity of population, which has resulted in either small inefficient schools or high transportation costs, the operation of an excessively large number of school districts, many of them Negro, high educational costs levied frequently against a poor tax base, and poor secondary and feeder roads within the counties. Urban financial problems have arisen from rapid population shifts from rural to urban areas, and also from districts that frequently are too small to provide economically the necessary special services such as guidance, psychological aids, health, attendance, supervision of instruction, and special training.[15]

JUNIOR COLLEGES

The people of Mississippi maintain an extensive system of junior colleges more closely related to secondary than to higher education.* The

* These colleges are as follows: Copiah-Lincoln, East Central, East Mississippi, Hinds, Holmes, Itawamba, Jones, Meridian, Northeast, Northwest, Pearl River, Perkinston, Southwest, Sunflower, and Coahoma.

junior college system has been formed, in fact, to continue the work of agricultural high schools through the sophomore college year, thereby providing a complete educational unit. These colleges derive funds through an annual state distribution, now $800,000 or more, local taxes, and tuition and fees. Their operation is nominally under the Junior College Commission consisting of three junior college presidents, who are selected by their colleagues, the state superintendent of public education, the chancellor of the University of Mississippi, and the presidents of Mississippi State College and Mississippi State College for Women. This commission studies their needs, determines the junior college districts, and fixes the standards the colleges must meet in order to qualify for an allotment from the state appropriation.

A supervisor of junior colleges and agricultural high schools operates from the State Department of Education. This officer serves as a coordinating agent in administering the system of colleges, assists in the development of courses of study, inspects the schools to determine compliance with standards, provides consultative administrative services, acts as executive secretary for the Junior College Accrediting Commission, and assists the presidents of the respective colleges in resolving problems necessary to attainment of the over-all program. This work is done through school visits, individual conferences, and participation in junior college evaluation studies. Most of the junior colleges are members of the Southern Association of Secondary Schools and Colleges, the regional accrediting organization.

None of the junior colleges has a large enrollment. In the 1952-53 sessions, for example, there were 5,282 students in the college departments, ranging from 698 at Jones Junior College to only 120 students at Coahoma Junior College. The agricultural high schools in the junior colleges had an enrollment of 1,993 the same year, and there were also 1,920 special students. Total students served by the system thus exceeded 9,000.[16]

HIGHER EDUCATION

The oldest public institution of higher learning in Mississippi is the University of Mississippi, now in operation for more than a century. In 1878 two land grant colleges were added, Mississippi Agricultural and Mechanical College (now Mississippi State College) and the Alcorn Agricultural and Mechanical College, the latter for Negroes. Six years later Mississippi State College for Women was created and in 1908 Mississippi

Southern College (formerly Mississippi State Normal College) opened at Hattiesburg. Delta State Teachers College began operations at Cleveland, Mississippi, two decades later. Additional senior colleges for Negroes have been founded, the Mississippi Negro Training School (Jackson College) in 1940 and the Mississippi Vocational College in 1946.

Higher education in Mississippi thus centers about one university and four colleges for white students and three public colleges for Negroes, with total enrollment of somewhat more than 11,000 students. Three other educational programs include a scholarship program for Negroes who seek special education, a research program conducted at the Gulf Coast Laboratory, and participation in the work of the Southern Regional Board of Education, whose headquarter offices are at Atlanta, Georgia.

Governing Body

Control of the state university and the colleges is placed in a constitutional body, the Board of Trustees of Institutions of Higher Learning.[17] Before 1912 each legislative act establishing an institution of higher learning provided for a separate board of trustees. In that year, however, a unified board was created to supervise the administration of the University of Mississippi, Mississippi State College, the State College for Women, and the Alcorn Agricultural and Mechanical College. Supervision of Delta State College and the Teachers College at Hattiesburg was added in 1932.

The present constitutional Board of Trustees of Institutions of Higher Learning has thirteen members, all of whom are appointed by the governor by and with the advice and consent of the senate.* Terms of office are long—twelve years—with one third of the board retiring every four years. The LeBauve trustee serves four years.

General administration of board policies is the responsibility of an executive secretary, who is selected by the board and serves at its will. In general this official is charged with maintaining a continuous study of the problems of higher education, studying and surveying the organization and management of each institution governed by the board and reporting on his findings, and making recommendations for improving the operation and economical administration of the university and the colleges.

* Members of the board are appointed as follows: one member from each congressional district, as they existed in 1942, one from each of the three supreme court districts, two from the state-at-large; and one member from DeSoto County. The latter is known as the trustee for the LeBauve Fund and votes only on matters concerning the university.—Constitution of 1890, art. 8, sec. 213A.

The executive secretary is a key officer because through him the Board of Trustees of Institutions of Higher Learning secures the necessary degree of coordination among the colleges of the system. He is a professional educator, and, in practice, his office seems to have developed into a liaison device between the board and the college presidents, the executive secretary representing the board in the administration of the institutions of higher learning and the professional viewpoints of the college presidents and deans in the governing body.

Institutional Administration

The chancellor of the University of Mississippi and the presidents of the remaining public colleges are selected by the board. These executives are usually appointed for four-year terms, the board retaining full authority to terminate their employment at any time for "malfeasance, inefficiency, or contumacious conduct, but never for political reasons."[18] Appointments for positions in the university and colleges are made by the board of trustees on the recommendation of the heads of the institutions.

The various institutions have been allowed a large measure of autonomy in determining their internal organizations. A definite pattern has emerged, however, and each of the colleges shows marked similarity. The university and each of the colleges have been organized somewhat generally along functional lines, the three main bases of organization usually being academic or instruction, student personnel, and finance. Depending on the particular institution, the academic division may be organized into schools and colleges, each headed by a dean; for example, the University of Mississippi has the following schools: liberal arts, medicine, law, pharmacy, education, commerce and business administration, engineering, and the graduate school. The fiscal division, under a comptroller or business manager, carries on the accounting, budgetary execution, purchasing, and other fiscal functions; sometimes the maintenance of buildings and grounds as well as the operation of auxiliary enterprises, such as cafeterias, is vested in this division. Probably the least functional integration is found in the field of student services and welfare, although five of the institutions have organized student personnel units.

Financing Higher Education

Funds for the support of the system of higher learning are derived largely from biennial appropriations and student fees. Other significant sources include Federal aid—now restricted chiefly to the State Extension

Service and the State Agricultural Experiment Station, both located at Mississippi State College—income from sales and services, and receipts from auxiliary enterprises. All sources except legislative appropriations accounted for $18,618,166 in the 1950-1952 biennium or 62 per cent of the total funds available.

The biennial appropriation—for 1952-1954, a total of $15,162,500 for all purposes, of which only $10,300,000 was for general support of the institutions of higher learning—is allocated by the Board of Trustees of Institutions of Higher Learning to the respective institutions on the basis of annual budget requests, the functions performed by each institution, the segregated income of each, enrollment, and legislative intent. Two per cent of the appropriation for support is retained by the board to cover its expenses and contingencies that may arise during the budget period. Substantial portions of the appropriation other than the general support appropriation are earmarked for special purposes, for instance, matching funds for the Agricultural Experiment Station Federal-state program.

Problems of a Unified Program

As recently as 1945, the system of higher education underwent general and thorough review. The report that emerged from this study indicated several causes of educational duplication, suggestive of Mississippi's system, among them the following: (1) unnecessary expansion of individual institutions; (2) unwholesome competition; (3) pressure of local communities to expand specific institutions for selfish local reasons; (4) failure of colleges to recognize purposes for which they were created; (5) failure of the institutions to provide functions of the type for which they are best equipped; and (6) failure of the institutions to recognize the needs of the state and to base their programs upon these needs.[19]

To solve such problems the *Gibson Report* suggested several formal allocations of functions among the public colleges and the university. For example, the study recommended concentration of graduate work and research at the university and at Mississippi State College. Certain types of coordination not requiring allocations were also recommended, and the report maintained that a greater degree of unity could be developed through a series of inter-institutional coordinating committees that would function both as policy forming and recommending bodies.* Without urging the

* Joseph E. Gibson, *et al., Mississippi Study of Higher Education, 1945* (Jackson: Board of Trustees, Institutions of Higher Learning, 1945), pp. 42-43. Among the various inter-institutional committees proposed was a council composed of the presidents of the institutions charged to propose and develop over-all inter-institutional

establishment of a consolidated university, the *Gibson Report* proposed an integrated University of Mississippi as another way to provide a unified program of higher education in the state, a proposal that had been made and disregarded several times in preceding decades. Whether or not the Board of Trustees of Institutions of Higher Learning will be able to resolve successfully the problems of duplication in educational effort and resist the pressure of one or another of the educational institutions remains to be determined by the future.

EQUALIZATION OF EDUCATIONAL OPPORTUNITIES

The Mississippi legislature took a step in the direction of ending discrimination against Negroes in the common school system in 1951 when it provided that, of a $7,000,000 increase in school funds, $6,000,000 should be earmarked for raising the salaries of Negro teachers, for state aid for new facilities and buildings, and for expanding the Negro school transportation system. Further evidence of the movement to terminate educational inequalities was offered by the 1952 legislature, which established the Recess Committee on Education and assigned to it the important task of studying the state's public school system and of submitting recommendations to achieve equalization between the races in instruction and facilities.[20]

Programs and Finance Proposals

The report of the eighteen man study committee recommended considerable reorganization of Mississippi's public school system. At the state level the committee proposed a State Educational Finance Commission of six persons, to be appointed by the governor with senatorial confirmation.[21] This body would disburse all state funds for construction, renovation, or repair of school buildings, approve locations for new schools, and distribute funds for transportation.

On the level of local government the committee would require the county boards of education to submit, by July 1, 1956, plans for the reorganization or consolidation of the present school districts. Satisfactory equalization of facilities between the races is a requirement of these plans,

---

policies, recommend a consolidated budget, and undertake coordinating duties generally. Inter-institutional committees were also proposed for developing policies to coordinate graduate work, a program of general education for social and civic effectiveness, undergraduate work in home economics, teacher education, summer school policies, and general extension activities.

and no school district would be eligible to receive state funds until its plan met the approval of the State Educational Finance Commission. The reorganization of schools generally would be on a county-wide or multi-county basis, but municipal or separate school districts might continue to function. The county superintendent of education, currently an elective officer, would be appointed by the county board of education.

The report proposed a "minimum" educational program for at least an eight-month term each year and also a minimum salary schedule. A somewhat complex financial arrangement was recommended, but the report indicated that the state would finance the minimum program on an equalizing basis. An annual state grant of $12 per student in average daily attendance would be made to finance the cost of construction and improvement of buildings under the reorganization and equalization programs.

The study committee estimated that the additional cost above the current level of common school appropriations would be $6,000,000 to $8,000,000 annually, and as much as $150,000,000 would be necessary to put facilities on a par for the two races. New plant and school construction would be a long range objective with immediate financial outlays for this purpose ranging upward from $5,00,000 annually.

To cover these financial increases, the recess committee originally made four specific proposals: (1) to increase the tax on incomes of $25,000 or more from 6 to 7 per cent; (2) to raise the sales tax from 2 to 3 per cent; (3) to raise the cigarette tax from four to five cents per package; and (4) to increase the oil and gas severance tax from six cents a barrel or 6 per cent of value, whichever is higher, to eight cents a barrel or 8 per cent of value. The committee estimated these changes would increase the annual yield from these sources by approximately $20,000,000. Shortly after presentation of these proposals, the increase of the income tax was withdrawn when the Governor expressed concern over all the proposed tax raises except that of the sales tax.

The 1953 Legislation

Governor Hugh L. White called the Mississippi legislature into extraordinary session November 3, 1953, to consider the legislative proposals made by the Recess Education Committee. The special session came at a time when the so-called segregation cases, involving continuance of the famous "separate but equal" rule for whites and Negroes[22] in the southern states, were being argued before the Supreme Court of the United States. It was inevitable that repercussions of this great national debate would be felt in Mississippi's special legislative session.

The 1953 legislature endorsed substantial portions of the recommendations of the Recess Education Committee by enacting a score or more measures that contained the enabling features of the equalization program. In this effort to realize the intent of section 207 of the Constitution of 1890 for separate and equal facilities for the two races, the legislature clearly sought equivalent educational opportunities for all children in such matters as improved school organization and administration, teachers' salaries, transportation, and buildings and equipment. The legislature also created the important State Educational Finance Commission, the statute providing for six members to be appointed by the governor for staggered terms of six years.[23]

This new commission is charged to receive and review plans for the consolidation or reorganization of Mississippi's school districts. Although present school units may continue to function as now constituted until July 1, 1957, after that date they must submit a plan of organization or reorganization that must be approved by the State Educational Finance Commission in order to qualify for state aid. This feature of the new school legislation accords with the proposals of the Recess Education Committee, even though the effective date of school reorganization and presumably reduction in the number of school units is postponed a year. Administration of transportation facilities remains with the State Department of Education.

The legislature also enacted, with some revisions, the minimum state-level equalization proposals, under which the state will assist in financing an eight-month term. During this term common school teachers will receive guaranteed salaries. If a school district adopts a nine-month term, local funds may be used to compensate teachers for the ninth month; otherwise instructors may be required to teach the extra month without additional salaries, if they have been offered and have accepted contracts from the school board.

State funds to supplement salaries of both white teachers and Negro teachers will be determined by the type of certificate held and the number of years taught—up to five years—by the individual instructor. The salary schedule thus attached to educational attainment specifies $2,200 annually for teachers with a master's degree and $2,000 annually for those who have received a bachelor's degree. Other salaries range downward from $1,600 annually for teachers who have completed three years of college work, to $700 for instructors who are only high school graduates.

An annual increment of $80 is provided for five years to teachers holding the two highest certifications. State aid also is offered for supplementing salaries of superintendents and principals, providing for the county superintendent's office, and for operating and maintaining the school plant.

As 1954 began, there was no assurance that the 1953 legislation authorizing educational opportunities would reach maturity, if only for the reason that financing the program was deferred until the regular session of the legislature. The costs of the Minimum Foundation Program are estimated at $46,000,000 annually, of which $10,000,000 will be supplied from local sources. Increased state revenues of $17,000,000 would be necessary to finance the program annually, including $6,000,000 for capital outlay.

These financial requirements caused the 1954 legislature to take action financing the equalization program only after four months of debate and even then on a trial basis of one year. The governor and legislators, in reaching this compromise decision, agreed to schedule a special session in the second year (1955-1956) of the school biennium to appropriate additional funds for the program as well as to legislate any necessary adjustments in the plan. The appropriation of $34,000,000 made for the trial year, together with required and authorized local support, will finance all phases of the program adopted at the 1953 special session except systematic financial support for school buildings.

Despite the intensity of opinions held on the traditional southern issue of segregation, the accomplishments of the 1953 extraordinary session were impressive. Certainly many of the recommendations of the Recess Education Committee embodied distinct educational improvements. Surely the action taken by the Mississippi legislature thus far in implementing these proposals reflects the emphasis upon education that has resulted in allocating to that activity the highest ratio of state expenditures. No doubt it has been an unfortunate historical development that "separate but equal" facilities for the two races has everywhere too often meant "separate and unequal" facilities. This heritage of a state and of a region, long impoverished by a destructive civil strife and populated with a large and poor racial minority, cannot obscure the real, if basically initial, steps that Mississippi has taken to give all children the best the state can afford in educating them for future citizenship.*

* In cases involving four states, *Brown* v *Board of Education* (Kansas), *Briggs* v *Elliott* (South Carolina), *Davis* v *County School Board* (Virginia), and *Gebhart* v *Belton* (Delaware), the United States Supreme Court on May 17, 1954, rendered an opinion holding segregation of races in the public schools of the states to be violative of the equal protection of the laws clause of the Fourteenth Amendment.—*New York Times,* May 18, 1954.

FOOTNOTES

[1] Art. 8, sec. 203.

[2] See, for example, *Mississippi Code, 1942,* secs. 6564-6575, *passim,* 6234-6241.

[3] Art. 8, sec. 202; see also Constitution of 1869, art. 8, sec. 3.

[4] For a full listing of the state superintendent's duties and responsibilities, see *Mississippi Laws, 1946,* ch. 297, sec. 7.

[5] *Report on a Survey of the Organization and Administration of State and County Government in Mississippi* (Jackson: Research Commission of the State of Mississippi, 1932), pp. 492-93.

[6] Compare *Report of the Joint Legislative Education Committee on the Public School System of the State* (Jackson, February 12, 1946) with *Mississippi Laws, 1946,* ch. 297.

[7] *Mississippi Laws, 1930,* ch. 278.

[8] State Department of Education, *Statistical Data 1952-1953,* Bulletin SD-53 (Jackson, 1952), p. 20.

[9] Constitution of 1890, art. 8, sec. 204; see also, Constitution of 1869, art. 8, sec. 4.

[10] *Mississippi Laws, 1953 Ex. Sess.,* ch. 10.

[11] The Recess Education Committee, *A Report to the Mississippi State Legislature* (Jackson, March, 1953), p. 16.

[12] *Mississippi Laws, 1950,* ch. 451, sec. 2.

[13] William P. McLure, *Let Us Pay for the Kind of Education We Need* (Bureau of Educational Research, University of Mississippi, 1948), p. 30.

[14] Summarized from John E. Phay, "A New Foundation for Mississippi Schools," *Public Administration Survey,* I (May, 1954). Compare with *Mississippi Laws, 1953 Ex. Sess.,* ch. 14; *1954,* House Bill 46.

[15] McLure, *op. cit.,* pp. 35-39.

[16] *Biennial Report of the State Superintendent of Education 1950-1951 and 1952-1953* (Jackson, 1953), p. 29.

[17] Constitution of 1890, art. 8, sec. 213 A. The amendment to the constitution went into effect in 1944.

[18] Constitution of 1890, art. 8, sec. 213 A.

[19] Joseph E. Gibson, *et. al., Mississippi Study of Higher Education, 1945* (Jackson: Board of Trustees, Institutions of Higher Learning, 1945), pp. 32-33.

[20] *Mississippi Laws, 1952,* ch. 453.

[21] This summary of proposals is taken from the Recess Committee on Education, *Digest of Legislative Proposals of the Recess Committee on Education* (Jackson, 1953), and from a memorandum prepared by David McKinney, Assistant Director, Bureau of Business Research, University of Mississippi.

[22] *Plessy* v *Ferguson,* 163 U. S. 537 (1896).

[23] This summary of legislation is made from *Mississippi Laws, 1953 Ex. Sess.,* House Bills: 2, 3, 6, 8, 9, 10, 11, 12, 13, 15, 16, 18, 19, 20, 21; Senate Bills: 1201, 1204, 1205, 1207, 1218, 1225.

CHAPTER 14

Public Health

IN 1877, nine years after the first state health agency had been established in Massachusetts, the Mississippi State Board of Health was created.[1] However, not until 1880 were funds appropriated for its support. Public health in the state even then had been long an object of control and regulation in the public interest. As far back as 1799 territorial legislation sought to deny admission into the territory of "infamous characters" who might bring with them the dreaded smallpox or other contagious diseases. Similar legislation was enacted again in 1805 and in 1807. The sale of foodstuffs came under legislative regulation in 1822, and two decades later a depot for smallpox vaccine was established in Jackson.[2]

Public health control developed simultaneously on the local level of government. The city of Natchez established a health department in 1818 after undergoing a severe yellow fever epidemic. In the years that followed, the counties and municipalities of the state received legislative consent to adopt a wide variety of health legislation. Finally, the boards of supervisors of three counties—Hancock, Harrison, and Jackson—in 1876 were authorized to appoint five physicians to act as the first local boards of health.[3] Two years before this action had been taken the president of the State Medical Association had strongly urged the establishment of state and municipal boards of health and passage of suitable registration laws.

Little was done, though, in the last years of the Reconstruction government. Early in 1877 the medical association by resolution decided to petition the legislature for passage of legislation to create a "State Board of Health," and on February 1, 1877, such an agency was established formally and charged to make inquiries into the causes of diseases, to investigate the sources of mortality, and to examine the effects of localities, employment, and other conditions upon the public health. From this beginning the State Board of Health has developed by a series of legislative acts and by positive leadership into a strong and effectively functioning public agency that enjoys both professional acceptance and widespread popular support.

STATE BOARD OF HEALTH

All physicians in Mississippi are designated members of the State Health Department, but the determination of public health policies rests with a smaller group, the State Board of Health. This body originally was composed of fifteen members appointed for staggered terms of office, twelve being selected by the governor. From 1892 until 1925 a full board was appointed by each governor when he entered office, but under this system political influences frequently retarded or disrupted the board's program.

Early in 1924 Governor Henry L. Whitfield approved the law under which the State Board of Health now operates.[4] The agency as thus revised consists of ten members. Of these, eight are physicians appointed by the governor from congressional districts and from a list recommended by the State Medical Association, one is a dentist appointed by the governor from candidates proposed by the State Dental Association, and these nine members in turn select the tenth member, who becomes the secretary and executive officer of the board. Terms of office are fixed at six years and are so arranged that those of three members expire every two years. Three members, selected by the full board, serve as an executive committee. Except for the executive officer, compensation is a nominal per diem payment.

The powers of the Board of Health are extensive. Among others, they include authority to make rules and regulations concerning public health for enforcement by the local health agencies, to appoint county health officers, to impose quarantine restrictions, to grant medical licenses, to gather vital statistics, and to study the control of epidemic diseases.

The executive officer of the Board of Health is secretary of the board and executes the policies that have been formulated by it. Like all other members he serves six years. His salary by statute cannot exceed $8,500 annually. The executive officer must meet the qualifications of a physician who is trained in bacteriology, hygiene, and sanitary science. He may be removed from office by a majority vote of the Board of Health.[5]

Departmental Organization

The State Department of Public Health, under the direction of the State Board of Health and including all the physicians of the state, now consists of ten divisions: laboratories, vital statistics, sanitary engineering, preventable disease control, the state sanatorium, maternal and child welfare, health education, county health work, industrial hygiene and factory inspection, and administration and library. Over-all administrative control is exercised by the executive officer of the board, and each division is headed by a director. The state sanatorium is concerned chiefly with the institutional operation of the tuberculosis hospital. Medical licensure is handled directly by the board rather than the central health department.

The allocation of major purposes or functions among the ten work units for two decades has appeared to make for an effective and an efficient program of public health. Observers have commented frequently on the coordination of the various services provided by the separate divisions, and the general respect that the health organization has engendered has sufficed to protect it in large measure from the political pressures and influences often exerted on less respected administrative activities of the state government.*

PUBLIC HEALTH ACTIVITIES

Local Health Work

Local health work in Mississippi has emphasized the development and operation of full-time county health units. The work is mainly the responsibility of the Division of County Health Work, though initiative in establishing county units rests with the locality.

Since 1920 counties have possessed authority to create and to maintain county health departments, and two or more counties have had legislative consent since 1926 to consolidate their health work in a sanitary district or district health department.[6] By 1950 forty-four counties were supporting county departments; thirteen local health units represented the joint

* In this connection the *Brookings Report* recommendation, prepared by officials of the United States Public Health Service, stated simply "that the present plan of organization of the State Board of Health should be continued without change."—*Report on a Survey of the Organization and Administration of State and County Government in Mississippi* (Jackson, 1932), p. 554.

efforts of twenty-six counties. An additional seven counties were embraced in the Southeastern Health District and the Tri-County District Health Department.* Only five counties had not provided local financial support for health departments, and these were being supplied essential health services by the State Board of Health in such basic fields as preventable disease control and sanitation.

The county health departments are the result of local action. Still the county health officer in each is appointed by the State Board of Health for a term of not more than four years, the selection merely being certified to the county board of supervisors for which it is made.[7] This health director must be a competent physician. He is charged with enforcing all of the county or health district rules and regulations, investigating health problems, and recommending the measures necessary to maintain the public health. He functions expressly "under the supervision and direction of the State Board of Health" and must report to it in the manner specified by the board.[8] The state agency is empowered to remove any county health officer for any conduct that it deems improper, for neglect of duties, or for any other offense that it judges to be detrimental to the public welfare.

Immediate execution of the local programs rests with the county health departments, no municipal health units being authorized. The governing bodies of the cities, towns, and villages of the state may, and do, appropriate moneys from their general funds, though, for the support of county or district units.[9] Supervision of the health programs of the various phases of health work is the function of the Division of County Health Work. This division acts as a liaison between the local units and the state department. It supervises the services required by the state, approves budgets for the local units, and provides assistance in securing buildings and equipment. It also participates in the extension of both Federal and state financial assistance, the state grants being designed largely to equalize the differences in the ability of counties to support programs.

Thirty years ago the main programs dealt with environmental sanitation, hookworm, and typhoid fever control. Later control efforts centered on tuberculosis, diphtheria, malaria, and venereal disease, though preventive services also were extended to expectant mothers, infants, and children. Major problems now include the high death rates in heart disease, determination of the cause of maternal and child deaths, and malnutrition. All of these programs, old and new, are considered basic. They are carried on by a minimum staff, in addition to the county health officer, of at least

* George, Greene, Perry, and Stone and Jefferson Davis, Covington, and Lawrence counties.

one full-time public health nurse, a sanitation supervisor, and a clerk. Other types of staff members employed in the several local departments include health educators, venereal disease investigators, laboratory technicians, veterinarians, and sanitation engineers. A field technical staff of medical, nursing, sanitation, and clerical personnel is maintained by the Division of County Health Work to aid the counties by making individual visits to them. Coordination of health programs in the counties is accomplished by this technical unit through individual conferences, group meetings, staff conferences, district meetings, and evaluation schedules.*

Communicable and Preventable Disease Control

Communicable disease control consists of combating diseases that are of special interest because of their ability to spread from one person to another or from animals and insects to human beings. Fifty such diseases are the object of attack by the Division of Preventable Diseases. In spite of reduction in the occurrence of many of these illnesses, notably diphtheria, typhoid fever, malaria, and smallpox, the State Board of Health estimates that the group still causes annually 3,000,000 man days of sickness in Mississippi. The responsibilities of the Division of Preventable Diseases include gathering and analyzing data related to the frequency and place of occurrence of illness, short-term and long-term planning for control, initiation of state-wide control programs, and facilitation of known control procedures. With the limited funds available for this work, the division has put emphasis upon selected diseases, whose control has the greatest yield in terms of public health.

Some of the special programs in communicable disease control merit brief indication. Thus a full-time liaison officer has been employed since 1948 to provide essential communication between private physicians, hospitals, and the central health department. An active tuberculosis control program has been carried on for many years, utilizing now mass X rays; and since 1946 a cancer control unit has been operating to supplement the efforts of the Mississippi Division of the American Cancer Society. Control of acute communicable diseases is evidenced by the low level of diphtheria, typhoid fever, and smallpox, which group reached their lowest level in the history of Mississippi in 1948. Malaria control has declined perceptibly in recent years, so that "it may be safely predicted that it will be reduced to only an occasional case in the next few years."[10]

* Orientation and training of personnel is an additional function of the staff. In 1947-1949 thirty health officers received their training, and fifty sanitarians were afforded field and class work.

A venereal disease control program is also carried on by this division. Reports of the division indicate that syphilis has declined by half since 1942. The state program utilizes the county health departments as case finding and informational centers and provides two rapid treatment centers for diagnostic and treatment services and for patient education. The tuberculosis control program employs bus-type X-ray units for both mass and special and selected groups, and a central register for tuberculosis cases now is in operation. Finally, there has been a transformation of control effort, necessarily partial, in the direction of mass education, since prevention and treatment knowledge is effective only if the general public is informed of it.

Vital Statistics

The general purpose of keeping vital statistics is to make and maintain on a systematic basis a record of important events, for instance births, deaths, marriages, divorces. Two corollary purposes are first, the preparation of statistical information to guide health officials, and second, retention of the original records for the persons affected by them. Since 1912 over four million vital records have been collected, half or more of them for births that have occurred within the state.* The collection of marriage records was authorized in 1926. In addition records are maintained of deaths resulting from the various communicable diseases, of infant and maternal mortality, and of stillbirths. The State Board of Health estimates that more than 96 per cent of births and deaths are recorded with its Division of Vital Statistics.

The collection of vital records demands working relations with physicians, funeral establishments, county health departments, and other public officials. The county registrar of births and deaths returns all birth certificates to the central State Health Department. Death certificates also are filed as permanent records. Each circuit court clerk is required to return monthly copies of marriage records for his county, and the chancery court clerk must file similarly records of divorces at the conclusion of every court term. Despite the difficulty of obtaining accurate records, which arises largely from the residence of the greatest part of Mississippi's people in rural areas, efforts to gain highest registration are essential if the data based on them are to be reliable guides to program planning.

* A vital statistics unit first was organized in 1878, but was discarded in 1880. The current Division of Vital Statistics was established November 1, 1912.

State Hygienic Laboratory

The State Hygienic Laboratory, established in 1910, was the first special division of the State Health Department. It provides tests for diagnosis and control of communicable diseases and functions chiefly as a service agency for other divisions of the State Health Department, though diagnoses and tests are afforded private practitioners. Additional services comprise examination of public water supplies (including stream pollution) and milk supplies to determine their fitness for human consumption, the manufacture and distribution of a few biological supplies, such as typhoid vaccine, and clinical advisory services. It renders also cooperative services to the Division of Sanitary Engineering by providing sterile containers for water and milk samples. An advisory for in-service or on-the-job training of local technicians is maintained by the laboratory, which employs a limited number of advisory and relief technicians to aid local clinic and hospital laboratories.

Sanitary Engineering

The sanitary engineering activities, administered by the Division of Sanitary Engineering, must be regarded everywhere as a fundamental aspect of public health work. They constitute primarily technical services rendered local officials and proprietary enterprises. Sanitation activities emphasize now eight activities: promotional and consulting work with communities regarding water supplies and sewerage, shellfish sanitation, milk control, development of sanitation standards for school lunchrooms, malaria control, typhus control, pest control, and inspection of frozen food locker plants. The division has encouraged also the enlarged use of the sanitary land fill as an improved method of garbage disposal.[11]

Plans for construction of water supply plants require state approval, and their operation is subject to periodic inspection and laboratory analyses. Similarly plans for sewerage systems must meet state approval and are subject to supervision. The policy of the division also requires the installation of properly constructed individual sewage disposal systems. Thus, plans and specifications are supplied prospective builders and home owners, and visits are made to property sites to furnish information concerning these systems. The Division of Sanitary Engineering functions as the approving agency for sanitary facilities in homes financed by the Federal Housing Administration where there is no organized municipal water supply or sewerage system available. The division acts in the same relationship to the Federal Housing Administration for all community water supplies and sewerage systems and establishes procedures to ensure the proper operation and maintenance of the systems as homes are sold.

The shellfish sanitation program was put into effect as a result of a damaging hurricane that swept the Gulf Coast in 1947, damaging most oyster plants and covering oyster beds with sand. To secure endorsement of the United States Public Health Service, the state conducted surveys to determine the areas unfit for growing shellfish, and the legislature passed measures to prevent oyster fishing in these areas.[12] A control program was put into operation, the State Sea Food Commission providing patrols and the Division of Sanitary Engineering supplying inspections.

Since 1927 milk control has been emphasized. This activity was expanded in 1947 when the State Board of Health took over the inspection services in southwest Mississippi that had been carried on previously by the Louisiana Department of Public Health because many Louisiana dairies purchased milk from this area. In general, the milk control program aims at a wider distribution of grade A pasteurized milk and milk products and a higher standard of operation and maintenance both in the processing plants and on the producing farms.

Additional sanitary engineering responsibilities include supervision of the construction and operation of places of public recreation so far as health matters are involved and the inspection of barber shops, hotels, and food producing and dispensing shops.

Maternal and Child Health

The operations of the maternal and child health program are directed toward training physicians and nurses in the specialized care of mothers and children, assisting the general public to an understanding of their problems, and cooperating with local communities in furnishing the necessary services. This work is the immediate responsibility of the Division of Maternal Child Health.

Services of the division cover a wide range of activities. They include among others a consultation service in obstetrics and pediatrics to both county health departments and private physicians, postgraduate meetings, provision of incubators and other equipment, and consulting medical and nursing services to the local health units. These services are supplemented by an essentially educational program that employs radio broadcasts, publications, seminars, schools for parents, and medical and nursing conferences to instruct mothers in the better care of infants and children, to detect early physical defects, and to promote mental health among children.[13]

The child guidance clinics provide psychiatric services. The state has been divided into three districts for this purpose, and permanent clinics are located now at Jackson, Greenwood, and Hattiesburg. Any child between the ages of three and eighteen is eligible for the service without charge,* and the clinics provide treatment of emotionally disturbed children and their parents. The clinics sponsor conferences of public health employees, prenatal and well-being clinics, and therapeutic interviews with social agencies, schools, and local health departments, as well as other devices.

Health Education

A Division of Health Education is now an integral part of the State Department of Health, though the health education function had been assumed a generation ago. By definition health education seeks to supply information concerning health matters to the people of the state so that they may participate in the development of action programs. It is founded, thus, on the premise that public health, medical, and allied services are effective in the degree that they are understood and employed by the public.

One aspect of the program is the school health service, which was inaugurated in 1942. It is administered jointly by the State Board of Health and the State Department of Education, these agencies sharing its responsibilities, and has as its major purposes the coordination of health and educational programs at both state and local levels of government, improvement of the health of school-age children, and development of an over-all school health program. The work program is executed through teacher training in school health and health education, advice provided health and educational employees at the different levels concerning the program, medical correction of physical defects in children, school nursing and sanitation services, nutrition education and training programs, and improvement of the recreational programs of schools and communities through organized physical education activities.[14]

The expansion of educational activities increased the demands made for public health nursing, although the available personnel has not been equal to the requirements for service. In-service staff education, typical in most state health departments, is provided through training centers in selected

* Although mentally retarded and psychotic children are not accepted for treatment, this type of child is seen frequently by the clinic staffs and his parents receive a diagnostic and interpretative report of his behavior.

county departments, advisory nurses, school health institutes, district conferences, and special institutes.

A significant development has been the joint planning of educational activities not only with other divisions of the State Health Department, but also with voluntary health agencies, such as the State Tuberculosis Association. Among the devices employed to effectuate the work programs thus decided upon are press releases, bulletins and pamphlets, and lectures. As in other state activities, the radio is a medium for reaching still larger audiences.

Industrial Hygiene

Factory inspection was made a responsibility of the State Board of Health in 1929, and its program was expanded then to include industrial hygiene.* In the discharge of its task to promote industrial safety and the good health of workers, the industrial hygiene program takes three forms.

First are engineering services, which include routine inspections required by the state factory inspection law, request and specific engineering services, and special surveys or studies. In making the inspections required by law inspectors focus attention on such matters as ventilation, noise abatement, safe and adequate sanitation, water supplies, sewage disposal, and heat and humidity factors. Specific recommendations are made to the individual establishments.†

Second, a nursing consultant works with establishments in promoting plant nursing programs and in employment of qualified persons as industrial nurses. Since most Mississippi industrial plants employ less than 200 workers, comparatively few nursing programs are found, and much of the consultation work is done with first aid attendants. Nevertheless, a substantial number of industries recently have inaugurated nursing programs that emphasize preventive as well as curative care.

Third, a chemical laboratory operated by the State Board of Health provides service to industry. Analyses and studies are made of gases, vapors, mists, and other substances actually or potentially dangerous.

* Administered by the Division of Industrial Hygiene and Factory Inspection.

† During a recent biennium, for example, 2,114 plant visits were made, of which 2,016 were self-initiated by the Division of Industrial Hygiene and Factory Inspection. These visits covered 359 plants and concerned 43,322 workers. Of the total number of times service was rendered, 767 constituted routine factory inspection. Out of 541 recommendations for improvement of the working environment, only 60 were carried out. A higher percentage was recorded for recommendations to improve health and welfare, some 21 of 49 improvements being accepted.—State Board of Health, *Thirty-sixth Biennial Report,* pp. 174-75.

Among the labor laws whose enforcement is vested with the health agency are those that require inspections thrice yearly in establishments where women and children are employed, a maximum hours regulation, a twice monthly pay day, and safety and sanitation inspection of factories employing women.[15] Every plant employing five or more persons is required by statute to pay a registration fee, the funds thus obtained defraying some of the costs of the industrial hygiene program.*

HOSPITAL PROGRAM

The hospital program in Mississippi embraces three related aspects: hospital licensing, allocation of funds to hospitals for charity patients, and hospital planning and construction.

Licensing

Although practitioners and nurses everywhere are required to meet certain qualifications and to be licensed by the state, throughout the nation only minimum requirements have been imposed generally for the organizations or agencies that render hospital service. Nevertheless, many states have enacted measures requiring inspection and licensing of one or more phases of hospital care, as for example, care of mental patients, maternal care, or institutional care of the aged. As late as 1946 Mississippi was one of eight states that had established no hospital licensure.† In that year the legislature made the State Board of Health responsible for inspection of hospitals that receive public moneys for the care of charity patients. These totaled about half of the 121 institutions. Two years later the Mississippi Commission on Hospital Care was designated to inspect, regulate, and license most hospitals.‡ The power thus granted extends alike to private and public hospitals, whether or not operated for profit. A license fee of ten dollars is charged, and hearings and a review of administrative action are provided for the denial or revocation of licenses. An Advisory Hospital Council of nine members has been established by statute

* In 1952, however, only 170 plants of the 1,610 establishments employing eight or more persons were paying this fee. Thus, only 15,000 of the 83,969 industrial employees in the state in that year were covered.

† The others were Arizona, Arkansas, Florida, Georgia, Kentucky, New Mexico, and South Carolina.

‡ *Mississippi Laws, 1948,* ch. 398, sec. 1. Establishments excepted from this legislation were convalescent or boarding homes, children's homes, homes for the aged, and offices or clinics where patients are not kept.

to advise the commission on licensing policy and in the development of rules and regulations.

Distribution of Charity Funds

The State Hospital Commission was founded in 1936* and directed to establish uniform charges for the care, treatment, and hospitalization of charity patients, to stipulate minimum requirements for their care, and to inspect hospitals that receive charity funds. In addition it was to impose standards of efficiency for the five state charity hospitals, which are located at Jackson, Laurel, Meridian, Natchez, and Vicksburg.

Hospital Planning and Construction

The Hill-Burton Act passed the national Congress in 1946. A hospital construction measure, it appropriated $3,000,000 for the survey of hospital needs in the several states and $75,000,000 for construction of both governmental and nongovernmental hospitals annually for a five-year period. It provided also that funds would be made available to the states on a matching basis for three purposes, namely, the expansion, replacement, or remodeling of hospital facilities. Grants would be made, however, only when state-wide surveys indicated that any proposed facility would be part of a carefully prepared plan for the entire state.[16]

The 1946 legislature promptly created the Mississippi Commission on Hospital Care.[17] This agency is composed of seven members, three appointed by the governor from the state-at-large, and one from each of the three supreme court districts. The executive officer of the State Board of Health is an ex officio member. The appointive members serve for staggered terms of six years, and the commission selects its executive director, who is entrusted with execution of its policies.

In pursuance of the Hill-Burton Act, the state legislation designated the Commission on Hospital Care to formulate a complete plan for hospital construction that would ensure care of all citizens of the state on its completion. The agency was authorized to receive and administer funds that might become available for construction of hospitals or related facilities from the Federal government or from any other source. It also was made

* The creating statute made members of the following: the governor and four members appointed by him, one from each supreme court district and one from the state at large. Term of office was fixed at four years.—*Mississippi Laws, 1936,* ch. 118. The writers have been unable to locate any published report of this commission, and its duties now seem to have fallen on the Mississippi Commission on Hospital Care.

responsible for establishment of an integrated nurses' education program, for assisting in the development of a prepayment plan of hospital insurance, and for disposition of the five charity hospitals owned by the state. Finally, provision was made for administration of grants-in-aid to hospitals, nurses' homes, health clinics, and related establishments when these are either publicly owned or are nonprofit institutions that return no earnings to private shareholders.[18] A decision of the Mississippi Supreme Court in 1950 held that this provision did not exclude hospitals owned and operated by religious orders from receiving grants.

Shortly after its creation the commission began preparation of a state-wide hospital plan. This plan, preceded by the required study, was approved officially by the Federal government July 1, 1947, the first plan to receive national endorsement.[19] The survey of hospital needs showed that the 121 hospitals were clustered in only sixty-two of the state's counties, and that the remainder were entirely without hospital facilities. Of the 4,807 beds, 1,545 required replacement with modern equipment. The accepted minimum standard for hospital care is four and a half beds per 1,000 persons, and, since Mississippi's hospitals provided somewhat less than two beds for each 1,000 population, the survey concluded that the state was 50 per cent below the minimum accepted standard of hospital services.

The state plan proposed construction of facilities for more than 3,800 new hospital beds for general hospital services in addition to 474 beds for special use and twenty-seven buildings for county health departments. Effectuation of this program would reach an estimated cost of $26,000,000, which would be shared almost equally by the Federal, state, and local governments. By 1950 more than fifty hospitals and thirty health centers had been approved as projects, and grants had been made for them.

The hospital construction program cannot be viewed merely as a Federal-state program. It depends largely for its ultimate success upon a plan for community hospital services, locally owned and operated. A five-man board of trustees for municipal hospitals and a five- to seven-man board for county hospitals may be established locally and granted the power to maintain and operate the hospitals, regulate them, fix their schedule of charges, staff them, and provide financial support. Federal and state aid now appear to stimulate chiefly the construction of facilities that will adhere to an organized pattern or system for hospital care.*

The state hospital plan envisages seventeen regional hospitals, scattered

* Under controlling legislation the state may contribute up to 60 per cent of the construction costs after the Federal subvention is deducted.

throughout Mississippi. The community establishments will be clustered about and both serve and be served by them. Each regional hospital will have 100 or more beds, and together with nearby community hospitals serve an average of 100,000 persons.

Although Mississippi's hospital construction program, like similar programs in many states, rests essentially upon initial Federal legislation, it is not simply a national program. Extensive financial support has been given the program by the state legislature and by numerous Mississippi communities. Its base, therefore, rests upon a sound integration of governmental activities at all levels. An integration of this sort holds particular importance for Mississippi, whose per capita income has risen but is yet among the lowest in the nation.

The hospital survey, construction, and service program has resulted from something more than concerted governmental action, however. Evaluation of the joint efforts of community leaders and citizens in a program of local and state improvement is difficult to make, but especially important has been the attitude of localities and their leadership in mobilizing support to provide laboratories, housing, and the other facilities necessary to attract doctors and medical personnel into the rural areas. The hospital program has benefited from the favorable reception by the press as well as from the knowledge and experience that business, professional, hospital, and academic groups have contributed, but even more has it been helped by the public response. The state has provided more than 300 medical education scholarships in recent years, and the recipients of this assistance are now returning under their obligation to practice within Mississippi.[20] The number increases with each graduation. Foundations have provided funds to sponsor training programs so that many areas have medical services not hitherto provided them. The cooperative work of governmental official and private citizen has wakened a very real community consciousness, and the results now are being measured in improved hospital care and health programs.

FOOTNOTES

[1] *Mississippi Laws, 1877,* ch. 40.
[2] *Mississippi Code, 1823,* ch. 54; *Mississippi Laws, 1846,* ch. 33.
[3] *Mississippi Laws, 1876,* ch. 62.
[4] *Mississippi Laws, 1924,* ch. 313.
[5] *Ibid., 1948,* ch. 395.
[6] *Mississippi Code, 1942,* Recompiled volume 5A (1952), sec. 7082.
[7] *Ibid.,* secs. 7033, 7082, 7084.
[8] *Ibid.,* sec. 7084.

[9] *Ibid.,* sec. 7082.

[10] State Board of Health, *Thirty-sixth Biennial Report* (Jackson, 1949), p. 186.

[11] State Board of Health, *Thirty-sixth Biennial Report,* pp. 153-67.

[12] *Mississippi Code,* Recompiled volume 5 (1952), sec. 6072.

[13] For a full description of activities see the biennial reports of the State Board of Health for 1947-1949 and 1945-1947, "Maternal and Child Health." See also report for the 1949-1951 biennium, *passim.*

[14] State Board of Health, *Thirty-sixth Biennial Report,* pp. 233-40.

[15] *Mississippi Code, 1942,* Recompiled volume 5A (1952), secs. 6986, 6993, 6994.

[16] *Public Law* 725 (1946).

[17] *Mississippi Laws, 1946,* ch. 363, amended by *ibid., 1948,* ch. 433.

[18] *Mississippi Laws, 1946,* ch. 363, as amended by *ibid., 1948,* ch. 433.

[19] *Biennial Report of the Commission on Hospital Care 1948-1950* (Jackson, 1950).

[20] *Mississippi Laws, 1946,* ch. 436. The scholarship program is administered by the State Medical Education Board.

CHAPTER 15

Public Welfare

THE SECOND QUARTER of the twentieth century has brought vastly increased activities by American states in the field of public welfare. Acting under the impetus of national grants, the states have inaugurated or broadened services in this field until such services have come to be one of the major functions of government. As used in the modern sense, the term "public welfare" means the program of public care and service for particular groups of the state's population, such as the physically and mentally handicapped, indigent old people, unemployed persons, veterans, underprivileged and delinquent children, and certain others. A part of the program of public welfare is the system of social security, or the activities of the state designed to secure the people against hardships that may befall them in the future. The whole program will be treated here.

Prior to the economic depression beginning in 1929 public aid for unfortunates in Mississippi was confined chiefly to certain institutions maintained by the state and such programs as were maintained and paid for by counties and municipalities. As the depression deepened, the task assumed gigantic proportions and the national government came to the aid of local governments, through the state, in 1933. This temporary program was superseded by the national Social Security Act of 1935, which furnished the incentive for the establishment in 1936 of a State Department of Public Welfare and a program for financial support to aged citizens. In 1938 this program was extended to include aid for the blind and child welfare, and in 1940 dependent children were included. Thus, in the space of twenty years the task of welfare has passed almost completely from local governments to a state-Federal organization. At the same time is has broadened from very limited aid to a very few persons to a program of aid and services to almost 100,000 people.

DEPARTMENT OF PUBLIC WELFARE

The principal organization for the administration of welfare in Mississippi is the Department of Public Welfare. The department is under the direction of the State Board of Public Welfare, which consists of three members appointed by the governor and confirmed by the senate, one from each of

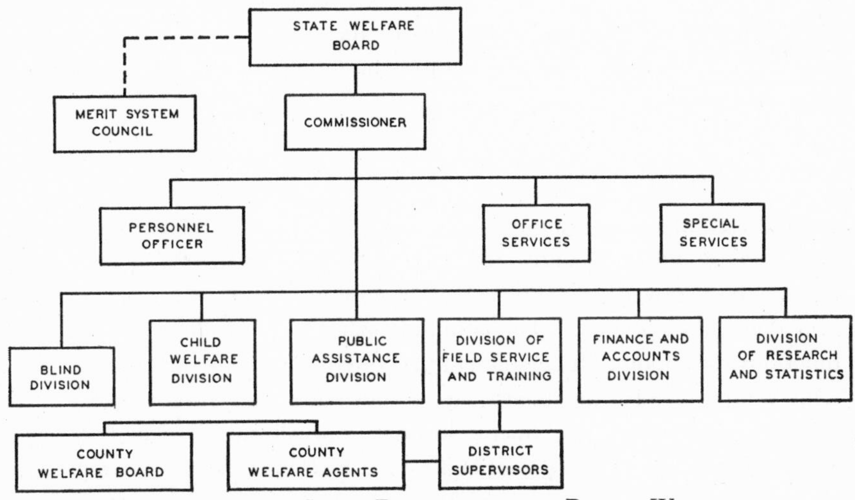

ORGANIZATION OF STATE DEPARTMENT OF PUBLIC WELFARE

the three supreme court districts. Members of the board serve for four years with no overlapping of terms.[1] One of the members is designated by the governor as chairman. Each person on the board receives per diem compensation of $10 and traveling and living expenses while engaged in official duties. The duties of the board as declared by law include: the appointment of a commissioner of public welfare who serves during the pleasure of the board and whose compensation is fixed by it; the making and publication of rules and regulations for the administration of the department, including county departments; the establishment and maintenance of a merit system covering all personnel in the state and county departments; the preparation and forwarding of necessary reports to the proper agencies of the national government; the establishment of rules and regulations concerning the use of records and files of the department; the preparation and publication of an annual report to the governor on the administration of the welfare program; and the fixing of proper bond for such employees of the department as it may determine. All information concerning payments and assistance under the welfare program are by law public records available at the office of the chancery clerk of each county.[2] The law prohibits use of the records for political, commercial, or advertising purposes.

Serving in an advisory capacity at the local level is the county board of welfare. This body consists of five persons appointed by the county board of supervisors to such terms as are fixed by the state department. Each member receives per diem compensation of $5, with a maximum of two days' pay per month. Functions of the county welfare board are to advise the county welfare agent and to plan the utilization and development of all resources in the county available for the promotion of public welfare.

Administrative Organization

At the head of the administrative staff of the department is the commissioner of public welfare, appointed by and responsible to the board. He may be removed by the board at any time for cause or for participating in a political campaign. The commissioner has the following duties and functions: to appoint all personnel in accordance with the rules and regulations established by the board; to establish the necessary administrative divisions within the department; to carry out all rules, regulations, and administrative provisions prescribed by the board; to make such reports to the board as it may require; to issue checks for welfare payments and administrative expenses; to procure necessary supplies; and to prescribe such forms and blanks as may be necessary in the work of the department. In addition the commissioner serves as a cooperating agency with the governor on matters of clemency and parole and provides legal service and consultation for the Children's Code Commission.

Within the department and under the supervision of the commissioner are six divisions. The three operating divisions—public assistance, child welfare, and the blind—administer services indicated by their titles. Two service divisions, finance and accounts and research and statistics, handle financial-statistical work for the whole department. The division of field service and training supervises county programs, trains local personnel, and acts as a liaison agency between the state and local staffs.

Administration of welfare at the local level is through the county department of welfare under the direction of the county welfare agent.* This officer is appointed by the state commissioner but is required to be a resident of the county. The county agent, with such assistants as may be necessary, administers within the county all forms of public assistance and welfare. The county department operates under regulations of the state department, and its personnel, with approval of the state department, may cooperate with other state and local agencies in work related to public welfare.† The complete administrative organization is shown on the chart on page 215.

The Welfare Program

The program of the Department of Public Welfare is embraced in five main functions. In the performance of these functions the department employs more than 600 persons and expends annually more than $24,000,000 from Federal and state sources.‡

The most important part of the welfare program is the administration of assistance to needy old people. Persons eligible for such assistance apply at the welfare office of the county wherein they reside. The county agent then investigates the applicant to determine whether he (or she) meets the following legal requirements: (1) he must be at least 65 years of age; (2) he must have lived in the state one year prior to the time of application; (3) he must live in the county in which he applies; (4) he must not live in a public institution; (5) he must not have transferred property within the past two years for the purpose of making himself eligible for assistance; (6) he must not have property, used as a home, the real value of which is more than $2,500.

If the applicant is found to be eligible under the above requirements, he is placed on the list by the county welfare board and receives payments in proportion to his needs insofar as the law and state appropriations permit. No person may receive more than $30 per month under the law. The

* In counties having two judicial districts the commissioner of public welfare may establish a county department in each district, under a single county welfare board.—*Mississippi Code, 1942,* Recompiled volume 5A (1952), sec. 7221.

† A few counties still maintain county poorhouses or farms for indigent old people. Some also maintain a limited program of outdoor relief. Such welfare is under the direction of the county board of supervisors.

‡ The amount of funds expended varies slightly. During October, 1953, the expenditures were $2,272,116. Monthly *Report of Division of Research and Statistics, State Department of Public Welfare,* October, 1953. Counties provide funds for expenses, from $40 to $100 per month, depending on the population of the county.

average payment for October, 1953, was $28.20 per month.* A check of recipients is made each twelve months by the county welfare department to determine whether any change in eligibility has occurred. Persons having greater needs than can be supplied under the program are eligible for assistance from other public sources, if available, although this additional aid is in no way controlled by the welfare department. The total number of persons receiving such assistance in October, 1953, was 62,877.

Another important function of the Department of Public Welfare is the administration of aid to dependent children. This program, although subject to the general supervision of another agency—the Children's Code Commission—is for all practical purposes handled by the regular welfare personnel. A "dependent child" is defined by the law as a needy person under sixteen years of age, regularly attending school, who has been deprived of parental support. The child must be living with a parent or relative. Applications are handled in the same manner as for old-age assistance and payments made in proportion to need and available funds. Maximum payments under the law are $15 per month for the first dependent child in a family, $10 for the second child, and $5 per month for each additional dependent child. The average payment in October, 1953, was $9.55 per child, or $27.88 per family. A total of 12,410 families with 36,239 children were receiving assistance under the program at that time.[3]

The welfare program also includes assistance to the needy blind and other persons who are deemed totally and permanently disabled and unemployable. These cases are administered similarly to those described above, though blind persons must be so certified after examination by an ophthalmologist or optometrist. Other requirements as to eligibility, such as need, residence, and nonresidence in a state institution, are fixed by law, and eligibility is determined in the usual way. Both classes of persons receive payments in proportion to need and available funds, though unemployable persons who retain their eyesight may not receive more than $25 nor less than $5 per month. The legal limit on the amount that may be paid to blind persons is $40 per month, though the law requires that the first $50 per month of earned income be disregarded in determining need. The average payment to the 3,112 blind persons on the rolls in October, 1953, was $34.14. At the same time 1,930 unemployable persons drew an average monthly payment of $24.39.[4]

A minor portion of the welfare program consists of the certification and supervision of persons receiving old-age assistance under the Confederate

* *Ibid.* The national treasury pays $15 of the first $20. Above that the state pays half the cost.

pension program. Veterans, their widows, and loyal servants are entitled to receive these payments according to a scale established by law. This type of assistance is rapidly disappearing. In February, 1953, only seven persons were on the rolls and the average monthly payment was $28.57.[5]

In addition to the above functions the welfare department renders various other services of a welfare or social nature. Most important of these is the service rendered to the State Parole Board in the investigation and supervision of paroled prisoners. The county welfare agent and the county sheriff are designated parole officers and have the duty of receiving reports from parolees and rendering service to them in the matter of securing employment. Other services rendered by the welfare department include assistance to war veterans, displaced persons, and persons being committed to the state mental hospitals.

CHILDREN'S CODE COMMISSION

A special agency devoted to child welfare has existed in the state since 1946, when the legislature established the Children's Code Commission. The commission is primarily a staff agency with the function of studying legislation relating to the children and recommending changes and improvements.[6]

The commission consists of nine persons appointed by the governor, one from each of the seven congressional districts (as they existed in 1946) and two from the state at large. Members have no fixed term and serve without compensation, though they are reimbursed for expenses incurred in connection with their duties. Functions of the commission may be stated briefly as follows: (1) to study the laws and conditions of the state affecting children as well as the functions and facilities of state agencies and institutions charged with the care, control, protection, and rehabilitation of children; (2) to investigate and examine studies and records of agencies and institutions dealing with children and enlist the aid of other private or public agencies engaged in such work with the view of obtaining necessary information on child welfare; (3) to make a biennial report to the governor and legislature on its work with recommendations for new legislation and for the repeal or amendment of existing laws; (4) to receive and administer public and private funds that may be made available to the commission.

The commission does not administer any welfare funds and has no employees, although it is authorized to employ professional personnel.

STATE VETERANS' AFFAIRS BOARD

The State Veterans' Affairs Board was created by act of the legislature in 1948 for the purpose of providing special service to veterans. It consists of seven members, one from each congressional district (as they existed January 1, 1952) appointed by the governor for staggered terms of seven years. Members are compensated $14 per day while in attendance at meetings and also are allowed travel expenses. The board annually selects a state service commissoner and six assistant commissioners who are full-time employees and administer the policies and program of the board. All members of the board, the commissioner, and his assistants are required to be veterans of wars in which the United States was engaged.

The functions of the board consist of assisting veterans or their dependents in securing any privilege or benefit to which they are entitled under national or state laws, cooperation with veterans' organizations in the prosecution of just claims on behalf of veterans, and generally the rendering of service to veterans or their families. The work of the agency, performed by the commissioners and a clerical staff, is primarily concerned with claims for benefits to which veterans are entitled under national and state laws and policies. The board works closely with other state agencies of its kind, with national agencies, and with the various veterans' organizations in order to expedite benefits relating to pensions, insurance, loans, and education. It is authorized to accept power of attorney for individuals in handling such claims as well as others that veterans may have. In addition, services are rendered to veterans and their families in such matters as the maintenance of an information service, visitation of hospitalized veterans, compilation of grave records of deceased veterans, and the distribution of memorial certificates to the next of kin of servicemen who lose their lives.

The more than 300,000 veterans living in the state make the task of this agency a large one. During the first three years of its existence it conducted 38,893 personal interviews, submitted 41,336 official papers to the national Veterans' Administration, and handled 15,111 new and reopened claims on which a total sum of $6,935,648 was paid. The county welfare departments cooperate in carrying out its program.[7]

EMPLOYMENT SECURITY COMMISSION

State assistance to the unemployed is administered by the Mississippi Employment Security Commission. This body consists of three members, one from each supreme court district, appointed by the governor for four-year terms, with the terms staggered so that only one vacancy occurs each two years. One member must be a representative of employees. The members receive salaries and reimbursement for necessary official expenses. The commission is required to designate a board of review of three persons to which its decisions may be appealed. Each member of the commission may appoint one member of the board. The commission also is required to appoint a state advisory council and local advisory councils, each consisting of an equal number of employees and employers, to assist it in the formulation of policies and settling of problems arising out of the administration of the program.[8]

The commission has the function of administering the laws relating to unemployment compensation and the promotion of employment. To carry out this function it is authorized by law to set up the necessary administrative organization, adopt rules and regulations, employ personnel on a merit basis, set up and maintain proper records, and generally to advise, recommend, and assist in matters promoting employment. It is specifically required to cooperate fully with the national Social Security Administration in the administration of the program. It is empowered to administer oaths, take depositions, issue subpoenas, and take similar steps necessary to the performance of its task.

Administrative Organization

The organization for the administration of this agency is headed by an executive director, appointed by the commission on a full-time basis. He has full responsibility for directing and coordinating the work of the different units and divisions of the organization, reviewing and approving administrative policies and procedures, and signing budgets, vouchers, fund transfers, and similar papers. He also serves as secretary of the commission.

The principal administrative divisions of the organization are the State Employment Service and the State Unemployment Compensation Commission, corresponding to the two main purposes of the program. The first of these finds and allocates jobs to unemployed persons, and the second makes payments of benefits to the eligible unemployed who qualify under the law or regulations of the commission. Other administrative units are designated as legal, research and information, field service, business management, training and procedure, and personnel. These divisions or units, with tasks indicated by their titles, are established so that the organization can accomplish better its two main functions.

The Program

The program of the Employment Security Commission is carried on by a total of about 400 persons. All administrative costs of the program come from the national treasury, though in the past the legislature has made biennial appropriations for this purpose, in the event the national allocation should be changed between sessions. A recent change in the national law makes such state appropriation unnecessary. The national grant for administrative costs in the fiscal year ending June 30, 1952, amounted to $1,700,218.

The work of the employment service division is done through the central office and through field offices maintained at various places throughout the state. In this manner the division compiles a list of workers, classified as to skill and training, to be available for immediate reference to suitable employment. Persons applying for unemployment compensation thus are added to the list where they may be given employment instead of compensation. This service also maintains contact with prospective employers, both in and out of the state, and learns their needs for employees. Proper records are maintained so that prospective employers may review the training and work history of applicants so as to select employees best suited to their needs. Field offices provide a convenient place where unemployed persons may go to locate job opportunities.

Unemployment compensation is based on the national Social Security Act of 1935 as amended, though the details of the program as well as its administration are left to the states. The national law levies a tax of 3 per cent on the pay rolls (up to $3,000 per person) of industrial employers for the purpose of financing the program. However, if the state has a law to this effect it may collect 2.7 per cent, or nine tenths of the tax levied by the national law, leaving only .3 per cent to go to the national treasury. With certain exceptions, private industrial employers, who employ eight or more persons for twenty weeks of a calendar year must pay the tax. The states may increase the tax and increase the benefits and coverage. The program in Mississippi conforms to the minimum program envisaged by the national law. The tax rate is determined by the state's unemployment experience rating formula and varies from .9 per cent to 2.7 per cent.

In order to be eligible in Mississippi an unemployed worker must register for work at an employment office of the Employment Security Commission, be available for work, and have been employed in an industry covered by the program for the proper time. The amount of compensation paid varies with the wages earned during employment, though it cannot be less than $3 per week nor more than $30 per week. No person may draw compensation for more than sixteen weeks during any year after the filing of a valid claim for benefit payments.

Average monthly employment covered under the program in the calendar year 1951 was 195,000 persons. In this same year the weekly insurance benefits amounted to approximately $4,556,000.[9]

WELFARE INSTITUTIONS

Certain phases of the welfare program are administered through institutions maintained by the state. Such institutions are those for the care and treatment of the insane and feeble-minded, the indigent ill, and training schools for the blind and deaf. Five separate administrative agencies exist for the state's welfare institutions.

The welfare institutions of Mississippi suffer from many of the handicaps common to such undertakings. By their very nature they are expensive operations, requiring large and well-trained staffs of technicians, physicians, psychiatrists, psychologists, and other specialists as well as large and specially equipped facilities. Appropriations to meet these needs usually are insufficient, with the result that the salaries offered are too low to attract enough qualified personnel and the funds inadequate to provide the facilities for proper care and treatment of inmates. Some of the institutions are overcrowded, which, together with inadequate staffs, makes their work more custodial than curative. Proper business and fiscal management of the institutions—which includes farms and other business operations—is difficult, not only because of personnel and funds, but also because the five separate administrations prevent over-all policy and supervision.

These considerations call for serious attention to the matter of grouping all welfare institutions under a single administrative body, which would make for uniform administrative policy and control and would effect a considerable financial saving that could be spent on improvement of staff and facilities. A recent report of a legislative committee recommends a similar arrangement.*

Mental Institutions

The three mental institutions of the state are under the supervision of a board of trustees of five persons appointed by the governor for staggered terms of six years. Three members, one from each of the state's supreme court districts, must be businessmen, and the other two must be physicians selected by the governor from a list of five recommended by the State Medical Association. The board exercises general supervisory powers over the finances, property, and administration of the institutions. It has authority to appoint an executive secretary, who maintains an office for the board. Administration of each institution is entrusted to a director, appointed by the board. The director, subject to the approval of the board, employs and dismisses physicians, nurses, and other employees, fixes their compensation and duties, and generally directs the institution.[10] Directors of the hospitals for the insane are required to be skilled physicians.

The Mississippi State Hospital at Whitfield, the largest and most modern mental institution in the state, is maintained for the diagnosis and treatment of the mentally ill as well as the care of the incurably insane. It also maintains a department for the treatment of diseases that may lead to insanity, and facilities for treatment of alcoholics and narcotic addicts. Mental patients are admitted only upon affidavit of a relative or other citizen, accompanied by the certificate of two physicians, appointed by the chancery clerk of the county, that the person is insane. Persons thought to be suffering from mental disorders may be admitted for examination without such affidavit and certificate, and if found to be insane, may be admitted as patients. Alcoholics, narcotic addicts, and persons incurably insane are segregated from other patients, and modern therapy is employed in all treatment. Patients who have estates or relatives who are financially able are required to pay part or all of the cost of care and treatment, though no patient may be denied admittance because of inability to pay.

The East Mississippi Insane Asylum at Meridian is operated and maintained in the same manner as the institution at Whitfield, although it does not offer treatment to alcoholics and narcotic addicts.

* This recommendation would establish a Department of Hospitals and Institutions, which would include all the institutions covered in this section except the mental institutions. These institutions would be continued under a separate board but would be served by the same bureau of administration serving the other institutions. See *Report of the Legislative Fact-Finding Committee on Reorganization of State Government* (December, 1950).

The State School for the Feeble-Minded at Ellisville provides care and training for feeble-minded persons and epileptics. It operates under a director who is responsible for the instruction of the inmates in such trades and occupations as they are capable of learning, with emphasis on farm, shop, and household occupations. A farm is maintained to provide training and employment and to reduce the cost of maintenance. Minors may be admitted to the institution upon application of a parent or guardian if the child, upon examination at the school, is found to be feeble-minded. Adults may be admitted on order of the chancery court of the county, issued after the filing of an affidavit and a certificate by two examining physicians that the person is feeble-minded. Patients in state insane institutions and inmates of the feeble-minded school may be interchanged, upon the decision of a director that the person may be cared for better elsewhere. The director of the school is authorized to parole or discharge inmates when, in his judgment, the person is capable of taking care of himself. Segregation of sexes, races, and different types of feeble-minded persons is required. Only persons whose parents or guardians cannot care for them are admitted, and the cost of maintenance of the institution is borne by the state, although the governing board is allowed to accept gifts for the school.[11]

Institutions for the Deaf and Blind

Two institutions are maintained by the state for the training of the deaf and blind. Both are located at Jackson, and both are under the direction of a board of seven trustees appointed by the governor for staggered terms of seven years. The board has general authority to determine rules and regulations of the institutions, to fix the general duties and salaries of employees, and to determine admission of persons in accordance with the law. Superintendents of the schools, who must be qualified as public school instructors, are appointed by the board for terms of six years. They may be removed by the board or by the governor for proper cause. Direct administration of the institutions is under the respective superintendents.

The Mississippi School for the Blind offers care and training for blind persons who are seven years of age or older. Students pay their board if financially able, although indigent blind children are admitted with no charges upon certificate of the superintendents of education of their respective counties. The number of nonpaying students admitted is governed by the amount of funds appropriated. Students are educated in the basic subjects by modern techniques for teaching the blind, including the Braille system, and are trained in skills and occupations. After completion of the course a blind person is furnished $150 worth of tools or equipment necessary to the trade or occupation for which he has been trained.

The Mississippi School for the Deaf offers similar training, though designed for the needs of deaf persons. The management of the institution is the same and the same rules govern admission, except that, apparently, persons may be admitted before the age of seven. Education by lip-reading methods is required, and training in skills and occupations is emphasized.

The work of these institutions does not conflict with the program of the State Welfare Department, which provides aid for the blind, unemployable, and dependent children. Persons in these institutions are not eligible for welfare payments.[12]

State Charity Hospitals

Mississippi maintains five institutions for the care and treatment of the indigent sick: the Mississippi State Charity Hospital at Jackson, the Mississippi State Charity Hospital at Vicksburg, the Matty Hersee Hospital at Meridian, the South Mississippi Charity Hospital at Laurel, and the Mississippi State Charity Hospital at Natchez. They are under the supervision of the Board of Trustees of Eleemosynary Institutions. This body consists of five members, one from each supreme court district and two from the state at large, appointed by the governor with the advice and consent of the senate. The term of office is four years. Members receive $10 per diem and travel expenses when engaged in the business of the board.

Each of the charity hospitals is administered by a superintendent appointed by the governor with the advice and consent of the senate for a four-year term. A superintendent must be a skilled physician and may be removed by the governor or the board of trustees, for proper cause, before the end of his legal term. The salary of each superintendent is fixed by the board but may not exceed $5,000 per year for part-time work or $6,000 per year for full-time duty. The superintendent employs and directs the staff of the hospital, supervises the buildings and land of the institution, requires maintenance of the proper records of admissions and financial operations, makes reports to the board of trustees, and generally is responsible for the proper operation of the institution and the care of patients.[13]

The program of the charity hospitals is the medical and surgical treatment of residents of the state who are financially unable to pay the costs of private treatment and hospitalization. To be admitted, except in emergency cases where immediate medical attention is necessary, a person must file a certificate signed by himself and three other residents of his county, one of whom must be a practicing physician, that the person is poor and needy and is unable to pay the cost of treatment. Patients admitted without certificate on an emergency basis may be charged for treatment if found to be able to pay, under such rules and regulations as may be established by the governing board. A statement of the cost of treatment of any patient, upon his death or discharge, is sent to the board of supervisors of his county of residence. The county board, if it determines that the discharged patient or those legally responsible for his support are able to pay the hospitalization costs, may enter suit to collect such charges. Any funds so collected are paid into the state treasury and charged against the appropriation for the hospital.

Generally the institutions maintain uniformity in standards of care, treatment, and hospitalization and in charges made for paying patients. Such standards are established by the Commission on Hospital Care. Naturally, the facilities and the flow of patients at each institution vary, with the result that there is some shifting of occupants from one institution to another for specialized treatment and for accommodation. In the biennium ending July 1, 1951, the Jackson hospital accepted only emergency cases, many of whom had been transferred from other charity hospitals because of a lack of facilities for specialized treatment and shortage of funds. Training schools for nurses are maintained at the Meridian and Laurel hospitals. All the institutions are authorized to accept private gifts for enlarging or improving their facilities.[14]

A large number of bed patients are cared for at the various institutions, and the Vicksburg, Laurel, and Meridian hospitals also operate large out-patient clinics. During a typical two-year period, 1949-1951, 26,678 bed patients were treated at the five hospitals, and 24,821 other persons were treated or examined in out-patient departments. This vast program of care and treatment is maintained at a relatively low cost to the state. The 1952-1954 biennial appropriation for all institutions was $1,475,000.[15]

State Tuberculosis Sanatorium

The state maintains an institution for tubercular patients at Magee. This institution, originally established in 1916, is under the direction of the State Board of Health.[16] The board has the authority to select the superintendent and other officials of the institution, to determine rules and regulations concerning the government of the institution and the admission of patients, to accept gifts and donations for the benefit of the sanatorium, and generally to exercise management and control. The superintendent chosen by the board has direct control over the institution and makes recommendations to the governing body on policies of operation. The law requires this official to be a well-trained physician who is experienced in public health work.

The program of this institution is the prevention and treatment of tuberculosis, including the collection and maintenance of statistical data pertaining to the disease and the cases treated. It has facilities for persons of all ages and for all stages of illness, including a program designed to prevent those susceptible to the disease from actually contracting it. Educational facilities are provided for persons of educable school age who are undergoing treatment.

The sanatorium is not maintained entirely by the state, and the law establishing it required the State Board of Health to conduct it "so that it may be as nearly self-supporting as shall be consistent with the purpose of its creation." Patients are charged from $5 to $21 per week, depending on their ability to pay. The 1952-1954 biennial appropriation for the institution was $1,955,000.[17]

Beauvoir Soldiers Home

A state-supported institution for the care and treatment of Confederate veterans and wives and widows of such veterans has long been maintained at Beauvoir, former home of Jefferson Davis, president of the Confederacy. This institution is under the direction of a board of six directors, appointed by the governor. The institution has very few inmates, and the current biennial appropriation for its maintenance is only $25,000.

FOOTNOTES

[1] Legal provisions concerning the Department of Public Welfare may be found in *Mississippi Code, 1942,* Recompiled volume 5A (1952), secs. 7214-90.

[2] *Mississippi Laws, 1952,* ch. 388.

[3] *Report of Division of Research and Statistics, State Department of Public Welfare,* October, 1953.

[4] *Ibid.*

[5] *Ibid.,* February, 1953. Current monthly reports do not include this entry.

[6] The statutory provisions relating to this commission may be found in *Mississippi Code, 1942,* Recompiled volume 5A (1952), secs. 7170-11–7170-16.

[7] *Mississippi Code, 1942,* Recompiled volume 5A (1952), secs. 7486-01–7486-09; *Mississippi Laws, 1952,* ch. 314; *Biennial Report of the Veterans' Affairs Board* (1951).

[8] The principal laws relating to the Employment Security Commission may be found in *Mississippi Code, 1942,* Recompiled volume 5A (1952), secs. 7368-7446.

[9] Mississippi Employment Security Commission, *Biennial Report* (January 31, 1952).

[10] *Mississippi Code, 1942,* Recompiled volume 5A (1952), secs. 6946-01–6946-16.

[11] *Ibid.,* secs. 6764-69; 6777-84.

[12] Laws relating to these institutions may be found in *Mississippi Code, 1942,* Recompiled volume 5A (1952), secs. 6785-6785-10.

[13] Legal provisions concerning the management of charity hospitals may be found in *Mississippi Code, 1942,* Recompiled volume 5A (1952), secs. 6942-56.

[14] *Ibid.,* secs. 6965-76.

[15] See the biennial reports of these institutions to the governor and legislature, June 30, 1951. See also *Mississippi Laws, 1952,* ch. 67.

[16] The State Board of Health is described in Chapter 14.

[17] *Mississippi Code, 1942,* Recompiled volume 5A (1952), secs. 6870–6880-01.

CHAPTER 16

Agriculture

IT IS NATURAL that the state government of Mississippi should interest itself in agricultural promotion and improvement. Agriculture is the principal industry of the state and provides, directly or indirectly, livelihood for most of its people. Obviously, whatever is beneficial to agriculture is beneficial to the entire state and its economy.*

The legislature has shown no reluctance to pass laws and create agencies to encourage and assist agriculture. Beginning in 1906 with the creation of the Department of Agriculture and Commerce, one agency after another has been established until there now exists a total of twelve bodies dealing directly with some aspect of the industry. This total does not include the extensive program of agricultural education and experimentation conducted under the direction of Mississippi State College, nor the various projects maintained by the national government. Some of these agencies were created to regulate various phases of agriculture; others exist for purposes of promotion and development and for service to farmers. Some agencies perform several or all of these functions.

DEPARTMENT OF AGRICULTURE AND COMMERCE

The Department of Agriculture and Commerce, despite its combined

* Income payments to individuals coming directly from agriculture in 1951 amounted to $410,000,000 or 24.3 per cent of all income payments. The indirect income from this source would be much larger.—United States Department of Commerce, *Survey of Current Business* (August, 1952), p. 13.

title, is concerned almost entirely with agriculture. It is under the direction of the commissioner of agriculture, statistics, and immigration, a popularly elected officer who serves for a term of four years. The law requires that this official have "competent knowledge of agriculture, mining, manufacturing, statistics and general industries" and that he be an experienced and practical agriculturist. Naturally, the judges of these qualifications are the voters who elect him. The commissioner is required to make bond in the amount of $5,000. Under his supervision the department is divided into eight administrative divisions: feed and fertilizer control, inspection, fruit and vegetable inspection, market bulletin, dairy laboratory, dairy and creamery, feed fertilizer and seed inspection, and seed laboratory. Approximately one fourth of the cost of operating the department comes from legislative appropriation; the remainder comes from fees and penalties, rents, Federal grants-in-aid, and miscellaneous sources. The 1952 biennial appropriation for the department, which employs twenty-six persons, was $265,700.

The work of the department includes the investigation of diseases and insects that affect agricultural crops and the study of remedies for them; the investigation and study of grasses and the compilation of reports on the varieties most suitable to the different sections of the state; the study of dairying, stock-raising, poultry-raising, fish and bee culture, wool culture, and the compilation of information on these matters that is of interest to the people; the establishment of grades and standards for farm products; and the investigation of drainage, irrigation, and subsoiling, and determination of what uses can be made of them to improve the soil of the state. Activities to promote the sale of agricultural products include study and report on broadening of the cotton market; the collection and compilation of information on agricultural specimens and other natural products suitable for manufacture; and the preparation of a handbook of information on the natural resources, climate, and facilities of the state for prospective settlers. The department does a great deal of statistical work, such as the collection, through county correspondents and cotton ginners, of figures on crops, acreage in production, and other information of value in the development of the state's agricultural resources. The *Market Bulletin,* monthly publication of the department, contains these figures as well as other market information. Further work of the department consists of cooperation with other state agencies concerned with agriculture, with the United States Department of Agriculture in securing agricultural grants-in-aid, and the encouragement of agricultural clubs and associations.[1]

PLANT INDUSTRY

State Plant Board

Assistance to agriculture through the study of plant diseases and insects and their control is provided by the State Plant Board, which has existed since 1920. The board is an ex officio body of three members: the commissioner of agriculture, the director of the State Experiment Station, and the chief entomologist of Mississippi State College. Members are not compensated for their services. The chief entomologist serves as the executive officer of the board and directs its activities. He is assisted by a chief inspector, an entomologist, twelve district inspectors, and other technical and clerical personnel, making a total of thirty-two employees.

The functions of the State Plant Board include conducting inspections and promulgating and enforcing quarantine regulations with regard to plants, plant diseases, and bees; studying insect and pest diseases and distributing information concerning their control; branding infected plants as a public nuisance and supervising their treatment or destruction; prescribing the manner of shipping plants and plant products; inspecting bees and the control and eradication of their diseases; and negotiating interstate plant agreements. In carrying out these duties employees of the board cooperate with other state and national agencies. The board has full power to enforce its decisions, though persons affected may be allowed a hearing.

This agency is financed chiefly by legislative appropriation. The appropriation for the 1952-1954 biennium was $318,895.[2]

The Lime Plant Board

The Lime Plant Board was established in 1942 but reorganized by the legislature in 1948. It consists of four members: the commissioner of agriculture, the director of the State Extension Service, the director of the State Experiment Station, and the maintenance engineer of the State Highway Department.

The principal function of the Lime Plant Board is the establishment of lime-crushing plants and the operation of these plants to supply limestone to farmers at actual cost. To perform this function the board may acquire and dispose of machinery, purchase limestone deposits, and make such rules as are necessary for the operation of lime plants. Such a plant has been established at Cedar Spring, under the control of a manager chosen by the board. The board, in its discretion, may use convict labor in the operation of lime-crushing plants. This agency is supported entirely by funds derived from the sale of limestone, which must be sold at cost. Proceeds of these sales are maintained in a separate fund for the purchase of new equipment, making necessary repairs, and paying other costs of the program. All money in excess of $15,000 in this fund at the end of each calendar year must be deposited in the state treasury to the credit of the state.[3]

State Soil Conservation Committee

Although the soil conservation program is almost entirely a project of of the Federal government, the state maintains an agency to coordinate this service on a state-wide basis. The State Soil Conservation Committee, established in 1938, is an ex officio body composed of the director of the State Extension Service, the director of the State Agricultural Experiment Station, the state forester, and the commissioner of agriculture. The committee is authorized by law to invite the United States Secretary of Agriculture to appoint an additional member, who is now the Federal soil conservationist stationed in Mississippi. Meetings are held monthly at which all business is transacted. Members receive no compensation but are reimbursed for official expenses and travel.

This committee receives petitions, holds hearings, conducts referenda, and makes decisions as to the establishment of soil conservation districts in the state. Two of the five commissioners of districts so established are appointed by the state committee. The other three local commissioners are elected by the farmers and landowners of the district. In addition, the committee provides information for the various districts, coordinating their activities and securing the cooperation and assistance of agencies of the national government. The legislature appropriates for this committee about $1,500 each biennium, which is spent for publicity in connection with the establishment of conservation districts. The sole employee of this agency is an extension worker located at State College who keeps the necessary committee records of the state program.

The soil conservation program of the state, staffed by Federal employees and financed by Federal funds, is a complete and valuable service to farmers and landowners who wish to make the most efficient use of the soil and prevent its depletion and erosion. In accordance with the plan described above the state committee has established seventy-three conservation districts of one or more counties, which embrace practically the entire area of the state. Each district has a commission of five resident landowners who act as an advisory body. A professional soil conservationist, with one or more subprofessional assistants, is assigned to the district to work with farmers in the improvement of land use. Services offered include land mapping, soil analysis, advice as to the proper crops, and technical advice on drainage and irrigation. Above the local districts, nine area offices have been established that have staffs including an experienced soil conservationist, a drainage engineer, and a soil scientist. Their services are available to landowners of the districts within the area. Specialized services, such as advice on forestry, tree culture, and agronomy, are available through specialized personnel who are supplied by the regional headquarters of the southeastern states. The whole state program is under the supervision of the state soil conservationist.

The success of this program is attested by its rapid expansion during the last twelve years, in response to the requests of farmers and landowners. Much of the improvement in soil fertility and crop yields in the state can be attributed to it.[4]

ANIMAL INDUSTRY

State Livestock Sanitary Board

Public aid in the control and eradication of infectious and contagious diseases affecting livestock and poultry is provided by the Livestock Sanitary Board, first created in 1917 and reorganized in 1950. This body consists of ten members, two of whom are the commissioner of agriculture and a professor of animal husbandry at Mississippi State College. The other eight are appointed by the governor and must include a graduate, accredited veterinarian, a general farmer, a breeder and producer of poultry, a breeder and producer of swine, two breeders and producers of beef cattle, and two breeders and producers of dairy cattle. Each of the various breeders' associations of beef cattlemen, dairymen, poultrymen, and swine producers submits to the governor a list of five names from which appointments are made. One appointive member must come from each of the state's congressional districts. All members serve for four-year terms. The board is required to meet at least four times each year, and it may be called into special session by the chairman or a majority of the members. Appointive members receive per diem compensation and traveling expenses for time devoted to their duties.

The board has the duty of making and enforcing such rules as it deems necessary to control diseases affecting animals in the state, certifying indemnity payments to owners for livestock destroyed, establishing and maintaining quarantine lines, maintaining laboratories, appointing as inspectors representatives of the United States Department of Agriculture and receiving financial assistance from this department, and appointing other veterinarians to assist in Federal-state programs of cattle-testing. The board employs a graduate, accredited veterinarian as executive officer who has charge of administering the program with such personnel as he may employ to assist him. An advisory commission of five persons appointed by the governor advises the executive officer and board in matters relating to tick fever of cattle.

Six administrative divisions of the board have been established under the executive officer in order to carry out its program. They are: (1) the administrative office, which maintains necessary records and general supervision over the various programs; (2) the diagnostic laboratory, which makes necessary tests to determine the presence of animal and poultry diseases in the main laboratory at Jackson and a branch laboratory at Tupelo; (3) the area brucellosis program; (4) the sheep scabies program, which works with diseases of sheep in quarantined areas; (5) poultry production and improvement, charged with the control and elimination of diseases of poultry and the development of a better program of poultry production; (6) general livestock inspection, a division that inspects livestock moving in the state and into the state in order to prevent the spread of disease.

The board employs around twenty persons, most of whom are veterinarians, inspectors, and technicians. This number is supplemented by Federal employees who work in the same program. In addition, the board makes use of certain personnel and facilities of Mississippi State College. Part of the cost of the activities of this agency is offset by sales and nonrevenue receipts. The 1952-1954 appropriation includes $190,400 for support and $172,500 for a fund to combat animal diseases and to indemnify persons for loss of animals through the work of the board.[5]

Livestock, Poultry, and Egg Production Assistance Program

A new program of assistance to agriculture was inaugurated by the 1952 legislature with the enactment of the Livestock, Poultry, and Egg Production Assistance Act. This law established a revolving loan fund of $2,000,000 for the encouragement of stock farming and poultry raising.

Administration of the program is vested in the dean of the Division of Agriculture, Mississippi State College, and an advisory committee of five persons: the chairman of the State Agricultural and Industrial Board, the state commissioner of agriculture, the chairman of the Board of Trustees of Institutions of Higher Learning, an active banker, and a businessman. The ex officio members may designate other members of their respective agencies to serve for them; the other two members are appointed by the governor. Members serve without compensation.

Loan applications must be accompanied by a plan of farm improvement and operations, both of which are approved by the county agent where the farm is located. The amount of such loans cannot exceed $15,000 and must be secured by real or personal property. The terms are limited to five years and the interest rate to 5 per cent.[6]

MARKETING ACTIVITIES

State Marketing Commission

Marketing assistance to farmers and producers groups is provided by the State Marketing Commission, established by the legislature in 1944. The commission consists of seven members, four of whom are the commissioner of agriculture, the director of the extension service, the extension marketing specialist, and the state director of vocational education. The other three members, one from each supreme court district, are appointed by the governor for staggered terms of four years. They must be experienced farmers. The commission elects a chairman from its members, and its secretary is the state marketing specialist. An office is maintained at the Mississippi State College, where meetings are held upon call of the secretary. Members receive per diem compensation and travel expenses while engaged in the work of the commission.

The functions of the commission are to aid in the establishment of proper, efficient, and economical processing, storage, and marketing facilities for handling and distributing agricultural products produced within the state, and to assist the farmers of the state in marketing their products. To accomplish this the commission makes grants of money to associations of producers of agricultural products or to federations of such associations. Administrative work of the body is entrusted to the secretary and to the director of the extension service. The latter officer makes surveys and studies regarding applications for financial assistance and recommends action to the commission. Most of the money expended by this agency is in the form of grants.[7]

Mississippi Central Market Board

Complementing the work of the commission described above is the Mississippi Central Market Board, which was established in 1946. It is a body of five members, of which the commissioner of agriculture is ex officio chairman. The other four members are appointed by the governor for staggered terms of four years, one from each of the state highway districts and one from the state at large. Of the four appointive members, one must be a wholesale groceryman dealing in fruits and vegetables, one a retail groceryman dealing in fruits and vegetables, one a farmer growing fruits or vegetables, and one a farmer producing poultry and eggs. The board is required to meet at least four times a year, and members receive per diem compensation and expenses for attendance at these meetings.

The duties of this board are concerned with the supervision and regulation of the Farmers Central Market, a million dollar enterprise in Jackson, which was officially opened on July 31, 1948. The board has charge of formulating a building and operating program for the market, fixing charges for facilities, making rules and regulations governing business, persons, and vehicles in the market, determining salaries of employees and hours of market operation, and similar duties. The board selects a state market manager who also acts as its executive officer. He manages the market, employs personnel, maintains records of leases, rentals, receipts, and disbursements and makes biennial reports to the legislature on market operation.

The Farmers Central Market, a fully modern supermarket, provides a central outlet for produce, a facility for grading, and a depot for the buyer. It contains ample space for handling, storing, and displaying produce. Important in its service to patrons is the Federal-state inspection service, which provides inspection and grading through cooperation of national and state agencies. On the same cooperative basis, it operates a market news service, furnishing daily reports on the fruit, vegetable, livestock, poultry, and dairy products market.

Although the legislature made an appropriation for the original construction of the market, it now operates on a self-sustaining basis and receives no money from the state except the matching funds for operation of the news service.[8] The 1952 biennial appropriation for this agency was $12,000.[9]

State Egg Advisory Board

The State Egg Advisory Board was created in 1944 to foster the development of the poultry industry and assist in the marketing of eggs. It consists of seven members appointed by the commissioner of agriculture for two terms—three representing egg producers, two representing egg consumers, one representing the hatchery industry, and one representing egg dealers. Members serve without compensation. The body makes recommendations to the commissioner of agriculture as to the regulation of marketing of eggs, including means of protection against fraud and misrepresentation. This body has purely advisory functions, with no administrative structure and no appropriation.[10]

MISCELLANEOUS PROGRAMS

Mississippi Agricultural and Industrial Exposition Commission

The Mississippi Agricultural and Industrial Exposition Commission, established by the legislature in 1946, exists for the promotion of agricultural and industrial development in the state. It is an ex officio body consisting of the commissioner of agriculture as chairman, the director of the Mississippi Extension Service, the president of the Mississippi Livestock Association, the director of the Mississippi Vocational Education Division, a representative of the Mississippi Association of Fairs, and a representative of the city commission of Jackson. Appointive members are designated by the governor, and all members serve for a term of four years without compensation.

The commission has charge of state lands and buildings used for exposition purposes and has the duty of making plans and arrangements for holding fairs and expositions to promote the state's agricultural and industrial program. It makes rules governing the use of state funds for premiums and awards and may accept donations to be awarded as prizes. The administrative work of the commission is done by an executive secretary. The secretary, appointed by the commission, directs the state fair held each year in Jackson and attends other Mississippi fairs and livestock shows where state premium money is awarded. He also holds an annual meeting of the Mississippi Association of Fairs and Livestock Shows and attends the annual International Association of Fairs and Expositions. Reports on the work of the commission, on fairs and expositions held, and on money expended for prizes and premiums are made by the secretary to the governor and the legislature.

The 1952 biennial appropriation for this commission was $89,910, most of which is spent in promoting county and district livestock shows. The state fair produces revenue that more than pays for its cost.[11]

Veterans' Farm and Home Board

Of primary interest to agriculture, though a part of the program of assistance to veterans as well, is the Veterans' Farm and Home Board. This agency, established in 1936 but reorganized and expanded several times since, is designed to aid veterans of World Wars I and II and the Korean conflict in the purchase of farms and homes. It consists of a board of six members appointed by the governor for staggered terms of four years, and a director and staff chosen by the board. The members of the board are paid expenses and $14 per diem for their services. Per diem compensation is limited to fifty days a year for the chairman and thirty-six days a year for other board members. The executive director is a full-time official.

The board administers a revolving loan fund for the benefit of veterans who wish to purchase farms and homes and who have been denied loans by national government or private lending institutions. Loans are limited in amount to $6,000, and the interest rate is fixed by the board, though it cannot exceed that allowed for loans under the National Servicemen's Readjustment Act of 1944. Terms of repayment may be up to twenty-five years. The board is empowered to purchase farms for resale, to appoint local committees in each county as advisory groups, and otherwise implement the act to fulfill its purposes. Loans made during the biennium ending June 30, 1951, totaled $4,617,792.99. The biennial appropriation was $2,000,000 in 1950 and $3,000,000 in 1952.[12]

Mississippi Rural Electrification Authority

An agency related to agriculture is the Mississippi Rural Electrification Authority, established as a public corporation and agency of the state in 1936. It is under the control of a board of three directors appointed by the governor for staggered terms of three years each, one from each supreme court district. Members receive compensation for expenses incurred in the performance of their duties and may also receive an honorarium of not more than $600 per year each, at the discretion of the governor.

Functions of this agency are the encouragement and promotion of the use of electric power in rural areas of the state. In carrying out this function it operates as a corporation with power to sue and be sued, to acquire and hold property, condemn land, easements, or rights of way for its facilities, borrow money and issue bonds, fix and collect rates and charges for service, and generally perform services necessary to the promotion and improvement of electric power systems. After the establishment of rural electrification systems in the state was completed around 1940 the greater part of the work of this agency was completed. It has not been active in recent years, but Governor Hugh L. White reactivated the agency in late 1953.[13]

State Chemist

The state chemist, although not entirely concerned with agriculture, performs services that assist farmers in many respects. This official, who is a professor of chemistry at the Mississippi State College, maintains a samples laboratory and makes analyses for the Department of Agriculture and Commerce, the Geological Survey, the Game and Fish Commission, and other state agencies. He also fixes and publishes standards of purity for food products under the state's pure food and drug laws. Fourteen persons, of whom twelve were technical and professional, were employed in 1951.[14]

AGRICULTURAL EXTENSION AND RESEARCH

Agricultural Experiment Station

Of great educational value to farmers and the agricultural industry is the Agricultural Experiment Station, a part of the program of Mississippi State College. Financed by both Federal and state funds, it constantly adds to the existing knowledge of agriculture through an extensive experimentation program in the use of soils, crops, and crop methods.

The extension program is headed by a director chosen by the Board of Trustees of Institutions of Higher Learning. Cooperating in its work are the following departments of the college: agricultural economics, agricultural engineering, agronomy, animal husbandry, chemistry, dairy husbandry, entomology, forestry, home economics, horticulture, plant pathology and physiology, poultry husbandry, and veterinary science and animal disease research. The station also maintains an editorial department and a library department.

The main experiment station is located at State College, but branch stations are maintained as follows: Black Belt Branch Station, Brooksville; Brown Loam Station, Raymond; Coastal Plain Branch Station, Newton; Delta Branch Station, Stoneville; North Mississippi Branch Station, Verona; Pontotoc Ridge-Flatwoods Branch Station, Pontotoc; South Mississippi Branch Station, Poplarville; Truck Crops Branch Station, Crystal Springs. Experimental pilot farms are maintained at Natchez and West Point. The location of these branch stations and farms is planned to cover all important sections of the state, so that each type of soil and crop specialty can be included in the experimentation program.[15]

Results of experiments conducted are circulated through regular and special bulletins, leaflets, and pamphlets issued by the experiment station or the extension service. This information is furnished to county agents and other employees of the extension service for distribution to farmers, or is available by direct individual request.

Agricultural Extension Service

Closely related to the experiment station program and also under the direction of the state agricultural college, the Agricultural Extension Service offers further assistance to farmers through its vast organization throughout the state. Fundamentally, the extension service is an off-campus teaching program that brings to the farmers of each county the knowledge gained through the various projects of the experiment station and other experimental processes.

Under the supervision of a director and an assistant director at Mississippi State College, the Agricultural Extension Service divides the state into five districts—northwest, northeast, east central, south, and southwest—each with a district agent. These district agents supervise the work of the county agents and county home demonstration agents. Each county, through its governing board, employs a county agent and a home demonstration agent from a list of persons approved by the director of extension as having a college degree in agriculture or home economics and experience in extension work. The county pays a part of the salary of these officials. Assistant agents are paid entirely by the extension service.

The work of the extension service embraces all kinds of instruction to farmers and farm housewives that will enable them to have better farms and homes. County agents provide pamphlets, bulletins, and folders, published by the extension service. They also conduct practical demonstrations on the farms and in the homes, give lectures, and otherwise further their program of education. Special attention is given to the 4-H Club program, an organization of farm youths who have projects in which they are taught better agricultural methods. Special state supervisory personnel are employed for 4-H Club work. Various specialists in other fields also are maintained at the state level. Negro agents are maintained in most counties who devote their time to Negro farmers and housewives.

The extension service is financed by Federal and state funds under the provisions of the Smith-Lever Act of the national Congress. More than 450 agents, assistant agents, and supervisory and specialist personnel are employed in the program.[16]

REORGANIZATION OF STATE AGRICULTURAL SERVICES

Any survey of the state's agricultural program brings out the large number of agencies that have been created and that operate more or less independently, with no general coordination. No part of the state administration is more decentralized and disorganized. The obvious result is duplication of effort, waste of money, and a lowering of the quality of service.

The broad nature of the program and the high cost to the taxpayers makes this matter of special importance. Legislative appropriations in 1952 for the direct support of agricultural agencies and services totaled approximately $4,500,000. If the appropriations for two loan funds directly related to agriculture are counted, the figure is more than doubled, amounting to almost $10,000,000. Such a large expenditure may well be defended. However, it seems highly necessary that as much as possible of this sum be spent for services rendered to the farmer and that the cost of administration be kept as low as possible.

Large sums are now dissipated through administrative inefficiency. Of the twelve separate agencies (not including those under the direction of Mississippi State College), eight have separate executive directors, separate facilities and office space, and separate staffs. Since there is no agency or official empowered to coordinate the activities of these agencies, each plans and effects its individual operating program within isolated statutory bounds. The lack of over-all planning and direction inevitably results in waste of time, effort, and money.

The most exhaustive study of state administrative organization in recent years, made by a joint legislative committee, examined the agricultural agencies in detail and recommended general reorganization in the interest of better service and reduced expenses. Briefly, the recommendations would abolish certain agencies such as the Egg Advisory Board and the Rural Electrification Authority, since they exercise no important functions. Most of the other independent agencies would also be abolished, but their functions would be transferred into a proposed Department of Agriculture. This department, headed by an appointive director with professional qualifications, would perform all present services through four bureaus, namely, Marketing and Standards, Agricultural Aid, Research and Statistics, and Regulation of Warehouses and Cold Storage Plants. In addition the department would maintain a State Chemical Laboratory. Heads of these bureaus and the head of the laboratory would be appointed by the director and removable by him in the interest of a coordinated program. An advisory board giving representation to the different sections of the state is included in the recommendations and liaison with Federal-state services is provided.[17]

A continuation of the broad program of state assistance to agriculture seems assured. Such action is justified by the vital position that agriculture occupies in the state's economy as well as by the improvement in agricultural conditions and farm income resulting from the work of public agencies. If one may judge by the acts of recent legislatures, a further broadening of the program and the addition of new services may be anticipated. The application of principles of sound administration to the state's agricultural services, thereby greatly enhancing the value of the program, is a pressing need.

FOOTNOTES

[1] For laws relating to this department and its work see *Mississippi Code, 1942,* secs. 4397-4575, 4835, 4943, 4978, 6022, 8936, 8961; 1952 Supp., secs. 4397-01–4397-31, 4424, 4545-08, 4545-09, 4560-03–4560-05.

[2] *Mississippi Code, 1942,* secs. 4978-5005; 1952 Supp., secs. 5000-01–5000-13; *Mississippi Laws, 1952,* ch. 52.

[3] *Mississippi Code, 1942,* secs. 4430, 4432, 4433, 4435; 1952 Supp., secs. 4428, 4431, 4434.

[4] The soil conservation law of the state may be found in *Mississippi Code, 1942,* secs. 4940-58.

[5] *Mississippi Code, 1942,* secs. 4837-4863; 1952 Supp., secs. 4835, 4836, 4847-5, 4863-01–4863-10; *Mississippi Laws, 1952,* chs. 50, 51.

[6] *Mississippi Laws, 1952,* chs. 120, 175.

[7] *Mississippi Code, 1942,* 1952 Supp., secs. 4435-01–4435-14.

[8] *Ibid.,* secs. 4435-31–4435-42.

[9] *Mississippi Laws, 1952,* ch. 57.

[10] *Mississippi Code, 1942,* 1952 Supp., secs. 4435-20–4435-29.

[11] The law pertaining to this commission may be found in *Mississippi Code, 1942,* 1952 Supp., sec. 4435-50; *Mississippi Laws, 1952,* chs. 54, 55, 56.

[12] The laws relating to this agency may be found in *Mississippi Code, 1942,* Recompiled volume 5A (1952), secs. 7517-7532; *Mississippi Laws, 1952,* chs. 119, 311. For figures on the financial operations, see *Report of the State Department of Audit, 1951,* p. 37.

[13] *Mississippi Code, 1942,* secs. 5500-5525.

[14] *Mississippi Code, 1942,* secs. 4448, 4470, 5127-30, 5929-06, 7123-27; 1952 Supp., secs. 5096-99, 5929-06.

[15] *Mississippi Official and Statistical Register, 1949-1952* (Jackson, Secretary of State, 1952), pp. 127-30.

[16] *Mississippi Official and Statistical Register, 1949-1952,* pp. 139-46.

[17] "Conservation and Recreation," *A Report of the Legislative Fact-Finding Committee on State Reorganization* (Jackson, 1950), pp. 68-72.

CHAPTER 17

Conservation

THE EFFECTIVE BEGINNING of state conservation in Mississippi dates from 1926 and the establishment of the State Forestry Commission. To be sure, a slight public interest in resources use and conservation had been manifested as far back as 1850, when the State Geological Survey was created, but no controls for the positive development or for the conservation of resources had been vested in an administrative agency. With the advent of the State Forestry Commission there began a movement that has continued to the present and that has witnessed creation of a dozen administrative bodies. Wildlife, mineral, water, and scenic and recreational resources are all within the scope of action allotted these agencies.

At least two stages have been present in the development of conservation as a public activity in Mississippi. The first attempted to achieve conservation of natural resources by simple statutory prohibitions, such as forbidding the killing of game in public places. Conservation was thus expressed in terms of familiar common law concepts. The second stage has been characterized by a shift of emphasis from mere negative legislative prohibitions to positive administrative measures in forest management, wildlife preservation, and minerals development and conservation. However, Mississippi has not yet completed the pattern of state administration of natural resources that ranges from legislative declaration of policies to the establishment of multiple resources agencies and thence to their coordination in a single department.[1] Despite the absence of an articulate interest in a unified administration of conservation activities, the volume of legislation dealing with natural resources indicates an emerging realization that economic opportunities in Mississippi rest largely upon the state's natural wealth and its wise utilization. This chapter will review, therefore, the administrative organization for the public administration of natural resources and demonstrate the main activities the state discharges in forest management, fish and wildlife, parks, water resources, and mineral resources.

ADMINISTRATIVE ORGANIZATION FOR CONSERVATION

Basis of Organization

The activities of state conservation agencies are based upon the individual resource, as forests, minerals, and water. In some instances a single board or commission deals with a given resource, as in the case of forestry; in others, like fish and wildlife or minerals, several agencies are active. The various fields of conservation activity, together with the agencies administering them, are indicated here.

STATE CONSERVATION AGENCIES AND FIELDS

Conservation Field	*Administrative Agency and Date of Establishment*
Forests	State Forestry Commission (1926)
Fish and wildlife	
Inland	State Game and Fish Commission (1932)
Coastal	Sea Food Commission (1901)
Parks and scenic resources	
Parks	State Board of Park Supervisors (1926)
Historical	Monumental Park Commission (1902)
	Brice's Crossroads-Tupelo Battlefield Commission (1936)
Water	Board of Mississippi Levee Commissioners (1890)
	Board of Yazoo Mississippi Levee Commissioners (1890)
	State Game and Fish Commission (1932)
Minerals	
Leasing	Mineral Lease Commission (1936)
Regulatory	State Oil and Gas Board (1932)
Research	State Geological Survey (1850)

The pattern or organization thus appears simple. Whatever the resource, there is an agency charged with at least some aspect of its administration in the public interest. Specialized techniques to meet the needs of specific resources are thereby facilitated; certainly the multiple agency system adjusts the government service or control to the persons affected by its activities. Since it is impossible to force all resources into a single agency, though, activities affecting a single resource are frequently divided among several bodies. Conflicts in work programs and sometimes duplication of efforts as well as isolation are found.

The use of many agencies instead of a single conservation department is affected, moreover, by the scope of activities and consequently the size of the administrative body. Of the various agencies only two function with field offices. Of the remaining ten, three agencies have very narrow functions,* two more are constitutional bodies that have only a sectional jurisdiction,† and one is concerned only with mineral research. The State Forestry Commission and the State Game and Fish Commission alone operate through field staffs of moderate size with area or regional offices throughout the state.

Characteristics of Conservation Agencies

The first characteristic of the conservation agencies, as preceding paragraphs have indicated, is a lack of any common pattern or organization. Organization around a central office is common to almost all the agencies except those administering forest and wildlife resources. In the case of the two latter conservation activities, sensitivity to local problems is desired as well as cooperative action with the local governments. However, local considerations are less compelling in the other agencies, such as those regulating oil and gas production or conducting geological research.

Second, there is no single method by which membership of the boards or commissions is determined, and the size of the membership varies widely. The largest body, the Board of Yazoo Mississippi Levee Commissioners, consists of ten members; the smallest agencies‡ have but three members each. Members of conservation agencies hold their office by appointment, by virtue of the ex officio principle, and by election. Of these methods, appointment by the governor is the most commonly employed, and membership of the State Game and Fish Commission, the Sea Food Commission,

* Monumental Park Commission, Brice's Crossroads-Tupelo Battlefield Commission, and Mineral Lease Commission.

† These agencies are the two levee boards concerned with flood control in the rich "delta" section of Mississippi.

‡ The State Board of Park Supervisors, Monumental Park Commission, and Brice's Crossroads-Tupelo Battlefield Commission.

Brice's Crossroads-Tupelo Battlefield Commission, and the State Oil and Gas Board is entirely determined by appointment. Six of the nine members of the State Forestry Commission hold office by appointment, and three are ex officio members. An additional seventeen ex officio resources commissioners or board members are scattered throughout four agencies. Members of the two sectional levee boards are chosen by election.[2]

Third, the conservation agencies in Mississippi are characterized by a reliance on a plural executive; that is, boards and commissions hold the final administrative authority. This plural executive is part-time, lay, unpaid, and for the most part merely advises the administrative agent employed to carry out policy. No uniform term of office is operative, but the longest is now six years and the common term four years. No statutory provisions cover removal; however, all members are subject to impeachment as prescribed by the Mississippi constitution.[3]

Fourth, structural patterns of these agencies are clear. As noted elsewhere, the State Forestry Commission and the State Game and Fish Commission are organized with regional offices between the central headquarters and the field forces. In the central offices of these agencies the functions of planning, organization, staffing, budgeting, directing, coordinating, and reporting fall to the chief administrative employee of the agency. This official is the state forester and the director of conservation, respectively. Communication in both instances flows from the field to the regional offices and thence to the Jackson headquarters. In all other agencies are found merely the central offices and occasionally a small field staff. The Mineral Lease Commission, however, has neither office nor staff; its records are kept and reports made by the state oil and gas supervisor. In other cases, both the size of the staff and the scope of the activity are small.

Implications of the Administrative Organization

Two major questions arise from this brief summary of the organizational pattern for conservation. The first concerns the desirability of the commission-board system and the second the evident scattering of conservation activities among many different agencies. Both of these questions arise in connection with the administrative organization of the state as a whole, and they are treated extensively in Chapter 7.

Here we may observe that the board-commission system ignores the real advantages that result from placing the responsibility for getting the job done upon a single official. In almost every conservation field standards, policies, and objectives have been so well developed over the past decade or two as to make the use of a single administrator desirable. The quasi-judicial nature of some oil and gas determinations, as they are prescribed by statute, would perhaps exclude the State Oil and Gas Board from this application.[4] Elsewhere, the plural executive merely tends to emphasize the disintegration that is found in Mississippi's general administrative system.

As it relates to conservation activities the use of many agencies instead of a single conservation department results in independent programs. The more agencies administering separate programs, the greater is the independence of action on the part of any one of them. The multiple agency system also destroys a unity or commonness of purpose, and the conservation of natural resources is diffused into specific programs for the conservation of forests, of wildlife, or of mineral resources. With this administrative organization there can be no realization that forest and wildlife resources, for example, are bound together closely and that solution of the problems of one will often meet the problems of the others. The inability of the Mississippi governor to control the sprawling administrative system nominally under his direction strengthens the normal tendency for independence of action.*

As a result of the administrative organization, then, Mississippi has a number of programs for conserving forest resources, wildlife resources, mineral resources, park and scenic resources, and water resources; thus the state has failed to develop a system for the conservation of natural resources except as the several agencies work cooperatively.

FOREST MANAGEMENT

The state forester estimated in 1950 that 19,126,451 acres, totaling 63 per cent of the land area of Mississippi, were in some type of forests.[5] Every county in the state has some woodland acreage. The total volume of sound saw timber in the state approached 33 billion board feet in 1942, of which 19 billion feet were in cypress or hardwood and 14 billion in pine. The total, expressed differently, reached 195 million standard cords, with 144 million of them in hardwood. In 1945, new growths of timber amounted to slightly more than three billion board feet.

The state's economic interest in forestry is reflected by an investment

* Although several resources administrators concede this point, few of them will concede need for unity at the policy-making level and hence need for a unified department of conservation.

value of $500,000,000. Stumpage alone was valued at $47,000,000; manufactured products exceeded a value of $200,000,000. Expressed in percentages, 15 per cent of Mississippi's annual income is derived from forests and forest products. Forest and forest industries employ approximately 60,000 persons with an annual pay roll of $87,000,000.[6]

These statistics indicate the importance that proper forest management and conservation have for Mississippi's people. Programs for forest conservation on the state level are chiefly the responsibility of the State Forestry Commission, but other agencies participate in them, and the work of the Forest Service of the United States Department of Agriculture is extensive.

Fire Protection Program

The principal forest conservation activity is the prevention and control of fire in public and privately owned forest lands. Fire protection is basic to good management, and complete coverage has not yet been obtained. From the creation of the forest agency in 1926 until 1932 fire protection activities were conducted on the basis of voluntary agreements concluded with the owners of timber lands. In the latter year the legislature empowered the boards of supervisors to assess and levy a special county tax of three cents or less an acre against the timbered and uncultivatable acreage of the county, the acreage then being designated as a forest protection area.[7] Under this legislation individual counties adopted fire protection measures, and systems of lookout towers, paid fire control crews, and other activities were established. By 1944 twenty-one counties were participating in the cooperative state-county program.

In 1944 a new statute authorized the commission to expend as much as three cents an acre to assist counties whose forests were under the fire protection system, and the maximum county tax was reduced from three to two cents. Authority was given to place under organized protection four million new acres every two years, these new accessions to receive the same financial assistance.[8] Five major supervisory areas, which conform to the timbered areas of the state, were established for supervision of the program, with each district divided into units under the charge of rangers. By 1952 fifty-one counties had come under the new program, and protected areas exceeded twelve million acres.

Considerable Federal assistance is provided the state under the terms of the Clarke-McNary Act. The Federal program also includes protection of private forest lands from fire, and this activity is carried on through the state agency, as indeed is most of the cooperative work involving the use of Federal funds on state and private timber land. For the period 1940-1945, almost 38 per cent of the funds expended for fire protection purposes was in fact derived from Federal grants.[9] Local forest programs center about the financial assistance made available by the action of the county supervisors and local law enforcement. Thus, the sheriff of each county is ex officio reforestation warden in his jurisdiction and is charged to enforce all statutes, rules, and orders relating to forestry.

State Forests and Nurseries

The state now owns one forest of approximately 23,000 acres in south Mississippi.* In addition, the W. W. Kurtz State Forest of 1,760 acres is directly administered by the State Forestry Commission under the terms of a bequest. Two nurseries capable of producing fifty million seedlings annually are the basis of a reforestation program. Under the Clarke-McNary Act Mississippi receives cooperative Federal aid in the propagation and distribution of seedlings to private woodland owners. Combined with careful management, the nursery program is designed to extend the present forested area.

Management Activities

The forestry agency is authorized to expend a portion of its state appropriation to encourage the growth of timber and its production, to encourage private ownership, and to foster forestry education. Much of this activity involves educational and demonstrational projects for rural schools and communities. Stand improvement is emphasized by demonstration of techniques for removing undesirable species, for reseeding, for cutting, and for adequate stocking. Mandatory cutting practices were imposed in 1944 by legislation applicable to specific tree sizes and species.[10] These practices are enforced by inspections.

Considerable activity in forest management and demonstration is included in the program of the State Extension Service. This service embraces assistance to farmers in determining the volume of timber upon their farms, in selecting timber to be cut, in restocking, and in marketing their products. The Federal program of assistance to private owners and non-farm timber owners upon problems of management, protection, and utilization of the resource is facilitated by the state agency.

* Title is in the University of Mississippi. The forest stretches over parts of George, Jackson, Harrison, and Stone counties.

WILDLIFE MANAGEMENT

Wildlife management in Mississippi has a dual task. First, it must provide constructive hunting and fishing together with the facilities that make it a recreational use, and second, the contribution that is made thereby must assist in the general development of the state. Although thirty-one states had recognized the importance of wildlife management by establishing administrative bodies before 1900,[11] Mississippi did not create the State Game and Fish Commission until 1932. Before that time inland wildlife conservation rested upon enforcement of prohibitory statutes. Evidently the state was well endowed with game and fish, and either a predominantly rural population threatened it but slightly, or Mississippi was tardy in recognizing the value of the resource. The regulation of sea food fishing, in contrast, began fully three decades earlier.

Game and Inland Fish

The State Game and Fish Commission, through its director of conservation, administers the system of game laws that has been adopted to give wildlife the optimum opportunity to reproduce. Law enforcement is attempted on a state-wide basis. Immediately responsible for enforcement are more than ninety game wardens who operate under the supervision of regional area officers systematically distributed over the area of the state. Among the statutes enforced are those concerning the various license fees, the open and closed seasons, and bag limits. Records of the agency show that arrests are not made indiscriminately or where there is no chance of conviction. Since game laws are frequently unpopular in specific localities, the intensity of their enforcement will vary with the local area.

A second phase of the inland game and fish program relates to the reservation of areas upon which hunting or fishing is prohibited. State reservation of lands began in 1932, when the new State Game and Fish Commission was empowered to lease cutover swamp and overflow lands belonging to the state for a twenty-year period. Refuges today fall into three categories: (1) public areas purchased or leased especially for game refuge and restoration purposes; (2) other public lands, such as the nine state parks, that have been designated game refuges; and (3) private lands that have been posted against trespassing after the wildlife agency has entered into agreement with the owners. Publicly owned refuges are provided with fire protection and predatory control.

Almost from the beginning the State Game and Fish Commission has conducted wildlife restoration projects. In 1938 the legislature enacted the necessary statute to permit the commission to participate in Federal aid restoration projects under the terms of the national Pittman-Robertson Act.[12] One of the more significant of these projects was a "coordination project" intended to adjust all governmental efforts, national and state, for wildlife restoration to a single program. Still other projects have included refuges where game is produced under the most favorable conditions. With somewhat similar purposes the state agency assists the Fish and Wildlife Service of the United States Department of the Interior in the distribution of excess fish from the Federal hatcheries and engages in an active fish rescue program. The latter involves taking fish from isolated water pits along streams and rivers and transplanting them to public waters and to privately owned fishponds.

A fourth aspect of the wildlife program centers about the control of industrial, agricultural, and forestry programs that directly or indirectly destroy wildlife. Among harmful practices are stream pollution, the silting of lakes and streams from erosion, the clearing out of fence rows serving as habitats, and the indiscriminate felling of "den trees" by loggers and cutters. In this connection cooperative relationships are maintained with Federal organizations, such as the Soil Conservation Service. Other practices are combatted through conservation education programs. Sportsmen's clubs, of which there are now upwards of sixty in the state,[13] and the Mississippi Conservation League contribute substantially to these programs.

Sea Food Conservation

The State Sea Food Commission administers statutes governing the sea food industry, which is concerned chiefly with shrimp and oysters. The importance of these products has been recognized for a half century as a resource that supports extensive employment on the Gulf Coast of Mississippi. The program of the commission is primarily regulatory, but it seeks also to replenish oyster reefs in the coastal waters. Hardly a conservation agency in the strict sense of the term, this commission yet performs an important conservation function.

PARKS AND SCENIC RESOURCES

Parks and recreational areas have been accepted as a public obligation because they both conserve natural resources and contribute to the health and well-being of Mississippi's people. Consequently, administrative action has been taken in recent years to establish a park system and to preserve historical sites.

State Park System

Until 1933 Mississippi had no state parks. Then the Federal government, as it had in other states, offered assistance in the development of recreational areas through the manpower of the Civilian Conservation Corps. Aid in the form of grants was also extended. Within eight years a state park system comprising more than 8,000 acres was constructed. This system today represents an investment of more than $2,000,000.

TABLE 11

MISSISSIPPI STATE PARKS, 1953

Name	*Location*	*Size in Acres*	*Date Opened*
Leroy Percy	Hollandale	2,442	July, 1935
Tombigbee	Tupelo	522	July, 1938
Clarkco	Quitman	793	June, 1938
Tishomingo	Tishomingo	1,404	May, 1939
Holmes County	Durant	444	June, 1939
Roosevelt	Morton	562	July, 1940
Spring Lake	Holly Springs	856	May, 1938
Percy Quin	McComb	1,673	May, 1939
Magnolia	Ocean Springs	250	June, 1941

Source: Biennial Reports of State Board of Park Supervisors.

State parks are well scattered: one services the Gulf Coast, three south Mississippi, two the rich Delta section, and three the more sparsely populated northern part of the state. Facilities vary somewhat with the park, but generally available are lakes, swimming and boating areas, picnic grounds and equipment, bathhouses, and, in most parks, vacation cabins. During the war period the physical condition of these facilities as well as the parks themselves deteriorated. In recent years a moderate program of repair has been undertaken to rehabilitate the parks.

Until 1936 park management was a duty of the State Forestry Commission. At that time the legislature established the State Board of Park Supervisors, which consists ex officio of three members of the forestry agency designated by the governor for four-year terms.[14] The board appoints a park director to serve as its executive officer. Hampered by insufficient financial support, the park system has much work ahead of it yet. Nevertheless, Mississippi parks are now visited annually by 25 per cent of the state's population. Their future development hinges, perhaps, on the continued orientation toward conservation rather than agriculture.

Memorials and Historical Sites

Major emphasis in the preservation of memorials has been a responsibility of the National Park Service rather than of the state.* On the level of state action, however, the Brice's Crossroads-Tupelo Battlefield Commission is charged to study and examine the two battlefield sites, to accept gifts and donations, and to cooperate with neighboring states in marking the battlefields as memorial locations. The Natchez Trace, first a primitive Indian path and then an historic highway linking Natchez with Nashville, Tennessee, has been partially restored by the United States government in cooperation with the governments of Mississippi, Alabama, and Tennessee. Important objectives of the restoration program are preservation of native scenes and historic sites along the parkway. The Natchez Trace Parkway Right-of-Way Commission, now inactive, was set up in 1938 to negotiate with the county boards of supervisors in the purchase of rights-of-way, which amount to 314 miles in the state. War brought activities to an abrupt halt in 1941 and left the project incomplete, although substantial progress has been made in recent years.

WATER RESOURCES

The water problems thus far encountered have not been related to the extent and utilization of available supplies so much as to the control of water carried by the many streams and rivers of the state. Although flood control has been thus of greater interest, evidence is ample that problems of water conservation require increasing consideration.

Water Conservation

The water potential of Mississippi is of doubtful quantity. Only in the southern portion of the state is water found in quantities sufficient to support large industrial establishments. In the north central areas there are definite limitations both as to locations and quantity. The alluvial plains of the Delta have enough water for current needs, but heavy indus-

* Historical sites under Federal jurisdiction include the Vicksburg National Military Park and Cemetery, the Brice's Crossroads Battlefield Site, Tupelo Battlefield Site, and the Ackia Battlefield Site.

trial use would reduce the pressure considerably and make pumping necessary.[15] Apparently with considerations of this sort in mind, the long defunct Mississippi Planning Commission recommended more than a decade ago that a Committee on Artesian Waters be established and empowered to issue rules and regulations for water conservation. Although the State Geological Survey and the Water Resources Branch of the United States Geological Survey conduct surface and ground water investigations, no state legislation is now in force to prevent needless waste. Research is the sole current effort in this direction.*

Stream pollution was attacked by a 1942 statute. The laws are broad enough currently to embrace all water sources in the state. Thus the State Game and Fish Commission is charged to prevent pollution that is destructive of aquatic life or injurious to the public welfare as well as to control all waste disposal.[16] Provision is made for inspection as a part of the enforcement process, for investigation and full hearings, and for punishment of violation of promulgated rules. Additionally, the State Board of Health is authorized to abate pollutions that endanger public health. In both instances, though, water conservation is approached from a police and negative point of view.

Flood Control

The main brunt of flood control programs is carried by the Mississippi River Commission, an agency of the United States Department of the Army.[17] The mission of this body is to protect from floods the alluvial valley of the Mississippi River, which stretches from Cape Girardeau, Missouri, to Louisiana. Several of its program activities are carried on with the constitutionally created Board of Mississippi Levee Commissioners and Board of Yazoo Mississippi Levee Commissioners,[18] and with the numerous local districts. The levee commissioners are local officers, popularly elected. They have been authorized to supervise the erection and maintenance of levees, but also have the power to cede rights-of-way, levees, and their management to the United States government. Current activities focus on the maintenance of flood control works, although they may construct ditches and levees. Without their active cooperation the Mississippi River Commission probably would not have undertaken many

* The legislature recently considered a Mississippi Water Resources Policy Commission to conduct a study of water resources that would assist the legislature in implementing a state policy for full utilization and protection of such resources.—Mississippi Legislature, 1954 Session, House Bill 194.

projects in the Delta that now safeguard rich agricultural lands from overflows and that have reclaimed others.

For almost a century the state has permitted the organization of local flood control districts in addition to the two sectional boards. From 1888 to 1939, 304 districts were organized to cover 2,988,460 acres,[19] but evil days fell upon many of them as a result of extensive financial obligations arising from construction work. Today no more than 170 are active. No central office exists for coordination of their activities in a comprehensive program or for the establishment of new districts on the basis of engineering feasibility.

MINERAL RESOURCES

In 1854 a "Report on the Geology and Agriculture of Mississippi," written by the first state geologist, called attention to the presence of large deposits of nonmetallic minerals. Although some interest in discovering and utilizing this potential mineral wealth was manifested in the 1930's, when the first Balance Agriculture with Industry Program was launched, the mineral resources of Mississippi received little attention until the discovery of oil in 1939. Aside from oil, few Mississippi minerals are spectacular. Common brick clay, crude sandstone, small deposits of iron ore suitable for paint pigments, some high grade bauxite, gravel and chert, bentonite, fuller's earth, and lignite are among the deposits.

A rapid expansion of the petroleum industry brought about a tremendous increase in the value of the state's mineral production in a single decade. In 1949, for example, the value of all minerals extracted was $95,300,000 as compared to a value of only $5,192,000 in 1939.[20] Mississippi now ranks 9th in oil production among the states and 28th in the total value of its mineral products. More than 3,500 workers are employed in extracting or processing minerals with an annual pay roll of $11,000,000. Of this total, oil accounts for as much as 90 per cent.

Mineral Policies for Public Lands

The Mineral Lease Commission, consisting of the governor as chairman, the attorney general, state land commissioner, and the state oil and gas supervisor,[21] dates back to 1932. Its objective, declared by statute, is to conserve, explore, and exploit mineral wealth in public lands. Attainment of this goal rests upon policies relative to the lease of state land for oil and gas or other minerals, to the execution of contracts for the drilling of oil or gas wells on public lands when required to protect the public interest, and to the construction of pipelines for state-owned fuels. So narrow are the powers of this agency that discretion as to when lands will be leased or contracts for drilling executed is almost the extent of its powers.

Oil and Gas Regulation

Protection of oil and gas resources against both waste and overproduction is the task of the State Oil and Gas Board. This body currently consists of five members. Three of them are appointed by the governor for staggered terms of six years from the three supreme court districts; one is appointed by the lieutenant governor, and the fifth by the attorney general, the latter two appointees serving four-year terms. The board appoints an administrative agent, the state oil and gas supervisor.

Production of petroleum is prorated among producers on a quota system that helps to keep a stable crude oil price and is motivated apparently by a desire on the part of the state to secure the maximum yield from the oil severance tax. Many experts prefer a field unitization system to the prorata plan. Under the unitization method producers pool their interests, space wells to secure the maximum oil from the field, and share profits on the basis of the acreage that each controls. The effect of this system is to eliminate the pressure of competition, in that holdings do not have to be rapidly exploited to ensure a return on the investment. The unitization system has been criticized, however, on the ground that it monopolizes the petroleum industry.[22]

In any event the board's program is stated in terms of regulatory activities. These activities are expressed in rules and regulations adopted under the terms of the laws governing production and distribution of mineral fuels. The state oil and gas supervisor devotes his full time to the issuance of drilling permits, supervision of oil and gas production in the various fields, and enforcement of the rules promulgated by the board. Notice and hearing are required by statute, and appeal may be taken from decisions of the board to the circuit court of Hinds County.[23]

Although both the private producers and the state have made a number of improvements in production and refining that have reduced waste, critical comment holds that "the most urgent need for conservation measures relative to mineral resources is in the petroleum and natural gas fields. . . . It is urgent that the public policy of Mississippi concerning oil and gas production be reviewed before it is too late to take adequate measures to protect the people's interest in these resources."[24]

Geological Survey

Nominally the work of the state geologist is directed by the State Geological Survey.* Actually this officer is free to plan and to execute the agency's program on the basis of his own initiative. In recent years the geological program has emphasized, although not exclusively, the location of oil and gas and the location and laboratory tests of clays suitable for industrial processing. During the depression years Federal funds assisted the preparation and financing of a dozen or more individual county surveys of mineral resources, but none of these have been completed recently. More than sixty-five bulletins of all kinds have been published by the State Geological Survey.

The work of the state geologist is designed apparently to bear immediate fruit for industrial development by providing detailed and technical knowledge of the state's mineral reserves. Clearly minerals cannot be developed until they are located and their quality and quantity have been summarized. Nevertheless, progress has been slow: "Unless the geological survey of the state proceeds at a faster pace than in the past fifty years, the survey will not be completed in this century."[25] Major needs for adequate geological investigation and research are now sufficient funds to employ staff and to test minerals that have been located.

FOOTNOTES

[1] Compare with Clifford J. Hynning, *State Conservation of Natural Resources* (Government Printing Office, 1939), p. 4.

[2] See Robert Baker Highsaw, *Mississippi's Wealth: A Study of the Public Administration of Natural Resources* (Bureau of Public Administration, University of Mississippi, 1947), pp. 62-63.

[3] Constitution of 1890, art. 4, sec. 50.

[4] See *Mississippi Code, 1942,* Recompiled volume 5A (1952), secs. 6132-01–6132-34.

[5] *Memphis Commercial Appeal,* February 5, 1950.

[6] *Mississippi Forests and Parks* (Published by the State Forestry Commission and the State Board of Park Supervisors, January and February, 1950), p. 2.

[7] *Mississippi Laws, 1932,* ch. 310.

[8] *Ibid., 1944,* ch. 238; replaced in part by *ibid., 1950,* ch. 210.

[9] Highsaw, *Mississippi's Wealth,* p. 112.

[10] *Mississippi Laws, 1944,* ch. 240.

* The survey is an ex officio body composed of the governor, state superintendent of education, chancellor of the University of Mississippi, president of Mississippi State College, and director of the Department of Archives and History.—*Mississippi Code, 1942,* sec. 8954. One member stated to the writers that the survey had not met in the decade or more that he had served upon it and that he "wondered what the state geologist did."

[11] Hynning, *op. cit.*, p. 25.

[12] *Mississippi Laws, 1938 Ex. Sess.*, ch. 39.

[13] *Mississippi Official and Statistical Register* (Jackson: Secretary of State, 1949), pp. 418-20.

[14] *Mississippi Laws, 1936,* ch. 194.

[15] Glen Francis Brown, *Geology and Artesian Water of the Alluvial Plain in Northwestern Mississippi* (University: State Geological Survey, Bulletin 65, 1948), p. 10.

[16] *Mississippi Code, 1942,* Recompiled volume 5 (1952), secs. 5929-01–5929-17.

[17] The Federal flood control program is discussed in Highsaw, *Mississippi's Wealth,* pp. 18-22. See also, Robert B. Highsaw, *The Delta Looks Forward* (Stoneville, Mississippi: Delta Council, 1949), pp. 67-76.

[18] Constitution of 1890, art. 11, sec. 228 ff.

[19] Mississippi State Planning Commission, *Summary Report of Planning Activities* (Jackson, December 31, 1939), p. 21.

[20] *The Blue Book of Southern Industry, 1949* (Baltimore: Manufacturers Record Publishing Company, 1949), p. 121; Bureau of the Census, *Statistical Abstract of the United States* (Government Printing Office, 1949), p. 761.

[21] *Mississippi Code, 1942,* Recompiled volume 5 (1952), sec. 5947.

[22] Summarized from "Mississippi's Mineral Resources," *Resource Use Notes* (Department of Resource Use, Mississippi State College, February, 1950), II, p. 5.

[23] *Mississippi Laws, 1948,* ch. 256.

[24] "Mississippi's Mineral Resources," pp. 5-6.

[25] *Ibid.*, p. 6.

CHAPTER 18

Transportation

MISSISSIPPI'S SYSTEM of roads and highways started with the primitive Indian trails that the first settlers followed, widened occasionally into crude roads as the traffic increased. Gradually other roads were constructed where necessity arose and resources permitted, although the waterways of the Yazoo, Big Black, Pearl, and Tombigbee rivers established the pattern for much of the early settlement of the state. Sometimes roads and waterways were combined, like the Natchez Trace, which the crews who piloted the flat-bottomed boats of the early river trade to New Orleans used on their return journeys.

Early attention to transportation needs was reflected in territorial statutes of 1799 that established basic road widths and provided the first road districts. Not long afterwards turnpike and toll road companies were created by legislative incorporation, the Homochitto Turnpike Company, established in 1809, being an early example. From the first, public road management was vested in local officials and in 1834 finally was placed with the county governing boards.

Not until 1916, though, was the State Highway Commission created and then only in anticipation of passage by Congress of a Federal aid program for highway construction. Even then the powers of the local units of government were carefully guarded.* Within a decade the Mississippi

* *Mississippi Laws, 1916,* ch. 168. The sum of $13,000 was appropriated for the first two years' operation of the new agency. Its duties were restricted to apportioning Federal funds and rendering technical advice to the counties. Four years later an act of the legislature, which enlarged the membership of the commission, provided that its powers would be "advisory to the boards of supervisors, whom the commission may assist with its engineering forces . . ." in road planning, location, and construction.—*Ibid., 1920,* ch. 26.

constitution had been amended to allow the legislature to designate state highways and to place them under the jurisdiction of the State Highway Commission.[1]

Long before the state acted directly to construct highways, it was concerned with water transportation. The first legislature in 1817 sought to assure improvement of water transportation, and appropriations for constructing or improving canals date back to 1823.[2] This interest resulted in the establishment in 1829 of the Board of Internal Improvements, an early planning agency that survived only until the middle of the century. Since its demise no state agency has been concerned with water transportation, although port commissions are authorized for several coastal and river cities.

The rapid development of air transportation in our century and the progress in aeronautics led to the creation of the Mississippi Aeronautics Commission in 1946. This agency is charged to encourage and to assist the development of air transportation in Mississippi and to act as a regulatory agency in matters that do not conflict with Federal air policy.[3]

STATE HIGHWAY ORGANIZATION

State Highway Commission

The United States government announced in 1928 that Mississippi did not meet the requirements for Federal highway aid and that no further allotments would be made to the state after June 30, 1929. Governor Theodore G. Bilbo immediately called a special session of the legislature to reorganize the State Highway Commission and to begin a hard-surfaced road program. Only 443 miles of paved road had been constructed by that date in a state system totaling 5,053 miles, and the legislature responded to the gubernatorial summons by setting up a study committee headed by Representative Horace Stansel, a registered civil engineer. The report of the Stansel Committee and the legislation of 1930, which was based upon it, set the course of highway administration in Mississippi for the next twenty years.

The legislature of 1930 transformed the State Highway Commission from a body of eight commissioners to one of three and vested in the new agency complete supervision and control over all roads in the state highway system.[4] Its action made Mississippi the only American state to elect the membership of its highway commission.* One member is chosen by the voters of each supreme court district, which thereby becomes a highway district, for a term of four years. The commissioners, whose tenure of office is concurrent, are compensated by per diem payments plus traveling expenses for days spent on their official duties. Annual per diem compensation may not exceed $6,600 each nor expenses $2,750 each.[5]

The commission appoints a director of the State Highway Department, who must be "a practical businessman" and who must not have been one of the commissioners within two years of his appointment. This official serves a four-year term that now is staggered with those of the commissioners. Even though the commission operates with an administrative officer, full responsibility for departmental management rests upon the State Highway Commission, which acts collectively as a legal entity, speaking only through the official minutes. Policy-making and administration thus are merged; the advantages that a plural body has of calm deliberation of broad considerations are mingled with the acute disadvantages of responsibility for administrative management. Accordingly, the director serves chiefly as an agent of the commission in approving bids and requisitions, in purchasing, and in signing contracts in the name of the state.

Under the director, and appointed by him with the approval of the commission, is the chief engineer. The engineer must meet specified professional qualifications and possess additionally five years of experience in highway construction. His term of office, also staggered with those of the commissioners', is four years. The director appoints, with the approval of the commission, additional engineers who are the heads of the principal divisions: construction, maintenance, and bridges.[6] The chief engineer, in turn with the director's approval, may appoint not more than nine district engineers; six are now employed. Any of these engineers may be removed for cause at any time by the director with the approval of the commission.

The administration of the department, subject to commission action, rests with the director in such matters as fiscal control, public relations, and office management and with the chief engineer for the engineering function. The administrative position of the chief engineer is weakened by the fact that the heads of divisions need not be responsible to him. However, he may formulate plans for the commission's approval, supervise and control construction and maintenance activities, and develop necessary research information. Beyond strengthening the position of the chief engineer, other

* Twenty-three states provide for appointive commissions, fifteen for departments headed by single administrators, and nine for single executives with advisory boards or commissions.

improvements that appear desirable for the highway agency include formulation of state-wide programs rather than those now based on apportionment of funds by the three highway districts; the development of continuity of policy and experience in the State Highway Commission, which can be accomplished only by staggering the terms of its members; an expansion of the public information function, supplying citizens with full reports of program activities and policy decisions; and achievement of uniform policies and standards of maintenance throughout the state.[7]

Federal Highway Systems

Federal highway funds are expended upon those systems that the state and the counties have selected with national approval. Three such systems are operative in Mississippi, with a total of approximately 12,000 miles.

The first is the interstate system, composed of four principal highways having 695 miles within the state. The Federal Highway Act of 1944 required designation of these roads to promote national defense by connecting cities, industrial centers, and metropolitan areas by as direct routes as possible. The second system, Federal-aid primary roads, is intended to link the major population centers of the United States. Highways for it were first designated in 1922 and 1923 by the State Highway Commission under national legislation that restricted grants to no more than 7 per cent of the total rural mileage in any state. Federal-aid primary highways now exceed 4,000 miles in Mississippi.

The third Federal system, the secondary roads, was started during the depression largely as a means of relieving unemployment. Mississippi has received and spent funds on the Federal-aid secondary system every year since 1934, with the exception of the World War II period, and this system today is a major part of the Federal program. Increased funds made possible the Public Roads Administration's program of expanding aid for secondary roads in 1944, when Congress required the designation of the principal secondary and feeder roads as a secondary highway system. In Mississippi today the Federal-aid secondary system embraces slightly more than 7,300 miles.[8]

Local Highway Administration

The county boards of supervisors are directly responsible for local highway activities and have control of county roads and bridges.[9] The supervisor from each beat exercises supervision of the roads in his district.

Although the boards of supervisors may establish a unit highway system under which all county roads are superintended by a road commissioner or county engineer, this system has remained largely unused. In general the individual supervisors have immediate control and direction, although alternatively special road districts may be created directly by the boards of supervisors or upon the petition of the local residents.[10] Each district is governed by three road commissioners selected by the board of supervisors for four-year terms. These districts are special taxing units and frequently are under the domination of the supervisors. They are usually small in area, ten or more to the county being common where they are found.

Mississippi has made little progress toward centralization of local highway administration. However, in 1949 the legislature provided a Division of State Aid Road Construction in the Highway Department. This division, headed by a state-aid engineer appointed by the governor, was created to render advice and technical assistance to the boards of supervisors on matters affecting the newly designated system of state-aid roads.[11] The state-aid engineer also may promulgate reasonable rules and regulations for designation of state-aid roads, issue uniform standards of design and specifications for their construction, approve or disapprove state-aid road contracts let by the boards of supervisors, and supervise and inspect the road projects receiving state assistance. These powers do not extend to roads entirely under jurisdiction of the county boards.

Municipal street administration deals with such factors as traffic planning and land use, design of arterial roads, and improved traffic engineering functions. The general law charter provides a street commissioner for municipal corporations, and in the larger Mississippi cities public works departments sometimes discharge this function. Statutes require the State Highway Commission to maintain all municipal streets used as a part of its primary system, and 1948 legislation extended state powers over municipal street construction to permit construction and maintenance of these streets at the department's discretion.

HIGHWAY FINANCE

Highways consume a larger ratio of the state dollar than any other function except education. At the same time, the state, its counties, and the municipalities have drawn highway funds from relatively few sources, namely, the motor fuels taxes, bond issues, Federal funds, motor vehicle fees, general fund and miscellaneous local revenues, and the property tax.

Of these sources the first three provide the major part of state highway moneys. So long as the counties were responsible for highway construction and matched Federal-aid funds, the State Highway Department was financed chiefly from motor fuels revenues. Since 1932, however, bond issues and Federal aid, along with the fuels taxes, have increased the amounts available for highway purposes.

State Highway Funds

Prior to 1932 annual funds for the State Highway Commission rarely exceeded $2,500,000. In the prewar period 1936-1941 average annual amounts for highway use exceeded $23,000,000. During World War II highway activities and highway funds both were curtailed. By 1952, however, highway expenditures from all sources were above $41,000,000.

Borrowing for state highways dates only from 1936, when Mississippi issued $23,000,000 in bonds to inaugurate construction of its present system of highways. Two years later most of these bonds were refunded from a $60,000,000 issue that authorized additional funds to continue the new program, and in 1946 the Mississippi legislature authorized another issue of $30,000,000. By the end of 1948 the state had actually borrowed somewhat more than $87,500,000 for highway purposes. Under the 1938 statute, which is still in force, bond issues must not exceed the amount where the total of annual payments and interest on the bonds will be greater than one third of motor fuel revenues estimated on the basis of the sums received from this source for the three years preceding the issue.[12] This revenue is pledged to their retirement. Highway debt service now exceeds $4,000,000 annually, and the highway bonds outstanding June 30, 1952, amounted to $61,945,000.

Motor fuels taxes are the sole tax revenue segregated in part to the State Highway Commission's use, yielding in 1952, $32,450,000. Receipts from the tax are now divided 9/14 to the State Highway Department and 5/14 to the counties. From its adoption in 1922 through 1952 the motor fuel revenues have brought more than $300,000,000 for highway purposes and more than $10,000,000 annually since 1936. This increase is attributable in part to the growth of automotive transportation and in part to periodic rises in the tax rates. Now taxed at 7 cents per gallon, gasoline was originally taxed at 1 cent; the tax was raised to 3 cents per gallon in 1924, 4 cents in 1926, 5 cents in 1928, and, finally, 6 cents per gallon in 1932. Other applicable rates are: oil, ½ cent per gallon; oil for motor vehicles, 8 cents per gallon; liquefied gas, ⅛ cent per gallon; and liquefied fuel other than gas, if used to propel motor vehicles, 8 cents per gallon.[13] Limited funds from motor vehicle fees also are available.

Motor fuel taxes and vehicle fees, along with others, are collected by the motor vehicle comptroller, who is appointed by the governor with senate consent for a four-year term. Not only is this officer responsible for collection of the motor fuels revenues, but he also enforces the motor vehicle privilege tax, which is returned to the counties, and enforces legislation providing regulation, inspection, standards, and specifications of gasoline, oil, and petroleum products. In addition to the share that the counties receive, the gasoline tax supports the Highway Safety Patrol, the office of the motor vehicle comptroller, the Mississippi Aeronautics Commission, and refunds to nonhighway users.

Federal Aid for Highways

The effects of national interest in highways have been apparent in the administrative organization for transportation in Mississippi, its financing, and the language of all major legislation for highway programs since 1916. Indeed, as this chapter notes, the State Highway Commission was established in expectation of Federal legislation, and the far-reaching *Stansel Report* resulted from an unfavorable Federal appraisal of Mississippi's highway organization. Moreover, acts providing revenue for state highway programs normally imply as their intent the matching of grants from the national government.

In 1917 Federal funds authorized for highways in all the states totaled $6,000,000. For a number of years thereafter the annual amounts approximated $80,000,000, rising to a new height, with emergency relief authorization, of $548,936,000 in 1933; by 1951 the annual Federal funds available amounted to $490,000,000. Altogether, in the three decades or so the Federal government made available more than $6,969,000,000 for highways.[14]

Mississippi received its first Federal-aid funds in 1917, and by the time of the great depression, before the 50-50 matching conditions of the early legislation were suspended, more than $25,000,000 of Federal highway money was invested in Mississippi highways. An equal sum was allocated the state between 1930 and 1936. Meanwhile, in 1934 the Congress of the United States re-enacted the matching principle upon which earlier highway grants had been made.

The Federal Aid Highway Law of 1934—the first Hayden-Cartwright Act—contained a number of additional provisions affecting public highways in Mississippi. First, it stipulated that any state would forfeit up to one third of future Federal-aid funds if further diversions of motor vehicle revenues were made for nonhighway purposes after the enactment of the new law. Second, the statute provided a specific distribution of funds to construct secondary or feeder roads, directing that not less than 25 per cent of the money allocated to any state was to be used for secondary roads. Third, permission was given for employment of 1.5 per cent of regular Federal-aid funds for surveys, investigations, and plans for future projects;[15] such application later was made mandatory, and under it the State Highway Commission in 1938 established a planning division. Throughout the decades of the thirties and the forties Federal highway legislation was passed by Congress to aid the states, and Mississippi shared in the assistance proffered by the various acts.

Federal assistance for elimination of grade crossings thus was inaugurated in 1936, and the Federal Highway Act of 1944 authorized $1,500,000,000 for highway construction in the first three postwar years. As a result of this legislation Mississippi received more than $23,000,000, of which 45 per cent was earmarked for utilization on the Federal-aid rural and urban primary systems, 25 per cent for employment in urban areas, and 30 per cent for construction of a secondary Federal-aid system.[16] The Federal Highway Act of 1948 extended this policy and made further authorizations for 1950 and 1951.

Altogether, as Table 12 shows, more than $106,000,000 of Federal highway funds have been available to Mississippi. Of this total, 59 per cent has been segregated for the Federal-aid primary system, 17 per cent for secondary Federal-aid highways, 15 per cent for emergency special grants, and the remainder for the Federal-aid urban system, grade-crossing elimination program, and military access. Special note should be taken of the ratio devoted to emergency relief grants, because with matching state funds these grants largely financed the construction of Mississippi's present highway system.

In 1936 the legislature acted upon the opportunities afforded by the Federal grants and embarked upon a large-scale construction program. Legislation of that year authorized issuance of $23,000,000 of highway notes, $18,500,000 of which were to be used in matching on a 55 to 45 per cent basis a $15,000,000 Federal allocation from the Public Works Administration.[17] The remainder of the bonds was to match Federal-aid funds then available for highway construction, making a total of $42,000,-000 available for this purpose. A system of primary and secondary roads

TABLE 12

FEDERAL AID TO MISSISSIPPI FOR HIGHWAYS

(In thousands of dollars)

Year	*Amount Authorized*	*Year*	*Amount Authorized*
1917	89	1936	2,197
1918	178	1937	2,191
1919	1,168	1938	3,504
1920	1,709	1939	3,413
1921	1,807	1940	2,332
1922	1,295	1941	2,755
1923	863	1942	5,976
1924	1,127	1943	2,407
1925	1,294	1944	None
1926	1,304	1945	None
1927	1,293	1946	7,975
1928	1,308	1947	7,976
1929	1,310	1948	7,898
1930	1,939	1949	None
1931	3,647	1950	7,183
1932	2,210	1951	7,184
1933	7,557		
1934	3,489		
1935	10,239	TOTAL	106,817

Source: Legislative Highway Planning Committee, *Today and Tomorrow* (Jackson, 1949), p. 31.

traversing each of the state's counties thus was facilitated by the combined Federal-state program.

The Federal relationship established by the highway programs has been highly significant for the state government. Intergovernmental relations with the state, the cities, and the counties have been created by it, the state aiding the local governments in system selection, construction, and financing in order to meet national requirements. The state government, in addition to maintaining an adequate administrative organization to administer Federal funds effectively, to matching grants-in-aid, and to refraining from diversion of highway funds, has assumed financial responsibility for adequate maintenance of roads on which Federal funds are expended, classified mileage in eligible systems, and established adequate highway standards. The State Highway Commission also has met Federal inspection prior to reimbursement for expenditures.

MAJOR HIGHWAY ACTIVITIES

Altogether Mississippi has more than 64,000 miles of highways, roads and streets. Of this mileage, 54,000 are in some way a responsibility of the counties, somewhat more than 3,000 miles constitute municipal streets, and the remainder is the state highway network. Highway activities embrace four major areas, namely, construction, maintenance, safety provisions, and traffic engineering.

Construction

Since 1945 state highway construction has been tied closely to the availability of matching funds and Federal aid and has taken the form largely of projects long delayed or made necessary by the ever-increasing traffic load of more than 400,000 registered motor vehicles. The Highway Commission's construction work is limited to the state highway system, which includes the Federal-aid systems together with the highways, roads, and streets placed under the commission for construction and maintenance purposes.

Mississippi legislatures frequently have designated additional highways to be included within the state system. The 1948 legislature reversed this trend and limited the state primary and secondary systems to 5,000 miles each. The report of the Legislative Highway Planning Committee in 1949 recommended that the state system further be reduced to 6,500 authorized miles, of which 5,880 miles would be rural highways serving every municipality of 1,000 or more population, with one through state highway. In the ensuing special and regular sessions, the legislature fixed the system at 8,600 miles,[18] which stands today as the maximum authorized mileage of the state plan.

Highway construction is under the supervision of the construction engineer of the State Highway Commission. Typical biennial data for this activity are reflected in Table 13.

Among the problems involved in highway construction are the selection of surface types in relation to soil conditions, availability of materials, and probable maintenance costs as well as the volume and nature of the traffic traveling over the highways, surfaced widths, grade and drain, bridges, road protection, and many other technical matters.*

* *Mississippi Laws, 1938,* ch. 130, established a formula for allocation of bonds and other construction funds to the three highway districts. This formula distributes 37.5 per cent to the northern district, 25 per cent to the central district, and 37.5 per cent to the southern district.

The Legislative Highway Planning Committee also recommended adoption of a system of state-aid roads comprising 13,600 miles. This plan

TABLE 13

STATE HIGHWAY CONSTRUCTION, 1949–1951

Type	*Miles*	*Cost*
Federal-aid primary and urban projects	517.1	$21,761,202
Federal-aid secondary projects	1,224.6	16,713,854
State projects	175.5	4,004,929
Projects completed and accepted	95.5	2,964,918
Projects under contract	669.2	29,663,362
TOTALS	2,681.9	$75,108,265

Source: *Eighteenth Biennial Report of the State Highway Commission* (Jackson, 1952), pp. 49-61.

was founded on the premise that all of the important secondary roads should be grouped into a single system and that division in management between the State Highway Commission and the counties should be eliminated.[19] The general proposal was adopted, and accordingly the legislature in 1949 established a state-aid system of 11,656 miles. Although the state is not directly and immediately responsible for highway construction in this system, state authority through the grant-in-aid principle extends to promulgation of rules and regulations for designation of the system in each county, preparation of plans and specifications, adoption of a uniform accounting system, setting up standards of construction, approval by the state-aid engineer of all contracts, and establishing specified measures of fiscal control. By 1952 more than fifty-five counties had adopted approved state-aid systems, and Mississippi had accepted the commitment of extending financial assistance to them on a basis somewhat similar to the Federal-aid program for the states.

The legislative divorcement of the state and state-aid highway systems left 43,000 miles of local roads to complete local supervision, maintenance, and construction. The rural roads thus built, though sometimes so rarely used that they might be abandoned, often provide direct access from farm to market and facilitate school transportation, the delivery of mail, and other services so that sound rural construction programs are significant.

Maintenance

The 1953 cost of repair and maintenance of state highways approximated

$631 a mile. The four main activities of highway maintenance are: (1) preservation of travel surfaces to defer replacement and prevent travel hazards; (2) roadside and shoulder maintenance to keep original highway widths and to furnish a surface level with that of the permanent surface; (3) provisions to ensure adequate drainage; and (4) traffic service maintenance, for instance repainting of center traffic stripes, replacement of signs, guard rails, and similar measures. Rapid stream flows that cause erosion and undermining of bridge supports introduce an additional maintenance problem.

The Maintenance Division of the State Highway Department has established a central office and six maintenance regions, two in each supreme court district, to cope with these problems. State highways in each county are divided in turn into maintenance sections, and a maintenance patrolman is made responsible for the inspection and upkeep of each section. Total maintenance costs on state highways alone exceed $4,000,000 annually.

Highway Safety

Adequate highway maintenance is essential to the safe use of public roads, but the highest possible standards in safety measures and traffic engineering also are important. Accidents on Mississippi's highways cost each year the lives of 400 or more persons. In the first three years following World War II the monetary expense to citizens of the state involved in traffic accidents, measured by insurance payments, hospitalization, damaged property, and other indices, averaged annually over $100,000,000.

Such records of course have not been confined to Mississippi. As far back as 1946 the President's Highway Safety Conference adopted—and reaffirmed in 1949—a nine-point safety program that embraced uniform state laws and ordinances, compilation of accident reports, traffic education, improved law enforcement, and other devices and measures. The conference sought to mobilize public support in the states for this program, and Mississippi soon thereafter formed a coordinating committee of representative state departments and agencies.

Administration of the highway safety function is the immediate responsibility of the commissioner of public safety and of the State Highway Patrol, which operates as a part of his office. The commissioner is appointed by the governor with senate approval for a four-year term. He is removable for cause. An assistant commissioner, who serves as chief of patrol and operations officer, also is designated by the chief executive.[20]

Administrative units within the office are maintained for major activities such as accident prevention, patrol records, drivers' licensing, identification, and auto theft recovery.

The State Highway Patrol, whose jurisdiction has been limited in recent years to operations on the highways, is composed of more than 174 patrolmen assigned among nine districts. Patrolmen are employed by the commissioner of public safety with the approval of the governor; they may be dismissed by him at will within the first twelve months of service, but thereafter only the governor may remove them for cause and after hearing. Members of the patrol are charged with the enforcement of the traffic laws on highways and also of any state laws on any public roads in Mississippi when directed by the chief executive.

The laws of Mississippi governing the use of motor vehicles conform with a few exceptions substantially to those of the Uniform Motor Vehicle Code.* In them are definitions of highways, minimum and maximum speeds for the different types of vehicles, restricted districts and zones, traffic signs, signals and markers, and the requirements for safe vehicle conditions, which are demanded normally for highway safety.

The present statute fixes the maximum for private automobiles at sixty miles per hour, for buses at fifty-five miles, and for trucks at forty-five miles; the minimum open highway speed is thirty miles per hour. Hand signals are required for stopping and turning, and safety markings are provided on hills and curves, vehicle operators being enjoined from overtaking and passing at such places. Many provisions relate to the equipment that a vehicle must possess.

Mississippi required no drivers' licenses before 1938. In recent years it has been recognized that an effective safety program rests in part upon a careful issuance of original licenses as well as an efficient system for handling renewals and duplicates, records of warning tickets, arrests, accident reports, and license revocations. Today all persons driving motor vehicles, except those specifically exempted and those prohibitively excluded,† must secure an operator's license before driving upon the highways or streets of the state. A license is obtained after application and

* *Mississippi Code, 1942,* VI, ch. 2, art. 1; *ibid.,* 1952 Supp., secs. 8091 ff. The statutes do not contain provisions covering titles, although the most recent report of the commissioner of public safety recommended enactment of a titling statute lest the state become a dumping grounds for stolen vehicles.

† Examples of the former are service personnel operating official vehicles, nonresidents licensed or registered in their home states, and operators of farm vehicles; the latter embraces, among others, minors under fifteen years of age, persons whose licenses have been revoked, habitual drunkards, and narcotics addicts.

examination by the Highway Safety Patrol, involving a vision test, a rules of the road test, and a driving test. Licenses now extend for a two-year period, but the commissioner of public safety, as well as the courts, has the authority to revoke or suspend a driver's license for cause.

Another important safety measure is the collection of adequate statistics concerning motor vehicle accidents. Every driver who has an accident that causes death or injury, or that entails damages of $50 or more, is required to report the facts of the accident to the commissioner within twenty-four hours. The latter may require supplemental reports. All of this information, other than the names of the persons involved, is confidential material and by statute may not be employed in court suits.[21] Accident reports then facilitate prompt investigation to determine the cause of the accident and to fix the blame.

The Highway Safety Patrol devotes considerable attention to traffic education. The director of the Public Relations and Safety Education Bureau is also executive secretary of the governor's Official Traffic Safety Coordinating Committee, and this dual position permits the bureau to cooperate with other interested state agencies. The need for care on the highways by driver and pedestrian is explained through school safety patrols, school-bus driver training programs, safety programs in the schools and with civic organizations, the national traffic safety contest, and radio, newspaper, and theatre publicity. Emphasis has been placed also upon a school training program, the supervision of the program being shared jointly by the State Department of Education and the Highway Safety Patrol. This program includes classroom driver education taught in the junior high schools and behind-the-wheel driver education taught in the high schools. This training has been initiated in only a small percentage of the schools, but it has been facilitated by the cooperation of motor clubs and other private associations. Several hundred schools additionally teach the rules of the road.

Traffic Engineering

Traffic engineering is concerned with studying highway use and control and regulatory measures through which easier and safer driving can be developed. A limited traffic engineering function has been assumed in Mississippi by the Division of Maintenance of the State Highway Commission. Nevertheless, the 1949 report of the Legislative Highway Planning Committee listed a number of engineering defects characteristic of the state's highways. Among them are a lack of uniformity in markings, signs, and control devices; poor driver protection at main intersections; inadequate lighting at dangerous points along the highways; lack of automatic gates and an insufficient number of flasher signals at rail-highway grade crossings; inadequate distance and directional markers; and absence in part of properly planned and enforced speed zoning, which results in excessive speeding through school districts and small municipalities.[22]

On the basis of these findings the committee recommended that traffic engineering activities be increased to a full-scale program. Such a program would embrace the elimination of many danger spots on the highways; close cooperation between the State Highway Commission and the safety patrol in designing better highways and in determining the relationship between road design, accidents, and traffic control; development of uniformity in signs and other control devices; and state control of surveys for installation and maintenance of special devices for improving vehicle operation. Although Mississippi has done much in the last decade to emphasize safety, a great deal remains to be accomplished.

MOTOR VEHICLES

Four important aspects of highway transportation deal directly with motor vehicles rather than the highways themselves: titling, licensing, inspection of private automobiles, trucks of all kinds, and other motor carriers, and the financial responsibility of vehicle operators. Since Mississippi has not complied with the provisions of the Uniform Motor Vehicle Code concerning titling, only three subjects—licensing of vehicles, inspection, and financial responsibility—are covered here.

Licensing

Privileges taxes are imposed upon both commercial and noncommercial motor vehicles. With a few exceptions these levies are based on a graduated scale. For example, the annual registration fee for all passenger vehicles is based on the horsepower and gross weight of the automobiles, with buses paying an additional tax measured by seating capacity.* The annual privileges charge for trucks is measured by gross weight, and different rates apply to common and contract carriers of property, private

* *Mississippi Code, 1942,* secs. 9352-03–9352-04. The Motor Vehicle Privilege Tax Act was amended in 1950 to clarify certain definitions, to eliminate an inapplicable tax classification upon passenger coaches, and to specify when excess weight permits shall be obtained by certain vehicles.—*Mississippi Laws, 1950,* ch. 474.

commercial carriers and drays, and private carriers. Trailers and semi-trailers are subject to license fees on the same basis as motor vehicles, depending upon whether they are employed to haul people or property. Registration fees must be paid in October of each year. License tags are sold by the county tax collector for private passenger vehicles, school buses, private carriers of property, commercial carriers, and drays of less than 8,000 pounds as well as for publicly owned vehicles operated by a county or lesser subdivision of government. All other tags are issued by the comptroller of motor vehicles.*

In addition certain fees required by the Motor Carrier Regulatory Act of 1938 must be paid by common and contract carriers whether engaged in interstate or intrastate commerce.[23] The charge for issuance of the necessary certificate or permit is paid but once. Annually, however, fees are charged for identification plates and for inspection. The latter as well as the charge for the plates are flat fees, but carriers of two tons or less have a lower inspection charge. Certificates and permits are issued by the Public Service Commission, and the identification tags are issued after inspection fees charged by the motor vehicle comptroller. Reciprocity in these, as well as other motor registration fees, is extended to those states with whom agreements have been concluded.

Inspection

Mississippi's statute governing motor vehicle inspection is in substantial accord with that of the Uniform Motor Vehicle Code. It has not been operative, however, because funds have never been budgeted for that purpose.

Mississippi's Uniform Highway Traffic Regulatory Act, adopted in 1938 at the time of great highway construction,[24] provided for appointment of official inspection stations and required the inspection of all motor vehicles at least once, but not more than twice each year, the time of inspection to be designated by the State Highway Commission. The act provided that these stations should inspect brakes, lights, steering equipment, horns, mirrors, and windshield wipers. In addition, police officers were authorized to stop and inspect vehicles, which must be put in safe condition within five days if defects are discovered.† Though not implemented, the law

* Municipalities are prohibited from imposing registration fees except upon drays and are excluded thereby from a lucrative revenue source allowed municipalities of several other states. *Mississippi Code, 1942,* Recompiled volume 7 (1952), sec. 9352-12; *Opinion of the Attorney General,* October 15, 1943.

† The legislation required that authorization from the commission is necessary for such action.—*Mississippi Code, 1942,* sec. 8263.

appears satisfactory as a statute, in that it includes equipment other than brakes and headlights and in that provision is made for annual or even semi-annual inspection. Also, it provides for supplementary road examinations by the highway patrol and police officers so that mechanical defects can be discovered between the formal inspections.* A program for periodic inspection assumes even greater significance today as the volume of traffic upon the highways continues to grow.

Financial Responsibility

In 1952 the legislature enacted the Mississippi Motor Vehicle Safety Responsibility Act, [25] thereby following the lead of more than three fourths of the states seeking to protect their citizens from financially irresponsible vehicle operators. The statute, which is administered by the commissioner of public safety, requires that drivers involved in accidents in which any person is killed or property damage exceeds $50 must report the accident in writing to the Department of Public Safety; if, within twenty days after receipt of such a report, the department does not have evidence satisfactory to it that the person subject to liability has been released from liability, that the matter has been adjudicated, or that a written and acknowledged agreement has been made with respect to claims and injuries, the Department of Public Safety is authorized to determine the amount necessary to satisfy the claims or injuries arising from the accident.

Within sixty days after the accident report has been filed, the license of the driver is suspended unless the security assessed against him has been deposited. This suspension, however, does not apply to vehicles covered by proper liability insurance or involved in accidents where no injuries or damage to person or property other than the owner occurred, to automobiles legally parked at the time of the accident, or to vehicles being operated without the owner's permission. Nor does the suspension of license take place in cases where, prior to the time of suspension, liability is released or agreement reached and acknowledged upon damages or where evidence is presented to the department that the vehicle operator was not guilty of negligence and hence not legally liable for damages.

The statute permits also a variety of forms of security. Although many

* *The Biennial Report of the Mississippi Highway Safety Patrol, 1947-1949,* p. 47, recommended that the motor vehicle inspection law be "strengthened with an enabling act permitting the State and Cities to enforce this Law." Apart from the absence of a budget, which apparently precludes state enforcement, the Mississippi Supreme Court in *Davenport* v *Blackmur,* 184 Miss. 836, 186 So. 321 (1938) held that a municipality cannot contract for the purchase of inspection equipment in the absence of a special charter provision authorizing it to establish a testing station.

operators prefer to carry insurance against damage to person or property as a matter of course, surety bonds, individual sureties, cash, or securities as specified are permissible. Other proof of financial responsibility may be required when the original proof no longer fulfills its purpose.

Although the financial responsibility statute marks definite progress in traffic administration in Mississippi, it does have several weaknesses. Chief among these no doubt is the fact that the statute is not applicable until after an accident has occurred; the operator who is careless in his driving habits and the maintenance of his vehicle is not required to show responsibility as a prerequisite to use of the state's highways, roads, and streets. The irresponsible operator and the dangerous vehicle thus cannot be removed from the highways as a preventive measure. Coupled with weak motor vehicle inspection, the 1952 statute may well prove inadequate.

AIR TRANSPORTATION

Mississippi lies directly on the system of commercial airlines that extends between Chicago and New Orleans as well as on the airways of several east-west lines. Postwar concern for the growth of both interstate and intrastate air commerce resulted locally in establishment of the Mississippi Aeronautics Commission in 1946.[26] This body comprises three members selected by the governor with senatorial confirmation. One member must be chosen from each of the supreme court districts, and all members serve six-year terms. The commission appoints its director, or administrative officer, to execute the policies of the commission, which functions as both a regulatory and promotional agency.

The Mississippi Aeronautics Commission is empowered to encourage the development of intrastate aviation and to facilitate the establishment of airports and navigational aids. Among the powers granted to realize this objective are those of recommending legislation, providing financial assistance for airports, supplying air markings and a civil patrol out of funds appropriated by the legislature, conducting hearings to determine the location, cost, and type of state-supported airports, and regulating wholly intrastate air traffic.[27] The commission may also receive and apportion Federal-aid and other moneys for the state or its cities in development of aeronautics facilities.

The commission registers annually, and at a nominal fee, aircraft operating within Mississippi, the chief requirement for registration being the appropriate Federal certificate of license. It holds public hearings, exercises a power of inspection, and licenses airports as well as enforces generally the aviation statutes. The scope of commission activities has not been great, the narrowness of its programs being indicated by current annual expenditures of no more than $20,000. With the projected development of intrastate secondary airlines, its regulatory functions will no doubt expand so long as they do not conflict with national legislation. Until such an expansion the function of the commission will likely remain chiefly promotional.

FOOTNOTES

[1] Constitution of 1890, art. 6, sec. 170.

[2] *Mississippi Laws, 1817,* p. 145; *1823,* ch. 57.

[3] *Mississippi Code,* 1952 Supp., secs. 7536-7540.

[4] *Mississippi Laws, 1930,* ch. 47.

[5] *Mississippi Code,* 1952 Supp., sec. 8019.

[6] *Ibid.,* sec. 8016.

[7] Summarized from Legislative Highway Planning Committee, *Today and Tomorrow—An Engineering Analysis of the Highway System in Mississippi* (Jackson, 1949), pp. 117-20. Hereinafter cited as *Today and Tomorrow.* The Legislative Highway Planning Committee was established by the 1948 legislature to survey highway needs and conditions. It reported back in the above study, made with the assistance of the Automotive Safety Foundation, which has been relied upon extensively in this chapter. The legislature of 1950 terminated the committee's life.

[8] For discussions of the various Federal systems, both generally and locally, see *Today and Tomorrow,* pp. 27 ff., and Austin F. MacDonald, *American State Government and Administration* (4th ed., Crowell, 1950), pp. 561-64.

[9] *Mississippi Code, 1942,* secs. 8386-8496; 1952 Supp., secs. 8328, 8349, 8362.

[10] *Mississippi Code, 1942,* secs. 8382-85, 8389, 8392-96, 8399-8404.

[11] *Mississippi Laws, 1949 Ex. Sess.,* ch. 6, sec. 5.

[12] *Mississippi Laws, 1938,* ch. 144.

[13] *Mississippi Code, 1942,* Recompiled volume 7A (1952), sec. 10013-06.

[14] The Council of State Governments, *Federal Grants-in-Aid* (Chicago, 1949), p. 218.

[15] *Ibid.,* pp. 221, 228; *Today and Tomorrow,* p. 26.

[16] *Today and Tomorrow,* p. 26.

[17] *Mississippi Laws, 1936,* ch. 182.

[18] *Ibid., 1949 Ex. Sess.,* ch. 6.

[19] *Today and Tomorrow,* pp. 79-80.

[20] *Mississippi Code,* 1952 Supp., sec. 8078.

[21] *Mississippi Code, 1942,* secs. 8166-72.

[22] *Today and Tomorrow,* p. 65.

[23] Amended by *Mississippi Code,* 1952 Supp., secs. 7633-83.

[24] *Mississippi Laws, 1938,* ch. 200.

[25] *Mississippi Laws, 1952,* ch. 359.

[26] *Mississippi Code,* 1952 Supp., secs. 7536-01–7540-01.

[27] *Mississippi Laws, 1948,* ch. 189.

CHAPTER 19

Business and Labor

UNTIL RECENT YEARS, the government of Mississippi was not greatly concerned with the problems of business and industrial labor. With an economy almost entirely agricultural there was little occasion for legislation affecting other kinds of economic activity, and the state confined its regulation to the minimum agencies for granting charters, supervision of public utilities, licensing, and inspection. The advent of a greatly enlarged program of national regulation of economic activities, coupled with recent emphasis on industrialization in the state, has made necessary a much broader program of state regulation of business and labor, and legislation of this sort promises to increase. The state has experienced considerable industrial growth in recent years. In the decade 1940 to 1950 employment in manufacturing plants with eight or more employees increased from 56,872 to 78,500, and the wages of these workers rose from $44,000 annually to $158,000 per year. Sales or receipts from manufacturing in 1950 amounted to $914,000,000. A continuation of this growth is generally predicted.[1] Mississippi is one of the few states that has engaged in a state-wide program of direct encouragement and subsidization of new industries.

Generally the regulation of business in Mississippi falls into two broad categories: the regulation of general business and corporations, and the regulation of special kinds of business, such as banking, utilities, and insurance. This distinction is based on the accepted doctrine that certain businesses are "affected with a public interest" and are thus subject to a higher degree of regulation than business in general.[2] Since all business enterprise is subject to the state's police power and may be regulated to protect the public health, safety, morals, and welfare, the distinction is really only one of degree. Separate agencies are maintained in this state for the regulation of business affected with a public interest.

CONTROL OF CORPORATIONS

Issuance of Charters

Any corporation desiring to do business in Mississippi, other than railroads and insurance companies,* must submit its proposed charter to the secretary of state. This charter must contain the name of the company, names and addresses of the incorporators, amount of capital stock and description with sale price, the period of existence of the company, the purpose of incorporation, the number of shares of stock to be sold before commencing business, and, if a utility company, a description of the line and points to be traversed. Upon receipt of the proposed charter the secretary of state refers it to the attorney general for examination. If, after examination, the instrument is found to be in conformance with the laws of the state it is then referred to the governor for approval. If disapproved by the governor, it is returned to the secretary of state with the governor's objections and the company has a period of thirty days in which to amend the provisions to which the governor has objected. When approved by the governor, it is officially certified by the secretary of state and returned to the applicants, who must have it published in a newspaper with circulation in the county of domicile. Fees required for incorporation, varying according to the amount of capital stock with a top limit of $500, must be paid in advance. Corporations applying from without the state are subject to the same general requirements as domestic corporations. Amendments to and renewals of charters are handled in the same manner as when the company was originally incorporated. No charter may be granted for a period exceeding ninety-nine years.

Supervision of Companies

Once chartered, a corporation is subject to little regulation or supervision. Sixty days after organization a report on the officers must be made to the secretary of state. The law guarantees the right of stock-

* Street railways and mutual insurance companies for insuring property of members are not excepted. Railroads are chartered by the governor upon approval of the application by the attorney general.

holders to vote in the election of directors in proportion to the number of shares held; prohibits the withdrawal or diversion of capital stock from its purpose if such action is during or results in insolvency; prohibits corporations, except those engaged in the loan business, from lending money to stockholders; fixes the financial responsibility of stockholders to creditors of the corporation; prohibits corporations from interfering with the social, civil, or political rights of employees; requires a statement of solvency and full information on assets of foreign corporations withdrawing from the state; and regulates the manner in which a charter may be surrendered. In normal operations, however, no reports are required and no financial supervision is exercised. Provisions for enforcement of the laws mentioned above are the same as for any other general laws.

BANKING AND SECURITIES REGULATION

Banking

Mississippi has experimented at length in the regulation of banking. Notable among these experiments was the state guarantee of deposits, a venture that proved a failure and was repealed in 1929. Administration of banking laws was formerly under an elective superintendent of banking, but this office was abolished in 1935, when the present Department of Bank Supervision was established. This department consists of a State Banking Board as a policy-forming and advisory body and the state comptroller, who administers the program of state supervision. The state comptroller is appointed by the governor for a term of four years and must have the qualifications of five-years' banking experience. He is further required to have no interest in any banking business while in office. The State Banking Board consists of the state comptroller and four other members who are appointed by the governor for staggered terms of four years. One of these persons must be the active senior executive officer of a state-chartered bank; the other three must be qualified electors. One is appointed from each supreme court district and one from the state at large.

New banks and banking institutions seeking incorporation in Mississippi must file articles of incorporation and full information with the state comptroller. If after examination the comptroller finds that the proposed institution conforms to the law in regard to public need for the bank, capital, provision for reserve funds, and organization, he recommends authorization of the new bank to the banking board. The board, after a hearing of the proposed incorporators and the procurement of any additional evidence it may desire, makes a decision as to the authorization of the new institution. If authorization is approved, the Department of Bank Supervision issues a certificate of public convenience and necessity that allows the bank to incorporate and organize. After the capital stock has been paid and the bank has paid an assessment amounting to .1 per cent of its capital stock, the department issues another certificate authorizing the institution to begin operation.

The Department of Bank Supervision further regulates banking by fixing the amount of interest to be paid on savings accounts and issuing rules and regulations on banking operations. It has authority to close insolvent banks and supervise their liquidation, as well as to re-open closed banks under specified conditions. Supervision of banks is carried out through examiners appointed by the comptroller who make regular and special examinations of state banks and their operation. The cost of operation of the state's supervision of banking is borne by the banks of the state through annual fees, levied in proportion to their assets.*

Regulation of Securities

The sale of securities by corporations, associations, or persons in the state is subject to fairly detailed regulation under the so-called blue-sky law, originally enacted in 1916. Securities issued by a government, banks, public and quasi-public corporations, domestic corporations organized for educational and charity purposes, and those under regulation by the Securities and Exchange Commission of the United States are exempt from its provisions. Dealers in other securities must file with the secretary of state an application and a plan of the proposed sale, along with a prospectus, full information on the financial condition of the company, its charter or constitution, and any other information that may be required. A fee based on the amount of securities to be sold is charged at the time of application. The secretary of state is empowered to make such examination of the company seeking to market securities as he may consider necessary. If, after examination and investigation, this official believes that the proposed sale will work any fraud, deception, or imposition upon purchasers, or that the company issuing the securities is not in sound financial condition, or that the securities are unreasonably priced, he must

* In 1953 these fees were fixed at $75 for the first $100,000 of assets and fifteen cents per thousand for each additional $1,000. The law authorizes the department to raise fees to a maximum of fifty cents per thousand for assets over $100,000. The banking laws of the state may be found in *Mississippi Code, 1942,* secs. 5153-5287; 1952 Supp., secs. 5159–5278-03.

disapprove the application. On the other hand, if the company and its proposed sale of securities are found to be proper, a permit is issued after the company furnishes bond payable to the state in the amount of 10 per cent of the securities to be sold, with a limit of $100,000.

The secretary of state has the responsibility of seeing that the sales of securities under the permit granted are in accordance with the terms under which it was issued. If he has information of any violation in regard to sales, or of insolvency, bad reputation, or illegal business practices by the company issuing the securities, he may, after notice and hearing, suspend or cancel the permit. Any purchaser of the securities is entitled to bring suit in the chancery court of any county on the bond of the company that has misrepresented the securities purchased and recover the money paid for such securities.[3]

INSURANCE REGULATION

In keeping with most other states, Mississippi has elaborate and detailed legislation regulating insurance. It is one of the few businesses that is regulated almost entirely by the states. Although a recent decision of the United States Supreme Court, reversing an earlier decision, has held that insurance is interstate commerce and thus within the power of Congress to regulate,[4] the Congress has since that time enacted legislation declaring state regulation to be in the public interest and exempting insurance companies from the Federal antitrust laws. For the time being, at least, this important business, affected with a very vital "public interest," is almost exclusively under state regulation.

The general purpose of regulatory insurance laws is the protection of purchasers of insurance policies by requiring reasonable rates, payment of claims for insured losses, and security of savings. To accomplish these objectives, the laws require state approval and supervision of any company as well as its agents who offer insurance policies for sale in the state. Domestic companies organizing in the state are limited to specific types of insurance, though this list contains all forms of legitimate insurance. The laws further require certain capital before companies can be organized and specify the investments in which a domestic company may place its capital, surplus, and other funds. A company from outside the state or the United States seeking to do business in Mississippi must meet requirements as to amount of capital, must file a copy of its charter and full information with state authorities, and make a deposit with the state treasurer to insure the payment of claims. If the application is approved, a permit to do business is granted. Any company operating in the state is required to furnish regular reports on its business, its financial condition, and any other aspect of its operations. For violation of any of the laws regulating insurance or for failure to maintain the company in a sound financial condition, permits of companies may be canceled and licenses of individual agents may be revoked.

Department of Insurance

The administration of the insurance laws in Mississippi is mainly entrusted to the Department of Insurance, established by law in 1902. This department is directed by the state insurance commissioner, elected by the people for a four-year term. The only qualifications for the office are that the incumbent be at least twenty-five years of age, a citizen of the state for five years, and have no connection with an insurance company. This official must furnish bond in the amount of $25,000 to ensure faithful performance of his duties.

As director of the department the insurance commissioner receives applications of domestic companies seeking incorporation in the state, requests of these companies to increase or reduce their capital stock, applications of foreign companies seeking to do business in the state, and applications of all persons who wish to act as insurance agents. It is his responsibility to examine these applications in the light of laws applying to capital, investments, kinds of insurance offered and rates charged, nature of organization of companies, and any other matters relating to the protection of potential policy-holders. If the commissioner is satisfied on these matters, he issues certificates authorizing the companies and agents to sell insurance after payment of the proper fees and deposits. This certificate serves as a charter for a domestic company. Thereafter, it is the duty of the Department of Insurance to supervise the transaction of insurance business by companies and their agents, chiefly through annual reports to the department from the operating companies, though the department may require special reports or make special investigations. Any complaint of a citizen that a company has acted illegally in any respect must be investigated. The commissioner has full power to cancel permits and revoke licenses when it is found that companies are not complying with the law. He also may force a company believed to be insolvent into bankruptcy proceedings.

In addition to the supervision of insurance operations, the Department of Insurance collects all fees and taxes levied on insurance companies and is required to report monthly on these collections to the state auditor and pay the proceeds over to the state treasurer. An annual report on all official acts, the condition of all insurance companies, licenses issued, and taxes received must be made to the governor. The law also makes the insurance commissioner the state fire marshal, in which capacity he works with local fire or police chiefs and county sheriffs in determining the causes, origins, and circumstances of fires.

Insurance Commission and State Rating Bureau

Special provisions for the regulation of fire and casualty insurance companies and their operations are found in the laws establishing the Insurance Commission and the Rating Bureau, which is under its direction. The commission consists of three businessmen, one appointed each by the governor, the attorney general, and the insurance commissioner, for terms of two years. The insurance commissioner is ex officio chairman of the group without the power to vote. The principal duty of the commission is to supervise the State Rating Bureau for Fire Insurance. This bureau, composed of representatives of stock fire insurance companies doing business in the state, establishes rates for such insurance based on basic factors governing risk, such as type of construction, location, and safety provisions. The bureau, with approval of the Insurance Commission, changes these basic rates from time to time, according to the rate of loss and the adequacy of protection. All agents and companies operating in the state are governed by these rates. All stock fire insurance companies doing business in the state are required to be members of this bureau, and mutual fire and casualty companies may subscribe to it. Expenses of the bureau and the commission are paid from assessments levied on companies in proportion to gross premiums collected.[5]

PUBLIC UTILITY REGULATION

Public utilities, generally considered to mean those enterprises engaged in providing water, gas, electric light and power, telegraph and telephone service, and public transportation, are the most highly regulated of all the state's business. This situation is typical of most states and arises from the fact that such businesses supply an esesntial public service and are, by their nature, likely to be natural monopolies. Further grounds for stringent regulation may be found in the grants of state power, such as that of eminent domain, which are bestowed on business organizations of this nature.

Prior to 1938 state regulation of public utilities in Mississippi was under the railroad commission. In that year, however, the old body was superseded by the present Public Service Commission with greatly expanded powers. This commission is an elective body, one member from each of the three supreme court districts, chosen by the voters for a four-year term. A member must be at least twenty-five years of age before election and have no connection with a company coming under the supervision of the commission. Members devote full time to their work.

The principal functions of the commission are as follows:

1. To grant franchises for operation of motor transportation companies, to approve applications of utility companies, and to issue certificates of convenience and necessity.
2. To adopt, promulgate, and enforce rules and regulations with respect to utilities under its supervision, including the abandonment of service.
3. To regulate traffic and freight rates on intrastate lines and to fix, regulate, and supervise rates of motor transportation carriers.
4. To require that the rates charged by utilities be reasonable and just, to require adherence to rate schedules, and to approve rate changes.
5. To conduct safety inspections of intrastate lines and carriers under its jurisdiction and to establish rules and regulations concerning these matters.
6. To require utilities to furnish adequate service.
7. To hear all complaints by and against utilities, railroads, or other common carriers in the state and to conduct hearings on these complaints.
8. To collect fees for inspection, control, and supervision of carriers, equipment, and service related to holders of certificates of convenience and necessity.
9. To visit each county through which a railroad runs and inquire into such matters as complaints and violations.
10. To apply to the courts for assistance in enforcing the statutes entrusted to its supervision and the rules and regulations promulgated under its authority.

The commission holds regular monthly meetings, as well as some special meetings, presided over by a chairman who is elected from the membership. There are eight employees on the staff of the commission, including a secretary, a rate specialist, and an assistant rate specialist. The secretary, who must possess the same qualifications as a commissioner, has custody of records, documents, and the seal, with the duty of issuing citations, subpoenas, and other papers of the commission. He also collects fees and penalties from motor carriers and performs such other duties as the commission may require. The rate specialists check and investigate the schedules filed with the commission and advise the body and the attorney general regarding increases and changes. Formal decisions of the commission may be reviewed by the circuit court with appeal to the state supreme court.

On June 30, 1951, 691 motor carriers, 18 railroads, and 45 other utilities were under the jurisdiction of the commission. The legislative appropriation for the body for the 1952-1954 biennium was $34,700. The fees and penalties collected by the commission also are used to pay expenses of its operations.[6]

TRADE REGULATION

Food and Drug Regulation

Food and drug regulation in Mississippi consists of laws designed to prohibit adulteration of drugs or articles of food manufactured or offered for sale, as well as the mislabeling or misbranding of such products and the use of nonstandard weights and measures. The laws also require the enrichment, by addition of vitamins, of degerminated food products made from corn and wheat and of oleomargarine and provide for inspection of locker plants where frozen foods are stored.

The original regulatory law on foods and drugs was enacted in 1910. It defined "adulterated" drugs as those not conforming to the standards of the United States pharmacopoeia or similar works; "adulterated" foods were defined in greater detail, and the manufacture or sale of both was prohibited. The law further prohibited misbranding, mislabeling, or insufficient labeling or branding of foods and required that proper standards of weights and measures be maintained.[7] More recent legislation, passed in 1944 and 1946, extended the regulation to require vitamin enrichment of certain food products and the approval and periodic inspection of storage facilities for frozen foods. As in the case of the earlier law, these statutes are detailed and comprehensive.[8]

State enforcement of the law regarding adulterated drugs is almost entirely disregarded, since Federal statutes enforced by the Food and Drug Administration of the Federal Security Agency furnish adequate protection. The secretary of the State Board of Pharmacy cooperates with this agency in reporting violations. Enforcement of the regulatory acts on foods is divided among two state agencies and local inspectors. The state chemist (discussed in Chapter 16) is required to fix standards of purity, which are the same as those required by national agencies. This officer also is charged with the responsibility of inspecting, collecting, and analyzing specimens of food with the further duty of publishing the results of such work. Although the state chemist is responsible for the enforcement of this law, the principal task of inspection is placed in the hands of local food inspectors appointed by the governing boards of counties and municipalities. Inspection by the office of the state chemist thus results from violations reported by the local inspectors. Local inspectors also are responsible for maintaining the standards of weights and measures. Enforcement of the laws requiring the enrichment of corn and wheat products and food locker inspection is lodged in the State Board of Health and the state health officer.

Although the division of responsibility for enforcement appears to be serious, it is overcome, in some degree, by the employment of representatives of county health departments as local inspectors, a practice that appears to be general. Thus the State Health Department, either through its own representatives or through the representatives of county health departments, provides most of the inspection services, and the state chemist provides the facilities for testing and analysis. Considerable aid in this work is obtained through the cooperation of the inspection services of the national Department of Agriculture.

Penalties for violation of the various laws regulating drugs, foods, and food facilities include fines ranging up to $500 and imprisonment up to six months. Proceedings against violators are instituted by the district attorney upon evidence supplied by the state chemist or the state health officer.

Antitrust and Fair Trade Laws

In addition to the specific regulation of business described above, some regulatory legislation is administered by the regular law enforcement authorities. Antitrust legislation prohibits a "trust or combine" in intrastate business that restrains trade, limits, increases, or reduces the price or production of a commodity, hinders competition, monopolizes production or sale of a commodity, or engages in similar practices inimical to the public interest. Agricultural cooperatives and agreements made in connection with the sea food industry are specifically exempted from the act. Enforcement of the law is the responsibility of the attorney general and the district attorneys of the state, and power to compel witnesses, books, records, and accounts to establish the fact of violation is authorized by law. Penalties for violation may be fines as well as the forfeiture of the right to do business in the state. The Fair Trade Act of 1938, permitting contracts between producers or wholesalers and retailers to the effect that an article will not be sold except at the price stipulated by the vendor, specified that such contracts are not to be deemed violations of the anti-trust laws.[9]

Incidental regulation of business, naturally, is found in other agencies not directly concerned with business as such and has been described elsewhere in this book. Various agencies primarily engaged in such activities as conservation, agricultural and industrial promotion, and taxation affect the business community and indirectly restrict or facilitate its operations.

LABOR REGULATION

General Provisions

Labor regulation in Mississippi has lagged behind that in most other states in somewhat the same manner that industrial development elsewhere has exceeded that in Mississippi. Agricultural labor—always the major portion of the state's workers—has been consistently without regulation or protection. For a long time the more general laws applying to industrial labor, such as those on safe and sanitary working conditions, child labor, and payment of employees have been in effect, but the small number of workers affected made the amount of regulation unimportant. The large body of Federal labor legislation of the past two decades, such as the National Labor Relations Act of 1935, the Fair Labor Standards Act of 1938, and the Labor-Management Relations Act of 1947, legalized collective bargaining, established minimum wages and a basic work week, and prohibited child labor for all workers in employment related to interstate or foreign commerce. Although the labor force has increased, the number of intrastate workers remains small, and the need for further state legislation affecting them has not been considered pressing. The principal recent laws concerning labor have pertained to employment security and workmen's compensation.*

The first important labor legislation in Mississippi was enacted in 1914. This law, with subsequent amendments, prohibits the employment of persons under fourteen years of age in any "mill, cannery, workshop, factory, or manufacturing establishment" and limits the hours of work for minors above that age in those places. Night work is outlawed for persons under

* Another recent law provides that "the right of persons to work shall not be denied or abridged on account of membership or nonmembership in a labor union or labor organization. . . ."—*Mississippi Laws, 1954,* Senate Bill 1394.

sixteen. Hours of work for women are limited to ten hours per day and sixty hours per week, except in cases of emergency or public necessity. Factories employing five or more persons that include women and children are required to register and pay an annual fee ranging from $10 to $200, depending on the number of employees.

Enforcement of these laws is largely in the hands of a factory inspector chosen by the State Board of Health. This official conducts inspections three times a year of plants affected by the law, collects the registration fees, requires inspection of steam boilers from factories using them, and makes an annual report on his work to the State Board of Health. Evidences of violation found must be reported by the inspector to the county or district attorney. The county sheriff also is required to inspect factories in his county employing child labor once each month, and the county health officer inspects them twice each year and reports to the sheriff on violations of the law relating to health and sanitary conditions. The sheriff is empowered to issue orders correcting unlawful conditions. Violation of these laws or failure to obey the order of a sheriff correcting them is a misdemeanor.

Inspection fees collected from these laws amount to approximately the cost of operation of the office of the factory inspector. These fees are remitted directly to the state treasury, and the agency is supported by legislative appropriation. The appropriation for the 1952-1954 biennium was $32,000.[10]

Workmen's Compensation Law

In 1948 Mississippi enacted a workmen's compensation law, thus being the last of the states to adopt such legislation. This law, like that of other states, is designed to provide a systematic means by which employees can be compensated for injuries received at their work without the necessity, and uncertain results, of bringing suit in the courts. It thus abrogates the common law defenses of employers in such cases and makes them liable for injuries to employees, without regard to fault as to the cause of the injury.

The employers subject to the act include all persons, firms, private corporations, and public service corporations that employ eight or more persons. State agencies, institutions, or departments, and local governments may come under the act if their governing officers so decide. Religious, fraternal, and nonprofit charitable corporations are excluded, as are farmers and farm and domestic labor. Employers may provide the funds for compensation by carrying insurance with private companies, or, upon furnishing evidence of financial ability, may be "self-insurers."

Compensation paid for injuries begins with unlimited medical care during the period of recovery. Payments for disability, whether temporary or permanent, are computed at two thirds the average weekly wage of the worker with a minimum of $10 per week and a maximum of $25 per week. The total period of compensation cannot exceed 450 weeks, and the maximum total amount that may be paid an employee is $8,600. This sum is in addition to the cost of medical care. Compensation for permanent partial disability is at the same rate, though the period of payments ranges from 15 to 200 weeks, depending on the amount of disability. Payments for partial disability of a temporary nature are also at the rate of two thirds the average weekly wage, less the weekly amount the worker is able to earn while partially disabled. The maximum amount and period of compensation are the same as for total disability. Payments begin fourteen days after notice to the employer, but no compensation, except medical benefits, is paid for the first five days of disability if the total period of disability does not exceed fourteen days. Disabled persons undergoing vocational rehabilitation may draw additional compensation up to $10 per month for a period not exceeding one year. Second injuries are compensated for as other injuries; however, if the injury results in permanent total incapacity, the worker may receive the maximum benefits under the law from a "second injury fund." This fund is created by the assessment of $500 on employers for each death of a worker without relatives or dependents eligible for compensation.

Compensation for death of a worker includes a lump sum payment of $100 to the widow, funeral expenses up to $350, and payments to the widow, children, or dependent husband or other dependent relatives, the payments varying in amount according to the number and relationship. The total death payments to all beneficiaries cannot exceed $25 per week; compensation cannot extend beyond 450 weeks, and the total amount paid is limited to $8,600, not including the lump sum death payment and funeral expenses. All compensation for injuries and death benefits are doubled for minors under eighteen years of age who are employed in violation of the labor laws of the state.

Administration of the law is vested in the Workmen's Compensation Commission. This body consists of three persons appointed by the governor with senate confirmation for staggered terms of six years. The chairman is selected by the governor. Commissioners may be removed by the governor for cause, after notice and hearing, but the law declares that the public interest will be served by retention of commissioners in office "as long as efficiency is demonstrated." Commissioners receive annual salaries of $7,000 each; the chairman receives $7,500. The commission employs a staff of fifteen persons. Cost of the operation of this agency is met by assessments on the insurers, and no legislative appropriation is made for its support.

The function of the commission is to direct the administration of the workmen's compensation statute. The commission has the power to adopt and publish rules and regulations to implement the law that are binding on participating parties, to hold hearings and compel witnesses and evidence, to conduct inquiries and investigations, to make awards and decisions, and generally to exercise such powers as are necessary to the proper administration of the system. Appeals from decisions of the commission may be taken to the circuit court of the county where the injury occurred.

During the calendar year 1951 a total of 35,919 reports was received by the Workmen's Compensation Commission. Of these there were 104 deaths, 8,177 major injuries, and 27,638 minor injuries. During this year the total amount paid in claims was $3,208,490.50.[11]

FOOTNOTES

[1] A detailed article on Mississippi's industrial program may be found in *Manufacturers Record,* June, 1951, pp. 66-104.

[2] *Munn* v *Illinois,* 94 U. S. 113, 126 (1877).

[3] The laws pertaining to corporations and securities may be found in *Mississippi Code, 1942,* secs. 5309-90; 1952 Supp., secs. 5310-82.

[4] *U. S.* v *Southeastern Underwriters Assn.,* 322 U. S. 533 (1944).

[5] The extensive legislation on insurance may be found in *Mississippi Code, 1942,* secs. 5616-5834; 1952 Supp., secs. 5626, 5628, 5647-49, 5653, 5669-01–5669-05, 5687, 5704, 5719, 5723-01–5723-07, 5738, 5759, 5834-01–5834-14.

[6] *Ibid.,* secs. 7632-7897; 1952 Supp., secs. 7633–7886-01. See also *Biennial Report of Public Service Commission* (June 30, 1951).

[7] *Mississippi Laws, 1910,* ch. 132.

[8] *Ibid., 1944,* ch. 272; *1946,* ch. 391.

[9] *Mississippi Code, 1942,* secs. 1088-1108.

[10] *Mississippi Code, 1942,* secs. 6977-98; *Mississippi Laws, 1952,* ch. 72.

[11] The workmen's compensation statute, with amendments, may be found in *Mississippi Code, 1942,* Recompiled volume 5A (1952), secs. 6998-01–6998-59. See also *Annual Report of Mississippi Workmen's Compensation Commission* (Jackson, 1952).

CHAPTER 20

Licensing

THE LICENSING of professions and occupations is not a new function of state government. Long recognized as a proper and legitimate exercise of the state's police power, it has been the subject of legislation that dates back more than a hundred years. In recent decades the growth of restrictions on the practice of tradesmen and professional persons has been multiplied. One authority attributes this increase to the attempt of the states to provide two kinds of service: protection of the public interest against unqualified practitioners, and protection of the various occupational groups against the same dangers. Both services may be construed as valid objectives of state policy.[1]

HISTORICAL BACKGROUND

Mississippi has had a professional licensing law almost as long as it has been a state. A legislative act of 1822 provided for the supreme court to appoint three members of the bar, one of whom was the attorney general, who would conduct examinations and license attorneys at the beginning of each term of court. Besides knowledge of the law, applicants were required to produce evidence of good character, United States citizenship, and an age of at least twenty-one years. Under this statute every lawyer was required to present a license before practicing in any court of the state: the penalty for practicing without a license was a fine of $200.* Sixty

* *Mississippi Code, 1824,* ch. 41. The author has found references to two earlier laws licensing attorneys, one passed June 21, 1818, and the other February 12, 1819, both of which gave this function to the supreme court. The references were to

years later the first licensing machinery for medical practitioners was created with the establishment of a "board of censors" in each congressional district of the state. These boards were ex officio, consisting of the two sanitary commissioners of the district. They were empowered to conduct written examinations in eight different fields of medicine for applicants for licenses and to forward their recommendations to the secretary of the State Board of Health, by whom the licenses were issued. In case of disagreement between the members of the district board the secretary of the state board cast the deciding vote on the application. In the same year a law was enacted providing for a board of dental examiners. This body, consisting of five practicing dentists appointed by the governor, was given the power to conduct examinations for prospective dentists and to grant or deny licenses to them. Both laws contained provisions making it unlawful to practice without proper licenses.[2]

In 1892 a similar law was enacted providing for and requiring the licensing of pharmacists. In the present century the older licensing laws have been rewritten and expanded and many additional occupations and trades have been regulated. The most recent group to be included was public contractors under a law enacted in 1952. At the present time the right to practice twenty professions, trades, or occupations is controlled in some degree by the state. Expansion of the list is still a matter of legislative concern, however, and bills providing for licensing of four additional occupations were introduced in the 1952 session of the legislature.[3] All these bills died in committee. One additional licensing agency was established in 1954.

PROFESSIONAL LICENSING AGENCIES

Generally the state has provided for the licensing of the various occupations by separate boards or departments. The only exceptions seem to be in those fields so closely related that separation would make for duplication. Thus, physicians, osteopaths, and podiatrists all are licensed by the same agency, though with different requirements and examinations. In a majority of cases the agency has no other function than the granting and revocation of licenses.

Toulmen's Digest of Mississippi Laws, pp. 29, 55. No copy of this work was available to the author. Mississippi, apparently, was the first state to have a licensing law for attorneys. See W. Brooke Graves, "Professional and Occupational Restrictions," *Temple Law Quarterly* XIII (April, 1939), 334-63.

TABLE 14

LICENSING AGENCIES

Name	Profession or Occupation Licensed	Date of Establishment	Number of Members	Method of Selection	Term (Number of Years)	Compensation
PROFESSIONS						
Board of Bar Admissions	Attorneys	1954	6	Appointed by governor	3	$20 per diem plus expenses
Board of Nurses' Examiners for Mississippi	Nurses	1914	7	Appointed by governor	5	$10 per diem plus expenses (from fees)
State Board of Architecture	Architects	1928	5	Appointed by governor	5	Fixed by board
State Board of Dental Examiners	Dentists, Dental Hygienists	1928	5	Appointed by governor	4	Division of fees
State Board of Education	Teachers	1890	3	Ex officio	4	None
State Board of Embalming	Embalmers	1918	7	5 appointed by governor 2 ex officio	4	Division of fees
State Board of Health	Physicians, Osteopaths, Podiatrists	1924	10	9 appointed by governor 1 ex officio	6	$3 per diem plus expenses (from fees)
State Board of Optometry	Optometrists	1920	5	Appointed by governor	5	$5 per diem plus expenses (from fees)
State Board of Pharmacy	Pharmacists	1922	5	Appointed by governor	4	$10 per diem plus travel expenses (from fees)

State Board of Public Accountancy	Accountants	1920	3	Appointed by governor	4	$10 per diem plus expenses (from fees)
State Board of Registration for Professional Engineers	Professional Engineers	1954	5	Appointed by governor	4	$20 per diem plus expenses
State Board of Veterinary Examiners	Veterinarians	1914	5	Appointed by governor	5	$10 per diem plus expenses (from fees)
State Insurance Commissioner	Insurance Agents	1890	1	Elected by people	4	$8,250
TRADES AND VOCATIONS						
Board of Barber Examiners	Barbers	1930	3	Appointed by governor	4	$10 per diem plus expenses (from fees)
State Board of Cosmetology	Cosmetologists	1948	3	Appointed by governor	4	$10 per diem plus expenses (from fees)
State Board of Public Contractors	Public Contractors	1952	5	Appointed by governor	5	Expenses (from fees)
State Game and Fish Commission	Commercial Fishermen	1932	4	Appointed by governor	4	$20 per diem plus expenses (from fees)
Mississippi Real Estate Commission	Real Estate Brokers, Salesmen	1954	3	Appointed by governor	4	$15 per diem plus expenses

Source: *Mississippi Code, 1942; Mississippi Laws.*

In Table 13 (pages 296-97) are listed the various state agencies engaged in licensing members of professions and vocations with the date of establishment of each in its present form and other pertinent data. It will be noted that the board type of organization has been followed generally in setting up these agencies. Selection of the boards usually is by gubernatorial appointments, although in some cases from restricted lists of nominees. Generally, too, the cost of operation is paid from the fees collected in connection with licensing. Naturally, each agency is a separate legal entity.

The system whereby separate agencies, created at different times with different organizations, regulate admission to professions or trades naturally precludes any central coordination or control of licensing policy. Each profession appears to have been considered by the legislature as an individual problem to be dealt with as seemed appropriate in view of the time, circumstances, and occupational group pressures. There is no necessary uniformity in either procedures or standards.

It is evident that increasing influence has been given to professional societies or organizations in the creation of licensing bodies. Of the agencies listed in the table on pages 296-97, the members of five are selected from lists submitted by the appropriate professional organizations. The fact that most of the licensing bodies operate without public funds also tends to enlarge the degree of control by professions over admission to their ranks. This development appears to have been an attempt to avoid political control over these boards, and in that respect it is to be commended. It raises the possibility, however, that the public interest will be sacrificed in the desire of the professions to restrict the number of licensed members. No abuses of this sort are evident in Mississippi.

State Board of Architecture

The State Board of Architecture was first established in 1928. Qualifications for membership are that a person must be a resident architect and have engaged in the practice of architecture for seven years. The officers consist of a president and secretary-treasurer chosen from the membership; the secretary-treasurer handles all the administrative duties of the agency.

The functions of the board consist of conducting examinations, issuing licenses and revoking them, and renewing the certificates of licensed architects each year. Examinations must be conducted twice each year after public notice of the time and place; approval by a majority of the board is necessary to pass the examination. Out-of-state architects may practice without an examination provided they hold licenses from a similar board in another state, are certified by the national registration boards, are graduates of recognized schools of architecture with three years' experience, or are long-established architects with creditable records. Licenses may be revoked by the board for incompetency, dishonesty, or commission of a crime after notice and hearing. Practicing without a license is made a misdemeanor by the law, punishable by fine or imprisonment.

This agency receives no appropriation from the legislature and is supported entirely by fees authorized by law. Applicants for license must pay an examination fee and $1 for recording the certificate with the secretary of state. A registration fee of $20 also may be charged. Licenses must be renewed annually at a fee of $5. The registration fee for out-of-state architects is $50. About fifteen licenses are issued each year.[4]

Board of Bar Admissions

As indicated earlier, Mississippi has had a licensing law for attorneys for well over a hundred years. Several different laws have been enacted, and various provisions for licensing have been employed during that time. The present Board of Bar Admissions was established in 1954. This body is composed of six licensed attorneys, two from each supreme court district, appointed from a list of eighteen submitted to the governor by the supreme court. The secretary of the Mississippi State Bar Association serves as secretary of the board, and all administrative work is carried on through his office.

The duties of the board are concerned almost entirely with the admission of applicants to the bar. The board meets twice each year, on the first Mondays of February and July, at Jackson to hold written examinations. Applicants must be United States citizens, residents of the state, and at least twenty-one years of age, and have good character. In addition, applicants must furnish evidence that they have successfully completed two years of college work in a standard college or junior college, and have successfully completed a general course in a law school that has been in existence ten years or one that has been approved by the board. Applicants with the required college work may also qualify if they have studied law for a period of two years under a reputable attorney with five years' experience who has been approved by the board. Persons seeking to take the examinations under the latter arrangement must notify the examining board two years in advance, and the attorney directing the reading course must make regular reports on the student's progress and certify to the completion of the course before the examination can be given. Examinations cover ten major fields of law as well as professional ethics, and the board is required to inquire into the moral character of the applicants.

Attorneys who have had five years' licensed practice in another state that has equivalent requirements for admission to the bar are exempt from examinations after two years' residence, if there is reciprocity with Mississippi. Graduates from the University of Mississippi Law School also are exempt. Applicants successfully passing the bar examinations as well as exempt persons are granted licenses by a chancery court upon receipt of proper certificates of eligibility. The board has no control over the revocation of licenses. Disbarment proceedings must be initiated by the governing board of the State Bar Association in a circuit or chancery court of the state.

Funds for the compensation and expenses of the Board of Bar Admissions are provided by the State Bar Association. Applicants for examinations are charged a $25 fee, which is paid to the secretary of the association.

State Board of Dental Examiners

Dentists and dental hygienists in Mississippi are licensed by a board appointed by the governor from a list of fifteen names submitted by the Mississippi Dental Association. Members must be licensed, practicing dentists of the state for the five years preceding appointment, graduates of a Class A or B dental college, and cannot be connected with any school of dentistry or dental supply business. The board annually elects a president and a secretary-treasurer. The secretary-treasurer is bonded and has charge of the administrative details of the board's affairs.

This board has the duties of conducting examinations for applicants for dental licenses, issuing and revoking licenses, and compiling each year a list of all registered dentists and dental hygienists in the state. It meets regularly on the third Tuesday of June of each year in Jackson for the purpose of conducting examinations, though more frequent meetings may be held, and at other places, at the discretion of the board. Applicants for examination must be high school graduates, graduates of a Class A or B dental college or school of dental hygiene, and must present evidence that they are at least twenty years of age and of good character. The examinations are written, though practical demonstrations may be required. Persons satisfactorily passing the examination are issued licenses by the board. These licenses may be revoked by the board if upon investigation of a complaint, a licensee is found to be guilty of immorality, malpractice, incompetency, or unprofessional conduct. Notice and hearing are allowed, and appeals on revocation of licenses may be taken to the chancery court of the county of residence. Practicing without a license is a misdemeanor punishable, upon conviction, by fine or imprisonment. Dentists or dental hygienists licensed by other states, or the District of Columbia, that maintain similar standards may be granted licenses without examination if reciprocal arrangements exist for Mississippi dentists.

The state provides no funds for the operation of this agency, though the law authorizes public facilities for giving practical examinations to applicants. Revenues are derived from fees, which are $50 for dental examinations and reciprocity licenses, $25 for dental hygienist examinations, and small fees for other papers. Members of the board receive no compensation, but fees are distributed among them, the secretary receiving twice the remuneration of other members.[6]

State Board of Embalming

Persons practicing the occupation of embalming in Mississippi must be licensed by the State Board of Embalming. This body, originally established in 1918, consists of seven members: the executive officer of the State Board of Health, the director of the Bureau of Vital Statistics, and five embalmers with five years' experience in the state. The board elects from its members a president, a secretary, and a treasurer, who serve for one year. The board meets at least once each year to administer examinations to applicants for licenses. It also has the power to adopt rules and regulations, consistent with law and the rules of the State Board of Health, concerning the work of the profession. Applicants for licenses must have a six months' course in embalming, a year's apprenticeship, and an age of at least twenty-one years. Upon passing the examination administered the applicant is issued a license for one year, renewable upon payment of a fee. The board may revoke licenses by two-thirds vote upon proof of violation of law or of its rules and regulations by an embalmer. All expenses of the board and compensation of its members are paid from fees collected. Practicing without a license is made a misdemeanor, punishable by fine.[7]

State Board of Registration for Professional Engineers

All professional engineers, except military or other United States government engineers, are licensed by the State Board of Registration for Professional Engineers, first established in 1928. This body consists of five registered engineers appointed by the governor from a list of fifteen persons nominated by the Mississippi Society of Professional Engineers. One member is selected from each of the supreme court districts, and two are chosen from the state at large. Members must be United States citizens, at least thirty-two years of age, with ten years' professional experience and five years' residence in Mississippi immediately preceding appointment. The board selects a president, vice-president, and secretary from its membership. The secretary is in charge of administrative affairs of the board with the necessary clerical assistance.

The board has the functions of licensing qualified applicants, revoking such licenses for cause, and of maintaining a roster of registered engineers. It holds two regular meetings each year, and may hold special meetings, to conduct its affairs. Licenses as "professional engineers" are granted to graduates of recognized four-year engineering colleges with four years of engineering experience or to persons with twelve years' engineering experience who are not less than thirty-five years of age. Such licenses require no examination. Persons with eight years' engineering experience may obtain licenses as "professional engineers" by taking examinations covering the approved four-year engineering curriculum. Licenses as "engineers-in-training" are granted to graduates of recognized four-year engineering colleges or to persons with four years of qualifying engineering experience who pass written examinations in the basic engineering subjects. Persons certified by national engineering registration agencies may be licensed without examination, as may engineers licensed by other states or countries, with equivalent requirements, on a reciprocity basis. Successful applicants are issued licenses, which must be renewed each year. They may be revoked, by majority vote of the board, after notice and hearing have been accorded the offender. Grounds for revocation are fraud, negligence, incompetence, or misconduct. Revoked licenses may be reinstated by the board, in its discretion, after six months. No state funds or facilities are provided this agency.[8] It is supported by fees charged to applicants, which are $25 for certificates as professional engineers, $10 for certificates as engineers-in-training, and $5 for annual renewal.

State Insurance Commissioner

The state insurance commissioner, described in Chapter 19, controls the licensing of insurance agents along with his other duties in regard to insurance regulation. Separate licenses are required for persons soliciting life insurance sales and those selling other types of insurance. No person may solicit without proper license.

An agent for life insurance, which may include health and accident and burial insurance, is licensed by the state insurance commissioner upon certification of a company authorized to transact business in Mississippi that such person is "fit, competent, and trustworthy" and has been appointed by the company to act as its agent. Agents for other types of insurance are licensed in the same manner, except that the commissioner may require a written or oral examination to determine the applicant's knowledge. Fees of $10 for a license and $2 for certificate of appointments are charged. The commissioner is authorized by law to investigate any agent at any time and may revoke licenses for such causes as incompetency, misrepresentation, or mishandling of funds. Notice and hearing must be allowed both company and agent and decisions on revocation of licenses may be appealed to the courts.[9]

Board of Nurses' Examiners for Mississippi

The Board of Nurses' Examiners for Mississippi, which controls the licensing of nurses, was originally established in 1914. Two members of the board must be licensed physicians, one of whom is connected with a hospital that maintains a school of nursing, three members must be registered nurses with two years' professional experience, and two must be licensed, practical nurses. The first five members must be taken from a list nominated by the State Nurses Association, and the latter two from nominations of the state organization of practical nurses. Practical nurse members sit on the board only on matters pertaining to practical nursing. The board meets regularly three times each year, and annually elects a president and a secretary-treasurer. The secretary-treasurer is bonded and is responsible for the records maintained by the body and the funds collected. The board has power to employ and control such persons as it may need for a staff.

Functions of the board are the examination of all nursing applicants, the issuance and revocation of licenses, and the maintenance of a register of nurses licensed. Examinations are held at Jackson for applicants who are at least nineteen years of age, who have a high school education or its equivalent, and who have graduated from an approved school of nursing. The examinations cover the subjects of the curricula of approved nursing schools. Practical nurses are examined when the board is satisfied that applicants are of good moral character and have successfully completed the course of study prescribed by the State Department of Education for practical nursing. Successful examinees are issued the proper licenses by the board. Nurses licensed in other states with equivalent standards are exempt from examination. Any license may be revoked by the board by majority vote after notice and hearing. Practicing as a registered or practical nurse without a license is made a misdemeanor, punishable by fine or imprisonment. Expenses of this agency, including salaries of employees and per diem compensation of members, are paid from fees collected.[10]

State Board of Optometry

Optometrists are licensed in Mississippi by a board established under a law of 1920. Members must be citizens who have engaged in the practice of optometry for the five years preceding appointment and who have no connection with a school of optometry. They are appointed by the governor with advice and consent of the senate, and cannot serve more than two terms. The board annually elects a president and secretary from its members; the secretary is a bonded official and receives a salary fixed by the board. Two regular meetings are held each year for examining applicants for licenses, and the board annually may hold two special meetings. The regular July meeting must be held in Jackson.

Duties of the board consist of administering examinations and the granting and revocation of licenses. Examinees must be at least twenty-one years of age and high school graduates with a two-year course in optometry conducted under standards recognized by the Federal government for vocational training. The board grants licenses to persons passing the examination. Optometrists licensed in other states with equivalent standards may be exempted from examination on a reciprocity basis. Licenses may be revoked or suspended by the board, after notice and hearing, for commission of a crime, intemperance, or use of narcotics. Practicing optometry without a license is a misdemeanor punishable by fine or imprisonment. Fees of $25 for original licenses and $5 for annual renewal are charged. All funds collected are paid into the state treasury, and all expenses, salaries, and per diem compensation of board members are paid by the state, though such payments cannot exceed the fees collected.[11]

State Board of Pharmacy

Persons practicing pharmacy in the state are required to hold a license granted by the State Board of Pharmacy. This board is composed of graduates of colleges of pharmacy, with five years' experience as retail pharmacists, chosen by the governor from a list of twenty-two names submitted by the Mississippi State Pharmaceutical Association. The governor must appoint the person on the list nominated by the association to be secretary and executive officer of the board. This body has powers to grant and revoke licenses to pharmacists, investigate complaints concerning drug sales, inspect places where drugs are sold, and generally to make and enforce such rules and regulations concerning the practice of pharmacy as are necessary for protection of the public. The secretary and executive officer of the board, who is a bonded officer, has control of records, finances, and administrative work of the agency.

Examinations for licenses are conducted each year in June in Jackson or at the state university. Applicants for pharmacists' licenses must be at least twenty-one years of age, graduates of a recognized school or college of pharmacy, and have good moral character. Pharmacists licensed by other states with similar standards and graduates of the University School of Pharmacy are exempt from the examinations. Successful examinees and exempt persons are issued certificates as registered pharmacists. The licenses are valid for one year, renewable upon application.* A temporary license, which will be valid until the next scheduled examination, may be issued to a person by a member of the board. The specific ground for revocation of a license by the board is conviction of unlawful sale of narcotics or intoxicating liquors, though the power in other cases may be inferred from the general authority to protect the public.

The costs of this agency, including the salary of the secretary, per diem compensation to other board members, and other expenses are paid from fees charged to applicants for license.[12] The fee for an original license, with or without examination, is $10 and the annual renewal fee is $2. Licensed physicians are not prohibited from compounding drugs by this act.

State Board of Health

Physicians, osteopaths, and podiatrists in Mississippi must be licensed by the State Board of Health, the organization of which is described in Chapter 14. This agency conducts examinations at least once each year in Jackson. Applicants for physicians' licenses must be citizens of good character, at least twenty-one years of age, and graduates of a recognized four-year medical college. Persons with two years of medical study may take part of the examination. Examinations are written and cover all major fields of medical study. Licensed physicians from other states with similar standards are exempt from examination, as are nonresident physicians whose practice extends into the state. The secretary of the board

* Persons holding licenses as "assistant pharmacists" at the present time are eligible to renew these licenses or to take the examination for pharmacists' licenses.—*Mississippi Laws, 1954,* Senate Bill 1584.

may grant to a qualified person a temporary license that is valid until regular examinations are given. Osteopaths' licenses may be granted to graduates of a reputable college of osteopathy without examination or they may be granted to applicants successfully passing examinations in anatomy, physiology, and hygiene. Examinations for licenses to practice podiatry, or chiropody, are granted to persons at least twenty-one years of age who are high school graduates and who have completed a course of at least three years in a recognized school of podiatry. Podiatrists licensed by other states with similar requirements are exempted from examination on a reciprocity basis. Examinations for the three types of licenses are given at the same time each year.

A license to practice as a physician, osteopath, or podiatrist is granted by the State Board of Health and may be suspended or revoked by this agency for conviction of a crime, fraud, immoral conduct, or unlawful or unethical practice. Notice and hearing must be allowed the offender and the board is authorized to issue compulsory process in obtaining evidence and testimony in such an investigation. Appeals from decisions on revocation of licenses may be taken to the courts on writ of certiorari.

This agency is supported by state appropriation, but the fees charged applicants for licenses are sufficient to defray the cost of administering examinations.*

State Board of Public Accountancy

The State Board of Public Accountancy, originally established by law in 1920, is the licensing body for certified public accountants in Mississippi. Its three members must be members of the Mississippi Society of Public Accountants and qualified electors. The board selects a member to fill each of its offices of president, vice-president, and secretary; the secretary handles the details of its administration. Duties of the body consist of conducting examinations and the issuance and revocation of licenses. The board meets twice each year at the state capital and administers the standard examinations prepared by the American Institute of Accountants to applicants who are resident citizens, at least twenty-one years of age, and who have good moral character. Successful examinees are granted licenses by the board. Accountants' licenses of other states with equivalent requirements may be suspended or revoked for unprofessional conduct, and the board is empowered to sit as a court, with full powers, to hear

* *Mississippi Code, 1942,* secs. 8878-8904. A physician's license covers the practice of surgery. Midwives are specifically exempted from the provisions of this law.

charges against any licensee. Appeals from its decisions on revocation may be taken to the courts. Practicing without a license is a misdemeanor punishable by fine or imprisonment, or both. This agency is supported entirely by fees, which cover the cost of examinations, certificates, and per diem compensation of members.[13] The fees are $25 for an original license, with or without examination, and $5 for annual renewal.

State Board of Education

Public school teachers in Mississippi are licensed under regulations established by the State Board of Education by authority of a 1948 statute. Various laws have governed teachers' licenses since the original act of 1924.

Present licensing requirements, fully effective on May 1, 1954, provide for seven types of certificates for elementary and secondary school teachers, classified according to the training and experience of the licensee. All applicants must be at least eighteen years of age, United States citizens or applicants for citizenship or exchange teachers from other countries, and must present certificates of good health. The licenses are designated as Class AAA, Class AA, Class A, Class B, Class C, Class D, and Class E and the educational requirements range from the Ph.D. or Ed.D. degrees for a Class AAA license to a high school diploma and six semester hours of college training for the Class E license. Different types of licenses are issued for elementary teachers, secondary teachers, special subject field teachers, supervisors, and administrators, with varying requirements as to training and experience. Present regulations require that all new and beginning teachers after December 1, 1954, must have at least two years of appropriate college training, and after December 1, 1956, all new and beginning teachers must have at least four years of appropriate college training. Generally, licenses are valid for limited periods of from one to ten years, the classes highest in the alphabetical rating holding for the longest period. Renewal of licenses, except for Classes D and E, which will not be issued after 1954, requires completion of additional training in the field in which the person is licensed. Licenses may be revoked by the county superintendent of schools for "intemperance, immoral conduct, brutal treatment of a child or other good cause" after notice and hearing, but appeals from his decision may be taken to the State Board of Education.

Administration of the complicated system of teacher licensing is by the Division of Instruction of the State Department of Education. Applicants apply directly to the department for original licenses or for renewal of a license, furnishing the necessary evidence of qualifications. The entire cost of the program is borne by the state, and no fees are charged except a $1 charge for each duplicate certificate.[14]

State Board of Veterinary Examiners

All persons practicing veterinary surgery, medicine, or dentistry in the state are required to be licensed by the State Board of Veterinary Examiners, originally established in 1914 but reorganized by law in 1946. This board has five members, no more than two from any supreme court district, appointed by the governor for staggered terms of five years from a list of nominees submitted by the State Veterinary Medical Association. The board elects a president, vice-president, and secretary-treasurer from its membership and holds annual meetings in Jackson to examine applicants for licenses. In order to take the examination a person must present evidence that he is at least twenty-one years of age, has good character, and has graduated from a recognized veterinary medical school. Applicants passing the examination are issued licenses, which must be recorded in the office of the circuit clerk of the county of residence or practice. Temporary licenses may be issued that authorize the holders to practice until the next regular examination. The board may revoke any license for fraud in connection with its issuance, or for unprofessional or dishonorable conduct. This agency receives no state funds and is supported by fees collected. The examination fee is $25. Veterinarians who had practiced in the state ten years prior to 1946 were authorized to obtain licenses without examination upon payment of a fee of $10. Cost of administration and per diem compensation of board members are paid from these funds.[15]

TRADE AND VOCATIONAL LICENSING AGENCIES

Few trades and vocations have come under the provisions of licensing laws. This fact would appear to make Mississippi lag behind most other states, since the trend generally is for more and more trades and callings to be included.[16] Perhaps this lag may be attributed in part to the prominence in the economy of the pursuits, such as farming, that are not considered proper subjects for such legislation. A nonindustrial economy means that there are fewer people in the skilled trades and consequently less need or demand for licensing. The pressure from members of various trades and vocations for additional licensing legislation is evident, however, in recent bills before the legislature.

Board of Barber Examiners

The members of the Board of Barber Examiners must be resident barbers with five years' experience in the state immediately prior to their appointment. The board elects a president and secretary. The secretary is a full-time, bonded officer and maintains an office at Jackson for administering the affairs of the board. Members of the board are compensated on a per diem basis.

The powers of the board extend to the making of rules and regulations for the execution of its powers, examination and licensing of applicants, inspection of barber shops and barber schools to determine compliance with the sanitary regulations of the board, and revocation of licenses for cause. Examinations, written and oral, are conducted three times each year, one in each supreme court district of the state. Applicants must present evidence of the proper age and of having satisfactorily passed a physical examination by a physician. Two kinds of licenses are issued, one for an apprentice barber and the other for a registered barber; the qualifications vary chiefly as to age and experience. Barbers licensed in other states may obtain temporary licenses allowing them to practice until another examination is given. The board may suspend or revoke the license of any barber, after notice and hearing, for incompetency, immoral or unlawful conduct, or violation of its regulations.

All funds of the Board of Barber Examiners are derived from fees charged for examination, certificates of registration, and renewal of these certificates each year. The fees vary from $1 to $5.*

State Board of Cosmetology

Cosmetologists† are licensed by the State Board of Cosmetology, established by law in 1948. Its three members, one from each supreme court district, must be licensed cosmetologists with five years' experience and must have no connection with a beauty school. A president and secretary are chosen by the board from its membership; the secretary is a full-time, bonded official who has charge of the agency and its staff of seven inspectors and stenographers. The board is responsible for the establishment of curricula for beauty culture schools in the state, the adoption of rules of

* *Mississippi Code, 1942,* secs. 8725, 8727-45; 1952 Supp., sec. 8726. The sanitary regulations of the board governing shops must be the same as those adopted by the State Board of Health.

† The word "cosmetologist" as used here includes cosmeticians, beauticians, hairdressers, manicurists, and those in similar occupations.

sanitation for beauty shops and schools with the approval of the State Board of Health, inspection of beauty schools and shops, the licensing of cosmetologists and beauty shops, and the suspension or revocation of licenses for cause. To be eligible for the license examinations, held at least twice each year, applicants must have completed a prescribed number of hours in training—the number varying for different types of beauty work—with specified experience in the trade, and also must present certificates of physical examination. Licensed operators from other states may be certified without examination. Licenses may be suspended or revoked by the board, after notice and hearing, for violation of the provisions of the licensing law or the regulations of the board. Appeals from the decisions of the board may be taken to the courts. The entire cost of salaries, per diem compensation of members, and expenses of this agency is derived from fees.[17] The fees charged to applicants vary from $3 to $25.

State Game and Fish Commission

The State Game and Fish Commission, described in Chapter 17, exists primarily for other purposes than for vocational licensing. It does, however, grant licenses to commercial fishermen. Such licenses are granted upon application and payment of an annual fee, which is in proportion to the size of fishing equipment used. No qualifications are required, and no clear provision is made for revocation, though this is plainly within the power of the commission.[18]

State Board of Public Contractors

Public contractors in Mississippi must be licensed and approved by a board established in 1952. The five members of the body, who are appointed by the governor for staggered terms of five years, must be contractors. A chairman, vice-chairman, and a secretary are chosen annually by the board from its membership. Four regular meetings are held in Jackson each year on the first Tuesday of January, April, July, and October, and special meetings may be held after proper notice. The executive secretary, chosen by the board, is a full-time, salaried official. Members receive no compensation but may be allowed official expenses.

The board has power to examine applications of contractors who seek contracts with state or local government agencies and to determine whether such persons are responsible. Certificates of responsibility are issued to persons recommended by the board, which has full power to suspend and revoke such certificates after hearing. Decisions of the board denying or revoking a certificate may be appealed to the chancery court of Hinds County. Contractors approved by the board must pay a special privilege license tax of $100 each year. Funds for expenses of this agency are derived from these fees.[19]

Mississippi Real Estate Commission

Real estate brokers and salesmen are licensed by a commission created by law in 1954. This body, which functions as a unit of the office of secretary of state, consists of one member from each of the three supreme court districts, appointed by the governor for staggered terms of four years. The group selects a chairman from its membership and a secretary to attend to the clerical work. Powers of the commission include the conduct of examinations for persons seeking licenses as real estate operators, the revocation of such licenses, and the encouragement of institutes and programs designed to improve the vocation of realtors.

Applicants for licenses must be United States citizens at least twenty-one years of age who have a year's experience in the real estate business. Recommendations as to character and reputation are also required. Such applicants must take written examinations on subjects relating to the real estate business. The examination for aspiring brokers covers more advanced knowledge than that given to prospective salesmen. These examinations are conducted at such times and places as the commission may direct. Persons passing these examinations are issued the proper licenses. Licenses granted by other states with similar requirements are recognized on a reciprocity basis. Any license may be suspended or revoked by the commission, after notice and hearing, for a variety of causes relating to unethical business or personal conduct. Engaging in the real estate business without a license is prohibited, punishable by fine and imprisonment.

Expenses of this agency are paid from fees charged applicants for licenses. These fees are $15 for a broker's license, $10 for a salesman's license, with annual renewal fees of $5 and $2.50 respectively.[20]

LICENSING PROCEDURES

Rules and Regulations

The regulations governing licensing procedure vary so much as to make an over-all description difficult. Generally, the statutes require that applicants take and pass written examinations to demonstrate their competence. However, important exceptions are found. Life insurance agents are licensed upon the recommendation of the company that employs them; teachers are granted licenses upon furnishing proof of certain college training; attorneys and pharmacists may offer the appropriate college degree in lieu of examination. Prerequisites for the licensing examinations differ widely. In some professions only age, residence, and good character are necessary; others require additional qualifications up to the appropriate college degree. The examinations themselves differ, or may differ, greatly as to length and comprehensiveness. In the case of dentists', sixteen subject fields of examination are set forth in the statute, and a practical test also is required; the bar examinations are required to cover ten separate fields of law. Engineers' examinations, on the other hand, are required to be only in "engineering design and construction."

The discretion of the licensing authority to issue or refuse to issue licenses would appear to vary somewhat as the legal provisions concerning the examinations. In the case of architects the applicant's examination must be satisfactory to a "majority of the board," though the usual requirement is merely that the examination be satisfactory. By its very nature the requirement of "good moral character" leaves much discretion with the licensing board, but the court decisions have tended to narrow this discretion. Thus, when the licensing authority had issued a person a license as an assistant pharmacist, the courts held that it could not refuse to grant him license as a registered pharmacist on grounds of moral character without proof of a change in the morals of the applicant.[21] Again, the courts held that a board had no discretion to deny license to a veterinarian who had the required years of experience to obtain a license without examination, even though this professional experience was unlawful.[22]

Revocation and Disciplinary Action

The power to suspend or revoke a license usually is stated along with the power to issue. In all cases the grounds for suspension or revocation are stated, though such statements differ widely with the different laws. In the case of dentists more than a dozen specific grounds are listed and described; similar provisions are found in the matter of physicians and barbers. In the case of veterinarians, however, the grounds are simply fraud in the procurement and "unprofessional or dishonorable conduct." The licenses of pharmacists, apparently, can be revoked only for illegal sale of narcotics and intoxicants. However, the State Board of Pharmacy has broad powers of inspection and regulation of the practice of pharmacy that would be equivalent to the power to revoke licenses.

The method of suspension or revocation is regulated more or less closely according to the particular law. In all occupations except those of law and teaching, it is done by the licensing body. In some cases a majority vote of the licensing group is required to revoke or suspend; in others a two-thirds vote is specified. In some of the laws the vote is not specified. Notice to the licensee and hearing on a proposed revocation are provided by law in most cases, but in four professions it is not mentioned, apparently being left to the discretion of the licensing boards. It is probable, however, that these licensees could compel notice and hearing as a matter of constitutional right, even in the absence of statutory provisions.[23] The amount of notice, where stated, varies from ten to thirty days. Some of the licensing bodies are given full powers to subpoena witnesses, compel testimony, and otherwise obtain information in connection with a revocation hearing; in others there is the simple provision for a hearing.

In few occupations the law specifically authorizes court review of a license revocation or refusal; elsewhere it is not specified. Where the highest state court has reviewed revocations, there appears a judicial tendency to insist on strict construction of the legal grounds for revocation. An example of this procedure was the case of a dentist who, in his application for license, gave references whom he did not know, stated that he was reared in the country when, in fact, he did not arrive here until his twentieth birthday, and anglicised his name without legal proceedings. The supreme court held that he had not "wilfully" misrepresented the facts about himself as was required in the ground for revocation of license.[24] In construing the legal procedures required for revocation, on the other hand, the court has taken a more liberal view. In reviewing a revocation of a physician's license, the court held that two members could act for the board in issuing notice of a revocation hearing and that the licensee was entitled only to know with "reasonable" certainty of the charges against him and to have "reasonable" opportunity to defend himself. Strict rules of pleading were held not to apply to revocation proceedings.[25]

Naturally the wide variation in the requirements for notice and hearing, the grounds and methods of revocation, and access to the courts make for similar variation in the disciplinary powers of the licensing bodies over their respective licensees.

EVALUATION OF PROFESSIONAL AND TRADE LICENSING

This survey of licensing requirements reveals that Mississippi, insofar as regulation exists, tends to follow the pattern of most other states. The growth of regulation has been steady; the courts have generally upheld it as a proper function of the state, requiring only that the regulation be reasonable and the enforcement fair. A notable feature of recent licensing laws is the tendency, also found in other states, to give greater authority to professional organizations in the determination of standards. Most of the statutes that have been enacted or revised recently have had the full backing of the members of the occupation affected by the laws.[26] Usually the standards of professional and trade competence have been raised by the licensing laws. With one or two exceptions the cost of licensing is derived from fees.

Large gaps in the program of licensing are evident in Mississippi. Few of the skilled trades are included, and some professional groups, such as chiropractors, are excepted. The inclusion or omission of certain occupations shows little relation to their importance. It would seem, for illustration, that the public welfare might be in fully as much danger from the work of unqualified plumbers as from untrained cosmeticians. In many cases where a law exists there are important exemptions.

Mississippi, like most southern states, has a broad program of state and local privilege taxes. These cover most of the occupations licensed as well as a great many others. Such taxes, often referred to as "privilege license taxes," are for revenue only, are not regulatory in character, and are not licenses in the sense that they are treated here.[27]

The number and variety of licensing agencies raise the question of coordination or consolidation of these bodies as has been done in New York, Pennsylvania, and some other states. Good administrative organization might dictate such a change. However, since the present laws providing for independent licensing bodies were passed, for the most part, with the support of the occupational groups affected, it may be expected that those same groups will oppose consolidation in the fear of losing the protection now provided. The idea of consolidating the routine portions of the process in a central agency while leaving the preparation of examinations and the determination of standards with the respective professional organizations might offer a solution that is satisfactory to the occupational groups and which also comports with sound administrative practice. Such a plan has been employed in California since 1929. Certainly combination of the administration of the licensing programs, as recommended by a recent report to the legislature, would accomplish this result.[28]

FOOTNOTES

[1] W. Brooke Graves, "Professional and Occupational Restrictions," *Temple Law Quarterly,* XIII (April, 1939), 334-63.

[2] *Mississippi Laws, 1882,* chs. 19, 23.

[3] S.B. 57, applying to plumbers; S.B. 225, applying to insect exterminators; S.B. 292, applying to general contractors; and H.B. 605, applying to small loan brokers.

[4] *Mississippi Code, 1942,* secs. 8632-46; *Mississippi Laws, 1954,* House Bill 75.

[5] *Mississippi Code, 1942,* secs. 8647-84, 8711-14; 1952 Supp., sec. 8660; *Mississippi Laws, 1954,* House Bill 99.

[6] Statutory provisions regarding this agency may be found in *Mississippi Code, 1942,* secs. 8746-48, 8750-54, 8756-63, 8766-70, 8772-75; 1952 Supp., secs. 8749, 8755, 8764, 8765, 8771. On revocation of licenses, see also *State Board of Dental Examiners* v *Mandell,* 198 Miss. 49, 21 So. (2nd) 405 (1945).

[7] *Mississippi Code, 1942,* secs. 8776-90.

[8] *Mississippi Laws, 1954,* House Bill 55. Surveyors are exempt from registration under this law.

[9] *Mississippi Code, 1942,* sec. 5722; 1952 Supp., secs. 5723-01–5723-07.

[10] *Mississippi Code, 1942,* secs. 8808-14, 8818, 8822-24, 8827-31; 1952 Supp., secs. 8806, 8807, 8814-5, 8815-17, 8819, 8825, 8826, as amended by *Mississippi Laws, 1954,* Senate Bill 1340.

[11] *Mississippi Code, 1942,* secs. 8832-46.

[12] *Ibid.,* secs. 8847, 8850-52, 8854-69, 8871-77; 1952 Supp., secs. 8853, 8870.

[13] *Mississippi Code, 1942,* secs. 8905-13.

[14] *Ibid.,* sec. 6263; Recompiled volume 5A (1952), sec. 6281; see also *Biennial Report of State Superintendent of Education* (January, 1952), pp. 57-59; *Teacher Education and Certification* (State Department of Education Bulletin 130, 1952).

[15] *Mississippi Code,* 1952 Supp., secs. 8914-01–9814-13.

[16] See Frank Hanft and J. N. Hamrick, "Haphazard Regimentation under Licensing Statutes," *North Carolina Law Review,* XVII (December, 1938), 1-18.

[17] *Mississippi Code,* 1952 Supp., secs. 8915-01–8915-19.

[18] *Mississippi Code, 1942,* sec. 5906.

[19] *Mississippi Laws, 1952,* ch. 329.

[20] *Mississippi Laws, 1954,* House Bill 262.

[21] *Watkins* v *Mississippi State Board of Pharmacy,* 170 Miss. 26, 154 So. 277 (1934).

[22] *Mississippi State Board of Veterinary Examiners* v *Watkins,* 206 Miss. 330, 40 So. (2nd) 153 (1949).

[23] Roger R. Tuttrup, "Necessity of Notice and Hearing in the Revocation of Occupational Licenses," *Wisconsin Law Review,* IV (1927), 180-86.

[24] *Mississippi State Board of Dental Examiners* v *Mandell,* 198 Miss. 49, 21 So. (2nd) 405 (1945).

[25] *Mississippi State Board of Health* v *Johnson,* 197 Miss. 417, 19 So. (2nd) 445, 827 (1944).

[26] See proceedings of the State Bar Association, *Mississippi Law Journal,* XIX (October, 1948), 450-59; XX (October, 1949), 500-506.

[27] For a list of these taxes, see *Mississippi Code,* Recompiled volume 7 (1952), secs. 9427–9696-236; *Mississippi Laws, 1952,* chs. 406-20.

[28] See report of the Legislative Fact-Finding Committee on Reorganization of the State Government. *Mississippi: A Report on State Reorganization* (Jackson, December 15, 1950), pp. 25, 59.

CHAPTER 21

Planning and Development

THE TERM "PLANNING," applied to governmental action, means different things to different people. Propaganda has given it an unpleasant connotation, but planning in its generic sense of investigating and forecasting future lines of both policy and program action is common to business and governmental organizations alike. Indeed, all individuals and all organizations must plan and thus have policies that they seek to fulfill. Life in a politically organized society demands at least a minimum of foresight and program arrangement.

State planning generally has been identified with the conservation of resources and with facilitation of the state's development. Thus it seeks to lessen, and often channelize, the unavoidable maladjustments that have resulted from our dynamic and exploitative civilization.[1] Sometimes this activity has been reflected in the establishment of state planning bodies whose primary tasks have been to inventory, appraise, and plan for the wise conservation and utilization of state resources. Other times the planning function is performed by a promotional agency whose chief assignment is to increase industrial development, attract increased trade and commerce, or exploit a supposed natural advantage that the state possesses.

Whatever the form state planning takes, formal organization for it in the American states is a comparatively recent development. State planning in its current sense began with the establishment of the National Planning Board, later the National Resources Planning Board, by President Franklin D. Roosevelt in 1933. Isolated examples of resources planning, however, long antedated the establishment of any state planning board. The history of administrative growth in Mississippi, as in other states, thus presents a paradox. The past reaches over into the future. Thus the Mississippi legislature in 1884 recognized the importance of planning for state development by creating an Exposition Bureau of Mississippi to provide for the "exhibition of the soil, climate, production, and resources of the State of Mississippi." However, planning of this or any other sort was generally isolated and came about only as first one and then another of the state resources obviously suffered from abuse, neglect, or depletion.[2] Occasionally the planning function was dramatized on a national scale, as, for example, with the intense interest aroused in conservation during the presidency of Theodore Roosevelt.

Planning as a continuous and organized function of state government awaited greater Federal stimulus. Shortly after the formation of the National Resources Planning Board, that body sent invitations to the governors of all the states to establish planning agencies with which the national board might work in surveying each state's needs for the projected long-range Federal public works program and which might make other studies, such as housing, population, and transportation reports. The National Resources Planning Board offered the assistance of Federal consultants to launch the new program. Within a short period almost every state, Mississippi among them, had established a planning board or commission.

State planning may be one or both of two kinds. The first type is long-range planning. This phase of planning requires consideration of basic proposed policies both by administrative officials and legislators. The administrative agency thus studies the given problem and prepares plans recommending desirable policy. It normally submits this report of its findings and recommendations to the executive. The determination and adoption of the proposed course of action as an official policy of state government, however, is quite properly left to the judgment of the legislature.

The second kind of planning is called program planning. It is concerned exclusively with the concrete measures that an administrative agency must take to effectuate a policy already adopted by the legislature. The purpose of program planning simply is to carry out most effectively and with the minimum friction the policies that the legislature has placed in the statute books. All active administrative agencies engage in this kind of planning, sometimes consciously and often without formal institutionalization of the function. The application of investigation and foresight to the daily discharge of the agency functions is normal to all management and cannot be escaped.

Our study is not intended to review the discrete planning activities carried on by the separate agencies of state government, important as they are, in the various functional fields like education and natural resources. Its purpose, rather, is to review the organization and procedures of planning that have been developed to ensure the fullest development and utilization of the state's potentialities. This review necessarily involves consideration not merely of the current industrial development agency but also of the commissions and boards that preceded it.

GROWTH OF THE PLANNING FUNCTION

Organized state planning in Mississippi reflects two separate lines of action: planning for over-all resources conservation and development and planning for industrial attraction and growth. Although these divergent objectives were maintained unsuccessfully for several years, by 1944 they merged, and the principal emphasis was placed then upon effectuating the Mississippi program of balancing agriculture with an equally strong industrial economy.

Mississippi State Planning Commission

The Mississippi State Planning Commission was created in 1936 and given broad authority to investigate and to plan in the interest of Mississippi's people and resources.[3] The commission consisted of the governor and eight members appointed by that official. By the terms of the statute one member of the commission was to be drawn from the State Highway Commission and two others from among the heads of the various state administrative departments. The remaining five members were to be chosen from the state at large for a four-year term.

The powers vested in the commission indicate well its relation to the nation-wide state planning movement stimulated by the National Resources Planning Board. The commission was charged with the primary duty of preparing and developing a "State Master Plan for the physical development of the State and prepare and keep current a proposed long term development program for major state improvements."[4] To accomplish this purpose the Mississippi State Planning Commission was instructed to cooperate with state and local administrative officials in order to coordinate all physical development programs related to comprehensive physical development of the state; to make studies of rural land utilization; to assist in determination of areas suitable for field crops, reforestation, watershed protection, recreation, and industrial and urban expansion; to prepare and release pertinent reports to the public; and to make recommendations to the governor and the legislature. The statute also required that state agencies give written notice of planned improvements to the State Planning Commission with a reasonable opportunity afforded the commission to study any major public improvement before the work was undertaken or lands for public use actually acquired. Provision was made in this legislation for a wide area of planning activities, the following subjects being included within the scope of commission action: soil conditions, land use and classification, population distribution, schools, parks and playground development, post, harbor, and waterway development, parkways, highways, traffic, transportation, water supply, flood control, drainage, housing conditions, and other matters related to physical development.

The first and principal step taken by the State Planning Commission toward the preparation of a master plan for physical development of Mississippi was the release on January 1, 1938, of its *Progress Report on State Planning in Mississippi.*[5] This report sought to isolate and appraise the problems confronting the state in terms of its resources and facilities, including land, water, and mineral resources, population, public welfare, recreation, and rural electrification. The commission summarized its approach in these terms:

> The problems with which Mississippi is confronted at this time may be conveniently divided into three groups: economic, social, and political. The political problems have to do with the government, its organization, functions and efficiency. . . . The activities of the State Planning Commission have been confined to social and economic problems. . . . In the face of such an array of economic and social problems, Mississippi can ill afford to allow them to pass unstudied, unattended, and unsolved. . . . In the consideration of these problems it is imperative that some organization be empowered to give deliberate study of them and offer aid in attaining their solution at the earliest possible hour. Such is the task of the State Planning Commission.[6]

The findings of the report were concrete, the document presenting specific suggestions for both administrative and legislative action.

First BAWI Plan

Also established in 1936 were the State Industrial Commission and the State Advertising Commission. Both of these agencies were designed to carry out the Industrial Act of 1936, more widely known as the first Balance Agriculture with Industry Plan.[7] The State Industrial Commission, consisting of three members appointed by the governor to serve until April 1, 1940, the expiration date of the statute, was charged to determine the desirability of industrial establishments seeking to qualify for local financial subsidization under the terms of the industrial act; to determine and to issue certificates of "public convenience and necessity" to municipalities that desired to construct industrial plants for qualified industries; and to otherwise encourage the industrial growth of Mississippi. The Advertising Commission, largely an honorary ex officio body, sought to bring favorable attention to Mississippi's resources and the economic opportunities they might afford.

Although the State Planning Commission was created partly as a result of Federal stimulus, the two agencies for industrial promotion clearly reflected the effects of the great depression upon a farm economy. The economic condition of Mississippi at the time of their establishment was poor. The depression had affected seriously the economic welfare of this state, like that of all other states, and in many communities the closing of lumbering and wood-working enterprises had destroyed the principal economic mainstay. The first Balance Agriculture with Industry program, sponsored by Governor Hugh White, sought to ameliorate these unfavorable conditions by community endorsement and the granting of industrial subsidies through an over-all coordinative control exercised by the state.[8] In the 1936-1940 period, twelve new industrial plants, employing a total that ranged from 4,500 to 7,000 employees at various times, were brought into Mississippi.

Mississippi Board of Development

Planning and industrial attraction were merged in 1940, when the three agencies discussed in preceding pages were abolished and replaced by the Mississippi Board of Development.[9] At the same time the Industrial Act of 1936 was repealed and industrial subsidization under state auspices discontinued with a change in political administration. The new board, composed of one member from each of the supreme court districts and appointed by the governor, was charged with essentially the same functions that previously had been vested in the State Planning Commission and was given, in addition, several responsibilities formerly allocated to the state industrial and advertising commissions. Thus, the new development board was charged to execute a program advertising manufacturing possibilities in Mississippi, to assist local and state agencies in stimulating development of industrial or commercial enterprises, and to collect information from firms interested in locating within the state relative to their financial responsibility, pay rolls, and similar data. The Mississippi Board of Development was abolished in turn in 1944 with the accession to office of Governor Thomas L. Bailey and was replaced by the Mississippi Agricultural and Industrial Board, which was founded to administer the Industrial Act of 1944. With this new legislative action a cycle was completed, and the shift from over-all state planning to limited state planning for industrial development was effected.

CURRENT PLANNING ACTIVITIES

Economic and Social Planning

State planning in the sense of development and utilization of Mississippi's human and natural resources rests once more with the individual agencies of government as well as with the legislature. These activities now are carried on usually by an operating official incidental to his primary duties and are involved inextricably with program planning. Occasionally, as in the State Tax Commission and the Department of Public Welfare, a division of research and statistics or similar administrative subunit is found. A few agencies, chiefly the Mississippi Agricultural Experiment Station and the Mississippi Geological Survey, have research functions for their primary purpose and plan for the scientific development of specific fields of governmental action. In still others, also primarily in resources administration, planning and research are an important, though subsidiary, activity. Frequently the state agencies are assisted by representatives of Federal agencies that also are concerned with planning their own programs, for example, the Southern Forest Experiment Station of the Department of Agriculture, the Fish and Wildlife Service of the Department of the Interior, the Soil Conservation Service, and the United States Public Health Service.

State planning as such, then, is no part of a unified program in Mississippi government, although some of the state's efforts, notably in the fields of agriculture, forestry, wildlife, public welfare, and employment security, are correlated well with Federal programs. A number of administrative officials have expressed the belief that this lack of coordination is harmful, especially where the functions of the agency are interrelated in their execution.

Administrative Planning

No board, commission, or office of state government, with the possible exception of the State Budget Commission, which deals mainly with financial controls, assists the chief executive in over-all administrative planning to improve the efficiency of governmental performance. When it is possible to alter the internal structure of an agency without statutory authorization, the task of planning for the change falls to the administrator and his immediate subordinates; in some instances, however, the alteration may be made on the initiative of a specially created legislative committee.* In the case of administrative planning by legislative committees and subsequent enactment, the piecemeal nature of the action taken usually deprives the change of much significance. Administrative planning in Mississippi, lacking both unity and direction, has been at best haphazard and spasmodic.

Industrial Attraction

In the field of industrial attraction, action has been most evident in Mississippi. The activities of the Balance Agriculture with Industry agencies in the 1936-1940 period hardly dented the basically agricultural economy. In 1940, 64 per cent of the state's population still lived upon farms, and the urban population, which might be employed in manufacturing concerns, constituted only 19 per cent of the total population. Agriculture, then a $400,000,000 investment, produced a gross annual income of $158,940,000. The 1,294 manufacturing plants in Mississippi in 1940 employed only 46,539 wage earners and paid them $27,437,088 in wages, or an average of $592. These concerns, moreover, were related closely to basic resources, some 498 being engaged in lumber and timber production and 392 in food processing.

By 1944 Mississippi was close to the bottom of the industrial ladder compared to other states. The per capita income stood at only $569. The state ranked forty-seventh in the value of manufactured products. Less than .002 per cent of all wages was derived from industrial employment. Worst of all, only a small portion, $46,000,000, of war production contracts had been let at that time to Mississippi businesses. Against this background the second Balance Agriculture with Industry program was

* For example, see the reorganization of the Game and Fish Commission in 1952. *Mississippi Laws, 1952,* ch. 186. The Legislative Fact-Finding Committee on the Reorganization of State Government, called for by Governor Fielding L. Wright, represents another example of administrative planning by a legislative committee. See Chapter 7, pp. 93-94.

adopted,[10] and Mississippi began anew efforts to lift itself by its own economic bootstraps.

The new industrial promotion statute created the Mississippi Agricultural and Industrial Board and set forth in detail the procedures by which it would operate. The board consists of twenty members, half of whom are ex officio. Membership includes ten persons appointed by the governor from the state at large for four-year terms, and the ex officio members, namely the governor, who is chairman, lieutenant governor, speaker of the house of representatives, two house members designated by the speaker, two senators designated by the lieutenant governor, the commissioner of agriculture, commerce, and statistics, state chemist, and state geologist.[11] One of the members selected by the governor is also appointed by him to be the board's executive officer and director. This rather large governing body functions through the director's executive staff and six committees: the executive, advertising and publicity, planning and research, agricultural, industrial, and legislative committees.

The executive officer of the board coordinates and supervises the work of the staff in effectuating board policy, selects and directs staff personnel, and prepares and submits reports of both the committees and the staff for consideration by the board. The staff of the agency is itself organized into work units that overlap the committees into which the board has divided itself.

The broad function vested by the legislature in the Mississippi Agricultural and Industrial Board is the achievement of a balanced economic development between agriculture and industry in the state. The board has pursued this objective generally by seeking to develop agricultural, commercial, industrial, and manufacturing enterprises. Although the board is concerned with both agriculture and industry, a recent report indicates its major emphasis:

> BAWI is in reality a program for industrial expansion and development—a program making possible the use of Mississippi agriculture, labor, and natural resources to raise the economic level of the State by: assisting present Mississippi industries to expand their facilities and employ more Mississippians; encouraging private Mississippi capital to be invested in "home grown" industries; attracting new industries which will provide their own facilities; attracting new industries by offering to build industrial buildings and provide sites to meet their specifications.[12]

This program is in fact a state-local program, even though it is administered under a state agency. Much of the action taken to secure industrial locations or relocations occurs at the local level of government, and the procedures of the Mississippi Agricultural and Industrial Board, fixed by statute, assure a cooperative yet supervisory state-local relationship. Subsidy funds thus are secured through local bonds issued with the authorization of the board. Furthermore, the bonds, which are pledged by tax revenue, can be issued only after a favorable vote by the citizens of the community seeking to attract some specific manufacturing concern. Plant sites and buildings purchased from such public money and leased to enterprises under the BAWI Plan are publicly owned.*

Safeguards are established around the issuance of bonds to prevent unfortunate mishaps. Before a bond election can be conducted and industrial facilities constructed or leased, each industrial subsidy project must be investigated by the Mississippi Agricultural and Industrial Board. If that agency finds that the project is both desirable and feasible within the terms of the BAWI statute, it issues a certificate of "public convenience and necessity." The explicit requirement of a prior certification from a legally constituted state agency is a significant control feature. No doubt it has served in practice to save local units from making commitments that were clearly rash or unwise.†

Activities of the board are financed entirely from general fund appropriations. These appropriations have ranged in amount from the modest $32,500 expended in 1945 to the $350,000 appropriated for the board's program in the 1950-1952 biennium. Substantial portions of available funds have been expended for advertisements, the total cost of this phase of the promotional program approximating $500,000 since 1944.

EVALUATION OF THE PLANNING FUNCTION IN MISSISSIPPI

General Summary

Clearly much remains to be accomplished in policy planning in our state. This blunt conclusion does not minimize the efforts of special legislative committees, the planning of particular state agencies, or the limited admin-

* The 1944 statute, as well as the 1936 law, also permitted municipalities to operate industrial facilities directly.—*Mississippi Laws, 1944,* ch. 241, sec. 12. This provision has never been used.

† Found also in the Industrial Act of 1936, this same provision did not escape notice. One observer commented that the law "provided the most centralized, systematic, and financially potent form yet taken by community subsidization in the South and at the same time carried the State of Mississippi, on paper at least, a considerable distance in the direction of socialistic theory."—Ernest J. Hopkins, *Mississippi's BAWI Plan* (Atlanta: Federal Reserve Bank of Atlanta, 1944), p. 5.

istrative research of the State Budget Commission. Mississippi simply has not assumed the much broader function of planning for over-all improvement in the use of its human and natural resources. In the decade of the nineteen thirties, when nearly all of the states were responding to Federal stimulus and establishing planning organs, Mississippi followed suit with its State Planning Commission. Although its work was significant, if only academically, for the first systematic report on social and economic problems in the state, the commission failed to develop to its possibilities, and, indeed, to endure. Its demise resulted partly from the lack of vision and imagination on the part of the political leaders of the principal factions alternating in the control of state government at that time, as well as from the unpopular connotation given the term "planning" by all too many people. The low per capita income in Mississippi, combined with the hard-felt effects of a major depression, served to focus attention on a narrow segment of planning—securing industrial locations and the pay rolls that go with them.

Today few signs indicate that Mississippi's governors and legislators feel an acute need for a staff agency to assist in planning major policies. Conditions characteristic of the local political atmosphere support this gloomy view. The state long has been tardy in adopting many of the formal accoutrements of good administrative management, such as a merit system for employing personnel, a strong executive budget, and a central purchasing program. Indeed, the nature of Mississippi's political factionalism is essentially hostile to these devices as well as to state planning. To the political leadership of Mississippi, an institutionalized planning agency and program are unacceptable.

Industrial Promotion

Industrial promotion has met with some success and a fair degree of public acclaim. The experiment of the Balance Agriculture with Industry Plan in stimulating industrial development in a rural state has been followed elsewhere by similar action; it may have economic signifiance for the entire South.

The long-range goal of the 1936 and 1944 industrial legislation has been more vividly emphasized by a current shifting of industrial enterprises from the New England states to the South. Under the first BAWI program a dozen plants were located in Mississippi with the assistance of local bond issues. By 1945 these plants accounted for 14 per cent of Mississippi's industrial employees and almost a fourth of its industrial pay roll. After nearly a decade of the second industrial promotion program, fully seventy-five BAWI plants are in operation. The number of workers in each establishment ranged from twenty to 2,000, and altogether a total of 16,846 persons were employed. Considerably more than fifty local governments have been serviced by the Mississippi Agricultural and Industrial Board, and four dozen of them have obtained one or more concerns. It is significant, perhaps, that total income payments to individuals rose from $436,000,000 in 1939 to $1,523,000,000 in 1950.[13]

How much the industrial subsidization program of Mississippi has influenced new industrial locations cannot be decisively answered. Plants that came to the state in some instances would not have come without financial inducements; and in other cases the BAWI Plan probably was a relatively minor factor in the ultimate plant location decision. The program no doubt has occasionally been a final determining factor in favor of a Mississippi location, especially where labor availability and wage rates were highly important, and somewhat less determinative where proximity to markets and raw materials were involved.[14]

The entire Balance Agriculture with Industry program, however, has raised economic issues of great importance. It rests essentially on the frank premise that industrialization offers a better future to thousands of Mississippians than a continued agricultural economy; it clearly is committed to local subsidization of industry from public funds granted under state authority and approval. Carried on to the fullest extent, it has placed tremendous if potential powers in the Mississippi Agricultural and Industrial Board.

Those Mississippians who endorse the program reason that once a given area of the nation has been entrenched as the center of a particular industry, plant expansions in that industry will tend to cluster there. Federal taxation and the minimum-wage laws are cited frequently as militating against the development of industry in the South. The proponents of the BAWI Plan have little time for those who condemn the program as an artificial subsidy; they claim that it is no more than a modest offset to artificial governmental measures thwarting Mississippi's industrialization. Certainly the program is a pioneer plan for state-sponsored and state-supervised local subsidization. It is also a direct attempt on the part of the state government to redress an imbalance in the Mississippi economy by minimizing the dangers inherent in a narrow agricultural system. Even so, the BAWI Plan is a phase, but no more, of state planning and development.

FOOTNOTES

[1] Benjamin H. Kizer, "State Planning," in George B. Galloway (ed.), *Planning for America* (Holt, 1941), p. 523.

[2] *Ibid.*, p. 525.

[3] *Mississippi Laws, 1936,* ch. 189.

[4] *Ibid.*, sec. 2.

[5] Assistance of the National Resources Committee and the Works Progress Administration was acknowledged. The latter provided financial assistance through Projects 65-62-4647, 265-6509, and 465-62-3-1.

[6] Mississippi State Planning Commission, *Progress Report of State Planning in Mississippi* (January, 1938), pp. 1, 2, 5.

[7] *Mississippi Laws, 1936, 1st Ex. Sess.*, ch. 1.

[8] Raymond F. Wallace, *Industrializing Mississippi: An Analysis of the Balance Agriculture with Industry Program* (Bureau of Public Administration, University of Mississippi, 1952), pp. 12-17.

[9] *Mississippi Laws, 1940,* ch. 147.

[10] *Mississippi Laws, 1944,* ch. 241.

[11] *Ibid., 1944,* ch. 241; *1950,* ch. 190.

[12] Mississippi Agricultural and Industrial Board, *Fourth Report to the Legislature, Biennium 1950-1952* (Jackson, 1952), pp. 6-7.

[13] *Survey of Current Business* (August, 1951).

[14] For a more detailed summary, see Wallace, *op. cit.*, pp. 38-52.

CHAPTER 22

Municipal Government

MUNICIPAL GOVERNMENT now concerns more than a third of Mississippi's people. Since 1890 a noticeable leveling off of population increases has occurred, and the population of the state has stabilized at slightly more than two million. Although this general trend has persisted until the present, the rate of urban increase has remained almost constant. Since 1940 farm population has fallen by almost a fourth, and as a result of this decline municipal population accounts for 35 per cent of the total.

As early as 1720 Natchez was settled, although the community did not become a municipal corporation until 1803. With the conclusion of the Louisiana Purchase, immigrants poured into the territory, and fourteen communities received charters. By 1892 some 325 charters had been granted to active municipal corporations. Three decades later the total of active municipalities had declined to 313, and by 1953 only 263 were operative.[1]

Mississippi always has been and remains predominantly rural and agrarian. Only one of its municipalities had a 1950 population in excess of 100,000, the capital city of Jackson. Meridian, the next largest city, had then but 41,709 inhabitants. Only 28 cities had more than 5,000 population. Conversely, 213 of the incorporated places had less than 2,500 inhabitants, and 150 of these contained 1,000 or fewer residents.

The problems of these municipalities consequently are somewhat different from those of the larger cities found in other states. It is nevertheless difficult for them to resolve these problems, for the small municipality must establish some fire and police protection, provide for education of children, and establish many of the services of large municipalities. To finance these varied activities Mississippi municipalities levy annually more than $12,000,000 in ad valorem taxes.

MUNICIPAL CHARTERS

A municipality comes into being when it is granted a charter that gives it a name, defines its bounds, sets forth the form of its government, and expressly provides the political and corporate powers it may exercise. Before 1892 all Mississippi municipalities received special charters from the legislature. These charters reflected the powers that individual communities felt necessary, and a consequent lack of uniformity as to both powers and methods for their exercise resulted. Although the special charter system permitted municipalities to secure charters adapted to their peculiar needs, there were a number of disadvantages involved in it. It imposed a heavy burden on the legislature, which had to approve both the original charter and amendments to it, a burden that from 1817 to 1892 embraced 802 separate statutes for 325 municipalities.[2] Abuses crept into the municipal government in such matters as taxation, granting of franchises, special favors to selected species of property, and injudicious pledging of the faith of cities or towns.[3]

Method of Incorporation

The Mississippi Constitution of 1890 sought to eliminate those evils by restricting legislative action dealing with municipalities to "general laws, . . . under which cities and towns may be chartered and their charters amended, and under which corporations may be created, organized, and their acts of incorporation altered; and all such laws shall be subject to repeal or amendment."[4] A general law charter was accordingly drafted for all municipalities, but those already in existence were given the option of retaining their special charters. The incorporated places that did not vote specifically to retain their private charters lost them and were subjected automatically to the provisions of the general law.[5] Few municipalities exercised this choice, and in 1950 about twenty private charters were in force.

A recent statute establishes the method of incorporation for municipalities. Any area may be incorporated as a municipality by filing in the appropriate chancery court a petition signed by two thirds of the qualified electors of the proposed municipality. This petition, which the law requires be published for three consecutive weeks, must state the proposed boundaries, the number of inhabitants, the assessed value of real property, and the corporate name desired for the new municipality. If these conditions have been met and the petition bears the required signatures, the chancery judge, after a hearing, enters a decree creating the municipal corporation and files a copy of the decree with the secretary of state.[6]

Type of Charters

There are two principal types of municipal charters in Mississippi, those granted under a general law and the special charters. By 1953, 240 of Mississippi's municipalities were governed under general law charters, and 23 cities operated under special charters granted before 1892. In addition, all municipalities with more than 2,000 population may adopt the general law commission charter of government whether they function under the general law or special charters, and any legal city or town may adopt the council-manager plan.[7] Since these latter forms allow some different powers to municipalities coming under their provisions, they are in effect different types of charters.

Home Rule

Home rule means simply that the inhabitants of a municipality have the right to frame their own charter for their own government. Home rule provisions may be of two types, either constitutional or statutory. Neither type is found in Mississippi, and all municipalities in the state, with some exceptions, have their powers determined by the general laws governing municipalities.

The constitution probably would not exclude statutory home rule, however, if such individual local independence can be provided through general legislation. Interpretations of the Mississippi courts uphold the principle that the legislature may commit to local agencies the framing of provisions to serve best varied local needs without reference to the legislature.[8] The requirement that laws shall be general in application has not prevented legislative interference with municipalities, the requirement being evaded by frequent classifications on the basis of population, location, or type of charter that are applicable often to a single municipality.*

Some voice in changing their local charters is permitted Mississippi's municipalities. The basic local law may be modified, of course, by legis-

* For example, a 1948 statute permitted Tupelo, chartered under the general law, to adopt what the legislature termed "the council form of government."

lative action, but it also may be amended through action initiated either by the governing body or by petition of the electors. The municipal governing authority prepares the desired charter amendment and publishes it for three weeks in a legal newspaper. The proposal then is submitted to the governor, who transmits it to the attorney general. If the latter rules that the proposed amendment is consistent with the Federal Constitution and laws and with the Mississippi constitution, the governor must approve it.[9] Should a tenth of the qualified electors of the municipality protest the amendment, the governor may not approve it until it has been submitted to and ratified by a majority of the electors in a special election. Alternatively, 20 per cent of the qualified electors of any municipality may initiate an amendment; in this case, the proposal must also be published for three weeks and an election held if there is sufficient protest. The amendment is then submitted to the governor, and the procedures outlined in the case of amendments proposed by the governing body are followed. These amending processes apply to all municipalities in the state, both general law and private charter, except in cases of conflicts between them and the provisions of a private charter or the statute establishing commission government; in such conflicts the provisions of the special charter of the commission law prevail.*

FORMS OF MUNICIPAL GOVERNMENT

An important factor in the efforts of Mississippi's municipalities to adjust themselves to the needs of their inhabitants centers in their attempts to achieve an effective and efficient daily performance. It is significant that the attention of the municipal citizens in several municipalities has been focused increasingly upon the form of government.

Most municipalities in Mississippi now operate under either of two forms of city government, the mayor-aldermen and the commission types. The third and more recent form, council-manager government, has been authorized only in recent years, and adoptions, though frequently discussed, have not been many.

* *Mississippi Laws, 1950,* ch. 491. Note, however, that the statute expressly provides that from its effective date, "no amendment to the private or special charter . . . shall be adopted or approved when such amendment is in conflict with any of the provisions of this act made expressly applicable to municipalities operating under a private or special charter, or is in conflict with any other act expressly made applicable to any such municipality."—Sec. 109.

Mayor-Aldermen Government

Government by mayor and aldermen, as it has developed generally in this country, is also the most widely employed form of municipal government in Mississippi. In 1953 a total of 247 municipal corporations in the state were governed under it. Of those cities exceeding 10,000 population by the 1950 census, only five used the mayor-aldermen form. All general law municipalities, except the few operating under the commission and manager statutes, employ the mayor-aldermen form.

As it is outlined by the general law, the plan is a weak mayor type, so called because the mayor's powers are few in number and carefully restricted in scope. This variation contrasts with the strong mayor-aldermen government under which the mayor virtually controls administrative matters.[10] A council composed of the mayor and board of aldermen comprises the governing body of the municipality. It exercises collectively powers for care, management, and control of the city, town, or village and its property and finances. Much the same provision is found in the private charters, although the charter of Greenville states that the city council shall exercise this power, with no mention of the mayor.[11] In both general law and private charter municipalities the mayor presides at meetings of the board of aldermen.

A single qualification is imposed for the office of mayor, namely, that the incumbent of the office be a qualified elector of the municipality.[12] The term of office is fixed at four years in all municipalities. This provision, found in the municipal code of 1950 along with a similar term for all other elective officials and aldermen, is intended to provide a uniform time for selection of city officials. Only in the larger municipalities is the mayor a full-time public officer. The compensation attached to the office frequently is nominal, but the larger cities pay more adequate salaries to mayors.

The mayor is the executive head of the city government. He is charged with the superintending control of all the city's officers and its affairs and has the responsibility for the enforcement of laws and ordinances. In general law municipalities he also has the power to require any officer to exhibit his accounts or other papers at any time. The mayor possesses little or no control over the appointment and removal of nonelective officers. These officers are chosen by the board of aldermen, and the mayor may vote in their selection only in case of a tie.[13] He is authorized to sign the commissions and appointments of all nonelective officers, but the pertinent statute specifies that his refusal or failure to sign them does not affect the validity of the officers when the council's minutes show the appointments were regularly made.

Although the mayor is a weak executive, he may influence policy formulation through the exercise of his legislative powers. In all municipalities he presides at meetings of the board of aldermen and votes in cases of equal division. More important is the general-law mayor's power to veto any ordinance passed by the board; this veto can be overridden by a two-thirds vote of the board of aldermen. He is empowered further to call special meetings of the board, limiting discussion to specified matters, and to communicate information in writing to that body with recommendations for its action.

The more powerful element of the municipal governing authority in general-law municipalities is the board of aldermen, which is composed of five members in municipalities having less than 10,000 population and of seven in the case of larger cities.* In the former municipalities, aldermen may be elected from the municipality at large, or, in the discretion of the municipal authorities, four may be elected from wards and one at large. In the cities having more than 10,000 inhabitants, six wards are established from which aldermen are chosen, and the seventh alderman is elected from the city at large. The term of office and qualifications are the same as those for the mayor with the addition that aldermen elected by wards must be residents of the district. Compensation is determined by ordinance and usually is nominal. Regular monthly meetings of the board of aldermen are held in addition to special meetings that may be called by the mayor or on the written notice of two members.

Other elective offices include the marshal, tax collector, clerk, street commissioner, and rarely, a treasurer. In certain of these offices individual members of the board of aldermen may be designated to serve. However, the offices may be made appointive by the mayor and board of aldermen.

Commission Government

The commission plan of city government seeks to concentrate governmental authority and responsibility, diffused by the weak mayor-aldermen form, in a small commission that replaces both the mayor and the council. Eleven of the twelve Mississippi cities employing the commission form of government have adopted it under the general laws of the state, and one,

* *Mississippi Laws, 1950,* ch. 491. Private charter municipalities, however, have boards ranging from four to eight members.

Vicksburg, amended its private charter to provide this type. Commission government has been popular with the larger cities, including Jackson, Hattiesburg, and Gulfport.

The general-law charter for commission municipalities provides for the office of mayor and two councilmen elected at large for a term of four years.[14] Candidates for any of the three offices must be qualified citizens of the municipality and have been residents of it for one year preceding the beginning of the term of office. The mayor is designated presiding officer of the council.

In keeping with the theory of commission government the exercise of "all executive, legislative, judicial powers" is entrusted to the city commission. Collectively it acts as the legislative body and determines the major policies of the municipality through ordinances.[15] Among the administrative powers that this body also exercises are the power to create, abolish, or fill by appointment all offices except those created by the legislature, to determine compensation for these offices, to promulgate rules governing the conduct of officers and employees, to issue and sell bonds, and to remove any officers whom it has appointed except as limited by law.

The mayor and the two councilmen individually serve as department heads and are responsible for the administration of policies that they as the city commission have decided upon. Administrative departments are allocated among the three officers by majority vote, but customarily the administration of specific functions is determined in advance. The mayor virtually always supervises the police departments and frequently has the finance and legal departments under his superintendence as well, as, for instance, in Jackson. The powers and duties of each department are prescribed by the mayor and the two aldermen functioning collectively as the city's legislative body.

Commission cities do not vest much power in the office of mayor. Although the mayor is president of the commission, he has no veto power and no appointing power that extends beyond that of the other members. He is, however, charged with superintending the general affairs and departments of the municipality and is empowered to report in writing to the legislative body on any matters that require its action.

Commission government in Mississippi is losing ground. McComb returned to the mayor-aldermen plan in 1947, and in 1948 the second largest municipality in the state, Meridian, abandoned commission government in favor of the council-manager form. There are no fixed and uniform standards for measuring the efficiency of municipal governments, but it is certain that the limited degree of integration that commission government brought with it resulted in some improvement in municipal procedures.

Council-Manager Government

The council-manager plan provides for a small council or commission, elected by the qualified voters, that is the municipal legislative body. The council enacts all necessary ordinances and is directly responsible to the electorate for the condition of city affairs. The plan also requires the city council to select a city manager and to hold him responsible for municipal administration. This pattern is followed closely by the restricted city manager statute enacted in 1948 and by the 1952 law that made the plan available to all legal cities and towns.*

The governing body in council-manager cities and towns consists of the mayor and the board of aldermen, who collectively are the city or town council. The mayor acts as ceremonial and titular head of the city, but he has no administrative powers. As a member of the council he has a voice and vote in its proceedings.[16] Term of office for both the mayor and the aldermen is four years, and compensation is limited to $1,200 and $600 annually for the mayor and aldermen respectively in cities of less than 10,000 and to $2,400 and $1,200 respectively in the larger cities. The mayor has no veto power over ordinances enacted by the council, in which all legislative power is vested.

The current statute specifies that the manager may hold office for any period not to exceed four years, as the council may prescribe, and that he shall be eligible for reappointment. He may be removed at any time by a majority vote of the council, provided he is furnished reasons for the proposed removal and afforded a public hearing before the council if he so requests.[17] Pending removal, the manager may be suspended from office.

The manager's powers are far-reaching. He is responsible to the council for "the entire administration" of the city or town government. He prepares and recommends to the council the annual budget, administers and

* Under *Mississippi Laws, 1948,* ch. 385, all cities having more than 30,000 but less than 40,000 population by the 1940 census and having the commission form of government could establish council-manager government; only one city, Meridian, fell within these requirements. In contrast, *Mississippi Laws, 1952,* ch. 372, authorizes any city or town to adopt the council-manager plan regardless of the form of government under which it is operating. It is the general legislation that is summarized here, since the 1952 statute amended *Mississippi Laws, 1948,* ch. 385, and hence is largely applicable to Meridian also.

enforces all laws and municipal ordinances, appoints and removes all department heads and other employees, and negotiates contracts and acts as purchasing officer, subject to the laws and the approval of the council. He may supervise directly all department heads and their employees, and he may make recommendations to the city council for improving municipal administration. The manager, however, has no authority over the organization of the police court or the public schools.

Although the council clearly is the supreme legislative body, the manager in Mississippi towns and cities is not excluded from all part in policy determination. Thus his recommendations may bear directly upon policy questions, as may also the reports and recommendations made upon request of the council and his annual financial report. Although the law properly subordinates the manager to the council, in practice the council may depend very largely upon his judgment, for he is a full-time official with the opportunity to be more familiar with municipal needs than anyone else.

By 1952 three Mississippi municipalities—Meridian, Grenada, and Picayune—had adopted the city manager form, and elections on its adoption were pending in several others. A number of obstacles confront the spread of this form of government. Although the council-manager statute is well-drafted, the absence of any home-rule provision in the state's municipal code is a barrier that is re-enforced by little feeling that the cities and towns can or should have the power to determine the details of their local government. Equally important is the absence of any large urban areas, Jackson excepted. With hardly more than a dozen municipalities above the 10,000 population classification and with the relative absence of large industrial development, a lack of consciousness for the need of good organization and sound practices at the municipal level prevails. Finally, many small municipalities have furnished the minimum of governmental services to their inhabitants, and local tax burdens rarely have been sufficient to focus attention on the need for sounder organization.[18] Expansion of manager government in Mississippi is conditioned upon overcoming these obstacles.

POWERS OF MUNICIPAL CORPORATIONS

Since cities are agents of the state for accomplishing the work of local government, they are dependent upon the state for all their powers. In the absence of constitutional restrictions the state legislature has complete control over them. Mississippi courts have never subscribed to the doctrine that cities enjoy an inherent right of local self government. On the contrary they have held that municipal powers are powers delegated by the state.[19]

Constitutional Provisions

The Mississippi constitution contains only two provisions concerning city-state relationships. One of these, section 88, simply provides that municipalities shall be chartered under general laws, and the other, section 80, requires the legislature, by general laws, to make provision against the abuse by municipal corporations of their powers of assessment, taxation, borrowing, and incurring debts. Neither of these restrictions upon legislative power is major, for the courts have stated definitely that "unless expressly limited by constitutional provision, the legislative department has absolute power over municipalities. The Constitution of 1890 contains no such specific limitation upon the power of the legislature in this regard."[20]

Grant of Powers

The general-law grant of powers provides that every municipal corporation governed under its terms shall possess four powers: (1) to sue and be sued; (2) to purchase and hold real estate and personal property; (3) to sell and convey property; and (4) to make all contracts and to perform all other acts in relation to the property and concerns of the municipality that are necessary for the exercise of its corporate and administrative powers.[21] The general-law charter also authorizes a number of specific ordinance powers of the municipal legislative body and defines the powers of municipal officers. These powers establish municipal authority relative to such matters as taxation and financial administration, public safety, including fire and police protection, elections, streets, and other public construction work, and the ownership and operation of specified utility services.

Not every one of these powers is available to all Mississippi municipalities. The prohibition upon legislative action affecting individual municipalities is flanked by the familiar device of classifying cities and enacting general legislation applicable to a class of municipalities. Since 1892 the general-law charter has divided municipalities into three classes for granting powers, cities, towns, and villages: cities have a population of 2,000 or more; towns more than 300 but less than 2,000; and villages more than

100 but less than 300 residents.[22] Different classifications have been employed for other legislation. Population is often used, as in the case of the council-manager statute and the municipal privilege tax code, which divides the municipalities into seven classes.

In general the powers of municipalities of all classes fall into two broad categories, governmental and proprietary. The municipality serves as the agent of the state, in the exercise of its public powers, to perform more adequately the work of local government than could the state itself. Where corporate or proprietary powers are employed, though, the municipality acts in the capacity of a legal person for the performance of commercial, or at least nongovernmental, functions. The distinction between the two types of municipal powers is significant for determining the liability of municipalities in torts, or wrongs. A municipality is legally responsible for the acts of its employees who are engaged in the exercise of its corporate powers, but it is not liable for wrongs committed by its employees working in a governmental capacity.

This distinction is logical but difficult in its application. The Mississippi courts have stated in general terms that the public or governmental functions of a municipality embrace those delegated by the state to the city as a part of the "state's sovereignty" to be exercised "for the benefit of the whole public," both the people living within the municipality and outside of it; everything else is a corporate or private duty. The courts have established thus in specific instances that fire protection, police protection, jails, workhouses, schools, hospitals, and poorhouses fall within the scope of public duties.[23] Powers and duties relating to the maintenance and operation of public parks and playgrounds, collection and disposal of trash, maintenance and operation of light plants and of water plants, establishment and operation of sewers, and the maintenance of gutters, drains, and streets have been held to be corporate and proprietary.[24]

Apart from the issue of liability, the powers of Mississippi municipalities are restricted by the judicial acceptance of "Dillon's Rule" for the construction of municipal powers, namely, that a city possesses only those powers expressly granted, those necessarily or fairly implied in its express powers, and those essential and indispensable to the accomplishment of its declared objectives and purposes.[25] Any fair, reasonable, or substantial doubt of the existence of the power is resolved against the municipality. Acceptance of the principle and elaboration on it have been clearly indicated by the Mississippi courts.[26]

Dissolution and Enlargement

Municipalities may be dissolved either automatically by the shrinkage of population and the failure to hold elections or official meetings, or voluntarily. When a census shows that a municipality has less than the legal minimum of 100 inhabitants, the secretary of state notifies the municipal and pertinent county officials of its abolition. If the records of the place show no official meetings for twelve months or if the records of the secretary of state show a failure to hold elections for municipal officials on two successive election dates, the municipality is automatically abolished. Any municipality with fewer than 1,000 inhabitants may be dissolved voluntarily by the combined action involved in an ordinance of dissolution and a petition and hearing before the chancery court of the county in which the municipality is located.[27]

Boundaries may be enlarged or contracted after passage of an ordinance by the municipal governing body and petition and hearing before the chancery court. A copy of the latter's decree must be sent to the secretary of state. Provision also is made for the combination of municipalities after separate ordinances have been adopted by the governing bodies of the combining towns or cities and a joint petition, filed in the chancery court, has been acted upon by the chancellor. Assessments and ad valorem tax levies in force at the time of absorption of one municipality by another remain in effect for the current fiscal year; in all respects the laws and ordinances of the largest municipality become operative throughout the enlarged jurisdiction.[28] Provision is made also for the qualified electors of territory adjacent to a municipality to initiate proceedings for enlargement. In the past, before the adoption of the 1950 municipal code, this kind of action was effected frequently by special legislation couched in the familiar form of general laws.

MUNICIPAL SERVICES

Mississippi's municipalities exercise controls over and provide their residents with the services made necessary by the concentration of population within corporate limits. As the density of municipal population has increased, so also have the functions that many of the state's cities provide. At the same time many Mississippi municipalities are still small rural communities whose functional problems are not as great as those of the larger municipal corporations. Review in general terms of several municipal functions is nonetheless important.

Public Safety

Among the major urban functions is that of supplying police and fire protection. Although almost every village, town, and city in the state furnishes some public safety activity, clearly the fire and police systems of Jackson and Meridian will be different from those of the smaller communities, such as Charleston and Hazlehurst.

Organized police forces are found in the larger cities. All municipalities of more than 10,000 population thus have organized police departments. Only two of these, Pascagoula, with a force of eight men, and McComb, with ten police employees, had departments of less than fifteen; in the other cities the size ranged upward from twenty-five members. The police department of Jackson in 1952 employed 138 persons, whereas Meridian, the next largest urban center, had 61 persons on its force, Greenville 46, and Vicksburg 36. These departments have grown because urban growth has brought with it problems of traffic regulation, control of crimes against property, abatement of nuisances, and regulation of gambling and other vices.

In the smaller municipalities police personnel usually consists of the marshal, who may be appointed by the governing body or more frequently popularly elected, a night marshal, and sometimes an additional patrolman. With the exception of patrol cars, which are common in most of the smaller municipal corporations, these departments possess little in the way of equipment. In contrast, several of the larger municipalities, such as Jackson and Meridian, have utilized for several years police radio systems to maintain communication with patrols. All of these cities have installed fingerprinting systems and devote considerable attention also to traffic regulation through lights and signal systems as well as traffic patrolmen.

Fire protection is somewhat less well organized throughout the state. All cities of 10,000 or more inhabitants, however, have organized fire departments. In one of these, McComb, the fire department consists of 9 paid firemen and 10 volunteer members. In most others all members of the fire department are full-time, paid firemen. These numbers range considerably, Jackson having 86 firemen, Meridian 51, Greenville 33, and Vicksburg 35. Columbus and Tupelo, smaller urban centers, have 22 firemen and 10 paid and 3 volunteer firemen, respectively.[29] In places of fewer than 10,000 persons the companies are almost always volunteer establishments, although it is common practice that one or two members, depending on the size of the community, will be full-time employees. Slight compensation is paid volunteer firemen in some cases.

Public Health

The chapter that reviews intergovernmental relations indicates that establishment of county health departments resulted in the transfer of many health functions to the counties and required the abolition of municipal health departments. The municipalities, though, still have several important health functions.

Mississippi municipalities may enact sanitation ordinances to protect the general health of their citizens, and most of the larger cities annually appropriate funds to help support the activities of the county health departments within the corporate limits. Virtually all the municipalities, large or small, collect and dispose of garbage, although this function in some of them is let on private contract. Most of the incorporated places also maintain sewage disposal plants, but a few rely still on cesspools and individual septic tanks.

Education

Free public schools are one of the most important services of municipalities. Any incorporated place can by proper ordinance establish a municipal separate school district, and today eighty or more maintain their own school systems. The municipal school district may either embrace only the area within corporate limits, or include territory beyond the jurisdiction of the municipality for other purposes. Many of the districts are limited to the municipal boundaries, but these districts usually accept pupils from nearby rural areas on a tuition basis.

Education of children of both the white and Negro races is a public responsibility. All of the municipal separate districts maintain, therefore, two systems of public schools providing separate elementary and high schools.

Public Utilities and Municipal Enterprises

Many municipalities have owned and operated various public utilities for several decades; others have more recently embarked upon a program of public service enterprises. The most commonly found utility in public operation is the waterworks system. Some 152 villages, towns, and cities reported ownership of this public service function in 1950, and more than 30 indicated municipal ownership of electric power systems exclusive of those that purchase electricity from the Tennessee Valley Authority. Twenty-four places owned airports, whereas only nine reported public ownership of gas plants. Thirty controlled recreational centers with swimming pools.[30]

Municipal ownership of power plants has declined somewhat since 1924. In that year the Mississippi legislature authorized the sale or lease of the plants after a majority vote of qualified electors. By 1927 the number of municipal plants actively functioning had declined from 72 to 33. The municipally owned power systems today are commonly administered under the supervision and direction of the mayor and board of aldermen, the city commissions, or, in a few instances, boards of public utilities. This latter type of governing body was authorized by the Municipal Electric Plant Act of 1936. This measure requires any municipality having 2,000 or more inhabitants and acquiring and operating electric plant systems under the terms of the law to place the management of the plant under a board of four persons who are residents and property holders of the municipality. Members are appointed by the mayor with the consent of the governing body for staggered four-year terms.[31]

Housing

Public housing programs in Mississippi have been stimulated largely by Federal action. Enabling legislation enacted in 1938 permits Mississippi municipalities to create local housing authorities after the governing body of the city has found that there is a shortage of low-rent, safe, and sanitary dwellings for persons of low income or that inhabited dwellings are unsafe and unsound.* By 1947 such cities as Biloxi, Clarksdale, Hattiesburg, and Laurel had established housing programs, although generally the housing units will be found in South Mississippi, where the degree of urbanization is highest. Administration of the municipal housing authorities is vested in a commission of five members appointed by the mayor for five-year staggered terms. The authorities are given sufficient corporate powers to construct, maintain, and operate housing projects, including the right to sue and be sued, acquire property, and issue revenue bonds.

* *Mississippi Code, 1942,* secs. 7296-97; *Mississippi Laws, 1938,* ch. 388. The legislature also authorizes county, regional, and consolidated housing districts.

Planning and Zoning

One of the results of the short-lived Mississippi State Planning Commission was creation of interest in the orderly physical and economic development of the state's municipalities through local physical and economic surveys. Today the standard state zoning law permits any municipality having more than 1,000 residents to control the use of property through zoning regulations on such matters as the size and heights of buildings and the location and use of physical structures for industrial, residential, and trade purposes. A number of Mississippi municipalities, among them the larger cities of Gulfport and Jackson and the smaller ones such as Leland, Louisville, and Starkville, maintain today both zoning and planning commissions; Clarksdale has established a planning body and Greenwood a zoning commission. These bodies are advisory in nature, and the current statute states simply that the legislative body of the municipality shall provide the manner in which the zoning regulations will be determined, established, and enforced. An increasing number of Mississippi cities now are developing comprehensive city plans, an action that has been made almost mandatory by their rapid growth.

FOOTNOTES

[1] Current figure based on *A Directory of Mississippi Municipalities* (Bureau of Public Administration, University of Mississippi, 1953), p. 87.

[2] M. H. Satterfield and Hugh W. Urban, *Municipal Government and Administration in Mississippi* (Jackson, 1940), p. 12.

[3] *Adams* v *Kuykendall,* 83 Miss. 571, 35 So. 830 (1904).

[4] Constitution of 1890, art. 4, sec. 88.

[5] *Mississippi Code, 1942,* secs. 3374-3825 contained the provisions of this act as amended; *Mississippi Laws, 1950,* ch. 491.

[6] *Ibid.;* see *Jackson* v *Whiting,* 84 Miss. 163, 36 So. 611 (1904).

[7] See *Mississippi Laws, 1948,* ch. 385, applying to Meridian alone; see *ibid., 1952,* ch. 372, for general council-manager statute.

[8] *Yazoo City* v *Lightcap,* 82 Miss. 148, 33 So. 949 (1903); see *Monette* v *State,* 91 Miss. 662, 44 So. 989 (1907).

[9] *Mississippi Laws, 1950,* ch. 491.

[10] Austin F. Macdonald, *American City Government and Administration* (4th ed., Crowell, 1946), pp. 172-73.

[11] *The Amended Charter of the City of Greenville* (1938), sec. 17.

[12] *Mississippi Laws, 1952,* ch. 491.

[13] *Ott* v *State ex rel. Lowrey,* 78 Miss. 487, 29 So. 520 (1901); *Mississippi Laws, 1950,* ch. 491. At least one private charter city permits the mayor to vote.—*Charter of Yazoo City,* sec. 7.

[14] *Mississippi Laws, 1950,* ch. 491. See also *Charter of City of Vicksburg,* sec. 7, as amended.

[15] *Mississippi Laws, 1950,* **ch. 491.**

[16] *Mississippi Laws, 1952,* ch. 372, sec. 14.

[17] *Ibid.,* sec. 16.

[18] Robert B. Highsaw, "City and County Manager Plans in the South," *Journal of Politics,* XI (1949), 507-14.

[19] *Steitenroth* v *Jackson,* 99 Miss. 344, 54 So. 955 (1911); *Adams* v *Kuykendall,* 83 Miss. 571, 35 So. 830 (1904).

[20] *Adams* v *Kuykendall,* 83 Miss. 571, 35 So. 830 (1904).

[21] *Mississippi Laws, 1950,* ch. 491.

[22] *Ibid.,* sec. 1.

[23] *Alexander* v *Vicksburg,* 68 Miss. 564, 10 So. 62 (1891); *Hattiesburg* v *Greigor,* 118 Miss. 678, 79 So. 846 (1918).

[24] See respectively the following opinions: *Byrnes* v *Jackson,* 131 Miss. 707, 105 So. 861 (1925); *Pass Christian* v *Hernandez,* 100 Miss. 76, 56 So. 329 (1911); *Yazoo City* v *Birchett,* 89 Miss. 700, 42 So. 569 (1906); *Greenwood* v *Pentecost,* 148 Miss. 60 (1927); *Brown* v *Meridian,* 102 Miss. 384, 59 So. 795 (1912); *Jackson* v *Anderson,* 97 Miss. 1, 51 So. 896 (1910); *Semple* v *Vicksburg,* 62 Miss. 63 (1884); *Senatobia* v *Dean,* 157 Miss. 207, 127 So. 773 (1930); *Atkinson* v *Decatur,* 131 Miss. 707, 95 So. 689 (1923); *Saxon* v *Houlka,* 107 Miss. 161 (1914); *Carver* v *Jackson,* 87 Miss. 583, 35 So. 157 (1903); *Natchez* v *Shields,* 74 Miss. 871, 21 So. 797 (1895).

[25] J. F. Dillon, *Commentaries on the Law of Municipal Corporations* (5th ed., Little, Brown, 1911), I, sec. 33.

[26] *Tullos* v *Town of Magee,* 181 Miss. 288, 179 So. 557 (1938); *Steitenroth* v *Jackson,* 99 Miss. 344, 54 So. 955 (1911); *City of Hazlehurst* v *Mapes,* 96 Miss. 656, 51 So. 890 (1910).

[27] *Mississippi Code, 1942,* 1952 Supp., secs. 3374-21–3374-23; *Mississippi Laws, 1950,* ch. 491.

[28] *Mississippi Code,* 1952 Supp., secs. 3374-10–3374-17.

[29] Police and fire personnel figures were derived from *The Municipal Year Book 1952* (Chicago, International City Managers' Association, 1953), pp. 391-404, 419-42.

[30] Figures taken from tabulated summaries of the Bureau of Public Administration, University of Mississippi.

[31] *Mississippi Laws, 1936,* ch. 185.

CHAPTER 23

County Government

THE COUNTY is a local unit of government in most of the forty-eight states. Although it is unimportant by comparison to municipalities for a great part of the country's population, it is everywhere, except in New England, the principal jurisdiction for rural areas.* Especially in the southern states, where the population is characteristically rural, the county is significant. Naturally it is the most important unit of local government in Mississippi.

DEVELOPMENT OF COUNTIES

Counties have existed in Mississippi since 1799. In that year the Natchez District was divided to form the original counties of Adams and Pickering. (The name of Pickering County was changed to Jefferson in 1802.) Later Amite, Claiborne, Franklin, Warren, and Wilkinson counties were created from the same district. Others were made from the early Choctaw and Chickasaw Indian cessions and the District of Mobile.[1] By the time the state was admitted to the Union in 1817 fourteen counties had been established. Later cessions from the Choctaws in 1820 and 1830 and from the Chickasaws in 1832 completed the territory of the state, and by 1836 it was all organized into counties. At various times some counties have been divided to form others, the last, Humphreys, being

* Rhode Island has no counties, and in other New England states counties have no governmental functions, serving only as judicial districts. In Louisiana counties are designated as "parishes."

created in 1918 from portions of five counties.[2] Today there are eighty-two counties in the state.

The Constitution of 1890 recognized the existence of counties in various places throughout the document. The seventy-five counties then in existence are listed by name in the sections dealing with legislative apportionment. Other sections refer directly or indirectly to county districts, officers, and powers. Section 260, without expressly authorizing the legislature to create new counties, contains limitations as to how this shall be done. Briefly, it requires that the qualified electors of any county or part of a county to be included in a proposed new county must approve the change by a majority vote of the persons voting. Elections on such a proposal cannot be held oftener than once in four years. New counties must be at least 400 square miles in area and existing counties cannot be reduced below that size.[3]

Acting on the generally recognized authority to do so, and within the limitations of the constitution, the legislature has created seven new counties since 1890. Although consolidation of counties, with approval of the qualified voters affected, is expressly provided for,[4] this power has not been exercised. The boundaries of counties may be changed without reference to the people.[5] Present counties vary considerably in size, from Montgomery and Walthall, each with 403 square miles, to Yazoo with 938 square miles.[6]

LEGAL POSITION OF THE COUNTY

Although the county in Mississippi is important as a unit of local government, legally it is but an instrumentality of the state. The state creates the county and gives it such functions as it deems essential; thus the state performs a great part of its functions through this medium. Except as restricted by constitutional provisions the legislature has virtually complete powers over local rural government.

The position of the county is somewhat different from that of cities. Consequently, it does not have the status of a municipal corporation. Rather the county may be called a quasi-corporation. It may sue and be sued by authority of the state legislature.[7] It is immune from liability to the same extent that the state is, thus having no liability in tort.[8]

Although certain aspects of county governments, such as provision for officers and their terms, school administration, and road administration, are fixed in the constitution, the greater part of its regulation is found in the statutes. The legislation on county organization, administration, and powers is voluminous. In spite of various constitutional provisions designed to prohibit it, much of this legislation is in the form of local and special laws.* The general law classifying counties is of importance. For purposes of determining salaries the legislature has divided the counties into eight classes on the basis of assessed valuation of real, personal, and public service corporation property: class one, $25,000,000 and over; class two, $20,000,000 to $25,000,000; class three, $15,000,000 to $20,000,000; class four, $10,000,000 to $15,000,000; class five, $8,000,000 to $10,000,000; class six, $6,000,000 to $8,000,000; class seven, $3,000,000 to $6,000,000; class eight, less than $3,000,000.[9]

ADMINISTRATIVE ORGANIZATION

For the purposes of administration each county has been divided into various districts or subdivisions. Some of these have little significance other than as territorial units. The township, an area of thirty-six square miles, is of importance as a governmental subdivision only for the handling of funds received from the sale or lease of sixteenth section school lands.† Other areas are of more importance.

Beats

Each county is divided into five districts called beats. These districts are the units for election of the county board of supervisors, one supervisor being chosen from each district. The selection of various other administrative bodies, such as the county school board, county board of health, and political party executive committees, is based on the beat. It is the unit for local highway administration and has a limited importance as an area for judicial administration, in that justices of the peace and constables are elected by beats. The law specifies that beats must be made with regard to equality of population and convenience for election of the supervisors. Changes may be made by unanimous vote of the board of supervisors at any time and are mandatory when ordered by a majority of the voters.[10] Nevertheless, the beats frequently are grossly unequal both in area and in population. There is also great inequality in the assessed valuation of property.

* See Chapter 5, pp. 55-56.
† A section is one square mile. Each sixteenth section was donated by the national government for public school purposes.

Court Districts

Nine counties of the state are each divided into two court districts. Circuit and chancery court sessions are held, or may be held, in both districts.* These counties also have two courthouses, one at the county seat and another in a county town of the other judicial district, with the result that county administration is carried on from both places.† The reasons for such districts appear to be chiefly historical and sentimental, having no necessary relation to the amount of judicial business of the county.

School Districts

For purposes of school administration counties have a large number of school districts. These are of five kinds: common school districts, consolidated districts, special consolidated districts, municipal separate districts, and rural separate districts. All are defined and established by law, and the number of different types as well as the total number of districts varies with the different counties.[11] Changes in the kinds of school districts under the new equalization statutes are discussed in Chapter 13.

Special Districts

Other districts have been established within the county, chiefly for state and national administrative purposes. These include water control districts and soil conservation districts. Although these additional units tend to complicate the structure of local government, they are not important to this explanation.

OFFICERS AND GOVERNMENT

The county, in addition to being an administrative area for the state, has important duties of local government. Since most of its officials are locally chosen, the autonomy of the county is more complete than its legal position would indicate. Most of the county officers are provided for in the constitution, but the manner of their selection is provided by law. The law generally requires their election by popular vote.

* The counties are Bolivar, Carroll, Chickasaw, Hinds, Jasper, Jones, Panola, Tallahatchie, and Yalobusha.—*Mississippi Blue Book, 1952,* p. 190.

† Some county officials have offices in both courthouses, whereas others have only one office.

Board of Supervisors

The board of supervisors is the principal governing body of the county. Its membership, organization, and general powers are set forth in the constitution. Its importance has been increased by numerous and frequent laws.

The county board is composed of five persons, one elected from each of the county beats for a term of four years. In order to be eligible a person must be a qualified elector, a resident of the district, and the owner of real estate valued at $300. The board meets regularly the first Monday in each month at the county seat, though in counties having two judicial districts it may hold monthly meetings at both courthouses. The board elects its president from among the members, and three members constitute a quorum. Special meetings may be called by any three members. The chancery clerk is the clerk of the board, and the sheriff is its executive officer. Both these officials or their deputies must attend all meetings. Upon taking office members must furnish bond in the amount of 5 per cent of the tax revenue collectible in the county for the preceding year. Vacancies in the membership are filled by the board for an unexpired term not exceeding six months; for longer periods a special election is held. Compensation of supervisors is on a per diem basis with the daily payment and the maximum total payment fixed by a complicated plan based on the different classes of counties. The maximum salary varies from $2,070 to $4,140 per year.[12]

The functions of the board of supervisors are so numerous that no full enumeration and description of them is possible here.[13] A brief description of the different types of powers should suffice. The types may be called financial, judicial, those pertaining to highways and public works, education, public health and welfare, agriculture and conservation, purchasing, and a group of miscellaneous functions.

Most important of the board's functions are those connected with county finance. They are broad and important and are related directly to other types of functions. Among them are the power to levy taxes for county purposes, appropriate money, equalize assessments, select depositories for county funds, settle claims against the county, prepare the annual budget, and issue bonds for a variety of purposes.

The judicial duties of the board also are important. Members are conservators of the peace with all the powers of justices of the peace. They may create additional justices of the peace and may establish county courts under legal limitations. The board also prepares the jury list for the circuit court.

County road administration is the exclusive task of the board of supervisors and includes the employment of crews and superintendents, the purchase or rental of equipment, inspection of roads and bridges, and similar duties. The board also lets contracts as specified by law for any other public works of the county and inspects and approves such projects. It is empowered to cooperate with any state authority in regard to these functions. However, the board has no control over state highways.

The board has numerous powers related to public education in the county. It also has general responsibility for public libraries and may levy a limited tax for their support. Many of the board's duties relating to education are in conjunction with the county superintendent of education.

The board of supervisors has general responsibility for the county public health program. Specific powers include the establishment, separately or in cooperation with other counties, of a health department. The board also may pass compulsory vaccination measures, establish community hospitals, and provide for food inspection. The board has responsibilities in connection with the county welfare program, including the care of paupers and the provision of county homes for this purpose.

Duties of the board in regard to agriculture and conservation generally look to the improvement of agricultural conditions and reforestation. For such purposes the board may establish drainage districts and appoint commissions for them, create flood control districts, parks, and game preserves, and cooperate with various state agencies in the promotion of such programs. The board may levy taxes and appropriate money for these purposes.

All supplies and equipment for the county are purchased by the board of supervisors, including furniture, record books, law books, machinery, and other materials needed for the conduct of the county's affairs.

In addition to the general classes of functions listed are miscellaneous duties and responsibilities such as the provision of facilities for the holding of elections and the general supervision and care of county buildings.

Sheriff and Tax Collector

One of the oldest offices in county government is that of sheriff. In Mississippi this officer is also the tax collector. He is elected for a four-year term and is ineligible to succeed himself. Any resident who is a qualified elector and is not a defaulter to the state is eligible. Compensation of the sheriff is on a fee basis and varies widely because of differences in tax revenues and numbers of fees.

The duties of the sheriff are of three main types. First, he is the chief law enforcement officer of the county with power to prevent criminal actions and to arrest offenders. Second, he is the administrative official who has direct charge of the courthouse, jail, and prisoners as well as responsibility for the county library. He is the executive officer for the district courts and the board of supervisors with the duty of preserving order, serving writs and citations, and performing similar services. Third, he is the tax collector for the county with the entailed duties of receiving and handling funds, seizing and selling tax delinquent property, and making reports to state authorities.

Chancery Clerk

The office of chancery clerk combines the work of the clerk of the chancery court and some of the duties of the county clerk. Naturally, this combination makes his duties diverse as well as numerous and important. The chancery clerk is elected for a four-year term and must have the general qualifications for county officers. Compensation of this official is a combination of salary, fees, and per diem wages and varies with the different counties. Aside from his duties in connection with the chancery court, the clerk's duties fall into three classes. He is clerk of the board of supervisors and has clerical and administrative work in that connection. He is also a county recording officer and maintains important records relating to property, taxes, and schools. In the third place he is the chief fiscal officer of the county having the duties formerly performed by the county treasurer as well as certain auditing functions.

Tax Assessor

The voters in each county elect a tax assessor who has the usual four-year term. Qualifications are the general ones for county officials and include no professional requirements. The assessor is paid a salary that varies with the different classes of counties, ranging from $2,600 to $5,000 a year. The duties of this official consist of making the annual evaluation of property within the county. Taxes for county and state purposes are levied on this evaluation, though the State Tax Commission makes its own assessment of the property of public service corporations. The Tax Commission also may order the county board to increase or decrease assessments on classes of property in order to equalize the evaluation throughout the state.[14]

Circuit Clerk

The clerk of the circuit court, like the chancery clerk, is a county official and has a number of clerical duties as such. Elected for a four-year term, he must possess only the general qualifications for county officers. He is compensated on a fee basis. His duties, in addition to those as clerk of the circuit court, consist of serving as registrar of voters, issuing marriage licenses, and other minor functions. On the whole, this office is less important and less remunerative than that of the chancery clerk. In counties not exceeding 15,000 population the board of supervisors may, in its discretion, combine the offices of circuit and chancery clerk. This has been done in five counties.[15]

Superintendent of Education

The chief officer of the county public school system is the county superintendent of education. He is elected for a four-year term with the general qualifications of four years' citizenship in the state and two years' citizenship in the county, the latter immediately preceding his election. Professional qualifications for the office include holding a certificate from the State Department of Education attesting that he possesses a bachelor's degree, holds or is eligible to secure a Class A certificate for school administrators, and that he has had not less than five years' experience in school administration in Mississippi or in a state extending reciprocity in licensing of teachers to Mississippi.[16] The county superintendent must also have these professional qualifications if he is appointed to the office in the manner described in Chapter 13. The minimum salary for this office ranges from $3,600 to $4,200 per annum depending on the school attendance. He is also allowed travel expenses.

The duties of the county superintendent in regard to the public schools may be grouped into three general categories. The first is that of advice to the schools of the county. In this connection he visits and inspects schools, furnishes information to superintendents, and maintains maps, files, and other materials. Second, the superintendent has financial duties in connection with the handling of funds from school lands in the county, the preparation of periodic school fiscal reports, and the certification of warrants for payment of teachers' salaries. Finally, he performs important duties for the state in the computation and handling of funds paid to the county under the state equalization law, the enforcement of the compulsory school attendance law, supervision of the annual school census, handling of free textbooks, and the maintenance of standards with respect to teacher qualifications and the physical conditions of school buildings and equipment.

County Attorney

Fifty-five counties of the state elect a county attorney.* He is chosen for a four-year term and, in addition to the general qualifications, must be a practicing attorney. The salary for the position is fixed by the county board within maximum and minimum limits established by law, based on classes of counties. Duties of the county attorneys are to prosecute cases for the state in the justice of peace courts and the county court and to assist the district attorney in prosecutions in the circuit court. He may also serve as attorney for the board of supervisors, for which he receives extra compensation.

Coroner

The office of coroner, though established by the constitution for each county, exists in only thirty-nine counties of the state where there were candidates for the position. In the remaining counties the duties of the coroner devolve upon the justice of the peace of the district.[17] The office is elective, with the usual four-year term, and there are no qualifications for candidates beyond the general ones for all officers of the county. Compensation is on a fee basis. The coroner has the duty of conducting inquests on all violent, sudden, or accidental deaths within the county for which the cause is not known. A sworn jury of six persons is impaneled for such inquests. Upon the request of a majority of the jury, medical or surgical witnesses may be summoned, and, on motion of the county or district attorney, an autopsy may be ordered. The coroner is also ex officio the county ranger and may act as sheriff if a vacancy occurs in that office where a deputy is not authorized to act.†

The absence of professional qualifications for the office of coroner, as well as other aspects of the office, indicates a lack of appreciation of its importance to the task of crime detection and law enforcement. Consid-

* The decision as to whether the county shall have this office is determined by majority vote of the qualified electors.—*Mississippi Code, 1942,* secs. 3910-12.

† The legal limit on fees for medical witnesses at an inquest is $10 and must cover any laboratory analyses. For an autopsy a fee of $75 may be paid.—*Mississippi Code, 1942,* 1952 Supp., sec. 3902. When the coroner acts as county ranger his duties pertain to the disposition of stray livestock.—*Mississippi Code, 1942,* sec. 4877.

erable sentiment for a medical examiner to replace the coroner has been evident in some states, particularly since the formulation of a model coroner law by the National Municipal League and other organizations in 1950. At its annual convention in 1953 the Mississippi Medical Association endorsed a proposal that would require coroners to be licensed physicians.[18]

Surveyor

The constitution also establishes the office of county surveyor. The surveyor is elected for a four-year term. There are no professional qualifications for the position, and compensation is in the form of fees for work performed. Duties of the surveyor are to make land surveys upon the order of a court or upon the request of landowners. The office is of no great importance and is filled, at the present time, in only thirty-six counties.

Miscellaneous Officials

In addition to the officers discussed above, there are a number of other county officials, most of whom are appointed. In five counties of the state the office of cotton weigher exists, but there appears to be no law governing his selection. Elective judicial officers, such as the county judge and justices of the peace, and court officers, such as constables, have been discussed in a previous chapter. The list of appointive officials includes the county agricultural agent, home economics agent, county drainage commissioners, county housing commissioners, county health director, county road engineer, county road commissioners, and county board of public welfare—all of whom are appointed by the board of supervisors. Other county officials, such as the county welfare agent, are appointed by state authorities. Still others are chosen by different county officials.[19]

COUNTY FUNCTIONS

An enumeration of the functions of the county might include the general subjects of agriculture and home economics, conservation, education, elections, finance, general supervision, health, highways and public works, justice, and welfare. Any statement that the administration of these matters is the function of the county government, however, would be misleading. A better explanation would be that the county has a function in regard to these services but that the state government participates to a greater or lesser degree in each of them.

In the field of local finance the county has important responsibilities. As indicated above, the board of supervisors levies taxes, issues bonds, makes appropriations, and generally has financial responsibility for the expenses of local rural government. Although these powers are regulated extensively by law, including the review of all county financial transactions by the State Department of Audit, the amount of expenditures and indebtedness of each county is still determined largely by its own board. The tax assessor of the county, through his power to place a value on most property within the county, determines to a considerable extent the amount of property taxes to be paid by each individual to the county as well as to the state. The tax collector collects the county taxes as well as such state levies as those on property, motor vehicle registration, privilege licenses, and the poll tax.*

In public education the main tasks of administration fall upon the county school boards within these units, although the county superintendent and the local school boards render important assistance. Of particular significance is the function of the county school boards as administrative agents in the program of state supervision and financial assistance. The program of state assistance and regulation, however, has not destroyed local autonomy, and the quality of educational facilities is still determined, to a large degree, at the county or school district level.

Highway administration in the county is limited to purely county roads. Although practically all counties have some highways that were built, at least in part, by state and Federal funds and over which the State Highway Department has full control, the construction and maintenance of the local roads is a function of considerable importance. As explained above, county highways are directly under the jurisdiction of the county board of supervisors, and in most counties the members of this body have chosen to administer this function individually. Thus there are usually five units within the county for road building and maintenance. Naturally, this situation makes for a vast amount of duplication and waste.†

Justice and law enforcement in the county are theoretically a part of the function of the state, though the system of decentralized organization makes them really local matters. Each beat in the county elects one or two constables and justices of the peace and each elects its own sheriff. Compen-

* State control over local finance is discussed more fully in Chapter 24.

† This subject is discussed more fully in Chapter 18.

sation of these officers is provided locally, and the sentiment in the particular locality has much to do with the quality of law enforcement and justice. Local autonomy in these matters is evident to the casual observer.*

The county's function in regard to elections is important. Although there are detailed laws governing elections, all officials administering both primary and general elections are locally chosen, and the county pays the costs. Enforcement of election laws is at the county level, and there is no important state administrative supervision.

In the fields of agriculture and home economics, health and public works, conservation, and welfare the county serves chiefly as a unit of state administration. The state pays most of the costs of these functions, and the selection of officials to administer them is either by the state or is limited to persons having approval of state authorities. The laws in regard to such programs are specific, although obviously local sentiment does affect their administration.

COUNTY GOVERNMENT REFORM

County government in Mississippi, as in most states, has changed little during the past hundred years. Although certain functions of the county in earlier times have been appropriated by agencies of the state, the basic structure and features of county government remain the same. Movements for governmental reform in other jurisdictions have affected it but slightly; it is still the "dark continent" of the state's political system.

The result of this neglect of a fundamental portion of the government is a system that is antiquated, inefficient, and devoid of the principles that make for responsible administration. Although no detailed plan for reorganization will be proposed here, it is suggested that any plan of reform should embody three main principles.

Consolidation of Units

The present boundaries of counties were established for an earlier period. Modern communication and transportation make them far more numerous than is necessary. The number of counties could be reduced at least to half the present figure, improving the quality of administration and effecting enormous savings in courthouses, supplies, equipment, and personnel.

* This matter is discussed more fully in Chapter 12.

Integration of Internal Administration

The diffusion of county government among a large number of officials, boards, and commissions—many of them chosen for separate districts within the county—makes the administration of county affairs free of any real responsibility to the people. Moreover, it makes possible, and probable, the selection of unqualified officials and the resulting wasteful administration. The task of the voters might well be limited to the election of the county board. Other officials, except those connected with school administration, should be appointed by and responsible to the board. Although this reform may take the form of board-manager government, similar to that employed in some cities of the state, such a plan is not absolutely essential. The important thing is the concentration of responsibility for county administration in a single body. The board, being responsible to the voters, aided by the employment of some sort of civil service examinations and a merit system, could select qualified persons to perform the various duties now in the hands of elective officers. Efficient and economical administration would be the obligation of the board to the voters—an obligation that would be direct and enforceable. The elimination of most intra-county districts, such as beats and drainage districts, would be involved in this reorganization.

Extension of State Supervision

Certain functions now performed by the counties could be improved by further state supervision and control. The local courts should be fully incorporated into the state judiciary. More complete state supervision of the administration of public health measures, welfare, bookkeeping, accounting, tax assessment and collection, and public education would make for more uniform and efficient services and, at the same time, relieve the county government of burdens it is not able to bear.*

Obviously reform of county government along these lines will not be easy. Some constitutional changes may be necessary, though it is significant to note that two of the essential changes—the consolidation of counties (with the consent of the people involved) and the appointment of county officers by the county board of supervisors—may be accomplished by acts of the state legislature. The changes, by whatever means, would

* Each session of the legislature now appropriates money from state revenues to be divided among counties and towns to enable them to meet their obligations. The 1954 session was an exception.

have to overcome entrenched political power in county officialdom as well as the lethargy of the voting citizens.

FOOTNOTES

[1] Dunbar Rowland, *History of Mississippi* (Jackson: Clarke Pub. Co., 1925), II, 673 ff.

[2] *Mississippi Laws, 1918,* ch. 348.

[3] Constitution of 1890, art. 14, sec. 260.

[4] *Ibid.,* sec. 271.

[5] *Lindsley* v *Coahoma County,* 69 Miss. 815, 11 So. 336 (1892).

[6] *Mississippi Official and Statistical Register, 1949-1952* (Jackson: Secretary of State, 1952), p. 200.

[7] *Mississippi Code, 1942,* sec. 2955.

[8] *Grenada* v *Grenada County,* 115 Miss. 831, 76 So. 682 (1917).

[9] *Mississippi Code, 1942,* 1952 Supp., sec. 4159.

[10] *Mississippi Code, 1942,* sec. 2870.

[11] These districts are explained in Chapter 13. See also Robert B. Highsaw and Carl D. Mullican, Jr., *The Units of Government in Mississippi* (Bureau of Public Administration, University of Mississippi, 1949), pp. 10-11.

[12] *Mississippi Code, 1942,* 1952 Supp., sec. 4166.

[13] For a full enumeration and explanation see Huey B. Howerton, *A Guidebook of the Board of Supervisors* (Bureau of Public Administration, University of Mississippi, 1948).

[14] *Mississippi Code, 1942,* secs. 9800, 9801.

[15] *Ibid.,* sec. 4064.

[16] *Mississippi Laws, 1953 Ex. Sess.,* ch. 10.

[17] Constitution of 1890, art. 5, sec. 135; *Mississippi Blue Book, 1952,* p. 210.

[18] See Richard S. Childs, "Rubbing Out the Coroners," *National Municipal Review,* 39 (1950), 494-96; *Memphis Commercial Appeal,* May 24, 1953.

[19] For a complete list of county appointive officers see Huey B. Howerton, *A Guidebook of County Appointive Officers* (Bureau of Public Administration, University of Mississippi, 1949).

CHAPTER 24

Intergovernmental Relations

THE RELATIONS that develop between both different levels of government and the administrative agencies operating on each level are a significant if relatively unknown subject of study in Mississippi. It is axiomatic that Federal, state, and local governments do not function in a political vacuum and that the probelms that arise when the interests of various governmental units touch, merge, or even conflict often cannot be resolved by any one of them acting alone. Sometimes intergovernmental relations are confused and numerous. Other times they have failed to emerge where logically they might be expected to grow. In still more instances, though, the relations between the different governments provide an effective guide toward program and policy unification. Intergovernmental relations are present in any case, and one way or another they force the attention of citizens.

UNITS OF GOVERNMENT

The number of governmental units operating at any one time indicates at least in part the quantitative scope of public and official relationships. It serves not merely to illustrate the presence of different levels of government, but also to emphasize the extent and variety of action possible at each level. Thus the total number of Mississippi's units does not appear large in comparison with that of other states. Mississippi now ranks twenty-seventh among the members of the American Union, and in its region—the Southeast—Mississippi is above both the median state and the average figure. North Carolina, with 608 units, holds the middle position in the region, whereas the average for the southeastern states is 639 units, a deceptive figure because Arkansas's total alone exceeds 1,000 governments.

TABLE 15

GOVERNMENTAL UNITS IN THE UNITED STATES AND MISSISSIPPI, 1952

Unit		*United States*		*Mississippi*
Federal		1		1
State		48		1
Counties		3,049		82
Municipalities		16,677		263
Townships, towns		17,338		—
School districts		70,452		92[a]
Special districts		11,900		254
Highway	674		—	
Fire protection	1,965		—	
Housing	838		10	
Drainage, flood control	1,934		163	
Irrigation	582		—	
Soil conservation	1,967		73	
Water and sewer	881		—	
Other	3,059		8	
TOTALS		119,465		693

[a] Not included as governmental units are the more than 3,000 school districts that are classified as administrative districts, and the numerous road and bridge districts in Mississippi's counties.

Sources: United States Department of Commerce, Bureau of the Census, *Governments in the United States in 1952,* State and Local Government Special Studies, Number 31 (Washington, 1953), Table 1, p. 11, and Table 10, pp. 20-21.

Compared to Minnesota with 9,026 units of government and Nebraska with 7,981 units, the quantity of Mississippi government is comparatively slight.

The long established, commonly accepted, and dominant governments are those that actually exercise controls and provide the services of general government—the Federal, state, municipal, and county governments. Special purpose units such as the soil conservation districts, however, have developed significantly as a result of Federal programs designed to find both constitutional and economical units of administration.[1] The relations that inhere between the levels of government provide the administrative cement that holds programs and services together and constitute the "functional federalism" characteristic of American government today.

Perhaps the most significant trend in intergovernmental relations has been the development of centralization, that is, the shift of political power from a subordinate to a central unit of government. Just as the national government exercises broad powers in activities once thought to belong to the states alone, so the American states themselves have tended to drain substantial authority for public action away from the city halls and the county courthouses. The reasons for this trend are not hard to find if they are sought.

First, the bases of our economy have changed from a local economy to a state and national economy. Economic authority is concentrated, and this concentration with its result of a vast growth of urbanism and of modern means of transportation and communication, along with inevitable maladjustments of the social and economic system, has produced demands for governmental action that cannot be met on a local or even state basis. Secondly, the very multiplicity of governments—in Mississippi a citizen may reside within the jurisdiction of a dozen or more units—has made for a complex, disintegrative framework often unable to meet the demands placed upon it. Third, the move toward centralization has been hastened, if not caused, by a lack of confidence in the standards of administration in subordinate governmental units. Local personnel conditions frequently deny the premises of sound administration, and the level of administrative competence sometimes has been too low to deal with current problems. For these reasons resort has been had to the state capitals and to Washington.[2]

LOCAL RELATIONS

Although local governments have lost some of their powers in recent years, they still continue to grow. The cities, the counties, and the special districts perform more services, spend more money, and employ more people in their efforts to meet the growing demands for more and better local services. The municipalities and the counties have cogent reason for cooperative action, for they are, for many purposes, too small—too small in area to facilitate efficient operations and too slight in financial resources to raise individually the money they need for many of their services.

City-County Relations

Public health is primarily a state function, although it is shared with the counties. Its transferral to the counties from the municipalities has prevented duplication of services and ensured uniformity of administration. The municipalities have cooperated in two ways, by making appropriations to the county health departments for work within the corporate limits and by providing office space. Since municipalities are forbidden by the state to organize separate health departments, they are without authority to provide additional protection and must cooperate with the county department, which seeks to control communicable diseases, examine milk and inspect dairy farms, inspect food, and abate health nuisances.

A number of cities maintain public hospitals jointly with the county, whereas others receive financial support from the counties wherein they are located. Municipal separate school districts receive one dollar of the poll tax from the counties toward their support and in turn make available their facilities to rural pupils for whom the county pays tuition. Provision also is made for municipal-county cooperation in maintaining libraries, airports, and other facilities.

Extramural Municipal Activities

Municipalities are empowered by statute to extend several services beyond their territorial limits. Health and quarantine regulations are enforceable within five miles of the city limits, and agreements may be made with the county to extend fire protection to rural areas. Other legislation allows the extension of utility services such as water, sewers, electric power, and airports beyond municipal limits.[3]

Special Districts

A final area of local relations is occasioned by the special purpose districts in Mississippi, which, for the most part, operate in rural areas. Occasionally these districts present special problems to the counties and municipalities.

The Mississippi constitution created the Yazoo-Mississippi Delta Levee District in northwest Mississippi and the Mississippi Levee District in the central west, the former consisting of nine counties and the latter of five.[4] These districts are charged to supervise the erection, repair, and maintenance of levee systems within their jurisdiction for protection against flood and overflow of waters. Each is governed by an elective board of commissioners, and each has powers to levy taxes and to appropriate lands.

Port commissions are authorized for any seaport or harbor designated as a port of entry by the Federal government. Six commissions have been established under the current statute. Among them are three separate port commissions at Biloxi, Gulfport, and Pascagoula. Each of these separate commissions is constituted of one member appointed by the governor, one chosen by the county board of supervisors of the county wherein the port is located, and three selected by the governing body of the municipality. The commissioners are empowered to levy privilege taxes, receive county and municipal aid, and expend funds under their own direction.[5] In Natchez, Greenville, and Vicksburg, all located on the Mississippi River, the respective mayors and commissioners or boards of aldermen are assigned the functions of port commissions, so that these cities have no special port agencies.

More than 160 drainage districts function in Mississippi, mostly in rural areas. All of them may issue bonds and levy and collect taxes. Other special purpose districts having significant intergovernmental relations are the road and bridge districts, which may construct and maintain roads within municipalities, and electric power districts, which have the status of municipal corporations and may operate within or beyond municipal limits. Although the latter districts may borrow funds, they have no taxing powers.

STATE-LOCAL RELATIONS

State officials in Mississippi exercise a number of controls over and supervise, often in detailed fashion, the performance of local functions. State supervision of local government relies upon both techniques to secure information and permit state leadership and compulsory devices intended to obtain local compliance with state-wide standards. Either group of devices of local government runs counter to strongly prevailing attitudes of local "self-government," and both have been resisted stubbornly in Mississippi. Nevertheless, state supervision or control is found in several functions, among them local finance, education, industrial promotion, highways, public health, and public welfare.

Supervision of Local Finance

The aspects of local finance over which the state maintains a watchful eye are numerous, including supervision of tax assessment and local accounting, mandatory financial reports, the requirement of annual audits, supervision of the budget, limitation on indebtedness and supervision of debt retirement programs, and financial assistance in the form of either shared taxes or outright subventions.

The devices by which Mississippi's government exercises these controls are varied. Some are authorized by constitutional provisions, such as section 80 of the Mississippi constitution. This section states, for example, that the legislature shall make provision by general laws "to prevent the abuse by cities, towns, and other municipal corporations of their powers of assessment, taxation, borrowing money, and contracting debts." In pursuance of this authorization much of the state's supervision of local finance has been effected through statutes that establish either legislative prohibitions, for example debt limits based upon the ratio of debt to assessed valuation, or administrative supervision of local fiscal acts. In still other instances, quite informal relationships are established as a result of formal requirements.

A few examples illustrate the nature of the control over local finance. Although the municipal governing body serves as the equalization body reviewing assessments of real and personal property, except that owned by public utilities, substantial supervisory authority is vested in the state with regard to county assessments. The State Tax Commission thus is charged to make equalization of county assessments of real and personal property, to require the information necessary to enable it to perform this function, and, in addition, to hold an annual conference of county tax assessors. The ad valorem tax commissioner supervises the collection of information concerning the quantity and value of property in each county and prescribes forms on which the data are supplied in order that the commission may act as an effective equalization body.[6] In the area of tax collection, in contrast, payment of taxes in installments is provided by general law.

Although the chief inspector of the state accounting department had authority for many years, on direction of the governor, to prescribe a uniform system of accounts for municipalities of more than 1,000 inhabitants, the power was never utilized, at least through 1940.[7] Under 1952 legislation, however, the State Department of Audit was vested with full authority to formulate and to require installation in all counties and municipalities in the state of uniform "systems of accounting, budgeting, and reporting . . . [which] shall conform to acceptable standards and legal requirements."[8] This statute went further and authorized the Department of Audit, when necessary, to postaudit, preaudit, and investigate the financial affairs of county offices and county departments on a fee basis to be paid partly by the state and partly by the county. Two years earlier, in 1950, the legislature acted to require the preparation and publication of an annual budget of expenditures for municipalities. Under this statute the state prescribes the form of the budget, the municipal accounting system, and an annual audit.[9] No prior review by the state of county budgets has been required, although the *Brookings Report* of 1932 recommended a department of local government in which this function would be vested.

Tax rates are imposed by the legislature for both counties and municipalities.* Actually the state controls local tax rates in two ways, first, by prescribing the taxes that the local units may levy, and second, by determining the maximum rates that they may assess. The limits imposed on ad valorem millage vary with the unit of government. Considerable doubt may be raised with respect to the efficacy of these tax limitations, which were originally intended to compel efficiency in assessing methods and to eliminate some possibilities of graft or corruption. Renewed agitation for more rigid tax limits marked the depression years. Under impetus of growing tax delinquencies the states took some measures, such as the Mississippi Homestead Exemption Law of 1938, to provide relief.† The local units of government, largely dependent upon the property tax, have been especially hard-pressed with the rising price level of the postwar years. Since the state usually has pre-empted the more lucrative tax sources, which are normally those local units cannot tap effectively, a reallocation of tax sources or a system of state-collected locally-shared taxes has been urged.

Local indebtedness is controlled by the state also. This control is in the form of legislative prohibitions of indebtedness exceeding a given percentage of assessed valuation, 10 per cent of the assessments in counties after 1950 plus the then outstanding bonds of the county and a similar figure for the municipalities, with the proviso that after certain types of indebtedness already contracted—bonds for municipal utilities, special improvements chargeable against property benefits, or the municipality's share of such a program—all outstanding indebtedness shall not exceed 15 per cent.‡ Advice to the local units is provided by the state's bond at-

* For example, see *Mississippi Laws, 1946,* ch. 280, establishing the county general ad valorem tax levy; *Mississippi Code,* 1950 Supp., sec. 9882 *et seq.,* establishes the general ad valorem levy for municipal separate school districts, municipalities, and other subordinate units. Other statutes prescribe rates for municipal privilege taxes and other sources.

† This measure exempted homesteads up to $5,000 from ad valorem taxes levied by the state and from ad valorem taxes levied for current and maintenance purposes by the counties and by school districts.—*Mississippi Code, 1942,* Recompiled volume 7 A (1952), sec. 9714; *Mississippi Laws, 1946,* ch. 261, *1950,* ch. 302. Since these exemptions materially reduce local revenue, the state makes reimbursement payments to the local units, totaling in 1951 $7,495,000. The state has not entirely vacated the ad valorem property tax; although limited by statute to four mills, in recent years the state levy generally has been only two mills.—*Mississippi Laws, 1942,* ch. 117.

‡ *Mississippi Laws, 1950,* chs. 241, 493. Certain other exceptions are made—for example, school bonds, revenue bonds for utilities.

torney, who examines legal papers connected with bond issues, gives opinions concerning the validity of the issues, and attends validation hearings when issues are contested.

Several other state controls apply to local indebtedness. Bond issues of counties, municipalities, and other local units thus must have approval by the voters, although some issues, such as refunding bonds and small issues, are excepted; the statutes prescribe that a three-fifths majority of those voting in the election is necessary to carry bond issues in both counties and municipalities. Moreover, the bonds must mature serially over a maximum twenty-five year period for both types of units. In both units proceeds of the bonds must be deposited in the local treasury and segregated for the purpose for which they were authorized. Similiar restrictions apply also to other local units. Finally, municipalities, counties, and all other local governments must file with the state auditor of public accounts tabulated statements of bond issues showing dates of issues and maturities, along with other information.[10] The purpose of this requirement no doubt is to facilitate central review of observance of debt limitations and regulations.

Although not related to administrative control or supervision of local governments, financial assistance is provided municipalities and counties by the state. Grants-in-aid are made, for example, for health work in the counties, but no grants are provided municipalities. Recent legislation has allowed all legal municipalities voluntarily to levy a municipal sales tax that is collected with the state sales tax and returned to the city levying the tax.[11] As far back as 1946 the legislature authorized the apportionment of any state surplus in the general fund above $5,000,000 in excess of any nonrecurring appropriations. This surplus was to be allocated on the ratio of one third to the state, one third to the counties, and one third to the municipalities. Since that year so-called pork barrel distributions have been made biennially. Counties share in or are returned the proceeds of several taxes, among them the gasoline excise tax, the truck and bus privilege tax, and the oil and timber severance tax. As recently as 1951 Mississippi's counties received more from these sources and from state educational funds and homestead exemption reimbursements than they did from all local sources, the comparative figures reaching $41,155,000 in state assistance and only $29,032,000 in local collections. Whether local officials like it or not, the implication of financial realities may well be that the counties no longer can pass a test of economic sufficiency, and that oft-heard claims of "county autonomy" are wearing thin.

Supervision of Education

Although local control over schools is an established tradition in Mississippi no less than in other states, the state supervises the educational function in at least six ways, namely, through financial subsidies to education, general supervisory powers, control over personnel, limited curriculum services, control over textbooks, and control over school buildings.

A most important governmental activity is public education. The organization of the various types of school districts has been alluded to in an earlier chapter of this study, and brief mention was made there of the sources of school finance. The Mississippi constitution, it must be noted again, states that there shall be a state common school fund that, together with local school funds, will be sufficient to maintain a minimum four-month school year. Any district may assess ad valorem taxes to maintain longer terms and, in practice, all districts do. The State Board of Education distributes, according to the constitutional requirement, the common school fund to the local school districts on the basis of the number of educable children in each district.[12] In 1954 the legislature repealed the statute providing an equalization fund and established the Minimum Education Program Fund, which, with the common school fund, will constitute the state's share of the cost involved in equalizing educational opportunities in the state. The provisions for distribution of this fund and substantive features of the new program, such as the guarantee of a minimum education to all children, guaranteed minimum salaries for teachers, free transportation to many students, and grants for administrative expenses and operation, and for maintenance of school buildings will result in new intergovernmental relationships between local, county, and state officials.[13] The first state appropriation of $34,000,000 for the program, made for a trial year, indicates the fiscal importance of the integrated educational program to the state.

Powers of general supervision over the public school system are vested in the state superintendent of education, including those to collect information on the basis of which state funds are apportioned locally; to issue rules and regulations for the efficient organization and conduct of the schools; to require annually or more frequently reports of the county superintendent; and to prescribe the forms on which reports shall be submitted.[14] Controversies arising from the construction and interpretation of the school laws are subject also to his decision.

Regulations for the certification of teachers in the common schools are administered by the Division of Instruction within the State Department of Education. These regulations are designed to assure that all new teachers beginning in 1954 have at least two years of appropriate college training and after December 1, 1956, at least four years of college training.

A rigid curriculum is specified for all public schools in the state, but a degree of flexibility has been added to the legislative curriculum by the permission given to the State Board of Education to appoint a curriculum committee of not more than seven persons to review the course of study in the public schools and make recommendations for changes.[15] A limited and advisory program of curriculum services also is maintained by the State Department of Education.

Mississippi is one of thirty-odd states in which control over textbooks used in the public schools has been established. Textbook rating committees are appointed by the state superintendent of education to review all books offered for adoption and to recommend three texts for each adoption. The Mississippi Textbook Purchasing Board may reject the recommendation of any rating committee and call for new recommendations, but it may not adopt any volume not recommended by a rating committee. The textbook purchasing agency functions, then, to adopt, purchase, and distribute texts for the common schools with a substantive professional check exercised upon it by the rating committees.

Finally, considerable state supervision and assistance is furnished the local school districts in school plant planning and construction, school building inspection services, and transportation services. Within the past few years state financial assistance has been provided school districts that applied to the State Building Commission for grants-in-aid for school construction; applications were reported on by the State Department of Education and reviewed by the Building Commission. Prior approval of plans and specifications also was exercised by the state agency. With increased attention upon equalization of white and Negro educational facilities, supervision of school buildings and state financial aid in their construction assumes a new importance, which was recognized by the establishment in 1953 of the State Educational Finance Commission. This agency now is empowered to approve or disapprove plans for locating and constructing new elementary and secondary school buildings, to approve surveys of educational needs, and to distribute available funds for construction, renovation, or repair of school buildings.[16] However, the 1954 legislature failed to appropriate funds for the systematic support of school buildings.

Supervision of Industrial Promotion

Attracting new industries to Mississippi and extending to them subsidies and tax exemptions is carried on jointly by the state and its local units. Although the Mississippi Agricultural and Industrial Board actively seeks to induce industry to locate within the state, it supervises closely the acts of local governments supplying specific subsidies. Counties and municipalities are authorized by statute to acquire lands and erect buildings that may be leased for industrial purposes, but it is the duty of the Mississippi Agricultural and Industrial Board to determine whether the public convenience and necessity require in any single case that the local government take such action. In order to grant a certificate of public convenience and necessity, the board must determine affirmatively the sufficiency of natural resources necessary to operate the proposed plant for a ten-year period, adequacy of labor supply within a twenty-five-mile area, and extent of property values, so that any bonds voted for industrial purposes will not exceed 20 per cent of the assessed valuation of all property within the local unit.[17]

If the board grants the certificate, it must determine (1) the extent and amount of bonds or expenditures that may be issued or made for the project; (2) what property may be acquired; (3) terms of the acquisition of property; (4) what expenditures may be made for the construction or acquisition of buildings and equipment; and (5) the method of operation of the project by the locality. After the certificate has been granted and the local government has accepted these determinations, the proposed plan must be ratified by two thirds of the qualified electors voting in a special election. The net effect of these regulations is to preserve local determination of industrial promotion policies under state supervision so that location of desirable and economically feasible establishments may be assured. This arrangement offers, perhaps, a more satisfactory device than the exemption from taxes of industrial enterprises by municipalities, which had been permitted since 1892.

Supervision of Highways

Note has been taken in Chapters 18 and 23 that the county boards of supervisors have control of county roads and bridges and that rural roads are administered usually within the county on a district basis. Substantial financial assistance is provided the counties from the return of motor vehicle taxes and from the return of the truck and bus tax, which is shared on the basis of one third in proportion to population, one third by area, and one third by the number of registered vehicles.

Considerable state supervision is exercised over highways designated as "state aid roads," that is, secondary roads of importance that have been grouped by the legislature into one system and have been located under county management with supervisory powers of promulgating rules and regulations for designation of such roads in each county, for preparation of plans and specifications, and for accounting systems placed with the state aid engineer.* Statutory relations between the State Highway Commission and the municipalities have been established under which the state must maintain all municipal streets used as parts of the Mississippi primary highway system and may construct them.

Construction and maintenance of all roads included in the state highway system is vested exclusively in the State Highway Commission. The alternative faced by the state today in its highway relationships is simple: the state may centralize and control all roads, as in North Carolina, or it may provide financial assistance in the amounts and under the controls that it deems wise and politically feasible. Mississippi has chosen thus far to return taxes for local highway purposes and provide state aid under supervision for highways having a general but secondary purpose.

Supervision of Public Health

A widened concept of the public health function has witnessed an expansion of health work on both the national and state levels of government. For all practical purposes local health departments are joint state-county operations, the controlling statutes providing that when a single county or two or more counties create a health department, other municipal or local health bodies are abolished.† These county or district health departments have full control over local health matters subject to "the supervision, direction, and jurisdiction" of the State Board of Health. Although the county health directors are appointed locally, on the recommendation of the State Board of Health or its executive committee, they may be suspended summarily or removed after investigation by the state agency. With the authority to promulgate and enforce reasonable rules and regulations, the State Board of Health is paramount.

The general health powers exercised by the state in public health matters

* This relationship is discussed extensively in Chapter 18, p. 265.

† *Mississippi Laws, 1918,* ch. 194; *1926,* ch. 309. Municipalities may appropriate funds to support county units, however.

are considerable. Thus the state board may require local health authorities to supply sanitary information on prescribed forms; it may and does inspect the sanitary conditions of local schools, public institutions, and all public buildings within municipalities; and it distributes health literature and advises local units on health education problems. Among the more coercive devices employed by the State Board of Health is the review of local health ordinances, which it may accept, amend, or reject. Prior permission of the board is required for construction or improvement of municipal water and sewer systems, as well as for jails. Similarly the State Board of Health may direct local health or other officers to begin proceedings for the abatement of health nuisances, or it may issue orders requiring improvement of local jails, water and sewer systems, and other matters directly affecting the general health of the community.[18] Similarly, the State Board of Health has full authority to establish quarantines.

Control of Public Welfare

Administration of virtually all welfare functions in Mississippi is vested in the State Department of Public Welfare. There are no municipal welfare departments, and the county departments are so organized that they constitute local extensions of the state department. The county board of public welfare, locally appointed, serves as an advisory body to the county welfare agent. This official, however, is designated by the commissioner of public welfare to serve as the executive officer of the local department and is responsible to the state commissioner for his administration. Although the counties may assist in the discharge of the various state welfare programs, they neither finance nor control them.[19] Counties may appropriate small amounts to help defray the expense of the county welfare agent. In short, except for scattered poor farms maintained by some counties, the welfare function has been allocated to the state.

INTERSTATE RELATIONS

An important medium of interstate relations among the members of the American Union is the Council of State Governments, which was established in 1925. This body functions as a clearing house of research and information among the states, provides encouragement for improving state legislative and administrative practices, and seeks to facilitate better Federal-state relations. Perhaps its most important service, though, has been to encourage full cooperation among members in the solution of interstate problems, thereby affording an effective alternative to Federal action in several spheres. Mississippi is a member of the Council of State Governments and has established a Commission on Interstate Cooperation to promote the state's participation in its work. The commission is composed of the governor, five members of the House Committee on Interstate Cooperation, and five members of the Senate Committee on Interstate Cooperation. The commission is authorized to formulate proposals for interstate cooperation and to arrange conferences with officials of other states and of other units of government.*

Tangible evidence of interstate cooperation is found in compacts made with other states, mostly in recent years. In 1948 Mississippi ratified the Interstate Oil Compact, which is designed to conserve oil and gas in twenty-two member states by preventing physical waste; this compact requires the states to enact and enforce certain statutes designed to conserve these important resources. Also in 1948, Mississippi adopted the Interstate Parole and Probation Compact establishing interstate supervision of parolees and probationers, and in 1952 the legislature approved the Interstate Civil Defense and Disaster Compact, which authorized the governor to execute compacts with the several states under its terms.

Perhaps the most significant of the current agreements are the compacts creating the Southern Regional Education Board and the Gulf States Marine Fisheries Commission. The former, made with thirteen southern states, is interstate cooperation intended to upgrade the quality and quantity of graduate, professional, and technical research and education in the South. The program, which now includes regional work in medicine, veterinary medicine, dentistry, and other areas, is directed by a regional board consisting of the governor and three representatives appointed by him from each state. Member states without adequate facilities in the fields into which the board has entered may contract with it to place students in out-of-state institutions, certify that the students are residents of the state sponsoring them, and pay a stipulated amount for each student actually enrolled. The board contracts with the educational institution to accept the students if they meet admission requirements and in the 1951-1952 school year placed approximately 900 of them. In addition, the board has planned a major expansion of its work into the area of graduate

* *Mississippi Laws, 1936,* ch. 198. The Commission on Interstate Cooperation is not to be confused with the Mississippi representation in the National Conference of Commissioners on Uniform State Laws, which encourages legislative action to secure uniformity among the states in a wide range of legislative subjects.

studies. It has thus appointed one commission to assist in the development of interstate and interinstitutional efforts to improve graduate programs related to the needs of the South. Another has been established to stimulate and guide the educational institutions of the region in their relationships with industry and public agencies so that not only will service be broadened, but educational facilities will be expanded.

The Mississippi legislature ratified in 1950 the Gulf States Marine and Fisheries Compact, which endeavors to promote and protect fisheries of Alabama, Florida, Louisiana, Mississippi, and Texas through the Gulf States Marine Fisheries Commission, now located at New Orleans, Louisiana. Substantial progress has been made toward the objective of the compact. In cooperation with private interests and the United States Fish and Wildlife Service the commission has completed research essential to exploratory fishing and biological research, collected statistical data related to the compact states, reviewed current state laws and regulations governing inshore fin fish, requested the governors and legislatures of member states to consider beginning new research programs, and suggested the enactment of statutes in the compact states permitting reciprocal fishing agreements.[20]

Reciprocal agreements are permitted in a number of activities with somewhat less than the formality of an interstate compact. Thus the motor vehicle commissioner, the attorney general, and the governor may promulgate reciprocity agreements with the other states and Canada concerning the operation of motor vehicles from Mississippi or from the other states and Canada in Mississippi. Other reciprocal agreements include those concerning plants, livestock, motor vehicle taxes, and unemployment compensation.

FEDERAL RELATIONS

Although the Federal government has maintained relations with subordinate units of government since the founding of the Republic, the greatest expansion of these relations occurred during and after the years of the great depression of the 1930's. Federal-state cooperation, made a necessity in lean years, was strengthened during World War II, while at the same time direct contact was being established between the national government and local units. Federal relationships with subordinate units of government have generally centered around two principal categories:

(1) financial assistance, largely in the form of the familiar grants-in-aid; and (2) the supplying of information and technical assistance.

Financial Assistance

The term "grants-in-aid" usually is defined to denote payments made by one government to another, conditioned upon acceptance of specified programs and upon adherence to specified procedures to attain the program objective. The Federal grants-in-aid are a lucrative source of revenue for Mississippi, accounting with other payments for 24.7 per cent of the state's revenue in 1952 alone.[21] Of the $40,557,000 the state government received in Federal funds that year, distribution among the functional fields of public activity included $14,152,000 for public welfare; $8,321,000 for educational functions; $8,189,000 for highways; $5,519,000 for public health and hospitals; $1,986,000 for the conservation of natural resources; $1,941,000 for employment security; and $449,000 for other purposes. At the same time local units also were receiving grants-in-aid and in-lieu-of-tax payments.

The pattern by which the national government administers grants-in-aid is well defined. Usually through legislation the state indicates its willingness to accept formally the grants-in-aid. The organization to administer the program and the initiative in preparing plans also are left to the state, but the Federal government reviews and approves the plans through an appropriate administrative agency. Provision is made for joint Federal-state financing of the program, often on an equal basis but with the national government sometimes supplying the larger share. Execution of the project plans then is made by the state or local unit concerned, subject to a separate audit and inspections by Federal officials. Upon satisfactory completion of the project by the local unit the Federal government makes full payment of promised funds.[22] Frequently the state or local governments receive partial payment before the project has been completed.

A few examples illustrate the use of the grants-in-aid device in Mississippi. A major instance of the impact of Federal programs upon the state is found in those established by the Social Security Act of 1935, as amended by subsequent legislation. This statute in effect created a national-state plan to aid some of the less fortunate persons in the American society and a truly Federal system for administering it, the national government to supply some of the necessary funds and the states to organize and conduct specific programs. Congress has made it the function of the Social Security Administration to approve all state plans for old-age assistance and for aid to the blind and dependent children; to approve state unemployment compensation plans; to certify to the United States Secretary of the Treasury Federal grants made to state agencies administering approved plans; and to administer directly the old-age and survivors' insurance system. In approving the Mississippi plans for these programs and maintaining the necessary supervisory relationships the Social Security Administration now works closely with the Mississippi Employment Security Commission and the State Department of Public Welfare. The obvious effect of the financial assistance in this case has been to place the social welfare programs on a constitutional basis, to secure acceptance by the state of nation-wide minimum standards, and to improve the administrative practices employed to attain program goals. In accomplishing these effects, grants-in-aid also have unified governmental programs.*

Conservation and agriculture are related activities wherein the grants-in-aid have been employed effectively. For years funds under the Federal Clarke-McNary Act have been allotted to Mississippi for forest fire protection. A formula is employed for the allocation of Federal moneys that recognizes need based upon the total estimated cost of a state-wide fire protection system and the expenditures of the state, including accredited county and private funds. Before any money is made available for expenditure, however, the Mississippi Forestry Commission submits to the United States Forest Service a proposed budget that details the proposed expenditures for the fire control program. After agreement to the program by Federal and state authorities, the state agency acts as the body immediately responsible for executing the projects for which funds have been made available; the national government audits and inspects the work of the state commission prior to reimbursement. Under somewhat similar arrangements the State Game and Fish Commission receives Pittman-Robertson Act funds to purchase land for wildlife purposes and to conduct research into wildlife management problems.

Concerned with conservation as well as with agriculture and education are the various programs that revolve about the State Extension Service, the Agricultural Experiment Station, the counties, and the soil conservation districts. Federal financial assistance for agricultural research and extension work is furnished under the Hatch, Adams, Purnell, and Bankhead acts, the relationships of the United States Office of Experiment Stations and of the Federal Extension Service necessarily being supervisory and administrative.[23] The State Extension Service especially, as well as its

* For an analysis of specific welfare programs, see Chapter 15, pp. 215-19, 221-23.

Federal counterpart, is related closely to agricultural and educational work in the local units of government. The Smith-Lever Act of May 8, 1914, by way of example, established a system of Federal grants-in-aid for the promotion of cooperative extension work in agriculture and home economics. Under this legislation county agricultural and home demonstration agents have been located in each of Mississippi's eighty-two counties, with the county paying a share of the program's expenses and the state and Federal governments the remainder. The daily activities of the county agents and their staffs include the dissemination in popularized form of scientific information related to agriculture as well as actual demonstrations. In a recent fiscal biennium in Mississippi (1950-1952) the extension program expenditures amounted to $4,699,271, of which sum Federal grants accounted for 54.6 per cent, state support 21.9 per cent, county funds 21.7 per cent, and miscellaneous sources 1.8 per cent.[24] Thereafter, however, a considerable increase in state support and a decrease in Federal and county support were anticipated.

The Soil Conservation Service represents an additional illustration involving Federal-state-local relationships. This service works with the Agricultural Experiment Station, the State Extension Service, and the ex officio State Soil Conservation Committee at the state level of government, but its primary relationships are with the local soil conservation districts, which are organized under state law and which numbered seventy-three in Mississippi in 1952. The Soil Conservation Service prepares surveys for these local units, and they act in turn for the national agency in projects conducted by the latter, receive grants, and expend such funds for conservation programs. Similarly the Production and Marketing Administration has administered soil erosion and fertility programs with the assistance of local county committees. In each county the Federal administration supplies the over-all planning and direction of the program. The county work of all Federal agricultural agencies is coordinated by local United States Department of Agriculture councils composed of representatives from each of the agencies operating in the county. In few other programs, observation indicates, have Federal-state-local relations been so effectively integrated as in agriculture.

Clearly there are several other programs involving Federal grants-in-aid in Mississippi. They include the assistance to highway construction carried on by the Public Roads Administration, programs for public health and for vocational education and rehabilitation, and the important hospital construction program, which has resulted in the improvement and expansion of hospital facilities in Mississippi. Some involve the state primarily; others, such as the program of the Federal Hospital Survey and Construction Act of 1946, include both state and local participation; and some, such as the airport assistance and the housing programs, allow for direct Federal-local relationships with the municipalities and counties.*

Largely of historical import today are the Federal relationships that the years of the depression witnessed. Many of the points of contact were between local governments and Washington directly. Under the Emergency Relief Appropriation Act of 1935 and subsequent legislation considerable money flowed into the state's cities and towns. Through March 1, 1938, for example, the Works Progress Administration inaugurated or completed projects in Mississippi's municipalities whose total costs were $38,126,674, of which no less than $28,907,302 or 76 per cent, were in national grants.[25] In the same years the national public housing program to assist subordinate governments, including counties and municipalities, was begun. World War II intensified these initial direct Federal-local relations when urban areas everywhere found themselves unable to meet new and excessive demands on educational, water, sewage, and other facilities and turned to Washington for assistance. Today, sixteen housing districts, local airports, and other agencies are well-established beneficiaries of Federal grants.

In addition to grants-in-aid the state and its local units receive other financial amounts from the Federal government. These returns are payments made by the Federal government or its agencies in the form of in-lieu-of-tax payments. The Tennessee Valley Authority offers an example of this form of payment. If all state and local taxes had been collected on TVA property in Mississippi in 1951-1952, yields would have amounted to $91,130; in-lieu payments to the state and counties totaled $92,452 for the same year and distributor payments in lieu of taxes, $233,484. Other Federal agencies making in-lieu payments are the Mississippi River Commission and the United States Forest Service.

The amounts received in lieu of taxes will vary with the year and the

* For example, see *U. S. Stat. at Large,* ch. 251 (1946), by which Congress authorized a $500,000,000 appropriation for airport improvements. Under this legislation the national government pays 50 per cent of the cost of improvements and 25 per cent of the cost of land. Seventy-five per cent of the annual appropriations, which were to run for seven years, is allotted for airport construction. In executing the statute the Civil Aeronautics Administration has maintained close relationship with municipalities and supervised administratively their grants. In the 1950-1952 period fourteen airport projects with a total Federal aid of $299,000 were activated.—Mississippi Aeronautics Commission, *Biennial Report 1950-1952* (Jackson, 1952), p. 11.

agency. Payments in every case are governed by Federal statutes, but the Mississippi legislature has also enacted measures governing distribution of in-lieu payments. Thus, since 1911 Congress has provided that the income from national forest lands shall be shared with the counties wherein these lands are located in order to compensate the loss of revenues; 25 per cent of the gross receipts of sales from timber and other resources of the national forests is returned accordingly to the state to transmit to the counties for the benefit of schools and public roads. A state statute affirms the terms of the Federal law.[26] Intergovernmental payments, however, have not always been sufficient to balance local tax losses. This problem is serious because approximately 1,400,000 acres of Mississippi's total area are owned by the Federal government and so exempt from state and local levies. Extensive national ownership of land, together with the discovery of valuable minerals on public holdings and a number of less tangible political factors, has developed much opposition among Mississippi's legislators to additional Federal acquisitions. Against such opposition must be measured the value of cash payments made to the state and counties, the general value to Mississippi of the flood control program of the Mississippi River Commission protecting the fertile Delta area, the increased timber production on national forest lands, and the road construction and general maintenance that have characterized Federal ownership.

Information and Technical Assistance

Various technical and informational services also are found in Federal relations with Mississippi's state and local governments, some of them flowing quite naturally out of the grants-in-aid relationship and others operating independently of it. The Surplus Property Procurement Commission, since its establishment by the legislature, has maintained a relationship of cooperation with the appropriate Federal agencies in negotiating and contracting to purchase surplus property for the state and in assisting local units in securing such property. The State Department of Agriculture and Commerce and the proper administrative subunits of the United States Department of Agriculture maintain jointly a statistical service for the benefit of farmers, and projects of the Water Resources Branch of the United States Geological Survey in surface and ground water investigations usually are made in consultation with the director of the state survey. However, in both cases the responsibility as well as the disbursements for the program is Federal.

Federal technical assistance in the field of law enforcement is evident in both the state and local governments. The Highway Safety Patrol has utilized the available cooperative services of the Federal Bureau of Investigation in discharging its law enforcement functions, and the FBI has made a twofold contribution to local governments through the services of its Identification Unit in criminal identification and its National Police Academy, which is maintained to train personnel of state and local police departments. Many of the larger municipalities have sent students in recent years to the academy. Further evidence of the value of this relationship was given by the director of the Identification Bureau of the Highway Safety Patrol, who stated in his 1952 report that investigators in his bureau must be, as part of their qualifications, graduates of the National Police Academy.

Similar technical assistance is provided by the Civil Aeronautics Administration in airport drainage, by the United States Office of Education in problems of school finance and administration, and by a host of other Federal offices. Although these are obvious illustrations of a type of relationship that is difficult to measure quantitatively or qualitatively, they indicate that a constant and healthy flow of information concerning program objectives and techniques passes between Federal officials and Mississippi's public employees.

FOOTNOTES

[1] Robert B. Highsaw and Carl Mullican, Jr., *Units of Government in Mississippi,* (Bureau of Public Administration, University of Mississippi, 1949), p. 19.

[2] Compare Leonard D. White, *Introduction to the Study of Public Administration* (3rd ed., Macmillan, 1949), p. 130; W. Brooke Graves, *American State Government* (4th ed., Heath, 1953), pp. 795-96; and Lane W. Lancaster, *Government in Rural America* (Van Nostrand, 1937), Chapter V.

[3] Summarized from M. H. Satterfield and Hugh W. Urban, *Municipal Government and Administration in Mississippi* (Jackson: State Planning Commission, 1940), pp. 43-46. See also *Mississippi Code, 1942,* sec. 2912; *ibid.,* 1952 Supp., sec. 3374 *passim; Mississippi Laws, 1936,* ch. 185.

[4] Constitution of 1890, art. 11, secs. 227-39.

[5] *Mississippi Code, 1942,* sec. 7546.

[6] *Ibid.,* sec. 9198.

[7] Satterfield and Urban, *op. cit.,* p. 54; compare *Mississippi Code, 1930,* secs. 3754 ff.

[8] *Mississippi Code,* 1952 Supp., sec. 3877-05; *Mississippi Laws, 1952,* ch. 176, amending *ibid., 1948,* ch. 202. In 1951 the State Department of Audit released *A Manual of Accounts* designed to facilitate establishment of a system of uniform municipal accounts.

[9] *Mississippi Laws, 1950,* ch. 497.

[10] *Mississippi Laws, 1938,* ch. 295.

[11] *Mississippi Laws, 1950,* ch. 516; amended by *Mississippi Laws, 1954,* House Bill 359.

[12] Constitution of 1890, art. 8, sec. 206. See also Chapter 13.

[13] *Mississippi Laws, 1953 Ex. Sess.,* chs. 11, 12, 14, 15, 18-20.

[14] *Mississippi Laws, 1946,* ch. 297; see also Chapter 13, p. 176.

[15] *Ibid., 1946,* ch. 478; *Mississippi Code,* 1950 Supp., sec. 6217.

[16] *Mississippi Laws, 1953 Ex. Sess.,* ch. 11.

[17] *Mississippi Laws, 1944,* ch. 241.

[18] *Mississippi Code, 1942,* sec. 7037.

[19] *Ibid.,* sec. 7221; *Mississippi Laws, 1946,* ch. 233.

[20] *Book of the States, 1950-51* (Chicago: Council of State Governments, 1951), pp. 26-31. For the legal basis of Mississippi's participation in several of these compacts, see *Mississippi Laws, 1948,* chs. 436, 284; *1950,* chs. 383, 556; *1952,* ch. 313.

[21] United States Department of Commerce, Bureau of the Census, *Compendium of State Government Finances in 1952* (Washington, 1952), Table 8, p. 14. Of neighboring states, Tennessee with 19.9 per cent and Louisiana with 21.6 per cent received a lower ratio of general revenue from Federal sources.

[22] Summarized from White, *op. cit.,* pp. 143-44.

[23] Summarized from Robert Baker Highsaw, *Mississippi's Wealth: A Study of the Public Administration of Natural Resources* (Bureau of Public Administration, University of Mississippi, 1947), pp. 128 ff.

[24] State Budget Commission, *General Fund Budget Discussion for the Fiscal Biennium 1952-54 for the State of Mississippi* (Jackson, December 20, 1951), p. 30.

[25] Satterfield and Urban, *op. cit.,* pp. 55-56.

[26] *Mississippi Laws, 1950,* ch. 269, accepting provisions of the Weeks Law, approved by the President, March 1, 1911, and amendments thereto.

CHAPTER 25

A Look Ahead

BEFORE THE CONSTITUTIONAL CONVENTION OF 1832 finally adjourned, President Rutilous Pray hopefully declared:

> We have now formed a new Constitution for the State of Mississippi; we have enlarged the duties and the liberties of the people; we have pushed forward the bounds of legitimate democracy; . . . Our children, who are to succeed us in the government, will find themselves unshackled by the immutable laws of precedent, which have so long bound us down to earth, to follow the footsteps of anterior generations; and, commencing where we have paused, their march will be onward.[1]

Nothing, perhaps, is more certain in government than change. Successive generations of Mississippians have witnessed the growth of their state government and the enlargement of its activities. Indeed, Mississippi has followed the typical pattern of development pursued by the members of the American Union; from small governmental structures and organizations have evolved the complex twentieth century states. Mississippi no less than the others has been sucked into the vortex of national development. The activities of the state are many, and the range of its official interest broad.

Yet the growth of Mississippi state government, influenced also by these wider causes, has unfolded against a peculiarly local setting—a geographic, social, and economic backdrop, as it were, which has conditioned political evolution. The development of Mississippi government has not been without problems, some of which have been resolved and some of which are today pressing. The issues as well as the Constitution of 1832, of which President Pray spoke, have passed into the oblivion of history, but new and no less demanding problems now test the force and vitality of public official and citizen alike. It is upon the resolution of these problems that the future of Mississippi's state government and administration rests.

PROBLEMS OF MISSISSIPPI GOVERNMENT

The Constitutional Problem

Constitutional revision is basic among the political problems that confront the state. From it stem a myriad of lesser problems, the solution of which are prevented or discouraged by the difficulties of constitutional change.

Like that of many other states, the Mississippi constitution contains many sections that would be more properly enacted in the form of statutes. Antiquated and restrictive regulations concerning suffrage, elections, taxation, and education are found in the basic charter. In like manner the details of legislative ill-apportionment, a decentralized state administration, and an atomized local government structure are imbedded in constitutional provision. Provisions of this nature are rapidly outdated, and frequent amendments are necessary to keep them even approximately abreast of the changing times and conditions. Such amendments are not always proposed; when proposed they are frequently defeated by the requirements for ratification. The lack of popular opposition is not enough to ensure ratification; the vote requirements demand popular interest as well. Yet it is difficult to see how popular interest can be aroused in many of the details of government that require change. In short, constitutional amendment is not the solution.

The problem is more than the matter of getting the necessary legislative vote for proposal of an amendment and the popular votes for ratification; it is more than inducing the legislature to call a constitutional convention. Constitutions are expressions of popular sovereignty; constitutional revision must be the result of popular demand. Until there is widespread feeling on the part of the voting public that constitutional reform is necessary, efforts to accomplish it will end in stalemate.

Popular interest and support for constitutional revision will not come easily, as attested by the difficulties encountered in recent movements for constitutional change in the southern states of Kentucky and Tennessee.

The natural inertia of people, their innate reluctance to experiment, is accompanied in Mississippi by a deep-seated suspicion of political change. The oft-quoted phrase from Hamlet, "rather bear those ills we have than fly to others that we know not of," describes quite accurately the attitude of a great many people toward any modification of the institutions and practices of government.

Obviously, a campaign to publicize the need for a new charter of government will be required. The specific defects of the existing document must be made crystal clear; the remedies available through a thorough revision or rewriting of the constitution must be made equally plain. A campaign for constitutional revision will be a major project in education. It will demand the cooperation of newspapers, radio stations, and all the other media of public information. The support of civic groups, fraternal orders, women's clubs, and similar organizations will be necessary. Prominent citizens must be enlisted who will devote their time and effort to the cause. Public forums must be held in which citizens may hear the case for constitutional reform, ask questions, and voice objections.

The immediate outlook for such a development in Mississippi is not encouraging. From time to time interest in the subject has been aroused, but it subsides before reaching the proportions of a state-wide movement. The last such period of interest was in 1950, and it failed to gain any widespread popular support.

The Legislative Problem

In one respect, the state's legislative problem may be considered as a part of the larger problem of constitutional revision. For, in the opinion of most students of the subject, the essential reforms in the legislative branch can be effected only by rewriting major portions of the basic charter. The point may be argued; certainly it is untrue that legislative ills cannot be alleviated by statute and constitutional amendment.

Fundamental among legislative ills in Mississippi is the failure to reapportion the membership. This deficiency inhibits a vital legislative function—that of representing the people. To the degree that the body is poorly apportioned, to that extent the people are ill-represented. An unrepresentative legislature casts doubt on the validity of basic legislative functions such as lawmaking and the supervision of administration. Although minor adjustments may be made by legislation, reapportionment is primarily a matter of amending provisions of the constitution. To make these changes either by constitutional amendment or by constitutional convention requires positive action on the part of the legislature. Moreover, since reapportionment will run counter to the vested interests of the over-represented areas of the state, the mere proposal of such an amendment requires considerable political courage and a renunciation of localism on the part of a large number of representatives. Only by such resolute action, however, can a start be made on the solution of this problem.

The solution of the reapportionment question is not unlike that of other problems, such as multiplicity of committees, antiquated procedure, and lack of expertness, that continually plague the legislative branch. Some are the result of constitutional provisions; some are the result of statutes or rules of the legislators' making. In each case, however, as in the case of reapportionment, the first step toward solution must be taken by the legislature.

Naturally, in most matters legislators move only as public opinion moves them. Yet in some fields, such as legislative procedure, there is little public knowledge of the situation and little popular interest in its improvement. In other fields popular interest in, and support for, reform can be stimulated by firm legislative decision and action. To say that legislators have shown no disposition to tackle their problems is, of course, false. Legislative salaries have been increased, a start on a bill-drafting service has been made, and a constitutional amendment providing for annual sessions has been proposed, though unsuccessfully. Yet all the major problems and most of the minor ones remain. Their solution calls for long and persistent effort on the part of many elements in the government and society. The first step, however, necessarily must be a determined attack by the legislature.

Solution of the larger legislative problems, such as attracting a more competent membership, reducing the rapid turnover among members, developing stronger resistance to the constant importuning of pressure groups, and attaining greater prestige and esteem in the public mind, will not come from specific improvements or changes. Attention to the matters within the legislators' power, nevertheless, is the best approach to these broader questions.

The Administrative Problem

A change of emphasis on the functions performed by the state has taken place in the last century. For a time after Mississippi's entry into the Union, state functions were narrowly limited to those of general government. A changing economy and different social patterns created new objects of legislative attention that resulted in the expansion of administrative machinery to meet satisfactorily the demands of the citizens for new services. Although the War between the States and the Reconstruction Period temporarily halted administrative growth, toward the latter half of the last century administrative functions once more were emphasized, particularly public education and health. Since 1900 weight has been placed in state government on the various service and regulatory functions, and recent accretions have been almost entirely of a service nature.

In organizing for increased governmental services and controls the state has usually created a new agency rather than assigned administration of the function to an operative administrative body. Considerable diffusion of administrative functions is found in the fields of general government, protection to persons and property, education, conservation, and agriculture. A most rapidly growing field of state operations—occupational licensing—reflects the disintegrative effect of emerging professionalization, and today fully twenty administrative agencies operate in this area. In contrast, the state's administrative efforts have been admirably integrated in public welfare, an area heavily influenced by Federal funds, and in public health.

The result of diffusing administrative authority is a large number of agencies, most of which rest upon a statutory basis. From 8 offices, boards, and commissions the state administrative structure grew to 16 by 1848, almost 40 by 1900, 93 by 1940, and more than 100 today. This trend has had serious consequences. Not merely powers and duties have been split, but the governmental functions themselves have been divided among too many agencies, a trend that has resulted in a destruction, to a large extent, of direction, unified governmental objectives, and responsibilities. This basic fact conditions the entire administrative problem in Mississippi today. Through the intermittent creation of new agencies, governmental machinery has evolved that is rigid, complex, and difficult to adjust to rapidly changing conditions. This structure in turn, with the absence of coordination among operating activities of the state government, makes it hard, if not impossible, to offer the legislature and to secure enactment of a well-rounded program; on the one hand, the legislature cannot get a clear grasp of the administrative picture, and on the other, the virtually independent administrative boards, commissions, and offices cannot supply one.

The net result is that Mississippi has a large number of state agencies that administer specialized functions or segments of functions without reference to any over-all state program. This result is mirrored in the lack of effective direction, supervision, and control on the part of the governor, who is largely chief executive only in name. Too many important administrative officials are elected independently of him. There are too many agencies, whose boards or commissions he appoints, for any real policy and program control, although a few steps in this direction have been taken by the State Budget Commission. Moreover, the Mississippi executive has substantially no staff aids in planning and administrative research, which today must be supplied by the individual agencies.

Areas are found, to be sure, where the governmental services are of high quality. Among these are public health, public welfare, highways, and various of the conservation functions. Others, such as state services in education, have shown consistent improvement. It is the total picture that is poor, the entire administrative structure that reflects a lack of planning and direction, a wide diffusion of authority and responsibility, and duplications of organization and function.

Within recent years two attempts have been made to reorganize the state's administrative system. One was the *Brookings Report* of the 1930's and the second the 1950 report of the Legislative Fact-Finding Committee on the Reorganization of State Government. Only minor modifications in administrative structure and practices have resulted from these reorganization movements, although the neighboring states of Tennessee, Alabama, and Louisiana as well as many others throughout the nation have streamlined their administrative structures. Both legislators and people, perhaps more strongly than in other states, have feared to group related functions into large departments and then to place the departments under the executive direction of the governor lest too much power be placed in the hands of a single official. The maze that is Mississippi government makes for neither good nor responsible administration simply because concerted governmental action is inhibited in spite of the best efforts of capable public servants to discharge the tasks assigned to them.

The administrative problem and its solution in Mississippi hinge on the general acceptance of the proposition that it is no escape from political domination and public irresponsibility to atomize powers among so many different agencies that no executive can act in accordance with a common plan. As long as there is government, there will be the possibility that a single officer may seek to wield power in an arbitrary fashion. The remedy to this possibility lies in the ballot box and responsible citizenship. A further refinement of the administrative structure of Mississippi will be required before the state machinery can be regarded as sound.

The Problem of Personnel

With more than 14,000 state employees, it is highly important for Mississippi's government that persons of character, training, ability, and initiative be attracted to the service of the state. Mississippi has been singularly fortunate in the number of capable public servants it has had over the years, but the state today is operating increasingly through specialist divisions, each of which is charged with some particular technical work. The divisions of government and the specializations that necessarily accompany them underline emphatically the need for sound and modern personnel practices.

Signal progress toward improved personnel administration was marked by the Public Employees' Retirement Act of 1952. This legislation, though, is only a beginning step, for currently only a few agencies—notably the State Board of Health, the State Department of Public Welfare, and the Employment Security Commission—have established even a semblance of comprehensive personnel systems. In state agencies generally the rudiments of good personnel administration are still absent. Lacking adequate employment and selection techniques, effective methods of determining rates of pay, a position classification plan, service-wide control of promotions and advancements, and other commonly accepted devices covering re-employment, dismissals, vacations, and other matters, the field for development is open for progressive leadership. Suffering a relatively low level of prestige and secure working conditions, state employees have done remarkably well in discharging the tasks entrusted to them.

Basic personnel improvement in Mississippi can come only with passage of legislation recognizing the importance of personnel in administration and establishing a state personnel office. A number of state agencies, to be sure, have succeeded in creating high personnel standards, but more have not. The curious dichotomy that is Mississippi's social and political heritage—government by the aristocracy versus government by the artisan and small farmer—stands as a barrier. One views state government as a closed concern, and the other reflects the Jacksonian view that public functions and hence positions are susceptible to best performance by amateurs in government. The effects of the nascent industrialization of Mississippi may introduce new factors and bring with them a fruition of the trend, evident now in such functions as public health and highways, toward professionalization of the public service.

The Problem of Finance

Financing government is a double-edged problem involving both expenditures and revenues. In no state of the South and perhaps of the nation has public finance been better managed in recent decades than in Mississippi. From the dark days of 1932 when the state had outstanding treasury warrants and unpaid appropriations balances totaling more than $5,000,000 with only $1,326 in the general fund to pay them, Mississippi has traveled the hard road to fiscal solvency and recurring biennial general fund surpluses.

The success the state has had in meeting its financial needs should not obscure the basic fact that there are grave issues. On the expenditure side of the ledger, both the needs and the demands of specialist agencies for funds have risen at a much more rapid rate than have revenues. Although general fund receipts continue to increase somewhat, state expenditures in Mississippi today consume 9.2 per cent of per capita personal income, a ratio well above the 5.7 per cent average for the forty-eight states. Highways and education now account for almost two thirds of all expenditures—a combination found in many other states. The attrition of a once new transportation system and the equalization of educational opportunities in Mississippi bid well to increase the ratio somewhat. A reduction in total Federal-aid payments, which now approximate a fourth of state income, would increase the pressure already placed upon limited funds.

The nature of the revenue system, complicated by multitudinous exemptions, also points up the fiscal problem. The sales and various gross receipts taxes account for more than 70 per cent of all state taxes, and the income levies add another 14 per cent. In a period of generally rising prices and increased incomes, these sources have returned heavy yields; the sales and gross receipts taxes, though, are essentially regressive and, along with the income tax, are unusually sensitive to fluctuations of the business cycle. Neither tax, moreover, has or could keep pace with the changing price level in recent years, even though total state revenues now equal 9.1 per cent of the per capita income in Mississippi compared to only 5.4 per cent for all forty-eight states. A diminution of revenue yields or the necessity for considerably larger outlays in any of the governmental functions might well throw Mississippi once more into severe financial straits.

Finally, the organization for fiscal administration and control poses questions. Although the Mississippi budget has been well prepared since

1932, its strength depends upon the prestige of the man who prepares the budget rather than on the law; it has not been and is not today a strong executive budget. Revenue collection is spread among a large number of agencies, a problem of diffusion common to the entire administrative framework. A clear and pervasive distinction between the executive function of expenditure control and the legislative function of the audit remains to be made. The total unity of fiscal administration is segmented by the large ratio of segregated funds earmarked for special purposes.

Although Mississippi's financial administration thus has achieved impressive results and has made the faith of the state, as well as its credit, sound, no doubt the great test is yet to come. The way in which the expenditure and revenue structures react to this unknown test will determine the consequences. It is still too early to predict confidently the outcome.

State versus Local Control

Of major importance in the more fundamental aspects of government is the matter of state direction and control as opposed to local autonomy. In certain functional fields, notably those where national aid is present, the problem has been solved by freeing local governments of most of the cost and thus effectively removing local interference. In others, such as judicial administration, law enforcement, and financial management, the concept of local rural autonomy seriously impedes efficient state government.

The idea of local autonomy is implicit in the whole concept of democratic government. The political parlance of democratic peoples is replete with such phrases as "right of self-determination" and "the strength of democratic government is inversely proportional to its distance from the people." In the United States this concept reveals itself in a strong belief in federalism and states' rights. The problem in Mississippi government today is that this idea, valid in its proper sphere, has been carried to extreme ends. Federalism ends at the state level; the idea of "states' rights" has no application to counties. No principle of American government is more firmly established than that local governments have only such powers as the state chooses to give them. The matter, then, is not one of principle but of policy. Policy in this respect calls for a realistic definition of "local government."

Clearly, the state government is as near to the people of the present day as were the counties during the last century. Modern means of transportation and communication have shrunken the state into a closely-knit community with common interests and common problems. The approach to these matters from a state level does no violence to the principle of local autonomy; it is merely a modern application of the principle. It is the only approach that can lead to a solution of many problems that vex the people.

The difficulties arising from county or local control of matters that are of state-wide concern are numerous. They reveal themselves in costly and inefficient duplication of officials, services, and facilities. They are evident in expensive, but poor, local road systems, in notable gaps in law enforcement, and in a public school system where inadequate funds are made more inadequate by costly local direction. Nor is it easy to see how extreme local control gives the average citizen any greater voice in the management of his roads and schools or in the enforcement of the laws. Except for those with a peculiar political concern, the citizens' interest is in better roads, better schools, and better law enforcement for the lowest possible cost. That interest certainly is not served by the endless duplications and contradictions that surround local control of these functions.

The loosening of community bonds by shifting political control from the local to the state level is a danger frequently pointed out by opponents of state direction. This argument assumes that all community bonds are political, ignoring the fact that social and religious ties also are important. It also assumes that the county, the principal subdivision for local political control, is a community. Such is not the case. Counties inspire few of the loyalties and associations that are identified with communities. Indeed, it is hard to see how state direction of what are essentially state functions can disturb local communities that are concerned with local matters.

This view of federalism does not deny any of the arguments that have been advanced for municipal home rule. Obviously, in compact city communities autonomy may be desirable in fields of purely local concern, and a very high degree of self-government comports with sound administration at the state level. Mississippi has few cities that present the problem at this time, but the continued growth of urban communities may call for more attention to the powers of municipal governments and the desirability of effective home-rule provisions. Here, again, it is policy instead of principle that should prevail.

THE STATE AND THE NATION

Mississippi is a state with a specific environmental setting and a particular social, political, and economic heritage. It is also one of the states of the American Union, and the trends that have affected the nation have not passed by Mississippi. Much has been narrated in this volume about the details of state government and how it functions. Mississippi has established various departments, boards, and commissions to execute the programs enacted by its legislature and frequently passed upon by its courts. These agencies have been staffed and public funds made available to them. Enduring relationships with Federal and local governments in Mississippi have been surprisingly encouraging, although many problems now are grave. Here is the time and the place, then, to put Mississippi's state government and administration into the larger pattern of politically organized society that is American federalism.

Growth and Government

Governmental structures no longer are simple edifices concerned with simple problems. State governments in particular now must deal with issues that are complex in their nature and that more often than not transcend the geographical lines drawn upon a map. Public health, conservation, education, public welfare—to name a few—are not peculiarly Mississippi problems; issues concerning them arise in New York and California, Oregon and Florida, and are debated in the halls of the Federal Congress as well. The broadening of problems and the growth of state functions have presented Mississippi state government with a paradox: how to maintain basic autonomy as a state and at the same time to adjust governmental efforts into the new federalism that has developed.

The conditions that have led to this paradox are manifested in administrative organization for public services and controls. Increasingly is government organized into special agencies with highly technical divisions and work units; increasingly are these structures manned by specialized experts responsible not merely to their state or Federal employers but also to a wide variety of special clientele publics. This development has had interesting results. One is that political leadership has been withdrawn from public servants actually administering programs. A second is that the relationship of intimacy, even of solidarity, between government and citizen has been replaced by a more unwavering impersonality. Perhaps most important has been the replacement of area by function.

Illustrations for this point abound in Mississippi. The welfare specialist in the county unit, or even in Jackson, finds professional communion not with the conservationist across the hall in the county courthouse or with the district highway engineer; he has professional intimacy with his state and Federal counterparts. The conservationist is less concerned with the parole officer than he is with the biologist of the United States Wildlife

Service. The highway engineer is less interested in the State Budget Commission than in the Public Roads Administration. This emphasis upon function at the expense of area no doubt has been stressed by the vast growth of Federal grants-in-aid. In any event, Mississippi has much government by function, considerably less by area.

Impact of Functional Growth upon State Administration

The effects of vertical integration are clearly seen in the almost inchoate state structures created by constitutions and statutes for administering public programs. State operations have expanded enormously. The sheer number of administrative boards, commissions, departments, and other agencies in the forty-eight states is staggering. As functions have grown and with them the administrative structure, duties and responsibilities have been divided and then sundered again. Each agency shields its area of special competence from intrusion, and the total effect becomes one of independent organizations operating under the common rubric of a state name and with the historical pattern of a state government superimposed.

State government thus has become characterized by segregation of administrative functions into subject-matter fields, a result in part of the ragged and uneven growth of public interest and pressures in specific areas. There has seemed to be no consistent relationship between welfare programs and mineral resource activities, highway construction and the licensing of professions and occupations, workmen's compensation and soil conservation. Only as the problems raised by each function are localized within the limits of the state and one county, municipality, or governmental district does force appear in the concept of a closer relationship between all programs.

In this situation of administrative disorganization each state agency has tended in fact to develop its own relationships with other state agencies and with Federal authorities; each has created its own connections with its private public. Somewhere, but distantly so, in the background is the citizen—using the broadest term—rather than the special client to whom attention is paid formally or informally; even then the broader public represented by the term "citizen" is likely to be indifferent about state policies that seem to have no immediate concern.

Most state programs lack broad appeal to the rank and file of the population. Moreover, the operation of most agencies is not featured by political controversy. Yet in recent years the major national issues, hotly discussed in Washington and reprinted in a thousand newspapers, have concerned many functions about which state government revolves. Agricultural programs, public health, public welfare, and natural resource policies are all areas of spirited argument of states' rights versus the national interest. That these issues rarely occur in the state administration of the programs indicates the nonpolitical atmosphere of many of the agencies.

Relation of State Programs to Federal Policy

What has developed over the years is a state acceptance of many Federal policies, not merely in Mississippi but in every state of the Union. In a few functional areas the Federal government may have fallen heir to policy initiative by default; in some initiative may have been seized; and in still others the development may have come as a logical result of the growth of a national economy. Whatever the cause, one fact is clear. National policies have developed where state policies have failed to emerge. National policies have grown or are evolving for many of the great areas of governmental action with which the states have most intimate concern—public health, welfare, transportation, natural resources, and others—and the initiation as well as the amendment of these policies is often spelled out in national party platforms. Although the political heat generated by the states has affected these policies, they remain national policies.

Today the states—including Mississippi—assist in executing national policies. The theory that the states have become mere agents of the national government, of course, is not valid. It is more nearly valid in some functional fields than others, more definite in some states than others. National policies are adjusted to state capacities and requirements. The notable fact lies in the failure of the states to develop truly state policies in large and important areas of government service and control.

This failure has peculiar significance today. Both the Democratic and Republican parties in the 1952 presidential campaign advocated an increased assumption of powers on the part of the states, and the Eisenhower Administration is pledged to increase state responsibilities. Such a growth in powers can mean only that the affected programs in each state must become actual instruments of state policy. They cannot do this until a policy vacuum has been filled, until there is some foundation upon which the frame of a state policy can be erected.

A State Policy for Mississippi

Before Mississippi can assume its new responsibilities, pledged by the national government, it must formulate state policies in a number of significant fields of governmental activity. Several major elements can even now be discerned. First, the state's political leadership must determine and secure acceptance of long-range goals of state action—of objectives in conservation, in public health, in transportation, in public safety, and in all the rest. These objectives will, of course, reflect the place of the service in Mississippi's economic and political structure. Second, a decision must be reached upon the administrative organization and devices best suited to accomplish these goals; no doubt this element will involve considerable structural alteration in state organization and procedures. Third, definite financial policies must be established and decisions made with respect to revenue sources, expenditures, and other financial arrangements. Fourth, the new policy must seek to include all state programs in a comprehensive state administrative program. Finally, account must be taken both of state programs in relation to each other and their relation to Federal programs.

Major changes in American state governments are not accomplished overnight. It would be both unwise and unrealistic to argue that Mississippi or most other states will immediately adopt such state policies regardless of how many responsibilities or of how much authority is returned to them by the Federal government. Nevertheless, the development of a constructive state policy for Mississippi would provide a positive benchmark against which the progress of state government can be measured.

Determination of state policy where there has been none places an awesome burden on Mississippi's political leadership. To the extent that this leadership succeeds in its great task, state action and Federal funds may be merged in state programs. If Mississippi governors and legislators fail in the determination of state policy, initiative must return to the Federal government with centralization of political and administrative power the only alternative. A simplified, modernized, and improved system of government and administration in Mississippi offers the best assurance that the state will demonstrate true strength in the twentieth century.

FOOTNOTES

[1] Dunbar Rowland, *Encyclopedia of Mississippi History* (Madison, Wisconsin: Selwyn A. Brant, 1907), I, 506.

Appendix

CHRONOLOGY OF SIGNIFICANT EVENTS

1540–41 Explorations of Hernando de Soto in Mississippi.

1699 Period of French dominion begun with establishment of Fort Maurepas by d'Iberville near present site of Biloxi.

1763 English dominion established by French cession of West Virginia to England in Treaty of Paris.

1779 Spanish dominion established with occupation of Natchez area by Spain.

1795 Natchez area ceded to United States by Spain in Treaty of San Lorenzo.

1798 Withdrawal of Spanish from Natchez District.
Mississippi Territory created by Act of Congress, April 7.
Territorial capital established at Natchez.

1802 Territorial capital moved from Natchez to nearby Washington.

1805 Treaty of Mount Dexter by which Choctaw Indians ceded approximately 4,400,000 acres in South Mississippi.

1816 Cession by Chickasaw Indians of lands lying east of Tombigbee River totaling approximately 408,000 acres.

1817 Mississippi admitted to statehood by Act of Congress, December 10, with capital at Washington.

1820 Treaty of Doak's Stand by which Choctaw Indians ceded approximately 5,500,000 acres of land in central and western Mississippi.

1822 State capital located at Jackson.

1830 Treaty of Dancing Rabbit Creek by which Choctaw Indians ceded remaining lands in Mississippi.

1832 New constitution drawn up and put into effect by convention meeting in Jackson.
Treaty of Pontotoc by which Chickasaw Indians ceded more than 6,000,000 acres of land in northeastern Mississippi, thus completing Indian cessions.

1846 First general public school law.

1848 University of Mississippi, authorized in 1844, opened at Oxford.

1861 Ordinance of secession passed by constitutional convention, January 9. Constitution revised for membership in Confederacy.

1865 Revision of constitution to abolish slavery and nullify ordinance of secession.

1866 Rejection by Congress of representatives elected under Constitution of 1865.

1867 Beginning of Congressional Reconstruction with passage of acts by Congress on March 2, 23, and July 19.

1868	New constitution adopted by constitutional convention and submitted to voters, where it was defeated.
1869	Constitution of 1868 resubmitted to voters in different form, ratified, and proclaimed in effect.
1876	Resignation of Governor Ames, marking the end of Reconstruction.
1877	Establishment of State Board of Health.
1880	Mississippi Agricultural and Mechanical College, founded in 1878, opened at Starkville.
1885	Industrial Institute and College, first state college for women in the United States, opened its first session at Columbus.
1890	Present constitution drawn up and put into effect by convention meeting in Jackson, from August 12 to November 1.
1902	Enactment of mandatory, state-wide primary election law.
1903	New Capitol Building completed.
1908	State prohibition law enacted.
1912	Constitutional amendment making general trial court judges elective.
1916	First State Highway Commission created.
1926	State Forestry Commission, first major conservation agency, established.
1932	General sales tax levied.
	Law establishing State Budget Commission with governor as ex officio director.
1936	Inauguration of Balance Agriculture with Industry Program.
	Legislature authorized first of the bond issues in extensive highway-building program.
1944	Constitutional amendment making Board of Trustees of Institutions of Higher Learning a constitutional body.
	Establishment of Agricultural and Industrial Board and new program to balance agriculture with industry.
1948	First Workmen's Compensation Law enacted.
1952	General council-manager law for municipalities enacted.
	Constitutional amendment enlarging Supreme Court to nine members.
1953	Program for equalization of educational opportunities in public school system enacted by special session of legislature.

MISSISSIPPI GOVERNORS

Name	*Term of Office*
GOVERNORS OF MISSISSIPPI TERRITORY	
Winthrop Sargent	May 7, 1798 to May 25, 1801
William C. C. Claiborne	May 25, 1801 to Mar. 1, 1805
Robert Williams	Mar. 1, 1805 to Mar. 7, 1809
David Holmes	Mar. 7, 1809 to Dec. 10, 1817
GOVERNORS OF STATE OF MISSISSIPPI	
David Holmes	Dec. 10, 1817 to Jan. 5, 1820
George Poindexter	Jan. 5, 1820 to Jan. 7, 1822
Walter Leake	Jan. 7, 1822 to Nov. 17, 1825
Gerard C. Brandon	Nov. 17, 1825 to Jan. 7, 1826
David Holmes	Jan. 7, 1826 to July 25, 1826

Gerard C. Brandon	July 25, 1826 to Jan. 9, 1832
Abram M. Scott	Jan. 9, 1832 to June 12, 1833
Charles Lynch	June 12, 1833 to Nov. 20, 1833
Hiram G. Runnels	Nov. 20, 1833 to Nov. 20, 1835
John A. Quitman	Dec. 3, 1835 to Jan. 7, 1836
Charles Lynch	Jan. 7, 1836 to Jan. 8, 1838
Alexander G. McNutt	Jan. 8, 1838 to Jan. 10, 1842
Tilgham M. Tucker	Jan. 10, 1842 to Jan. 10, 1844
Albert G. Brown	Jan. 10, 1844 to Jan. 10, 1848
Joseph M. Matthews	Jan. 10, 1848 to Jan. 10, 1850
John A. Quitman	Jan. 10, 1850 to Feb. 3, 1851
John I. Guion	Feb. 3, 1851 to Nov. 4, 1851
James Whitfield	Nov. 24, 1851 to Jan. 10, 1852
Henry S. Foote	Jan. 10, 1852 to Jan. 5, 1854
John J. Pettus	Jan. 5, 1854 to Jan. 10, 1854
John J. McRae	Jan. 10, 1854 to Nov. 16, 1857
William McWillie	Nov. 16, 1857 to Nov. 21, 1859
John J. Pettus	Nov. 21, 1859 to Nov. 16, 1863
Charles Clark	Nov. 16, 1863 to May 22, 1865
William L. Sharkey	June 13, 1865 to Oct. 16, 1865
Benjamin G. Humphreys	Oct. 16, 1865 to June 15, 1868
Adelbert Ames	June 15, 1868 to Mar. 10, 1870
James L. Alcorn	Mar. 10, 1870 to Nov. 30, 1871
Ridgley C. Powers	Nov. 30, 1871 to Jan. 4, 1874
Adelbert Ames	Jan. 4, 1874 to Mar. 29, 1876
John M. Stone	Mar. 29, 1876 to Jan. 29, 1882
Robert Lowry	Jan. 29, 1882 to Jan. 13, 1890
John M. Stone	Jan. 13, 1890 to Jan. 20, 1896
Anslem J. McLaurin	Jan. 20, 1896 to Jan. 16, 1900
Andrew H. Longino	Jan. 16, 1900 to Jan. 19, 1904
James Kimble Vardaman	Jan. 19, 1904 to Jan. 21, 1908
Edmond Favor Noel	Jan. 21, 1908 to Jan. 16, 1912
Earl LeRoy Brewer	Jan. 16, 1912 to Jan. 18, 1916
Theodore Gilmore Bilbo	Jan. 18, 1916 to Jan. 20, 1920
Lee Maurice Russell	Jan. 20, 1920 to Jan. 22, 1924
Henry Lewis Whitfield	Jan. 22, 1924 to Mar. 18, 1927
Dennis Murphree	Mar. 18, 1927 to Jan. 17, 1928
Theodore Gilmore Bilbo	Jan. 17, 1928 to Jan. 19, 1932
Martin Sennett Conner	Jan. 19, 1932 to Jan. 21, 1936
Hugh White	Jan. 21, 1936 to Jan. 16, 1940
Paul B. Johnson	Jan. 16, 1940 to Dec. 26, 1943
Dennis Murphree	Dec. 26, 1943 to Jan. 18, 1944
Thomas L. Bailey	Jan. 18, 1944 to Nov. 2, 1946
Fielding L. Wright	Nov. 2, 1946 to Jan. 22, 1952
Hugh White	Jan. 22, 1952 to —

Source: *Mississippi Official and Statistical Register 1952* (Jackson, Secretary of State, 1951), pp. 14-15.

MISSISSIPPI ADMINISTRATIVE AGENCIES, 1954

Agency	*Legal Basis*[a]	*Date Created*
GENERAL GOVERNMENT		
Attorney General	Art. 6, sec. 173	1817
Auditor of Public Accounts	Art. 5, sec. 134	1817
Board of Trustees of the Public Employees Retirement System of Mississippi	7446-12	1952
Budget Commission	9103	1932
Capitol Commission	8952	1906
Governor	Art. 5, sec. 116	1817
Lieutenant Governor	Art. 5, sec. 128	1817
Mississippi Commission on Interstate Co-operation	3317	1936
Office of Motor Vehicle Comptroller	10008.01	1946
Secretary of State	Art. 5, sec. 133	1817
State Board of Election Commissioners	3204	1871
State Board of Public Contractors	8968-01	1952
State Board of Public Contracts	Art. 4, sec. 107; 8961	1892
State's Bond Attorney	4313	1907
State Bond Retirement Commission	*Laws, 1944,* ch. 140	1944
State Building Commission	9023-01	1944
State Department of Audit	3877-01	1924
State Bond Commission	4380	1936
State Depository Commission	9126	1908
State Land Office	4066	1892
State Motor Vehicle License Tag Commission	9352-14	1938
State Tax Collector	9177	1892
State Tax Commission	9197	1926
State Treasurer	Art. 5, sec. 134	1817
Surplus Property Procurement Commission	9028-01	1946
PROTECTION TO PERSONS AND PROPERTY		
Adjutant General	Art. 9, sec. 219	1823
Board of Bar Admissions	*Laws, 1954,* House Bill 99	1928
Board of Cosmetology	8915-01	1948
Commissioner of Public Safety	8076	1938
Department of Bank Supervision	5153	1935
Department of Insurance	5616	1902
Factory Inspector	6977	1914
Mississippi Employment Security Commission	7399	1940
Mississippi Real Estate Commission	*Laws, 1954,* House Bill 262	1954
Public Service Commission	7688	1938
State Board of Public Accountancy	8905	1920

State Board of Registration for Professional Engineers	*Laws, 1954,* House Bill 55	1928
State Insurance Commission	5816	1924
Workmen's Compensation Commission	6998-43	1948
State Board of Architecture	8632	1928
State Veterans' Affairs Board	7486-01	1948
Veterans' Farm and Home Board	7519	1936

HIGHWAYS AND TRANSPORTATION

Mississippi Aeronautics Commission	7536-02	1946
Natchez Trace Parkway Right-of-Way Commission	5990	1936
State Highway Commission	8014	1930

DEVELOPMENT AND CONSERVATION OF NATURAL RESOURCES

Board of Mississippi Levee Commissioners	Art. 11, secs. 229, 233	1890
Board of Veterinary Examiners	8914-03	1914
Board of Yazoo-Mississippi Delta Commissioners	Art. 11, sec. 229	1890
Lieu Land Commission	4116	1942
Lime Plant Board	4428	1942
Mineral Lease Commission	5947	1932
Mississippi Agricultural and Industrial Board	8936	1944
Mississippi Agricultural and Industrial Exposition Commission	4435-50	1946
Mississippi Central Market Board	4435-31	1946
Mississippi Geological Survey	8954	1850
State Marketing Commission	4435-01	1948
Mississippi Rural Electrification Authority	5502	1936
Sea Food Commission	6049	1902
State Chemist	4448	1892
State Department of Agriculture and Commerce	4415	1906
State Egg Advisory Board	4435-20	1944
State Forestry Commission	6023	1926
State Game and Fish Commission	5841	1932
State Livestock Sanitary Board	4835	1917
State Oil and Gas Board	6132-02	1932
State Plant Board	4978	1920
State Seed Improvement Committee	8010	1938
State Soil Conservation Committee	4943	1938

HEALTH AND SANITATION

Board of Nurses' Examiners	8806	1914
Mississippi Department of Public Health	7016	1897
State Board of Barber Examiners	8725	1930
State Board of Dental Examiners	8749	1928
State Board of Embalming	8776	1918
State Board of Health	7024	1877

State Board of Optometry	8835	1920
State Board of Pharmacy	8851	1922
HOSPITALS AND INSTITUTIONS		
Beauvoir Soldiers' Home	7447	1924
Board of Trustees for Deaf and Blind Institutes	6785-01	1944
Board of Trustees of Mental Institutions	6946-01	1947
Board of Trustees for State Eleemosynary Institutions	6942	1936
Mississippi Commission on Hospital Care	7146-01	1946
State Hospital Commission	7130	1936
Tuberculosis Sanatorium of Mississippi	6870	1916
CHARITIES		
Children's Code Commission	7170-11	1946
State Department of Public Welfare	7218	1936
CORRECTION		
Board of Commissioners of the State Penitentiary	7923	1944
Board of Trustees of the Mississippi Training Schools	6744-03	1948
State Parole Board	4004-02	1944
EDUCATION		
Commission of Junior Colleges	6478	1928
Board of Trustees of Institutions of Higher Learning	Art. 8, sec. 213-A; 6719	1944
Department of Archives and History	6180	1906
Mississippi Illiteracy Commission	6660	1924
Mississippi State Textbook Purchasing Board	6634	1942
State Board of Education	Art. 8, sec. 203; 6233	1890
State Department of Education	Art. 8, sec. 202; 6245-01	1869
State Historical Commission	6189-01	1948
State Medical Education Board	9054-01	1946
State Temperance Commission	6679	1934
LIBRARIES		
State Library Board	9037	1942
State Library Commission	6210	1926
RECREATION		
Brice's Crossroads-Tupelo Battlefield Commission	6016	1936
Mississippi Athletic Commission	8925	1928
Monumental Park Commission	6021	1902
State Board of Park Supervisors	5957	1936
War Veterans Memorial Commission	*Laws, 1938,* ch. 191	1938

[a] Article and section references are to Mississippi Constitution of 1890. Unless otherwise indicated, numbers in this column refer to sections of *Mississippi Code of 1942.*

Bibliography

GENERAL WORKS

Brookings Institution, *Report of a Survey of the Organization and Administration of State and County Government in Mississippi* (Jackson, 1932).

Butts, Alfred B., *Public Administration in Mississippi* (Jackson: Mississippi Historical Society, 1919).

Ellett, A. H., *The Federal Union and Mississippi: A Civil Government* (Richmond: Johnson Publishing Company, 1910).*

Ethridge, William N., Jr., *Modernizing Mississippi's Constitution* (Bureau of Public Administration, University of Mississippi, 1950).

Garner, James W., *Reconstructon in Mississippi* (Macmillan, 1901).

Highsaw, Robert B., and Mullican, Carl D., *The Growth of State Administration in Mississippi* (Bureau of Public Administration, University of Mississippi, 1950).

Key, V. O., Jr., *Southern Politics in State and Nation* (Knopf, 1949), ch. 11.

Kirwan, Albert D., *Revolt of the Rednecks: Mississippi Politics, 1876-1925* (University of Kentucky Press, 1951).

Lowrey, Robert, and McCardle, William H., *A History of Mississippi* (Jackson: R. H. Henry and Company, 1891).

Mississippi Agricultural and Industrial Board, *Mississippi: A Guide to the Magnolia State* (New York: Hastings House, 1949).

Mississippi Legislature, Fact-Finding Committee on Reorganization of State Government, *Mississippi: A Report on State Reorganization* (Jackson, 1950).

Rainwater, Percy L., *Mississippi: Storm Center of Secession, 1856-1861* (Baton Rouge: Otto Claitor, 1938).

Rowland, Dunbar, *History of Mississippi, the Heart of the South* (2 vols., Jackson: S. G. Clarke Publishing Company, 1925).

Satterfield, Millard H., and Urban, Hugh W., *Municipal Government and Administration in Mississippi* (Jackson: State Planning Commission, 1940).

MONOGRAPHS, REPORTS, AND SPECIAL STUDIES

Alexander, Julian P., *Mississippi Jury Instructions* (St. Paul: West Publishing Company, 1953).

Belcher, John C., and King, Morton B., Jr., *Mississippi's People* (Bureau of Public Administration, University of Mississippi, 1950).

* Secondary school text.

Bettersworth, John K., *Confederate Mississippi: The People and Policies of a Cotton State in War Time* (Baton Rouge: Louisiana State University Press, 1943).

Brandt, Louis K., *Mississippi Corporate Fees and Taxes* (Bureau of Business Research, University of Mississippi, 1948).

Brown, Calvin S., *Archeology of Mississippi* (University: Mississippi Geological Survey, 1926).

Bryan, Gordon K., *County Finances in Mississippi* (Social Science Research Center, Mississippi State College, 1950).

———, *County Revenues and Expenditures in Mississippi, 1949* (Social Science Research Center, Mississippi State College, 1951, and annually thereafter).

Burrus, John N., *Life Opportunities: An Analysis of Differential Mortality in Mississippi* (Bureau of Public Administration, University of Mississippi, 1951).

Cabaniss, J. Allen, *History of the University of Mississippi* (University of Mississippi, 1950).

Davies, Vernon, *Housing for Mississippians* (Bureau of Public Administration, University of Mississippi, 1947).

Davis, C. C., and others, *The Centennial Lectures in Commerce* (Bureau of Business Research, University of Mississippi, 1949).

Ethridge, George H., *Mississippi Constitutions* (Jackson: Tucker Printing House, 1928).

Fortenberry, Charles N., *A Handbook for Mississippi Legislators* (3rd ed., Bureau of Public Administration, University of Mississippi, 1952).

Gibson, Joseph, *et al.*, *Mississippi: A Study of Higher Education in Mississippi* (Jackson: Board of Trustees of Institutions of Higher Learning, 1945).

Harrison, Robert W., *Flood Control in the Mississippi Alluvial Survey* (Stoneville: Delta Council, 1952).

———, *Levee Districts and Levee Building in Mississippi; a Study of State and Local Efforts to Control Mississippi River Floods* (Stoneville: Delta Council, 1951).

Hathorn, Guy B., *Suffrage, Apportionment, and Elections in the Mississippi Constitutional Convention of 1890* (Unpublished M.A. thesis in the University of Mississippi Library, 1942).

Henderson, C. O., and Caldwell, John T., *Lands Owned by the State of Mississippi Through Tax Reversion* (Works Progress Administration for Mississippi, n. p., 1937).

Highsaw, Robert B., *Administering Mississippi's Wealth* (Bureau of Public Administration, University of Mississippi, 1949).

———, *The Delta Looks Forward: An Inventory of Natural and Human Resources* (Stoneville: Delta Council, 1949).

———, *Forms of Municipal Government in Mississippi* (3rd ed., Bureau of Public Administration, University of Mississippi, 1947).

———, *Mississippi: Moneys for the Cities* (Bureau of Public Administration, University of Mississippi, 1947).

———, *Mississippi's Wealth: A Study of the Public Administration of Natural Resources* (Bureau of Public Administration, University of Mississippi, 1947).

———, and others, *Handbook of Mississippi State Agencies* (Bureau of Public Administration, University of Mississippi, 1948).

———, and Johnson, Edward M., *Aids for Governing: An Analysis of Technical Assistance in Mississippi* (Bureau of Public Administration, University of Mississippi, 1948).

———, and Mullican, Carl D., Jr., *The Units of Government in Mississippi* (Bureau of Public Administration, University of Mississippi, 1949).

Hopkins, Ernest J., *Mississippi's BAWI (Balance Agriculture with Industry) Plan* (Atlanta: Federal Reserve Bank of Atlanta, 1944).

Howerton, Huey B., and others, series of guide-books for Mississippi county officials, such as *A Guidebook for the County Tax Assessor* (Bureau of Public Administration, University of Mississippi, 1948-1951).

James, Lee M., *Mississippi's Forest Resources and Industries* (Washington: United States Forest Service, 1951).

Lowe, Ephraim N., *Mississippi, Its Geology, Geography, Soil, and Mineral Resources* (Jackson: Tucker Printing House, 1919).

McCain, William D., *The Populist Party in Mississippi* (Unpublished M.A. thesis in University of Mississippi Library, 1931).

McLure, William P., *Financing Public Education in Mississippi* (Bureau of Educational Research, University of Mississippi, 1948).

———, *Let Us Pay for the Kind of Education We Need* (Bureau of Educational Research, University of Mississippi, 1948).

Mississippi Board of Development, *Mississippi—America's State of Opportunity* (Jackson, 1944).

Mississippi Department of Public Welfare, *Narrative Reports of Child Welfare Workers* (Jackson: Division of Child Welfare, 1952).

Mississippi Legislature, General Investigating Committee, *On the Executive Departments,* A Report to the Mississippi State Legislature (Jackson, 1948).

Mississippi Legislature, Highway Planning Committee, *Today and Tomorrow: State Highways, County Roads, City Streets; an Engineering Analysis of the Highway Transportation System in Mississippi* (Jackson, 1949).

Mississippi Legislature, House of Representatives, Tax Study Committee, *Report* (Jackson, 1952) and *Supplement* (Jackson, 1952).

Mississippi State Planning Commission, *Housing* (Mimeographed, Jackson, 1940).

———, *Progress Report on State Planning in Mississippi* (Jackson, 1938).

Mississippi Economic Council, *An Analysis of Income, Services and Operation of 24 Representative Mississippi Cities with Recommendations* (Jackson, 1951).

Morse, W. C., *Mississippi Minerals* (University: State Geological Survey, 1944).

Robertson, F. O., *Health Services in State Institutions of Higher Learning in Mississippi* (Washington: American Council on Education, 1950).

Rowland, Dunbar, *Courts, Judges and Lawyers of Mississippi, 1798-1935* (Jackson: State Department of Archives and History, 1935).

Slay, Ronald J., *The Development of the Teaching of Agriculture in Mississippi, With Special Emphasis on Agriculture as a Part of School Curricula* (Teachers College, Columbia University, 1928).

Sydnor, Charles S., *Slavery in Mississippi* (Appleton-Century, 1933).

Van Sickle, J. V., *Mississippi Population Trends and Their Implications* (Jackson: Mississippi Board of Development, 1943).

Wallace, Raymond F., *Industrializing Mississippi: An Analysis of the Balance Agriculture with Industry Program* (Bureau of Public Administration, University of Mississippi, 1952).

Wilber, Leon A., *Mississippi State Administration: A Summary of Constitutional and Statutory Provisions* (Hattiesburg: Division of Social Studies, Mississippi Southern College, 1949).

Wingo, Earle L., *Mississippi Criminal Law and Procedure: A Ready-Reference Book Covering All of the Statutes in Mississippi Relating to Crime and Criminal Procedure, . . .* (Atlanta: Harrison Company, 1951).

BIENNIAL REPORTS

The following officials, boards, commissions, institutions, and agencies issue reports every two years:

Adjutant General
Aeronautics Commission
Agriculture and Commerce
Agricultural and Industrial Board
Agricultural and Industrial Exposition
Auditor of Public Accounts
  County Receipts and Disbursements
  State Receipts and Disbursements
Blind, School for
Budget Commission
Central Market Board
Charity Hospital, Mississippi (Jackson)
Charity Hospital, Mississippi (Vicksburg)
Charity Hospital, Mississippi (Natchez)
Charity Hospital, South Mississippi (Laurel)
Charity Hospital, Matty Hersee (Meridian)
Columbia Training School
Deaf, School for
Education, State Department of
  Crippled Children's Service
Ellisville Training School
Forestry Commission
Game and Fish Commission
Geological Survey
Health, State Board of
Highway Commission, State
Highway Safety Patrol
Historical Commission
Hospital Care Commission
Hospital, Mississippi State (Whitfield)
Hospital, East Mississippi State (Meridian)
Insurance Commissioner
Institutions of Higher Learning, Board of Trustees of
Land Commissioner
Library Commission
Librarian, State Law
Livestock Sanitary Commission
Medical Education Board
Motor Vehicle Comptroller
Oakley Training School
Oil and Gas Board
Parole Board
Penitentiary, State Board of Commissioners of
Plant Board

Public Employees Retirement System of Mississippi, Board of Trustees of
Public Service Commission
Public Welfare, State Board of
Sea Food Commission
Secretary of State
Surplus Property Procurement Commission
Tax Collector, State
Textbook Purchasing Board
Treasurer, State
Veterans' Affairs Board
Veterans' Farm and Home Board

OTHER OFFICIAL PUBLICATIONS

General Laws of the State of Mississippi (Published after each regular session of the state legislature. Usually laws passed at extraordinary sessions are included).

Journal of the House of Representatives of the State of Mississippi (Published after each regular and extraordinary session of the state legislature).

Journal of the Senate of the State of Mississippi (Published after each regular and extraordinary session of the state legislature).

Local and Private Laws of the State of Mississippi (Published after each regular session. Usually laws passed at extraordinary sessions are included).

Mississippi Code Statutes, Annotated, 1942 and Cumulative, Biennial Supplement (10 vols., Atlanta: Harrison Company).

Mississippi Employment Security Commission, *Jobs* (Published quarterly).

Mississippi Reports, Cases Argued and Decided in the Supreme Court (Little Rock: Mississippi Reporter Company, publisher of recent volumes).

Mississippi State Tax Commission, *Service Bulletin* (Several different series of publications on state and local finances, all numbered consecutively with a number of each series issued annually).

Senate and House Rules and Joint Rules of the Mississippi Legislature (Published at the beginning of each regular session by the Secretary of the Senate and the Clerk of the House).

Index